AppleWorks
Tips and Techniques

AppleWorks®
Tips and
Techniques

ROBERT ERICSON

Second Edition

SYBEX®

San Francisco•Paris•Düsseldorf•London

Cover design by Thomas Ingalls + Associates
Cover photography by Casey Cartwright
Book design by Joseph Roter

To Ann, Grandpa, and good teachers

Acknowledgments

This book benefited most from timely encouragement, some of which predated AppleWorks. I am particularly indebted to Hunter Dupree and Tom Galloway. Carole Alden and Rick Talcott encouraged me to work with SYBEX. Dianne King suggested the second edition.

Many people provided helpful comments. Each of the following provided at least one important insight that would almost certainly have escaped me: Bruce Benedict, Richard Blanco, David Burger, Giorgio Cupertino, Lawrence Eaton, Tom Ewing, John Farley, Robert Fortuno, Bruce Huenard, Debra Hara, Frank Howell, Philip Kaplan, Jim Long, Sherry Lowry, Steven Morrisby, Ann Moskol, Robert Netro, Bill Newell, Bruce Ristow, Al Salerno, Susan Smith, Bruce Sprague, David Teskey, Rick Talcott, Paul Taylor, and Roger Vancil.

Each of the following provided at least one important insight for the second edition: Ralph Beckman, Randy Brandt, Jon Breslaw, Les Burton, Jim Dertian, Dennis Doms, Palmer Hanson, Lee Hayward, Cyndi Heller, Jim Hercules, Jerry Hewett, Leland Ho, H.G. Lawson, Paul Lucas, Fred McKiernan, Peter Meyer, Vedula Murty, Chuck Newby, W.M. Patterson, Wayne Paulson, Richard Reynolds, Paul Ross, Robert Sangster, Dexter Shaler, Mark Simonsen, Gary Travis, Chris Van Buren, Jim Willis, Norman Wirtz, and Robert Young.

Barbara Gordon managed the original project with competence, style, and understanding. Valerie Robbins edited both editions with insight and offered many helpful suggestions. Dan Tauber reviewed the first edition with a critical technical eye, and Olivia Shinomoto word processed the editing with skill and care. Other SYBEX people who contributed to the production of one or both editions include Brenda Walker, Donna Scanlon, and Cheryl Bettigole, typesetting, and Eileen Walsh, Jon Strickland, and Aidan Wylde, proofreading.

Finally, I was greatly encouraged by the concurrent development of substantive applications that can be used with AppleWorks. I would particularly like to note the work of Penny Alexander in management, Deane Arganbright in mathematics, Anthony Filipovitch in planning, and Jeffrey Jacques in statistics.

Table of Contents

Introduction

*T*he most gratifying part of writing a reference book is learning how people use it for constructive purposes. Readers tell me that their copies have become well-worn: friends share the book with friends, teachers with students, and parents with their children. The book has been a resource for engineers who design renewable energy systems, nurses who analyze medical data, farmers who manage crop production, librarians who track book circulation, and many other people who do many different kinds of work. It has been a resource for me as well, because the book has a memory more dependable than mine.

The first edition of the book covered AppleWorks through version 1.2. This second edition includes information on versions 1.3 and 2.0, as well as new techniques. It also includes an additional chapter on related macro programs. Macros record keystokes used for various techniques, allowing you to work quickly without having to rethink each step.

This AppleWorks project really began at a national planning conference in Minneapolis, in the spring of 1984, during a discussion with a planning professor who was developing much-needed spreadsheet templates for analytical methods used in town planning and management. He developed an eminently practical set of methods templates using VisiCalc notation, and I developed integrated applications for AppleWorks, including several based on his work.

AppleWorks quickly proved to be a very effective tool. I began a notebook to document everything I learned while transferring classic VisiCalc templates and developing integrated applications from scratch. The notebook grew larger as I learned more about AppleWorks, and I was surprised in several ways.

First, I found AppleWorks remarkably fun to learn. The programs in AppleWorks gently encourage thought: they have useful options waiting to be combined in new ways. This is an inherent benefit of integrated software, and the AppleWorks designer, Robert Lissner—remarkable architect that he is—has made the most of it. There is a theory in environmental design that says we find a special contentment in building things from an assortment of parts. That theory has always impressed me, but even more so in recent months. AppleWorks is very much an integrated assortment of parts, and it is, above all else, fun to learn and easy to teach.

Second, I found that AppleWorks has a number of undocumented options that make it easy to develop advanced applications. Experienced users can use these options to find interesting ways around apparent limitations. For example, there are ways to print multicolumn Word Processor text, manage more than 30 Data Base categories, and add additional functions to the Spreadsheet. These are among the many options documented in this book.

Third, I discovered that AppleWorks has undocumented problems that require some caution. For example, before you develop a Data Base application, read about specific problems with record-selection rules. And before you use wide worksheets, read about formula capacities in rows. Once understood, the undocumented problems can be effectively isolated.

Fourth, I learned that AppleWorks has an unusually large capacity. With additional memory in an Apple IIe or Apple IIc, AppleWorks can manage more than 6,000 database records in random-access memory (RAM). And it remains remarkably fast and dependable at that level. The traditional "small-yet-serious" image of the Apple II has been greatly enhanced by AppleWorks.

As the AppleWorks notebook grew, it helped others learn about applications development. Someone suggested converting the notebook to technical notes that could be easily shipped by airmail. The resulting package was primarily intended for people working in environmental design and information science. Experienced users found the documentation and tips contained in the notes helpful, and many of them kindly sent me their own insights along with information about interesting projects they were working on.

The technical notes attracted a far broader audience than I expected. I learned that many people master AppleWorks quickly, begin developing interesting applications, and find that they need additional AppleWorks information. When SYBEX wrote to me, the notes were being used in more than 20 countries, and we both knew that it was time for an advanced AppleWorks reference book.

USING THE BOOK

This book is designed primarily as a reference for intermediate and advanced users. I use these terms humbly, and only in a relative sense, because we all have more to learn. If you are new to AppleWorks, you can also use this book to learn the basics more efficiently. Begin by studying the AppleWorks manuals. Try things out on your Apple. Write questions and comments as you go along, and then refer to this book for specific additional information. In my experience it was that additional information that reinforced points in the AppleWorks manuals and made everything fit together.

In the pages that follow, I have outlined some keys to understanding and using the book.

Many people are beginning, intermediate, and advanced users in different ways at the same time.

These terms must always be used cautiously. Some people know a great deal about the Word Processor, but they rarely use the other AppleWorks programs. Some people have mastered Spreadsheet accounting applications, but they know little about other applications for the same program. Most of us learn according to our individual needs and interests, which means that we tend to learn somewhat unevenly. Almost everyone will find at least one thing in the book that they already know. Likewise, almost everyone will find something that they will probably never need to know.

The AppleWorks information applies to the Apple IIc, the IIe, the enhanced IIe, and the IIGS, all of which use exactly the same program.

Apple now calls these personal computers the Apple II series. At least three utilities are currently available to modify AppleWorks for the earlier Apple II and II+ models. If you are using such a utility, keep close at hand a list of the keys that correspond to the standard AppleWorks commands, and ignore all references in this book to memory expansion and allocation.

The Apple III uses a version of AppleWorks known as III E-Z Pieces. It can exchange files with the Apple II version of AppleWorks. If you are using III E-Z Pieces, read the cautions about undocumented problems first, test them on your version, and note the ones that apply. Ignore all references in this book to memory expansion and allocation.

All the tips in this book apply to AppleWorks through version 2.0 USA unless otherwise noted.

References to specific earlier versions are always noted. References to version 1.1 apply to version 1.0 as well.

I have included the most significant undocumented problems in earlier versions of AppleWorks. Note them when they are mentioned in the book, even if you have the latest version. When you develop a good template that others can use, it may not work well on earlier versions of AppleWorks. A surprising number of people continue to use the earlier versions for a variety of reasons.

The information in this book combines technical insights with management concepts.

Some people develop superb applications and then misplace their files. Others manage their files well but need to learn more about developing applications. This book addresses both sets of problems. Sometimes the information is simple and almost obvious; sometimes it is subtle and more difficult. In every case the intent is to document additional capabilities. In AppleWorks and in general, simple insights are often the most valuable.

Tips and techniques are utility information. The tips consist of useful pieces of information or simply reminders of some feature in AppleWorks. Techniques are procedures requiring special knowledge, often the result of using several tips in combination. Techniques appear within tip headings, although they are not always specifically noted.

Along with tips and techniques, the book includes cautic about undocumented problems and possible unwanted effects ot specific procedures. Each caution includes a suggested way around the problem. You may want to read the cautions first, just to make certain that undocumented problems have not affected work already completed.

This book uses a modular design.

The component tips, techniques, and cautions are grouped in ways that most readers will want to study them. If you want to find utility information related to financial applications for the Spreadsheet, you can check the Table of Contents and find the information in one place. If you want to find all the information related to the command for saving files, you can look in the Index under "Files, saving" or "Saving files" for page references throughout the book. By using the Table of Contents and Index to complement one another, you can quickly find almost anything.

This book focuses primarily on working within Apple-Works, although it includes instructions for transferring data to and from AppleWorks.

You will normally work within AppleWorks, and there is much information to cover at this level. When you need to go beyond AppleWorks, look for specialized software that offers Apple-Works design conventions and built-in data transfer capabilities. AppleWorks can also create and use ASCII and DIF files, both of which have been well documented in other sources. For specific references, read the annotated bibliography in Appendix D.

The research for this book followed this path: over a period of fifteen months, I developed and tested many large applications in environmental design and management, almost always as part of other work. This kind of real-world testing worked surprisingly well. It created a critical mass of information to which others added their findings. During the two years between editions, I kept an AppleWorks Data Base file of additional tips and cautions, mainly for versions 1.3 and 2.0.

There are other logical and potentially productive paths for studying AppleWorks. For example, I have included suggestions and references in Appendix A for those readers who want to explore AppleWorks byte by byte.

Learn to appreciate the subtle craftsmanship of AppleWorks.

AppleWorks gets things done efficiently. It has become a quiet workhorse in many professional fields, accomplishing more than almost anyone had expected. But surprisingly few people know that AppleWorks can perform the important common functions—replacing text, arranging records, calculating interest—faster than far more expensive integrated software running on far more expensive systems.

The templates and macros used in this book can be purchased on a disk.

The cost is $12 postpaid from Robert Ericson, P.O. Box 16064, Rumford, RI 02916. The templates and macros use both sides of the disk, and many are extended versions of examples used in this book. Template files can save time in applications development, particularly when the templates include complex formulas or large amounts of needed data.

Finally, and most importantly, comments and suggestions are welcome and appreciated.

Please send them to the address given above. I will send collected information on undocumented problems to Apple. Authors of tips and cautions published in later editions of this book will be gratefully acknowledged.

DESIGN OF THE BOOK

This book is, above all, a reference book for serious users. The main chapters follow the order of AppleWorks files on the Desktop: Word Processor, Data Base, and Spreadsheet. The chapter on printer configuration comes last, although you may want to read it first if you have problems getting your printer to work correctly. Note that the *AppleWorks Reference Manual* follows a similar order, except that its Data Base chapters came before the Word Processor chapters until the most recent edition—*Using AppleWorks*. Knowing this, you will find it easy to use this book and the *AppleWorks Reference Manual together*.

The tips, techniques, and cautions follow a logical order within each chapter. Most of the AppleWorks commands, functions, and options have been included in the book, but some receive more detailed treatment than others. There are several good reasons for any imbalance in the quantity of information provided on different topics.

First, the need for cautions varies from program to program within AppleWorks. For example, the Data Base record-selection rules have serious undocumented problems, whereas parts of other programs work flawlessly. This is certainly not an unusual situation. Almost every software package has undocumented problems that are unevenly distributed. These problems also tend to be discovered after the user manuals have been written.

Second, the level of documentation in the *AppleWorks Reference Manual* varies considerably from program to program, and within each program. For example, the exponentiation function in the Spreadsheet receives surprisingly little attention in the *AppleWorks Reference Manual,* whereas other functions, such as @CHOOSE, are explained in detail.

Third, some options have far more potential than others for advanced AppleWorks applications. Remember that the materials from Apple, which include excellent disk-based tutorials, were written primarily for beginning users. At that level it would serve little purpose to discuss, for example, @COUNT as a logic function. In fact, this particular subject has received little attention anywhere, because most other spreadsheets have a larger set of logic functions.

Fourth, AppleWorks was written for a 128K system. Several firms now offer extended-memory cards with 256K or more, along with software to modify the AppleWorks Startup and Program disks. These modifications make it possible to exceed specific limits described in the *AppleWorks Reference Manual,* enabling you to use AppleWorks in a broader range of applications. It also changes the ways in which the AppleWorks programs most effectively complement one another.

The tips, techniques, and cautions in this book have been arranged in ways that complement the *AppleWorks Reference Manual* most efficiently. At the beginning of each chapter I have provided an overview of the information that follows, as well as an explanation of why some options are more useful than others.

At the beginning of each section within a chapter, I have provided a more detailed overview. If you are reading the book from cover to cover, I think you will appreciate these overviews. If you are simply looking for an answer to a specific question, they are not required reading.

ORGANIZATION OF THE BOOK

However you approach the book, the following overview should be helpful. Almost everyone will want to read the Desktop chapter, because its tips and cautions are broadly useful in AppleWorks. Beyond that, there is no preferred way to approach the book.

Chapter 1 covers the Desktop and related subjects. Everything in AppleWorks goes through the Desktop—sometimes once, often repeatedly. The closely related subjects include ProDOS, the clipboard, and key commands.

Memory expansion for the Desktop has greatly increased the range of AppleWorks. Many readers will want to pay special attention to this subject, because a small investment in memory makes AppleWorks perform much more efficiently.

Chapter 2 covers the Word Processor, which has particular strengths and limitations that serious users should be aware of. The tips and cautions in this chapter cover form letters, printing, editing, proofreading, and extended report writing. Many readers will be surprised to find solutions to minor undocumented problems that sometimes occur without being noticed.

Chapter 3 covers the Data Base. This program has assumed new importance because additional memory can so greatly extend its capabilities. The chapter includes tips on using large databases and cautions on undocumented problems in the record-selection rules.

Chapter 4 covers the Spreadsheet. No other part of AppleWorks offers more flexibility for applications development. Readers interested in the Data Base will want to study the section on using the Spreadsheet for database management.

Chapter 5 is probably the most challenging in the book. It covers methods for transferring information between AppleWorks programs, to AppleWorks from other sources, and from AppleWorks to other sources. Before you read about transfers between any two AppleWorks programs, you should understand the two programs individually. Advanced Apple users will particularly appreciate the many complementing options offered by the Data Base, Apple-Works Mailing Program, Spreadsheet, and SuperCalc 3a.

AppleWorks can also serve as an editor for BASIC programs. Programming and external data transfers sometimes require disk format conversions from ProDOS to DOS 3.3 or vice versa. This subject has been covered in detail.

Chapter 6 covers printers. I have tried to distinguish between printing and printers. If you are having problems with your printer, read this final chapter first. Printer problems include such curious things as an "80N" printed at the beginning of a Word Processor file, or too many spaces between lines. When you have configured the printer correctly, you can then use the standard printing options described in the first five chapters.

This chapter also includes some control code techniques, but be sure you understand the basic options before you attempt these techniques.

Chapter 7 explains macros. It focuses on an integrated set of practical applications for Super MacroWorks and MacroWorks. In order to use macros effectively, you need to think carefully about how you work and what can save the most time. This chapter offers suggestions based on many hours of keyboard use.

Appendix A discusses a logical development path for the Apple II series and AppleWorks, as well as additional approaches to studying the programs. Appendix B provides insights on using the keyboard for configuring printers, entering text, entering numbers, and editing data. Here you will find a table of ASCII values and some keyboard templates that you may find useful. Appendix C reviews the general subject of sources, while Appendix D provides a bibliography of publications directly related to AppleWorks.

CONVENTIONS USED IN THE BOOK

In writing this book, I have used some conventions that are consistent with AppleWorks. If you make note of them now, you will be able to use the book more efficiently.

AppleWorks uses capital letters for specific purposes. The three programs within AppleWorks have generic names, but they begin with capitals so that you will know, for example, the difference between the Spreadsheet in particular and spreadsheets in general. The same convention applies to the Desktop and some other generic words with particular meanings in the context of Apple-Works. The spelling of clipboard is an exception to the rule.

I have also used capital letters to begin names of keys, such as Return, Escape, and so on. Arrow keys are indicated by arrows, as in →. Key sequences are sometimes noted parenthetically as brief reminders. For example, in the Word Processor you can underline text (Control-L) without accessing the Printer Options menu. For our purposes ProDOS volumes will be synonymous with 5¼-inch disks. ProDOS volumes have names preceded by a slash mark. In this book all disks will be designated /P (for ProDOS) unless otherwise noted.

The commands in AppleWorks use the key with an outline of the Apple logo on it. Almost everyone calls this key the Open-Apple key, and the AppleWorks Reference Manual consistently uses terms such as Open-Apple-S and Open-Apple-1. In Apple-Works, the Open-Apple and Solid-Apple keys are interchangeable until you use macros, so I have used terms such as Apple-S and Apple-1 through most of the book. The Solid-Apple key is often more convenient for commands that include letters on the left side of the keyboard. (However, it may take some time to overcome old habits.)

It is important to understand the meaning of specific words used throughout the book. For our purposes, these are the most important terms: command, option, function, number, value, arrange, sort, category, field, layout, format, standard, global, and utilities. The following paragraphs define these terms briefly; some of these words will be defined in greater detail in related tips and cautions.

AppleWorks includes commands, options, and functions. For our purposes a *command* begins with an Apple key, as in Apple-S for the Save command, or a Control key, as in Control-L for underlining. In many cases a command accesses a menu of *options*. The longest list of options appears on the Word Processor Printer Options menu. Note in this context that underlining can be either a command (Control-L) or an option within the

Printer Options menu. *Functions* are confined to the Spreadsheet. They include arithmetic and logical functions. Many begin with @, as in @SUM.

Numbers are numerals, the characters 0–9. In the Spreadsheet they can be labels or values. *Values* can be added and subtracted. Remember that simple rule of thumb, because it will serve you well throughout the book, especially in Chapter 5 ("Transferring Information").

AppleWorks uses several terms that are not well known. If you have used other spreadsheets and database managers, it may take some time to get used to the new terms. *Arranging* in Apple-Works is the same as *sorting* in other programs. Likewise, a Data Base *category* would be called a *field* in many other database managers. In AppleWorks you choose *layouts* instead of *formats,* and you specify *standard* values instead of *global* values.

Utilities are programs or files that perform useful functions in support of larger systems, in this case the Apple II, AppleWorks, and applications being developed on AppleWorks. In each case, I have tried to give the utility in question a descriptive title.

GENERAL APPLEWORKS TIPS

Some tips are generally applicable, beyond the boundaries of any single chapter, perhaps even beyond the boundaries of Apple-Works. Most of the tips that follow are reinforced with specific variations in one or more chapters.

Tip: *Learn about AppleWorks in bite-size pieces, according to your own needs and interests.*

There is much information in this book, and there will probably always be more to learn from other sources. If you take all this on at once, you can be overwhelmed. Take it in bite-size pieces, starting with whatever interests you most. If that is what you already know best, so much the better.

If you need AppleWorks for writing reports, spend your time with the Word Processor first. Then consider possible interactions with the Spreadsheet and Data Base. If you want to create reference tables for management reports, learn enough about the Spreadsheet to do just that. No one has to know everything about AppleWorks. It is important to define what you should and should not attempt to learn. Set priorities.

Tip: *Read about AppleWorks and encourage others to read.*

Some people own relatively few programs, but they accomplish much with what they have. They read the manuals, write in the margins, note undocumented problems, consult Apple journals, and study advanced books. Many otherwise competent people somehow forget about the manuals. The fact is that everyone needs at least the manuals, and Apple wrote good manuals for AppleWorks.

Those of us who read the manuals are often the ones who teach AppleWorks to those who don't. When you teach, explain the basics and strongly encourage your students to read enough to teach others something useful. It makes everyone more confident, and you avoid becoming a question-answerer forevermore.

Knowing that many teachers will be using this book, I have attempted to provide some examples and illustrations that can be adapted easily for beginning students.

Tip: *Add to the book.*

Throughout the book I have made brief suggestions about additional applications and possibilities for further study. It is my way of encouraging you to go beyond the book in using Apple-Works in your own field. For example, a technique abstracted from an environmental design application can later serve a completely different purpose in a scientific research application.

Write in the margins, highlight the text, and add tabs to the pages you use most. Abbreviate and modify wherever necessary. Remember that my comments may sometimes be inappropriate to your specific needs. Above all, have as much fun adding to the book as I had writing it.

Tip: *Start an AppleWorks notebook.*

Your notebook can hold the most important information you collect about AppleWorks beyond this book. It should be your own specialized reference. Include the following:

- Two copies of your printer control codes
- Samples of available character sets from your printer
- Hard copies of all the menu screens in AppleWorks

You get the point: this is where you keep what you use most often. Include documentation for the applications you develop. When you have too much for one notebook, start a hanging file system in a file cabinet, but keep the most important information in the notebook.

Time and time again you will need to consult your notes. You will often be able to use applications completed months ago, and you will always be thankful that you organized the information in a logical way.

Tip: *Use the hardware that makes AppleWorks function most efficiently for you.*

There is no need to acquire more hardware and software for AppleWorks than you really need and can afford. If you have a 128K Apple IIe or IIc, use two disk drives. If you have any II system with at least 256K, you can work efficiently with just one disk drive (see Chapter 1).

Try to think of the system as a whole. If you enter information with two fingers, the bottleneck in your system is probably right at the keyboard. Learning to type is the wisest investment you can make. After you learn to type, four dollars worth of chips for the printer buffer may be the most prudent choice. Think about what you really need. Ask yourself what you would do with additional hardware and software.

The first edition of this book was written on a 192K Apple IIe with two Apple-compatible disk drives, an amber monochrome monitor, a buffered Grappler card, and an Okidata 92P printer. There were some variations: I eventually installed the Apple IIe enhancement kit and increased memory to 384K, but the basic system was four years old when I wrote this second edition.

Tip: *Use a recent version of AppleWorks.*

If you use any program regularly, the most recent version is generally the most dependable. However, AppleWorks versions 1.3 and 2.0 have different undocumented problems, and the earlier version is slightly faster for some applications. The best choice depends on your needs. Apple offered the first upgrade, to version 1.2, through participating dealers at no cost. Many dealers simply copied the new version onto a customer's blank disk, which is the most logical method imaginable. Disks for the version 1.3 upgrade cost $20, but you could get them only from Apple, using forms obtained from a dealer. The upgrade to version 2.0 worked the same way, but the cost increased to $50. Whenever you need to upgrade, call an Apple dealer to determine current availability and cost.

Tip: *Use product descriptions as reference points.*

This book includes limited descriptions of hardware and software related to AppleWorks. These descriptions can provide generic insights about products of similar design. Use any given product note in this book as a reference point for judging other products that may be more recent or more appropriate to your needs. Study current issues of Apple journals, and look for specific information in reviews and advertisements.

Tip: *Make hard copies of the screens.*

AppleWorks has a command (Apple-H) for printing the contents of a screen to your printer. Use it for everything you can imagine: menu screens, Printer Options menus, error messages, lists of files on disk, key Spreadsheet formulas, quick Data Base record printouts. In fact, this book has been illustrated with hard copies printed with a daisy-wheel printer. (It prints the @ sign in place of the Open-Apple.) Specific versions of this tip appear throughout the book, because the concept can never be stressed enough.

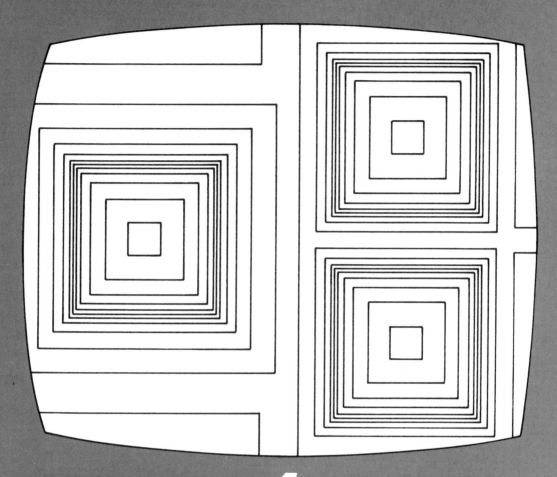

1
The Desktop

*T*he Desktop is the AppleWorks file-handling area. On it, you can load up to 12 files, access and display them quickly, create new files, save some to disks, discard others, and keep tabs on the status of each file. The Desktop can display an Index of available files, enabling you to change between files quickly, but it cannot display two files at the same time. The AppleWorks Reference Manual introduces the Desktop and clearly illustrates its functions, but it does not document the available shortcuts.

The overall performance of the Desktop is impressive, and it is very much an extension of ProDOS, Apple's fast and dependable operating system. Longtime users have run AppleWorks for thousands of hours without losing any information. You can learn how to use the Desktop on two levels: it guides beginning users safely with logical menu sequences, and it offers several file-handling shortcuts for experienced users. If you feel comfortable with the menus, it is time to start using the shortcuts.

The tips in this chapter address the problems that tend to slow people down most often: misplaced files, uncertainty about what to do next, and second thoughts about choices just made. They are among the most important tips in this book, simply because you can use them so often.

This chapter is divided into eight sections. The first section introduces general, broadly useful tips on using the Desktop. The second section concerns using the Desktop menus more efficiently. Everyone should read the sections on managing files and using the clipboard, because they contain essential information and a few surprises.

The fifth section describes options for expanding Desktop memory. No innovation has been more important to AppleWorks than memory expansion. The section on common AppleWorks commands covers previously undocumented options. The ProDOS section explains what experienced users need to know about the operating system and its utility programs.

The last section covers the problems of managing your own desktop—the one with real pencils and papers. Because AppleWorks lets you work more productively, you may have to manage more disks and paper.

GENERAL DESKTOP TIPS

The following tips are valuable for anyone using AppleWorks. The techniques will help you use the available Desktop options more efficiently. If you are a longtime Apple user, you may be surprised by the ease with which AppleWorks uses lowercase letters and prints copies of the screen display.

Tip: *Print and annotate hard copies of the Desktop menu screens.*

You can print a hard copy of any monitor screen by using Apple-H when the screen is displayed. Start by printing the Main Menu screen, then the Add Files menu screen, then the Word Processor, the Data Base, and the Spreadsheet menu screens. Highlight your most common choices with a yellow marker, and write notes about when to use each option. Keep the hard copies of the screens nearby so you can see the Desktop menus at any time. Figure 1.1 shows the Main Menu screen.

Tip: *Use lowercase letters wherever appropriate.*

AppleWorks will always accept lowercase letters for finding text, for setting layout options, for Spreadsheet formulas, and so on. Longtime Apple users who just winced may continue using uppercase letters forever, but the fact is that lowercase letters are easier to enter, simply because there is no need to depress the Shift key.

More importantly, lowercase letters are easier to read. We tend to make certain visual mistakes consistently, confusing the characters S and 5, for example. The Apple II creates each letter within a 56-dot matrix on the monitor screen. In contrast, some other personal computers use dot matrices with more than twice that density, thereby permitting more fully formed screen characters.

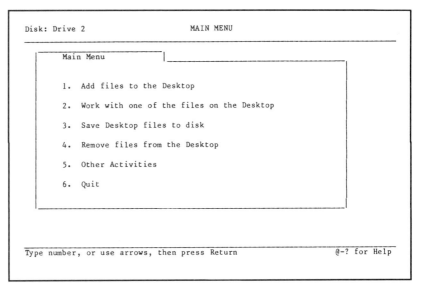

```
Disk: Drive 2                    MAIN MENU

    ┌─Main Menu──────────────┐┌──────────────────────────
    │                        ││
    │   1.  Add files to the Desktop
    │
    │   2.  Work with one of the files on the Desktop
    │
    │   3.  Save Desktop files to disk
    │
    │   4.  Remove files from the Desktop
    │
    │   5.  Other Activities
    │
    │   6.  Quit
    │
    │
    └

Type number, or use arrows, then press Return        @-? for Help
```

Figure 1.1: *Main Menu*

Given the Apple II screen character matrix, it is important to use a logical blend of capital and lowercase letters that makes text easier to read. It is rarely a good idea to use all capitals. I will note specific exceptions to this rule in other tips and cautions. (For example, you may choose to use all capitals for report headings and other circumstances where it is more important to differentiate between word groups than between letters.)

When you are searching for text in a Word Processor document, you can enter lowercase letters for the desired word or phrase, even if it begins with a capital letter (unless you choose case-sensitive text selection). In Spreadsheet formulas, lowercase letters are automatically converted to capitals when the formula has been completed.

Tip: *Find things to do while the disk drives are running.*

The Startup Disk takes a little more than ten seconds to load—more than enough time to insert your data disk in drive 2 and too long to wait around doing nothing. As a rule of thumb, an

AppleWorks file requires less than a second per thousand bytes to load from or save to disk. You will be saving files far more often than loading them, and each time you save a 30K file, you have 25–30 seconds to do something else. (For example, it takes about that long to look up a word that you suspect you might have misspelled.)

Tip: *Use the file utilities provided with AppleWorks.*

AppleWorks has three important utilities: two for disk cataloging and one for disk formatting. You can obtain a catalog of only AppleWorks files from option 1 on the Main Menu. You can obtain a complete catalog of all ProDOS files from option 2 on the Other Activities menu. Figure 1.2 shows the Other Activities menu.

Disk formatting is particularly convenient with AppleWorks. It can be used at any time, even when you have 12 files on the Desktop and information on the clipboard waiting to be moved to another file.

Although a file copying utility has not been included, you can effectively copy AppleWorks files by loading one or more files on

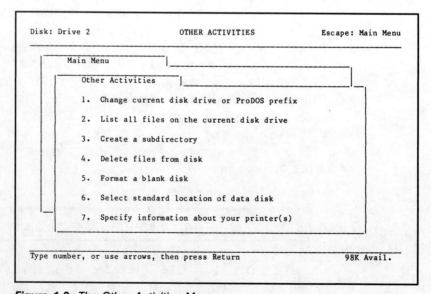

```
Disk: Drive 2              OTHER ACTIVITIES        Escape: Main Menu

    Main Menu          |
                       |_____
        Other Activities    |
                            |_____|

            1.  Change current disk drive or ProDOS prefix

            2.  List all files on the current disk drive

            3.  Create a subdirectory

            4.  Delete files from disk

            5.  Format a blank disk

            6.  Select standard location of data disk

            7.  Specify information about your printer(s)



Type number, or use arrows, then press Return             98K Avail.
```

Figure 1.2: *The Other Activities Menu*

the Desktop and then saving them to other disks. You cannot use this technique to copy other kinds of ProDOS files, however.

Caution: *AppleWorks can lock you out.*

Other cautions in this book describe various conditions under which AppleWorks can lock you out of the program. No matter which key you press, nothing happens. That means you have to turn the power off and back on to reload AppleWorks, or use Control-OpenApple-Reset for a warm restart. Of course, anything you have not saved from the Desktop is lost.

In such an emergency, you can press Control-Reset to enter the Monitor, which displays an asterisk (*) at the beginning of each line. Enter the following lines to return to the Main Menu in version 2.0. Press Return at the end of each line. These lines include six zeros to enter, but no letter O:

```
C073:0
3 Control-P
2F0:2C 83 C0 2C 83 C0 4C
:27 11
2F0G
```

For AppleWorks versions 1.1 through 1.3, use :33 10 in the fourth line (instead of :27 11). Practice this technique before you really need it. You should return to an 80-column screen after the second line. When you return to the Main Menu, save what you need to save before going any further.

In Chapter 7 we will discuss a macro program that makes Control-Reset work in AppleWorks version 2.0. It brings you safely back to the Main Menu every time.

Tip: *Use the Desktop to run a cleaning disk in drive 2.*

Many disk manufacturers recommend running a specially designed cleaning disk in both drives every two weeks or so. To run a cleaning disk in drive 1, simply insert the disk, turn the Apple on for about 30 seconds, and then turn it off.

There are two traditional methods for running a cleaning disk in drive 2. The first method is to change drives on the controller card and run the normal drive 2 in the drive 1 position. The second uses a BASIC utility program to activate drive 2.

Here is an easier method. Load AppleWorks, place the cleaning disk in drive 2, proceed as if to add files to the Desktop from drive 2, and hold down Return for the period of time needed for cleaning (usually about 30 seconds). AppleWorks attempts to catalog files from a data disk for about five seconds, finds no files, and sends an error message as shown in Figure 1.3. By holding down Return, you essentially ask AppleWorks to keep trying.

WORKING ON THE DESKTOP

The menu options and commands can work differently for beginners and experienced users. In this section we will take a

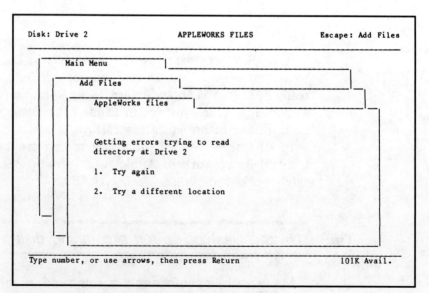

Figure 1.3: Try again option used for cleaning drive 2

closer look at the choices. The tips and techniques in this section define limits more precisely, so that you can work efficiently within those limits. Several tips explain why some options are more appropriate than others for specific purposes. You will find, for example, that the Apple-Q command offers many ways to move quickly within AppleWorks.

Tip: *AppleWorks loads as much of a program as it thinks you will need, and you can choose commands accordingly.*

When changing to a file that requires a different program, as from a Word Processor document to a Spreadsheet template, AppleWorks loads enough of the new program to get you started, more when you use additional functions. This is a good design choice, because you may want to load an application simply to check information on a file in that application.

In the Spreadsheet, for example, AppleWorks will load more of the program when you attempt to blank a cell. Using the Apple-B command usually indicates that you intend to spend some time revising the worksheet. If you actually intend to leave right away, use ", the Space bar, and Return to remove the entry.

Caution: *When Desktop files use enough memory, file changes slow down.*

It is fast file handling that makes AppleWorks a workhorse for professional applications. But if you have, for example, 24K of files loaded on a 55K Desktop, the Apple-Q command accesses the Program disk for more than four seconds before going to the Desktop Index, and then again for another four seconds before going to the new file.

By expanding the Desktop with extra RAM memory, you can maintain instant file access at much higher memory-use levels. For example, the Apple-Q command can provide instant access to more than 160K of files on a 229K Desktop. That makes a significant contribution to overall efficiency on a project such as this book. The options for memory expansion are covered in detail later in this chapter.

Even when file changes slow down, everything keeps working dependably. The Main Menu options for removing files from the Desktop, checking on what must be saved, and loading new files continue to work as efficiently as ever.

Tip: *Use Apple-Q instead of option 2 on the Main Menu.*

No matter how long you have been using AppleWorks, start thinking through your strategies. When would you use option 2 on the Main Menu? Probably never, because it gives you the Desktop Index, which is accessible with Apple-Q from anywhere. After loading two or more files, what do you do when the screen message tells you to press the Space bar? Use Apple-Q again, because the Space bar just takes you back to the Main Menu to select option 2. Note that AppleWorks version 2.0 automatically displays the Desktop Index when it loads two or more files.

Tip: *Use Apple-Q to return to the Desktop Main Menu.*

Whenever you press Apple-Q, the next Escape takes you back to the Main Menu. There are times, particularly in the Data Base, when you would otherwise need to press Escape four times to return to the Main Menu. That means waiting for each new screen to appear on the way. Use Apple-Q to save time.

Tip: *Use Apple-Q to check the remaining available memory.*

Apple-Q serves another useful purpose. When the Desktop Index appears, the Apple-? message disappears from the lower-right corner of the screen, and you can then see how much memory is available on the Desktop. The Desktop Index always highlights the file you are using, so if all you want to do is check the available memory, Return takes you directly back to the same cursor position in your document.

Tip: *Use the Main Menu Save Files option to check the size of any file on the Desktop.*

To see the amount of memory used by any given file on the Desktop, press Apple-Q and Esc to return to the Main Menu. Then choose option 3 to save Desktop files to disk, even though you have no intention of actually doing that.

If you add the memory requirements of each file to the remaining available memory, the sum may be less than the Desktop memory you started with. This is a normal occurrence in memory management—nothing is lost.

Tip: *Use Apple-S to save files often.*

If you recently purchased AppleWorks, this is so obvious that you may wonder why it has to be mentioned. The answer is simple: the Tutorial Manual for AppleWorks version 1.0 gave Apple-S a bad name. It was specifically called the "Ultimate Quick and Dirty Save Shortcut." In reality, it is quick and clean. Unless you need to check the status of your file at the end of a session, use Apple-S to save.

Use Apple-S often, at least every twenty minutes. Use it when you have just solved a difficult problem, such as a complex sentence construction, a Data Base report layout, or a long Spreadsheet formula. Use it instinctively when you will spend the next half minute away from the keyboard, because that is when a save costs the least time.

Tip: *Use the Main Menu Add Files option to see what is on the data disk.*

The Add Files option provides the easiest and safest method for finding out what you have on your data disk, how much space you have left, and so on. It is useful even when you have no intention of adding files to the Desktop. The Add Files option addresses such questions as the following:

Do I have enough free space on the disk? Proceed as if you are adding files from the primary data disk, but simply note the amount of disk memory available. The formatted disk began with 136K, so the files plus the remaining memory should add up to 136K, give or take a little. If they don't, you may have some unwanted non-AppleWorks files on the data disk. To find them, first select the Other Activities option on the Main Menu and then the option to list all files. If you find any unwanted Other (non-AppleWorks) files, delete them from the disk. These might include ASCII or DIF files that you used to transfer information

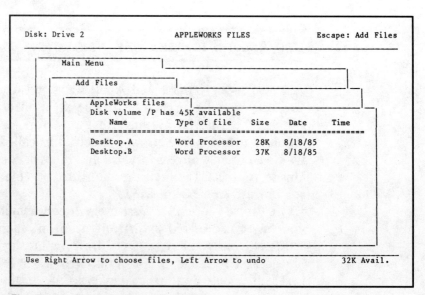

```
Disk: Drive 2                   APPLEWORKS FILES            Escape: Add Files
  ┌──────────────────────────┐  ─────────────────────────────────────────────
  │    Main Menu             │
  │  ┌────────────────────┐  │  ──────────────────────────────────────────
  │  │    Add Files       │  │
  │  │  ┌──────────────────┐ │  ─────────────────────────────────────
  │  │  │ AppleWorks files  │
  │  │  │ Disk volume /P has 45K available
  │  │  │    Name         Type of file   Size   Date     Time
  │  │  │ ===================================================================
  │  │  │ Desktop.A       Word Processor  28K   8/18/85
  │  │  │ Desktop.B       Word Processor  37K   8/18/85
  │  │  │
  │  │  │
  │  │  │
  │  │  │
  │  │  │
  │  │  │
  │  │  │
  │  │  │
Use Right Arrow to choose files, Left Arrow to undo          32K Avail.
```

Figure 1.4: *All AppleWorks files listed*

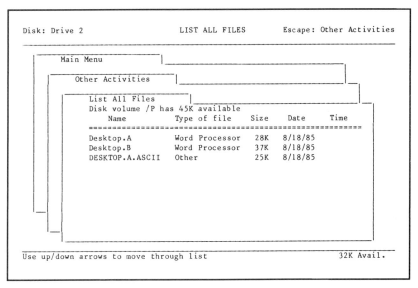

```
Disk: Drive 2                LIST ALL FILES        Escape: Other Activities
_____
   | Main Menu              |_____
   |   | Other Activities      |_____
   |   |   | List All Files       |_____
   |   |   | Disk volume /P has 45K available
   |   |   |    Name            Type of file    Size    Date    Time
   |   |   | ==============================================================
   |   |   | Desktop.A         Word Processor  28K    8/18/85
   |   |   | Desktop.B         Word Processor  37K    8/18/85
   |   |   | DESKTOP.A.ASCII   Other           25K    8/18/85
   |   |
   |   |
   |   |_____
   |_____
_____
Use up/down arrows to move through list                       32K Avail.
```

Figure 1.5: *All ProDOS files listed*

and then forgot about. Figures 1.4 and 1.5 illustrate a discrepancy caused by an ASCII file.

Did I save the file to both the primary and backup disk? Proceed as if you are adding files from the primary data disk, read the catalog, find the date for the file in question, note the file size, and press Escape. Then remove the primary disk, insert the backup disk, press Return, and compare your notes with the catalog information for this disk.

Do the primary and backup disks have the same files? This is an extension of the last procedure. It is not unusual to save a file to the data disk that happens to be in drive 2, even though that file may actually belong on some other disk. Print a hard copy of the catalog for the primary disk. Then remove the primary disk, insert the backup disk, press Return, and compare your hard copy with the catalog information for this disk.

Of course, there are times when you merely want to know which disk you have in drive 2. Then you can just open the disk drive door and look at the disk label, provided, of course, that the drive is not running.

Caution: *The act of printing causes the file to be listed as Changed.*

When you check the status of a file that has been printed, the file will usually be listed as Changed (even if you simply pressed Return to use the printer proposed). If you encounter a case like this, there is no need to save the file again before removing it from the Desktop. With large files this is well worth remembering.

How does the file change just by printing it? If you select any printer for the first time, AppleWorks must recalculate pages— that is the change. In the unlikely case that you save the file after printing and then print it exactly the same way again, the file will be listed as Unchanged.

There are times when you will make file changes simply for one printout. You may have no reason to save a file with the changes, so choose the option to "throw out" the changes when you remove the file from the Desktop.

Tip: *The Save Desktop files option is generally more useful than the Quit option.*

The Quit option (6 on the Main Menu) will tell you which files have been saved, which files have changed, and which remain unchanged (and hence need not be saved). The problem is that if a file needs to be saved, you will usually want to save it to a backup disk as well. The Quit option shows only one file at a time and provides for only one save.

By selecting option 3 (Save Desktop files to disk), you can see the status of all the Desktop files at once, and you can also save any file as many times as you wish. Figures 1.6 and 1.7 show information screens of the Quit and Save Desktop files options.

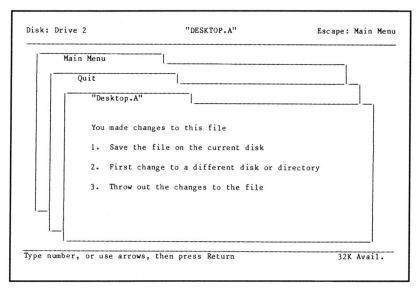

Figure 1.6: Quit option

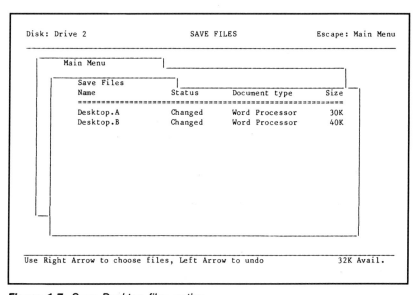

Figure 1.7: Save Desktop files option

MANAGING FILES

Few of us think about how we manage files, so this is another place where it is time to take a closer look at work habits.

The most important tip here is the advice about using small files. This book was assembled from dozens of files that were about 30K in size, despite the ready availability of large extended memory cards. Once you are comfortable with file management methods, using small files will clearly be the most sensible way to work.

This section also provides additional documentation on methods of cataloging and saving files. Pay special attention to file naming, because the rules will be important later.

Caution: *AppleWorks uses an indirect save that requires more disk space than you might expect.*

AppleWorks through version 1.3 saves files in a two-step process that I call the indirect method. When you press Apple-S, AppleWorks first saves the file to available free space on the disk, and then it deletes the previous file of the same name. If you attempt to save a 70K file to the disk from which it came, Apple-Works will tell you that there is insufficient room, because a disk holds only 136K.

When there is insufficient room for an indirect save, you can first delete the previous file of the same name. That creates some additional risk, but you do have a backup disk—right?

Version 2.0 follows the same process, but whenever the disk has insufficient room, AppleWorks notifies you and asks if you want to delete the previous version of the file. If the new version of the file is larger than the previous version, it may not fit on the disk even after AppleWorks deletes the previous version. In that case you must save to another disk.

Tip: *Use small files whenever possible.*

AppleWorks can save small files faster; they require less free space on a disk and use less memory on the Desktop. More importantly, small files let you take maximum advantage of the Desktop.

Think of the chapters in a book or report. If you keep a whole chapter in one file, what happens when you want to write in two different sections as you think of related information? If the chapter is in two files, you can use Apple-Q to flip back and forth between two related cursor locations. This method is generally faster and easier than setting markers within a single file.

How small is small? A small Word Processor file is something under 30K. Even at that size some of the commands, such as Apple-M, slow down noticeably. You can always assemble small files into large files for special printing needs. You can do this by moving 250 lines to the clipboard at a time, which is the maximum number permitted. In the case of a Word Processor file of 490 lines, which can be about 30K, that means two moves to the clipboard. You can find the approximate halfway point by pressing Apple-5.

A small Spreadsheet file is also something under 30K. At that size the recalculation times generally approach 30 seconds. Modular construction methods permit you to assemble small files into large files when you really need a large integrated model. Again, multiples of 250 lines (or rows in this case) can be moved to the clipboard.

Database applications generally use more memory than other kinds of applications, simply because they generally contain more information. In this relative sense, a small Data Base file is something under 60K. None of the commonly used Data Base functions have slowed down much by then, but it does take longer to save the file.

Some intermediate users think that they need to build at least one large spreadsheet template. Focus instead on small files and subtle craftsmanship—less is more, particularly when less is just enough.

Tip: *Learn how AppleWorks lists files.*

It is helpful to know where to start looking for files on Apple-Works catalogs. When you see a list of AppleWorks files on the current disk, the file grouping is always Word Processor, Data Base, and Spreadsheet, in that order. When Other files are listed from option 2 on the Other Activities menu, they are listed after Spreadsheet files. "Other" means ProDOS but not AppleWorks. If you remember this, you will know when to hold down ↓ before AppleWorks displays files, which can give you a fast start moving through the list.

Within each file group, file names are arranged alphabetically, or more precisely in an ASCII order that recognizes all letters as uppercase letters. You can use capitals and lowercase letters any way you want, but note that spaces and periods come before letters in ASCII order. See Appendix B for a complete ASCII table.

You can also use a prefix to group your file listings. For example, suppose you assign the prefix "A." to all Word Processor files in a project (A.Appendices, A.Index, and A.Text, for instance). They would then be listed together, in alphabetical order, before any files beginning with a "B." prefix. Figure 1.8 shows an example.

Caution: *AppleWorks has confusing file capacity limits.*

Like ProDOS, AppleWorks accepts no more than 51 files in a volume (or directory). When you attempt to save the 52nd file, AppleWorks will tell you that it cannot write to the disk. Once understood, this limit presents no practical problems, because you can always create subdirectories.

In versions 1.1 through 1.3, AppleWorks can catalog the first 170 files in a subdirectory. Version 2.0 catalogs only the first 85 files. Those numbers are the effective limits, although all versions have an incorrect error message indicating a 130-file limit.

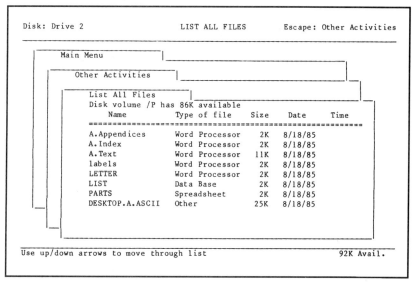

```
Disk: Drive 2                    LIST ALL FILES        Escape: Other Activities
    _____
   | Main Menu                 |_____
   |    _____|                                          |
   |   | Other Activities       |_____     |
   |   |    _____|                                     |    |
   |   |   | List All Files     |_____      |    |
   |   |   | Disk volume /P has 86K available                  |      |    |
   |   |   |      Name          Type of file    Size   Date    Time   |    |
   |   |   | ================================================================
   |   |   | A.Appendices       Word Processor    2K   8/18/85         |    |
   |   |   | A.Index            Word Processor    2K   8/18/85         |    |
   |   |   | A.Text             Word Processor   11K   8/18/85         |    |
   |   |   | labels             Word Processor    2K   8/18/85         |    |
   |   |   | LETTER             Word Processor    2K   8/18/85         |    |
   |   |   | LIST               Data Base         2K   8/18/85         |    |
   |   |   | PARTS              Spreadsheet        2K   8/18/85         |    |
   |   |__ | DESKTOP.A.ASCII    Other             25K  8/18/85         |    |
   |       |                                                           |    |
   |    ___|                                                           |    |
   |___|                                                               |    |

Use up/down arrows to move through list                           92K Avail.
```

Figure 1.8: *Alphabetical file listing showing use of the prefix "A."*

Tip: *The Desktop Index lists files in the order that they were loaded.*

Files are never listed alphabetically in the Desktop Index unless they were loaded in that order. You can easily load the Desktop in alphabetical order from one program group on a single disk by selectively loading the files.

Tip: *You can move the cursor backwards in the Desktop Index.*

If the cursor is on the first file and you want it on the last file, press ↑ once to move the cursor to the bottom of the list. To go back to the top of the list, press ↓. This technique saves time when you have four or more files on the Desktop. Note that it does not work with disk file catalogs.

Tip: *AppleWorks file naming rules are more liberal than those of other ProDOS files.*

AppleWorks file names can have blank spaces within them, but other ProDOS file names cannot. When Robert Lissner wrote AppleWorks, he created three special ProDOS file types: AWP for AppleWorks Word Processor, ADB for Data Base files, and ASP for Spreadsheet files. You will see those file type names when you catalog a disk from ProDOS BASIC.

Note, however, that Data Base report names have nothing to do with file names, even though a report name can be the same as a file name. A report always exists as part of an ADB file. Rules for naming Data Base reports are far more liberal than rules for naming ProDOS or AppleWorks files. Table 1.1 shows the differences in rules. We will discuss Data Base report and category names in greater detail in the Data Base chapter.

Tip: *Learn how to change Desktop file names.*

In AppleWorks, this option is as useful as the option for printing hard copies. By changing the name of a file on the Desktop,

Table 1.1: *Rules for file and report names*

Options	ProDOS Files	AppleWorks Files	Data Base Reports
Maximum characters	15	15	19
Lead numerals			X
Internal numerals	X	X	X
Lowercase letters	X	X	X
Symbols			X
Blank spaces		X	X

you isolate it from the previous version on disk. That means you can make all kinds of changes without worrying about destroying the previous file by accidentally saving the Desktop file. Specific applications of this tip appear throughout the book. The concept is broadly useful, and it cannot be stressed enough.

To change a file name, press Apple-N to put the cursor on the file name. Press Control-Y to clear the existing name, enter a new name, and press Return.

When you change a file name, the previous file name disappears from the Desktop, but the previous file of that name remains on the disk. If you do irreparable damage to the Desktop file, discard it, load the previous version again, and change the name again. If you make changes and want the new version to replace the previous version on the disk, change back to the original name before saving the file to disk.

Caution: *Never use the same name for two different files.*

If you name a Word Processor file Farm.Report and save that file on a disk named /P, AppleWorks will not let you overwrite it with a Spreadsheet (or Data Base) file that uses exactly the same name. An error message will appear telling you why you can't use that file name, and you will have to change the name. Figure 1.9 shows the error message screen.

If you name an ASCII or DIF file Farm.Report, AppleWorks will not prevent you from overwriting the AppleWorks file when you enter the path name /P/Farm.Report. That alone is reason enough to add special suffixes to ASCII and DIF files.

When loading files, you will be warned when a file name is identical to one already on the Desktop. However, AppleWorks will always let you do it, even if you have substantially changed the file already on the Desktop.

Lastly, you should know that AppleWorks considers FARM.RE-PORT and Farm.Report to be the same files. If you save Farm.Report to a disk that contains FARM.REPORT, Apple-Works will delete the file named FARM.REPORT.

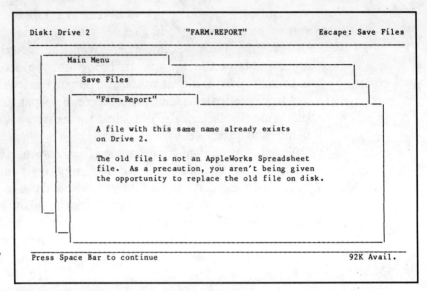

```
Disk: Drive 2                "FARM.REPORT"              Escape: Save Files

        Main Menu
            Save Files
                "Farm.Report"

                    A file with this same name already exists
                    on Drive 2.

                    The old file is not an AppleWorks Spreadsheet
                    file.  As a precaution, you aren't being given
                    the opportunity to replace the old file on disk.




  Press Space Bar to continue                               92K Avail.
```

Figure 1.9: *Same file name, different program*

Caution: *You can accidentally format the Program disk.*

Because AppleWorks writes date information on the Program disk each time you load AppleWorks, you cannot use a write-protect tab on the Program disk. When you begin using a new Program disk, you might forget to select drive 2 as the standard location of the data disk (with option 6 on the Other Activities menu). If you forgot to select drive 2 as the standard location of the data disk, drive 1 will remain the standard location by default. If you begin formatting disks without looking at the data drive location specified in the upper-left corner of the screen, AppleWorks *will* format its own Program disk.

Caution: *Desktop files generally require more space than disk files.*

Data in Desktop files is often further compressed when you save the file to disk. The corollary to this rule is that the Desktop will not always have room for a file, even if it seems to be small enough on the disk. When you attempt to load a file onto the Desktop, you may need to remove another file first.

Any discrepancy between Desktop file size and disk file size is understandably a matter of concern. Here are two examples of file size discrepancies that should make you feel more comfortable with AppleWorks.

A Data Base file named Members.List requires 90K on the Desktop, but only 76K on the disk. Discrepancies of this magnitude are common with Data Base files. When you load the file, make certain the Desktop has enough remaining memory.

A Spreadsheet file named Projections requires 16K on the Desktop and 17K on the disk. It is not unusual to find minor exceptions to the rule, particularly for Spreadsheet files with many copied formulas.

Tip: *When the Desktop has insufficient memory, remove the file AppleWorks requests you to remove.*

If you are close to the Desktop memory limit, the Desktop may run out of memory while you are entering information. (This may have happened to you already.) AppleWorks will tell you that you should save and must remove a specific file from the Desktop Index. It may not be the largest file, and it is almost never the one you would like to remove, but you have no choice. Figure 1.10 shows the screen message.

There is an easy way to avoid this problem: keep track of the remaining available memory. You may be wasting memory by leaving information on the clipboard.

USING THE CLIPBOARD

Apple-C permits you to copy information to the clipboard. The clipboard provides a temporary storage place where up to 250 lines of a file can be stored until retrieved. The clipboard borrows

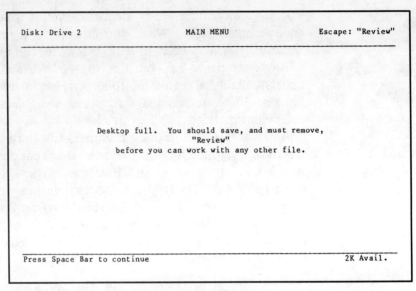

```
 Disk: Drive 2                    MAIN MENU                 Escape: "Review"




           Desktop full.  You should save, and must remove,
                                "Review"
                  before you can work with any other file.






 Press Space Bar to continue                                    2K Avail.
```

Figure 1.10: Request to remove a specific file

Desktop memory as needed, but AppleWorks never gives you direct information about how much memory the clipboard is using.

The clipboard is far more useful than the AppleWorks Reference Manual suggests. For example, it can efficiently move and copy information within documents, because it allows you to do other things while text is in temporary storage. The designated options for moving and copying within the document do not provide that capability.

In each chapter we will discuss specific additional applications for the clipboard. Some are surprising, while others are more obvious. Here we will review general approaches applicable throughout AppleWorks.

Tip: *Moving to the clipboard is often the most efficient way to move sections of information within a document.*

Place the cursor on the first line to be moved. Press Apple-M to access the Move menu, and then press T to indicate that the move will be to the clipboard. Move the cursor to highlight the desired lines, and press Return.

By using the clipboard you are free to do other things before deciding where to put the information. When you decide, place the cursor where you want the text to begin, and press Apple-M to access the Move menu again. Press F to move the lines from the clipboard. Copying lines to the clipboard is similar to moving, except that the text also remains in its original position.

If you use the designated option to move lines within the document, you cannot perform other operations until the move has been completed. If you move text to the clipboard, you can do almost anything before the move is completed. In fact, you can even move text within the document.

Tip: *By using the clipboard, you can copy two separate sections of information at once.*

If you copy one section of information to the clipboard, then immediately copy another section to it, the second section will replace the first. There is no way to keep two separate sections of information on the clipboard simultaneously, unless you first join the sections within the source document.

However, you can still copy another section within the document, while one section of information remains on the clipboard. Simply press Apple-C and select the first option to copy within the document. This option has no effect on the clipboard, but you must unload the "within" section before unloading the information on the clipboard.

Tip: *When you need to transfer anything between files, move to and from the clipboard whenever possible.*

The move and copy commands require different amounts of memory. Copying to the clipboard creates two copies of the text in memory. Copying from the clipboard leaves a copy on the clipboard (for a total of three). Moving simply changes the location of one segment, requiring almost no additional memory. Moving from the clipboard empties the clipboard.

Therefore, when you copy to the clipboard, move from the clipboard to empty it. When you move anything to the clipboard, you can still make multiple copies in the new document by copying from the clipboard more than once. The last use of the clipboard should be a move, again to empty it.

Tip: *You can empty the clipboard by moving or copying an empty space to it.*

There may be times when you copy lines from the clipboard and then realize that you really should have moved them from the clipboard instead. Suppose the clipboard has a 15K segment that you want to throw out. To do that, copy an empty space or line to the clipboard. The one-byte segment will replace the 15K segment, essentially emptying the clipboard and returning the needed memory to the Desktop. Figure 1.11 shows how the available Desktop memory decreases when 250 lines of text are copied to the clipboard.

Leaving copied information on the clipboard may bring you above the memory-use level at which file changes start to slow down. The copied information may even fill all the remaining available Desktop memory, forcing you to remove a file from the Desktop before proceeding further. The smaller the Desktop memory, the more important it is to use the clipboard efficiently.

EXPANDING THE DESKTOP

AppleWorks was designed to operate within 128K of RAM in both the Apple IIe and the Apple IIc. Several firms offer 80-column extended-memory cards with 256–1536K and more, however, and they also provide software that modifies AppleWorks so

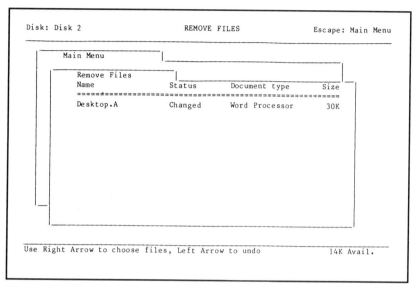

```
Disk: Disk 2                    REMOVE FILES            Escape: Main Menu


        Main Menu              |_____
                               |
        Remove Files          |_____
        Name              Status        Document type        Size
        ============================================================
        Desktop.A          Changed       Word Processor        30K












Use Right Arrow to choose files, Left Arrow to undo          14K Avail.
```

Figure 1.11: *56K Desktop, clipboard with 250 lines of text*

it can take advantage of the extended memory. We will look at an 80-column extended-memory card for the Apple IIe to understand the practical implications of this important innovation.

The descriptions that follow should be considered generically, because memory-expansion technology is evolving rapidly and innovations are appearing almost every month. Applied Engineering and Checkmate Technology have led the way in developing memory cards and in modifying AppleWorks to use additional memory.

Each AE RamWorks and Checkmate MultiRam card comes with a utility disk that adds capabilities to AppleWorks. Both firms offer inexpensive software upgrades. To run AppleWorks version 2.0 on an older card, you simply upgrade the software. That gives older cards (including mine) a long, useful life.

The information in this section is based on the AE AppleWorks 2.0 Expander version 2.01 and the MultiRam version 5.02 utilities. In this section we will refer to them simply as utilities and make distinctions only where they differ significantly. (For example, Applied Engineering uses a different disk for AppleWorks prior to version 2.0.)

Tip: *Extended-memory cards speed up the overall performance of a given task.*

This is often more important than the extended-memory capacity itself. The speed improvements come from the improved performance of Apple-Q.

In a previous caution we noted that with 24K of files loaded on a 55K Desktop, the Apple-Q command accesses the Program disk for more than four seconds before going to the Desktop Index, and then again for another four seconds before going to the new file. By adding enough RAM to the Desktop, you can change files within the same program almost instantly up to much higher memory-use levels.

Incidentally, there are two other hardware options for minimizing the time required for a given task:

1. With AppleWorks program files and data files on a hard disk, you can bring program segments and files to the Desktop in much less time than it requires to load them from a floppy disk. Hard disks for the Apple II generally come in 10- and 20-megabyte sizes, and although they greatly extend disk memory, they have no effect on Desktop memory capacity.

2. With an additional card that uses a 65C02 processor running at a faster clock speed, AppleWorks can execute processing operations faster. That option is important mainly for Spreadsheet recalculations and Data Base searches that use large files. It has no effect on the times required for loading and saving those files. If you have a IIGS, you already have a built-in choice of two clock speeds for its 65816 processor.

Tip: *Add memory yourself.*

Most cards have at least two memory banks that accept either 64K or 256K chips (you must be consistent within each bank of eight chips). You can find an older extended memory card with at least 64K installed for about $50, and a new one for $100–150. If you buy a card with one bank of 64K chips installed, add a bank of 150-nanosecond 256K chips. They cost about $30 for a set of nine, which provides a spare in case of any problem. The utilities for these memory cards include superb programs for diagnosing any problems.

If you buy a card with one bank of 256K chips, you have enough, but you may want to add the 64K chips from your original Apple 80-column memory card. Table 1.2 shows the minimum amount of Desktop memory you can expect to have when you use an 80-column extended-memory card of a specific size.

Inserting chips is simple enough, but there is one probable complication: you may find that the pins are slightly wide for the socket. To correct this problem, lay one side of pins on a firm, flat surface and apply just enough pressure to bend them slightly inward, all together. This should make them fit. Follow directions about where the notched end of the chip should be.

Caution: *Add only the memory you really need.*

A card with multiple banks can hold more memory if you need it later, but more memory requires more power, which generates

Table 1.2: Memory modifications to AppleWorks

	Extended Memory Cards			
	64K	**256K**	**320K**	**512K**
System Memory	128K	320K	384K	576K
Desktop Memory	55K	183K	229K	367K
RAM Option		X	X	X

more heat within your Apple II. Using large amounts of memory can also slow down AppleWorks. When you use large files on a large Desktop, it can take a long time—30 seconds or more—to remove a file.

For most AppleWorks users, a 256–320K memory card makes good sense. It can handle a large Data Base or Spreadsheet file when you really need one. It offers more than enough capacity for normal use with multiple files on the Desktop. (Recognizing this, Checkmate makes a small, inexpensive card with just one bank of 256K chips.)

Tip: *You can save a file onto sequential disks.*

With more than 136K of memory on the Desktop, it is obvious that files can grow too large for standard 5¼-inch disks. The utility software modifies AppleWorks to save such files to more than one disk in sequentially numbered segments.

If the file name is Budget, the second segment is automatically named Budget.2. When you reload, you load the segmented file in an orderly sequence. If your file already ends with the suffix .2 to denote the second version of the budget itself, the second segment is automatically called Budget.3. That may not be exactly what you had in mind. If you save very large files consistently, consider naming them differently. For example, a file named Budget.B would then be neatly segmented as Budget.B.2.

Limit the names of large files to 13 characters, because segmenting will truncate file names to fit the segment identification number within the ProDOS limit of 15 characters. Figure 1.12 shows some segmented file examples.

There is another possible complication with the segmenting process. If you try to save a new 60K file on a disk with room for only 50K, the modified AppleWorks will save what it can and ask for another disk to continue the save. In this case you should Escape from the save, find a disk with more room, and save the file as a single entity.

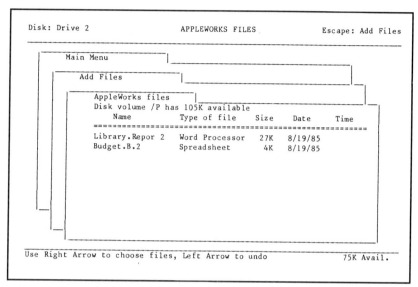

Figure 1.12: *Renamed file segments*

Tip: *You can expand the Desktop by adding memory to your Apple IIc.*

Apple IIc owners have not been ignored by firms offering memory expansion. Applied Engineering and Checkmate also offer extended memories of 256K and more for the Apple IIc, along with software to modify AppleWorks. The ability to load all of AppleWorks into RAM, described in the following tip, is particularly useful for Apple IIc users who want to use Apple-Works efficiently with one disk drive.

Tip: *You can load AppleWorks into RAM with a 256K memory card.*

The AE software can modify AppleWorks so that it automatically loads into RAM, providing instant access to each component program. It takes about 30 seconds to load everything from the Program disk into RAM, so there may not be a net benefit for short sessions.

Loading AppleWorks entirely into RAM has no effect on the available Desktop memory. If you have a 384K system, the Desktop has 229K whether you use the RAM option or not. In general, it makes sense to use the RAM option when shifting back and forth between programs (for example, to add several Spreadsheet tables to a Word Processor report). Rapid program access makes it easier to remember how to respond in one file to information you have just seen in another file.

Apple IIc owners will appreciate the option to load everything into RAM, because it allows you to efficiently use drive 1 as the standard data disk location. However, you should understand that if the Desktop is loaded to near capacity, a file segment may replace a program segment. After that point AppleWorks will need to access the Program disk in drive 1 for the necessary program segment.

Tip: *Utility software dramatically increases the Data Base record capacity.*

The standard Data Base can manage up to 1350 records. With the Utility software that capacity increases to more than 22,000 records. The complete Data Base file is stored in RAM all at once, so record selection and arranging are incredibly fast. The modified Data Base gives the Apple II series a significant advantage over other personal computer systems in a broad range of professional applications.

Increases in the record limit decrease available Desktop memory by about 2K per 1000 records, so it is generally best to work with 2000–6000 records. You can change that option quickly when loading AppleWorks.

Tip: *You can add other useful capabilities.*

Utilities more than double the maximum length of Word Processor files, which is more useful for assembling files to print than for editing. Applied Engineering can take the Word Processor beyond 22,000 lines and the clipboard to more than 2000 lines for the Word Processor and Data Base. The latter capability means you can copy complete files at a time. AE also lets you use available memory as a print buffer.

The Checkmate expander for AppleWorks versions 1.2 and 1.3 installs a save routine similar to that used by version 2.0. Another Checkmate program enables you to use extended memory for a RAM disk (it works with AE cards as well). An electronic "disk" in memory saves time by providing almost instant access. For example, with a spelling checker and its dictionary on a RAM disk, you can review and correct misspelled words in less than half the time it would otherwise take.

Tip: *You can minimize conflicts if you think ahead about AppleWorks modifications.*

Patches and programs that modify AppleWorks can create conflicts. You have to think ahead if you use more than one program at a time. The most important rule to remember is this: always use a copy of AppleWorks, not the original, and always archive at least one extra copy of the original.

Here is the order for using extended-memory card utilities and Super MacroWorks described in Chapter 7:

1. Copy the patched version of ProDOS onto the AppleWorks Startup disk.

2. Install the Super MacroWorks pre-expander patch.

3. Use the extended memory utility.

4. Install Super MacroWorks.

If you make the pre-expander patch without installing Super MacroWorks in step 4, AppleWorks will not work.

Tip: *You can make time-clock modifications to the Apple-Works disks.*

Several firms offer clock cards that can be used to add the date and time to any ProDOS file, including AppleWorks files. If you have installed a clock, the correct date will automatically appear when you load the AppleWorks program, and you will never have to consult a calendar.

Utility software for extended-memory cards includes software with its clock card that can modify AppleWorks in two additional ways. First, a corner of the screen can show the current date and time. This modification has no particular advantage over a wind-up watch, and some people may prefer not to be constantly reminded about time, but you can turn it off. Second, another modification allows you to enter the actual time and date into Data Base time and date categories by pressing a specified key. This can be particularly useful in specialized time-conscious applications, such as record-keeping for shipping and receiving operations.

After the AppleWorks program has been modified, you can use it with or without the clock card installed for additional flexibility.

Caution: *There is no design standard for memory cards.*

Software for one memory card will not necessarily work with another. Memory management methods vary among card manufacturers, but you can generally transfer segmented AppleWorks files.

Several firms, including Apple, offer RAM cards for the IIGS. Although these cards work differently than the ones we have described, they serve the same purposes. AppleWorks version 2.0 automatically recognizes these cards, expands Desktop memory, and increases Data Base capacity to 6350 records.

Unfortunately, AppleWorks version 2.0 uses Apple RAM cards inefficiently, reserving all the memory to itself. It never loads the printer segment, so it never completely frees a disk drive. Other RAM cards come with software that solves these problems while maintaining Apple compatibility.

Through all this the old Apple IIe has fared remarkably well. With an extended-memory card and coprocessor from third parties, it can store many more records and handle them faster than a IIGS with an Apple RAM card.

COMMON APPLEWORKS COMMANDS

About a dozen commands work the same way in each of the three component programs. These commands are as central to the operation of AppleWorks as the Desktop itself. The following tips supplement the information in the AppleWorks Reference Manual.

Tip: *AppleWorks has undocumented control commands.*

As with many programs, AppleWorks can use additional control commands that duplicate documented AppleWorks commands. One offers a particular advantage: Apple-Y functions exactly as Control-Y does, deleting the rest of a Word Processor line, Data Base category, or Spreadsheet cell. Apple-Y is often more convenient, because you use the Apple keys so often. You should also know that if your finger slips while using Apple-U to edit a Spreadsheet cell, you might clear the cell with a mistaken Apple-Y.

Some other control commands are standard commands on the Apple: Control-I for Tab, Control-J for ↓, Control-K for ↑, Control-H for ←, Control-U for →, and Control-M for Return. These offer no particular advantage, but if the cursor moves unexpectedly when you thought you pressed Control-B, Control-L, or Control-Y, you will know that it happened because you used an Apple rather than an AppleWorks command.

Tip: *When a screen message requests you to hit the Space bar, Return will do as well (but not vice versa).*

This tip is most worth remembering when you format a box of disks; using nothing but Return improves your response time. Space bar messages are generally used to make you slow down and think about your response. If you have been there a hundred times before, you may not need to think it over again.

Caution: *The Ruler is really a divider.*

The Ruler in AppleWorks divides a file into eight vertical parts. It is therefore really a divider, not a ruler. While it finds relative locations well, it cannot be used to locate precise positions within a file.

Apple-1 marks the beginning of the first section; Apple-8 marks the beginning of the eighth; Apple-9 marks the very end of the file. The locations of section markers 2 through 8 change as the file becomes longer or shorter.

To find precise locations, use fixed markers in the Word Processor and cell coordinates in the Spreadsheet. For locating precise points in Data Base files, there is no obvious all-purpose choice.

USING PRODOS

The Desktop is, in a functional sense, the operating system for AppleWorks. It depends on and extends ProDOS. AppleWorks performs efficiently because of the operating system, and ProDOS has gained wide acceptance because AppleWorks has become the most widely used Apple software package.

ProDOS loads and saves files quickly by any standards. It can load an 18K Spreadsheet file in less than ten seconds, which is less than 20 percent of the time required for a similar file using the DOS 3.3 version of VisiCalc. If you use only AppleWorks files, you can probably get by without knowing much more about ProDOS. Everyone else should read on.

If you have an Apple IIe, you probably have the ProDOS User's Disk Utilities. If you have an Apple IIc, you have a disk called the ProDOS System Utilities. In this book I will refer to both as the ProDOS utilities. They are used most often to copy disks.

Tip: *Learn the differences between DOS 3.3 and ProDOS files.*

DOS 3.3 and ProDOS differ in many ways, but one difference is particularly important here: a disk formatted for ProDOS has a volume name preceded by a slash (/) mark. That name is separated from any file name by another slash. The name can be brief, such as the /P used throughout this book. ProDOS volume names cannot be longer than 15 characters. The same rule applies to ProDOS file names. Volume names precede file names, as in /P/Filename. Together they are called the path name.

Tip: *Think of a ProDOS volume as a disk.*

For most AppleWorks purposes, a ProDOS volume is the same as a standard 136K floppy disk. Although a ProDOS volume can have subdirectories, there is really no need to use them with a two-disk-drive system. An AppleWorks data disk seldom has more than 20 AppleWorks files, so there is rarely any confusion. If you have a hard disk or a high-capacity floppy disk, subdirectories provide branching paths for finding your way through many files.

Tip: *If you use standard 136K disks, give each data disk a standard volume name.*

A brief standard volume name (such as /P) is easier to remember and enter when you write path names for ASCII and DIF files or for segmented Data Base files.

Formatted data disks can then be interchangeable on an Apple system with two standard disk drives. If you use the ProDOS utilities to compare or copy files or volumes, you can quickly rename one volume to avoid confusion or error. Note, however, that in most cases you will be copying files by loading them to the Desktop and saving them to another disk.

Note that this tip is limited to 136K AppleWorks data disks. Program disks should have distinct names. Each copy of an AppleWorks disk should be named /APPLEWORKS.

Tip: *If you use large-capacity disks, use short volume and subdirectory names.*

AppleWorks, the ProDOS utilities, and many other Apple II programs require you to type in both the volume and subdirectory names whenever you change subdirectories. The AppleWorks tutorials show long descriptive names that take advantage of the ProDOS 15-character limit. However, if you use anything more than minimal abbreviations for often-used volumes and subdirectories, you will quickly become frustrated by the number of characters you need to type.

Utilities included with macro programs offer automatic catalog listings with the option to use the cursor to select the desired file in a subdirectory (see Chapter 7).

Tip: *The ProDOS User's Disk Utilities can compare Apple-Works files and volumes.*

If you question whether two identically named AppleWorks files are in fact identical, the ProDOS Filer can compare them. Use the Filer first to quickly rename one of the volumes.

When should you compare files? Suppose you saved two important Spreadsheet files. You might want to make certain that both saves were perfect. Suppose you checked one Word Processor file for spelling errors, made corrections, and saved the file to two disks. You might want to make certain that both saves were perfect. In general, it is a test for perfection. If you simply doubt whether a file has been backed up, just save it from the Desktop again.

The ProDOS Filer will also run on the Apple IIc, even though it is not included with the ProDOS System Utilities.

Tip: *The ProDOS utilities can lock AppleWorks files.*

There are good reasons to lock AppleWorks files. For example, you may eventually use templates as the source for 80 percent of all new AppleWorks files. Sooner or later you will save a completed file over the template because you forgot to change the file name. If you lock the template file, that cannot happen.

The ProDOS utilities can lock any ProDOS file. Then, if you try to save a file to a disk that contains a locked file of the same name, AppleWorks will not permit it. You will see the screen message shown in Figure 1.13. If you later want to unlock the file, return to the ProDOS utilities.

Caution: *ProDOS 1.1.1 can destroy data on 5¹/₄-inch disks.*

Under highly unusual circumstances, ProDOS 1.1.1 can destroy data on track 0 of standard 136K disks. Track 0 is critically important because it contains directory information for the entire disk.

The *Open-Apple* newsletter for November 1986 provided a thorough explanation of what happens, along with a patch to correct the problem. To make the patch, use a copy of your original ProDOS Filer disk or System Utilities disk. Unlock the ProDOS file and then go to Applesoft BASIC. When the right bracket character (]) appears, enter the following:

```
BLOAD PRODOS,A$2000,TSYS
POKE 22211,189 : POKE 22214,189
POKE 22217,189 : POKE 22220,189
```

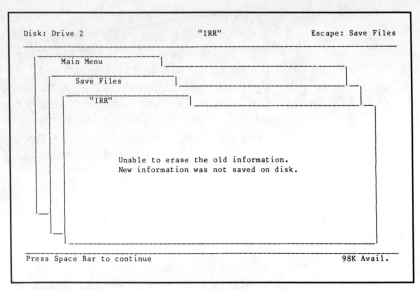

Figure 1.13: *Screen message indicating locked file*

```
POKE 20484,189 : POKE 20485,142
POKE 20486,192 : POKE 9463,208
BSAVE PRODOS,A$2000,TSYS
```

Reboot the patched ProDOS disk. It should now show ProDOS 1.1.1P (for patched) on the opening screen.

The ProDOS file on the AppleWorks disk should already be unlocked. Use the ProDOS utilities to delete the file. Then copy ProDOS from the Utilities disk to the AppleWorks disk. You will probably want to repeat the process for other program disks that include ProDOS 1.1.1 (or earlier versions).

MANAGING PROJECTS

This section covers the problems of managing your own desktop—the one with real pencils and papers. Because AppleWorks lets you work more productively, you may have more to manage.

If you want to work efficiently with AppleWorks, group your tasks into clearly defined projects. Give each project its own disks, notebook, hanging files, and so on. You can undertake many projects in the same time period, provided everything remains neatly partitioned.

If you spend time searching for papers lost in heaps, pay particular attention to this section. AppleWorks will eventually straighten you out, whether you want it to or not, but everything will be easier if you make a conscious effort to cooperate.

Tip: *Learn to manage disks efficiently.*

The important concept is to keep related files on the same disk. Use keywords to describe the contents of the disk. For example, Ames Project Letters could describe a disk of letter files, even though no single file uses that specific name. The keywords on the label need have nothing to do with the ProDOS volume names (all of which might be /P, for example).

Keep related disks in the same box. Some disks come in a hard box that can store up to 12 disks, and they last a long time. Use keywords to describe the box. For example, Ames Project could describe a box of disks, even though no single disk has that label.

Neatly typed file names on the label mean little in themselves. Twenty unrelated files on a disk will always be something of a jumble, even if the file names are typed alphabetically on the disk label—logical grouping is the key.

Tip: *Make a "working disk."*

At any given time you may be working on several projects, transferring information, and saving unrelated files on the same disk. A "working disk" allows anyone to break the rules in a controlled way.

The disk should include at least three files we will design later: a Word Processor template, a Spreadsheet parts file, and a multipurpose Data Base template. All of these together take about 6K on the disk, leaving another 130K free for the day's work. Figure 1.14 shows the catalog of a typical "working disk."

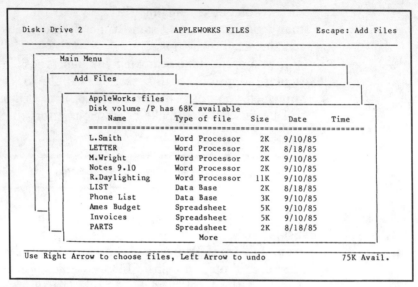

Figure 1.14: *Partial catalog of a "working disk"*

During the day, save files to the "working disk" if they cannot conveniently be saved to the proper disk. At the end of the day, save everything to its proper disk and delete any unnecessary files.

Tip: *Print hard copies of the screen to document your work.*

Documentation is, without question, the most tedious part of applications development; few people do it thoroughly. When you design a template, make copies of key screens and annotate them. In many cases your documentation will be a collection of these annotated copies.

Tip: *Use keyboard templates and make notes.*

Keyboard templates offer a simple but effective way to remember the things that count most, such as commands and formulas.

You can design a template sheet, print it on utility bond paper, and have it copied onto card stock. Highlight specific commands in yellow, and write comments in pencil in the margins. You can and should make your own templates for specific applications, or use self-adhesive Post-It notes for simple reminders.

The most common kind of keyboard template is for people who are learning AppleWorks or using it only occasionally. It should be designed for using the Word Processor and for working with existing Spreadsheet and Data Base applications. The commands in AppleWorks use the letter keys wisely for mnemonic purposes, but some people need time to adapt, particularly if they have used other programs. For example, VisiCalc users may have difficulty remembering Apple-L for layout (rather than F for format).

Specialized templates are also helpful for experienced users who design Spreadsheet or Data Base applications. Include what you need most: engineering formulas, selected commands, and so on. After several days away from AppleWorks you may need a template to remember obscure command sequences, such as the one to reset manual recalculation in the Spreadsheet.

No matter how experienced you are with AppleWorks, you will always be learning something new that you have not quite mastered. This is the kind of information that belongs on a keyboard template. There is no point in remembering information such as the number equivalent to column N in the Spreadsheet, even though you sometimes need to know that when designing applications. This kind of information also belongs on a template.

There are some patterns for templates in Appendix B. Before you spend as much as $20 on a plastic template, think about making one yourself (and make some copies for your friends).

Tip: *Put a note board on the wall near your Apple.*

You need a place to post information, especially hard copies of the AppleWorks menu screens. After a hundred hours on Apple-Works, when you can see the screens in your mind's eye, you can use the space for new information. People always need more surface area for information, and note boards conveniently provide that.

What else belongs on the note board? An Apple II reference chart is particularly helpful. Beagle Bros, a firm specializing in utility software, publishes one such chart that is a classic in graphic design. The chart comes with many Beagle Bros programs, including Extra-K, a program noted in Appendix A.

Tip: *Develop a method for differentiating programs, templates, and data files just by glancing at the disk label.*

One way to do this is to use different-colored pens to write the disk labels. For example, use a red soft-tip pen to write disk labels for programs. A ProDOS volume name may be different from the program name, so it is usually best to include both names on the disk label. Use a black soft-tip pen for templates and common data files, or use any color combination that makes sense to you.

To differentiate template files from common data files, you can write and enter the template file names entirely in uppercase letters. Though uppercase letters are harder to read, this is a case where it may be more important to differentiate between word groups than between letters.

Tip: *Assign a prefix to note the purpose of an Apple-Works file.*

Choose a prefix for denoting files of similar type (for example: LTR or L for letter). Use short prefixes to leave more space for descriptive names. The idea is to choose prefixes that make sense to you. Above all, be consistent. Include your own standard abbreviations on an editorial style sheet, and post that sheet on your note board.

Tip: *Add time records to critical files.*

AppleWorks provides an option to enter the correct date when the Program first loads. Use that option faithfully, because you will often need to compare file dates.

Sometimes you will need to know which of two files is the most recent when both have the same date stamp. A clock card can place a time stamp on a file, but rather than buying a clock card, why not write the date and time at the beginning of the file, so that you can find it with Apple-1. Use a consistent form, such as the AppleWorks convention (Oct 1 87 5:30 PM).

Printouts likewise need date and time stamps. We have all mistakenly used the wrong printouts as often as the wrong files. By entering the time in the file itself, you also print it on paper copies—something a clock card does not do.

Tip: *Use the Escape key to hide your work.*

If someone needs to talk to you while you are using Apple-Works, their eyes will inevitably be attracted to the flashing cursor on the screen. You may have some work displayed that you would rather not have others see. Simply press Escape to go to the Main Menu. Your work is off the screen, and pressing Escape again will bring it back just as quickly.

Tip: *Use both sides of 5¹/₄-inch disks.*

Think of each side as a separate disk, because that is how your disk drives see them. To write to the opposite side of any disk, lay another disk on it face down, outline the notch location, then use a common paper punch to make the new notch. Better yet, buy a disk punch that aligns itself perfectly and makes square notches—Quorum makes a great one.

If you have single-sided, double-density disks, you may want to use the ProDOS utility disks to verify the blocks on the reverse side. After verifying ten or so, you will probably feel completely confident.

Many people use both sides of the disk for archival storage and limited day-to-day use. In theory, using both sides can expose the magnetic surfaces to more dust particles. In practice this has not been a problem.

You can even install AppleWorks on both sides of a disk. I have used a disk that way for years with no problems. If anything ever does go wrong, just insert an identical backup disk and keep working.

Tip: *Find a small case to carry AppleWorks and data disks.*

AppleWorks used to come with a small plastic case that protected up to six disks. You could put your own address on the case and carry it in a briefcase to and from anywhere. You can find similar plastic cases in many computer supply stores.

Tip: *When available time on your Apple is limited, consider the things you can do by hand.*

In many cases, two or more people share an Apple for personal and professional uses. Sometimes it would be nice to use AppleWorks when someone else is using it, but it may not be all that necessary. Consider what can be done with a pencil and paper.

Preliminary report outlining can be done as efficiently on paper as on the Word Processor. Spreadsheet design can be done efficiently on graph paper, and you can make preliminary back-of-the-envelope calculations with a $15 scientific calculator. Database design can be done on hard copies of record layout, report format, and printer options screens.

SUMMARY

In this chapter I have addressed the common problems that tend to slow people down by presenting many tips and techniques that you can use repeatedly.

Practice using the tips for working on the Desktop and practice using the ProDOS utilities to do the things AppleWorks cannot do. If you use AppleWorks often, consider adding memory to match your needs. Remember that you can always install more memory later.

Above all, concentrate on bringing logical order to your work. That will save more time than anything else you do. AppleWorks can help you greatly: it is a superb model of order and efficient design in its own right.

As you understand more about Desktop operation, you can work more efficiently with the Word Processor, Data Base, and Spreadsheet. In the next three chapters, you can draw upon what you have learned in this chapter. There will be tips for changing file names, copying to the clipboard, and using AppleWorks commands for unexpected purposes. The tips and techniques in this chapter will help you build component parts that can be used again and again in many useful applications.

2
The Word Processor

ost AppleWorks users spend more time with the Word Processor than with the other programs, and for good reason. We generally exchange information by putting our thoughts into words and sentences, which we then use to construct letters, reports, manuals, and even books. In doing so we become, in effect, wordsmiths, for whom the Word Processor can be a valuable tool.

As word processors go, the AppleWorks Word Processor is easy to learn and teach, because what you see on the screen is essentially what you get printed on paper (especially if you keep the formatting simple). Most people feel comfortable enough with the Word Processor to begin typing without much instruction. If you are teaching others, encourage them to start writing on their own. AppleWorks has good error-trapping routines, so no one will get lost.

Although the Word Processor may lack some commands, it is large and fast. (In fact, one can make that comment about all the AppleWorks programs.) When you compare it to other respected word processors, AppleWorks does not look quite as powerful. But in day-to-day work, AppleWorks holds its own. Although the AppleWorks Word Processor cannot generate complex form letters, version 2.0 has a Mail Merge option that meets most common needs. AppleWorks does not provide exact word and character counts, but its line and character counts suffice for approximations. AppleWorks cannot use macros to substitute one keystroke for a block of text, but add-on macro programs are available.

The Word Processor has fast screen response, superb file-handling routines, and a large file capacity in RAM. Most people will find the Word Processor good enough, even for writing a book.

This chapter provides tips in eight sections for getting the most from using the AppleWorks Word Processor. The first section provides some general tips. The section on entering text provides some important insights about efficient use of the keyboard. The section on writing letters includes useful information on using letter templates, writing form letters, and printing mailing labels. In the large section on printer options, you should particularly note the Word Processor rules for paragraph and page integrity, as well as techniques for managing margins and character columns.

The fifth section provides some tips for using the copy command in ways you may not have considered. The following section introduces some useful applications for the find and replace commmands. The next section covers methods for handling problems presented by long files with complex formats. The final section in this chapter provides tips for using spelling checkers with the Word Processor.

GENERAL WORD PROCESSOR TIPS

This section contains general insights about how the Word Processor works. You will usually begin your work from scratch or by loading a file onto the Desktop. Writing is only as good as the thought and editing behind it. By using this program efficiently, you can have more time to do the work that counts. Figure 2.1 shows the Word Processor menu.

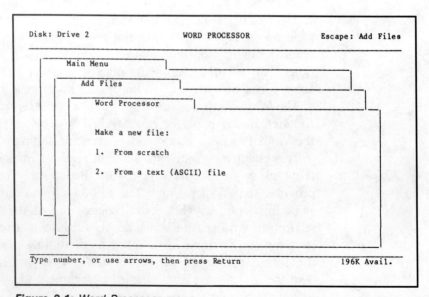

```
Disk: Drive 2                WORD PROCESSOR              Escape: Add Files

         Main Menu

            Add Files

               Word Processor


               Make a new file:

               1.  From scratch

               2.  From a text (ASCII) file




Type number, or use arrows, then press Return              196K Avail.
```

Figure 2.1: *Word Processor menu*

Tip: *Print and annotate hard copies of the Word Processor menus.*

You will need a hard copy of the Word Processor menu and the Printer Options menu, as well as the command menus for Apple-Tab, Apple-F, Apple-R, and Apple-P. If you have not yet done so, print copies of all these screens using Apple-H, and post the copies on a note board near your Apple. Pencil in notes about when you use each option. A hard copy of the Printer Options menu for version 2.0 appears in Figure 2.2. Earlier versions lack the Mail Merge option. Use a yellow marker to highlight the line showing the main printer options in effect.

Tip: *The cursor always appears at the beginning when you reload a file.*

A file is also always displayed in the normal display mode when you reload it, regardless of whether you were previously using the

```
File: Options                  PRINTER OPTIONS      Escape: Review/Add/Change
=====|====|====|====|====|====|====|====|====|====|====|====|====|====|====|===




          PW=8.0  LM=1.0   RM=1.0  CI=10  UJ   PL=11.0  TM=0.0  BM=2.0  LI=6  SS
     Option:                 UJ: Unjustified       GB: Group Begin      BE: Boldface End
                             CN: Centered          GE: Group End        +B: Superscript Beg
     PW: Platen Width        PL: Paper Length      HE: Page Header       +E: Superscript End
     LM: Left Margin         TM: Top Margin        FO: Page Footer       -B: Subscript Begin
     RM: Right Margin        BM: Bottom Margin     SK: Skip Lines        -E: Subscript End
     CI: Chars per Inch      LI: Lines per Inch    PN: Page Number       UB: Underline Begin
     P1: Proportional-1      SS: Single Space      PE: Pause Each page   UE: Underline End
     P2: Proportional-2      DS: Double Space      PH: Pause Here        PP: Print Page No.
     IN: Indent              TS: Triple Space      SM: Set a Marker      EK: Enter Keyboard
     JU: Justified           NP: New Page          BB: Boldface Begin    MM: Mail Merge
```

Figure 2.2: *Printer Options menu for AppleWorks version 2.0*

layout mode. (The Data Base follows similar conventions, but in the Spreadsheet the cursor remains where you left it.)

While the file is on the Desktop, the cursor and the display mode always remain as you left them, which is exactly as it should be. Make a note of this, because when you make a quick change to another file, you may return with text on the clipboard, and you almost always need to come back to precisely the same place.

Tip: *In AppleWorks, a "paragraph" is anything that ends with a carriage return marker.*

You always use Return to end a paragraph. You type sentences and let the Word Processor decide when to wrap words. At the end of the paragraph you press Return and begin the next paragraph on the following line.

Note, however, that there are times when Return serves other purposes. For example, it can end

- A title or heading line

- A line of text in a list (such as this list)

- A row in a table

Because each of these examples ends with a carriage return marker, AppleWorks sees them as "paragraphs," even though they are not paragraphs in the sense that we normally use the word. You have to remember the peculiar AppleWorks definition, because the Word Processor makes decisions about printer options based on the locations of carriage return markers.

It is important to consider the complications that this can create. For example, you can also end a "paragraph" by inadvertently entering a Return instead of letting AppleWorks wrap the word down to the next line.

Tip: *Format option values are saved with each file.*

When you save a file, you save all the specified printer options with it. When you load a file, use Apple-Z to make these options visible in the stack at the beginning of the file. Notice that when an option has been superceded, it nevertheless remains in the stack. You can delete the ones you no longer need with Apple-D.

Tip: *Printers are listed in the order you added them.*

When you first tell AppleWorks you want to print, the proposed printer is always the one at the top of the list. To have your printer there you must configure it first, even if that means removing the Apple Dot Matrix Printer and the Imagewriter that Apple has already added. It helps to have your standard printer on top, so you can use Return to step through the printing menu sequence.

Tip: *Save your work to disk at least every 20 minutes.*

Press Apple-S at least every 20 minutes to save what you have entered. Save it to a backup disk as well on every second or third save, especially when you have to look something up or stop to think about what to write next.

ENTERING TEXT

Most of your time with the Word Processor will be spent entering text, so it helps to know everything you can about working efficiently. With AppleWorks you spend more time on the lower rows of the keyboard than you would on a typewriter. That is where the arrow keys are located, along with the Apple-C, Apple-M, and Apple-Z commands.

Caution: *The Word Processor lacks several basic editing commands.*

The Word Processor has no command to delete the character directly under the cursor. This means that you must move the cursor one character to the right before pressing the Delete key. Likewise, the Word Processor cannot delete a whole word at a time. You have to use the Delete key for each character, which takes only a few extra seconds here and there, but the time adds up after a while.

The Word Processor cannot change the case of a letter under the cursor. It cannot restore a deletion made by mistake. It has no command to move the cursor directly to the first or last character of a text line.

Fortunately, you can have all of these capabilities with an add-on macro program (see Chapter 7).

Tip: *Use a text entry line wider than the default setting.*

At any given time, the screen can display up to 20 lines of text, less than half of a letter-size page. You can view more text on the screen if you change the default margins to allow more characters on a text line. Try 70–72 characters per line—this line length is easy for the eyes to scan, and it still leaves some empty space at the right of the screen.

In addition, changing the CI setting (characters per inch) will display more characters on screen without changing the margins.

The most practical line length for writing may not be the best for printing, but you can reformat quickly if you define the overall format at the beginning of the file.

Tip: *Move the cursor as efficiently as possible.*

Each method of moving the cursor has advantages in specific situations. Your choice of method depends on where you are in a document and where you want to move.

When moving the cursor most of a line forward or backward, hold down an Apple key and press → or ← to jump one word at a time. On wide lines, try this variation: hold down → or ← to start the cursor moving one character at a time, then press an

Apple key to increase speed as needed; you will quickly get the feel of it.

Apple-← will move the cursor to the left across a large space in a line with one move. You can use such moves often, because you will normally enter text at the end of a document, where the line below the cursor is empty. To move the cursor from anywhere in the last line of a document to the first letter of the last line, you can move down into the empty space with ↓, left all at once with Apple-←, and up to the first letter of the last line with ↑. Use these open-space moves whenever you can.

There is another way to move quickly from the end to the beginning of the line your cursor is on. Press ↑ to move the cursor to somewhere near the end of the previous line, then press Apple-→ one or more times to reach the first letter of the line where you started.

Tab and Apple-Tab also move the cursor quickly back and forth across lines of text. These keys are particularly useful for reaching a specific column in an empty line or empty part of a line. Try working with fewer tabs, so that the ones you have set are useful not only as tabs but also for moving the cursor quickly.

Tip: *Make a note of when you use the insert and overstrike cursors.*

The insert cursor is a blinking underline that inserts characters—place the cursor on a character, type in another character, and the original character is pushed to the right. The overstrike cursor is a blinking rectangle that types over characters—place the cursor on a character, type in another character, and the new character replaces the old. You can switch between cursors using Apple-E, and you will undoubtedly develop preferences for each in different circumstances.

You may find that you generally use the insert cursor for draft writing, because you need to add information and push text ahead of the cursor. The overstrike cursor works well for editing, particularly for changing individual characters within defined spaces, as in tables, for example. In overstrike mode you can use the Space bar to blank out characters with spaces.

Tip: *The overstrike cursor is useful for creating small tables.*

The overstrike cursor types over letters instead of pushing letters to the right. Use it to maintain alignments on small tables that you build in the Word Processor.

Use the insert cursor with the Delete key and Space bar to push entire rows back and forth within tables. Note also that you can copy spaces from the clipboard to create a whole new column. This technique is described in the section on moving and copying text.

For large tables designed and built by trial and error, use the Spreadsheet. We will discuss this "build-and-transfer" technique in Chapter 5.

Tip: *Delete characters as efficiently as possible.*

Apple-Y deletes everything from the cursor to the end of the line. For large deletions, place the cursor on the first or last character to be removed. Press Apple-D, move the cursor to highlight the text to be erased, and then press Return to complete the deletion. Note that when you highlight lines of text from the first character of a line using ↓, the highlighting continues one character beyond the final line specified. Therefore, you must remember to press ← once before you press Return to delete the material.

The Delete key works well for deleting one or two words, but Apple-D is more efficient for deleting more than two words (to the left or right of the cursor). Again, however, the highlighting goes one character too far when you use Apple-→ to highlight whole words, so remember to press ← once before you press Return.

One Delete will traverse all of the open space to the right of a carriage return marker and remove that marker if it is the first and only thing in the line. To delete any other carriage return marker, move one space to the right of it and press the Delete key to eliminate it. Make certain the return markers are visible when you do this.

Tip: *Use Apple-Z to display all text markers.*

Many printer options are visible on screen only when you use Apple-Z to display the file in layout mode. Files usually have a few format setting lines at the beginning and others scattered through the file. Each takes a line of its own, whether it is displayed or not. Note that caret (^) markings used for certain print enhancements always appear on screen.

When you move or copy text, you need format settings to highlight text accurately—it makes a difference whether you take format markers with you. Thus, when you move or copy text, the Word Processor always displays the format settings automatically, often displaying additional lines on the screen. When the display changes, the text line your eyes are following will shift down or even off the screen, and it takes time to adjust to the new display. Furthermore, when you write macros to automate keystrokes, the display changes faster, and the rapid shifts to and from the layout mode can be disorienting.

In most cases you will be writing text with simple formatting, and the marks displayed in the layout mode will not be obtrusive. Save the normal display mode for the Word Processor's best possible preview of what the printer will put on paper.

Tip: *Delete any spaces preceding carriage return markers.*

Spaces between sentence-ending periods and carriage return markers can cause mischief in printing, notably by adding unexpected empty lines to printed copy. You need to see the markers in order to find and delete the unwanted spaces; Apple-Z takes you to the display that shows these markers. If you are already using the previous tip, you will be in layout mode most of the time anyway.

You can search for spaces all at once before printing a document. With experience you will develop an eye for detecting them, and the experience will come faster if you use the layout mode consistently.

Tip: *Minimize word-wrapping distraction.*

If the last word on a line does not quite fit, that entire word moves down to the beginning of the next line. It will move back up to the previous line only if you delete enough of the characters in front of it. This process is called word wrapping; it can be confusing to watch continuously.

There is an easy way to prevent words from wrapping during writing and editing. If you plan to insert a sentence or more in the middle of a paragraph, press Return and type on an empty line until you finish that sentence. Then press Delete to eliminate the carriage return marker and close up the space that separates new text from what follows.

Tip: *Use the clipboard efficiently.*

Read all the clipboard tips in Chapter 1 if you have not already done so, because with the Word Procesor it is especially important to use the clipboard efficiently. Where the tips refer to lines, think of text. In the Word Processor, you can move or copy as little as one character or as much as 250 lines. The 250 lines are counted in the source document, even if the source document has wider lines than the destination document or vice versa. You can use a 77-character line in the source document to move the most text possible.

Tip: *Sticky spaces serve two important purposes.*

Sticky spaces are normally used to keep two words together on a line. For example, Apple II would look peculiar if Apple and II were split apart, so you can replace the space with a sticky space (Apple-Space bar) to keep them together. You will often need to do this for words with associated numbers.

Sticky spaces can also be used independently to make the Word Processor recognize an otherwise empty line. Two following tips explain the use of sticky spaces with page calculations and double spacing.

Caution: *The Word Processor has no soft hyphen.*

Many word processors include a soft hyphen, which allows you to hyphenate a word conditionally. You insert a soft hyphen when you need to split a word at the end of a text line. The soft hyphen appears as a regular hyphen when printed. If you subsequently reformat the text so that the word is no longer at the end of a line, no hyphen appears. AppleWorks lacks this capability, but there are ways around this limitation.

For the word in question you can enter a hyphen followed by a space. (Use a dictionary to make certain where the hyphen can go.) That solves the problem. For words already connected by a hyphen, enter a space after the hyphen. If you later add text or change side margins, check the hyphens, too. Use the find command to locate all instances of a hyphen followed by a space.

Most people print text without justifying the right margin, but even then an occasional long word can create an unusually large space at the end of a text line. If the printed text will have fewer than 77 characters per line and no line contains more than a few print-enhancement markers, what you see on screen is just about what you will get on paper.

WRITING LETTERS

Business letters are generally less than one page long, with simple formatting and printing requirements. You may want to use the same thought in more than one letter, or produce a dozen or more letters of almost exactly the same form. The following tips present useful information for those who write business letters.

Tip: *Left-justified letters are the easiest to format.*

Left-justification (or blocked style) is an efficient letter form for both the word processor and the reader. There is no need to spend time centering headings and closings (in fact, that style of letter writing is now considered dated). Leave at least three line spaces for the signature before the typed name.

Figure 2.3 shows a sample letter. You may want to enter the letter as a Word Processor document so you can try out some of the techniques discussed below.

Tip: *Use a letter template.*

A letter template need contain no more than an address heading, a greeting, a closing, and a signature name, along with some basic format settings (for example, tabs and margins) and any necessary printer option settings. You can save copies of the template on several disks, wherever it is needed. Use an uppercase file name, such as LETTER, for the template.

```
September 21, 1985

Dear Bob:

Here's a suggestion for using AppleWorks.  Maybe you can include
it in the next edition of the book.

A regular kitchen table is too high for the Apple.  After
refinishing our old table, we decided to saw more than two inches
off the legs and make it the Apple table.  The top is now less
than 28" high.  We also found a reasonably-priced secretarial
chair with pneumatic height adjustment.  Everyone in the family
works with the Apple, each using a different seating height.
Workspace comfort is important, and this is an affordable design
solution.

Sincerely,



Susan Smith
```

Figure 2.3: Left-justified letter

A basic letter template can be used for reports as well. Just add a footer that will begin printing on page 2. Then delete the address heading and related text.

Figure 2.4 illustrates a basic letter template without showing carriage return markers.

Tip: *Learn how to transfer paragraphs from letter to letter.*

A broad range of friends and associates can often benefit from the same information, although you may not say things exactly the same way to each of them; you can copy paragraphs from letter to letter when appropriate.

Suppose you want to include the paragraph about the Apple table (Figure 2.3) in an informal letter to a friend who also owns an Apple. Begin writing the letter and note the place where you want to import a paragraph. If the previous letter is not already

```
File: LETTER                        PRINT MENU        Escape: Review/Add/Change
=====|=============================|======================================
--------Right Margin:  0.5 inches
--------Pause Each page
January 1, 1986

Susan Smith
34 Meetinghouse Rd.
Jefferson, RI 02845


Dear



Sincerely,



Susan Smith
--------New Page
-----------------------------------------------------------------------
Print from?  Beginning  This page  Cursor
```

Figure 2.4: *Letter template*

on the Desktop or data disk, insert the proper disk into drive 2. Then proceed as follows:

1. Load the file with the previous letter onto the Desktop.

2. Find the paragraph you need and copy it to the clipboard.

3. Press Apple-Q to change files.

4. Place the cursor on the name of the file containing the new letter, and press Return.

5. Place the cursor on the line and column where the paragraph is to begin.

6. Move the paragraph from the clipboard.

7. Delete any unwanted spaces.

8. Save the new letter.

The beginning of the new letter might appear as shown in Figure 2.5. Notice that the first sentence of the copied paragraph has been moved to the end of the previous paragraph, and that several changes have been made to the wording of the copied paragraph.

```
September 30, 1985

Dear Jeff:

When are you coming this way again?  We have been steadily
converting the old farmhouse into workspace and have much to show
you.

Your father tells me you bought one of those classic old IIe's
with the white-letter keyboard.  Make sure you find a good place
for it.  A regular kitchen table is too high for the Apple.

After refinishing our old table, we decided to saw more than two
inches off the legs and make it the Apple table.  The top is now
not quite 28" high.  We bought a secretarial chair with pneumatic
height adjustment for less than ninety dollars.  Three of us work
with the Apple, each using a slightly different seating height.
Workspace comfort is important, and this is an affordable design
solution.
```

Figure 2.5: Paragraph copied into a second letter

Tip: *If you want to repeat more than two lines of text, transfer the text rather than rewrite it.*

The deciding issue on whether to transfer or rewrite is really not length but difficulty in reconstructing the thought. With practice you should be able to make transfers quickly enough to justify copying as little as two lines from almost any file already on the Desktop.

Sometimes it is faster to modify an existing letter. When you want to repeat almost all of a long letter, add it to the desktop, change the file name (with Apple-N), delete the unwanted parts, add the parts you need, and save the new file.

Tip: *The best way to proofread is from hard copy.*

When you finish writing a letter or any document, check it for mistakes by reading the printed draft. You can annotate printed copy, and it is much easier to read than text on the screen, especially if it is printed on a letter-quality printer or a high-quality dot-matrix printer.

Tip: *You can write several similar letters without a mail merge program.*

AppleWorks 2.0 has a Mail Merge printer option built in, and we will discuss it in Chapter 5. Earlier versions of AppleWorks work with several different mail merge programs.

Many people who use the Word Processor will want to write several similar letters at a time without setting up a mail merge system. If you have a buffered printer, this method is an efficient choice for up to a dozen letters at a time (some would say more). Consider the example of a letter announcing a meeting and agenda to ten members of a library association building committee.

Write inside addresses for each of the committee members, or load your file if you have previously written them. They should be stacked on top of one another, as shown in Figure 2.6. These small lists need not be kept in the Data Base. However, they can be produced from existing Data Base reports printed to the clipboard, a subject covered in Chapter 5.

Save the file if you have not previously done so. Then use Apple-N to change the file name, because you will be making significant changes to this file.

Enter the date at the top of the list, then copy it to the clipboard. Copy it from the clipboard repeatedly, above each name on the list. Then write the letter at the end of the file, including a general greeting, closing, and signature name, followed by a new page marker (NP). Copy that letter to the clipboard, then copy it from the clipboard repeatedly, below each name on the list. The file will then contain a series of identical letters beneath different addresses. When the file is printed, the new page option places each letter on a separate page, as shown in the partial printout in Figure 2.7.

```
File: Address List            COPY TEXT        Escape: Review/Add/Change
=====|====|====|====|====|====|====|====|====|====|====|====|====|====|===
--------Left Margin:  1.0 inches
--------Right Margin:  0.5 inches


Susan Smith
81 Main Rd.
Jefferson, RI 02845

Arnold Wright
52 Mill Rd.
Jefferson, RI 02845

Thomas Farmer
12 Field Rd.
Jefferson, RI 02845

Edward Joiner
19 Mill Rd.
Jefferson, RI 02845


-----------------------------------------------------------------------
Copy Text?  Within document  To clipboard (cut)  From clipboard (paste)
```

Figure 2.6: *Address list in the Word Processor*

```
September 8, 1985


Susan Smith
81 Main Rd.
Jefferson, RI 02845

Dear Friends:

The Building Committee will meet on Thursday, September 19, at
7:00 PM in the library meeting room.  The agenda will include the
following items:

Arnold Wright will tell us what he has learned about possible
modifications to the building that will increase available
daylight.  He will also discuss related lighting controls.

The working group on handicapped access will have copies of their
most recent progress report.  Thomas Farmer will discuss
additional improvements that will benefit all library users.

If you think of additional agenda items, please call me at
888-1182.

Sincerely,



Ellen Cooper




September 8, 1985


Arnold Wright
52 Mill Rd.
Jefferson, RI 02845

Dear Friends:

The Building Committee will meet on Thursday, September 19, at
7:00 PM in the library meeting room.  The agenda will include the
following items:

Arnold Wright will tell us what he has learned about possible
modifications to the building that will increase available
daylight.  He will also discuss related lighting controls.

The working group on handicapped access will have copies of their
most recent progress report.  Thomas Farmer will discuss
additional improvements that will benefit all library users.

If you think of additional agenda items, please call me at
888-1182.

Sincerely,



Ellen Cooper
```

Figure 2.7: *Two copies of a form letter*

There is another variation to the method described above that works well with a buffered printer. Write the body of the letter, beginning with a standard greeting and ending with the signature name. Type in the date at the top of the stack of headings and copy it to the clipboard.

Copy the date from the clipboard repeatedly, before each address in the stack. Set the cursor just above the lowest date in the stack, print from the cursor, and then delete that date and heading. Move the cursor just above the next date and repeat the process. Keep repeating it until the printer buffer is full.

With either of these methods, you might want to include specific greetings, such as "Dear Mr. Farmer," in the address stack and omit the general greeting from the body of the letter.

Tip: *Use address lists to print addresses on envelopes.*

There are several different ways to print addresses for envelopes. For more than a dozen envelopes, print from a Data Base labels report onto mailing labels. (See Chapter 3 for more on mailing labels.)

For fewer than a dozen envelopes, return to the list of addresses shown in Figure 2.6. Load the original address list file, because you will need the addresses together again.

For addressing envelopes you need wide left margins. Assuming ten characters per inch, specify 2.5 inches for small envelopes and 4 inches for business envelopes. Specify a new page after each address on the list and a pause for each page. Load the envelope as you would a sheet of paper, so that the print head is on the line where you want the address to begin. Remember that the default top margin is 0 inches.

The printer will print the address and eject the envelope. In fact, the roller will move far enough to eject an 11-inch sheet of paper. You may want to specify a shorter page length and tell the printer not to accept top-of-page commands when printing envelopes, but that is not absolutely necessary.

The formatted file for printing business envelopes appears in Figure 2.8 (without showing carriage return markers). Note that you can also print addresses on continuous 4 x 6-inch post cards, which are available for tractor-feed printers. Print the address on one side and the message on the other. In this case it is necessary to specify a page length of 4 inches, and to make certain that your printer is configured to accept no top-of-page commands.

Tip: *Use window envelopes.*

If you use a tractor-feed printer, printing envelopes can be a hopelessly clumsy process. Window envelopes save time, because you can fold the letter to use the letter heading as the address in the envelope window.

Business-size window envelopes commonly have a 1 × 4½-inch window in the lower-left corner. That gives you plenty of leeway to get the heading position right when you fold the letter in thirds.

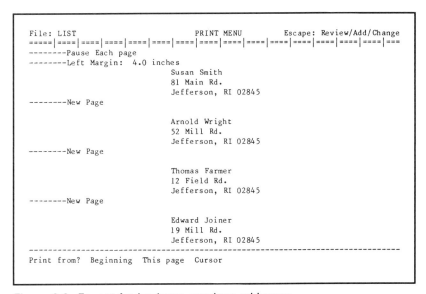

```
File: LIST                    PRINT MENU        Escape: Review/Add/Change
=====|====|====|====|====|====|====|====|====|====|====|====|====|====|====|===
--------Pause Each page
--------Left Margin:  4.0 inches
                            Susan Smith
                            81 Main Rd.
                            Jefferson, RI 02845
--------New Page

                            Arnold Wright
                            52 Mill Rd.
                            Jefferson, RI 02845
--------New Page

                            Thomas Farmer
                            12 Field Rd.
                            Jefferson, RI 02845
--------New Page

                            Edward Joiner
                            19 Mill Rd.
                            Jefferson, RI 02845
----------------------------------------------------------------------------
Print from?  Beginning  This page  Cursor
```

Figure 2.8: *Format for business envelope addresses*

PRINTER OPTIONS

Using the printer options requires some thought. Press Apple-O to review the Printer Options menu. It may appear confusing at first, but the 37 printer options are logically grouped. You will normally use only about half a dozen of these options anyway. AppleWorks version 2.0 includes an additional Mail Merge option (for variable text entry).

Tip: *Think of printer options in logical groups.*

The printer options are listed in logical groups from top to bottom in columns, but they are not arranged alphabetically. Because the AppleWorks manuals have not explained the logic, the list remains difficult to use.

The tips and cautions in this section refer to specific options; they follow the order on the Printer Options menu. Press Apple-H to print a hard copy of the menu screen if you have not already done so. Use a yellow marker to indicate the groups of options on the menu. Each group is defined in Table 2.1. AppleWorks version 2.0 includes one additional Variable Text Entry on the list: MM for Mail Merge.

Tip: *You can revise formatting lines without using the Apple-D command.*

Apple-D is the only command that can remove a text formatting line. With the cursor anywhere on the text formatting line, Apple-D highlights the entire line. (With the cursor on a character in a line of text, Apple-D highlights only that character until you use the arrow keys.)

Table 2.1: *Printer Option Groups.*

Group	Option	
Line Length, Print Density	PW	Platen Width
	LM	Left Margin
	RM	Right Margin
	CI	Characters per Inch
	P1	Proportional-1
	P2	Proportional-2
Text Positioning	IN	Indent
	JU	Justified
	UN	Unjustified
	CN	Centered
Page Length, Line Density	PL	Paper Length
	TM	Top Margin
	BM	Bottom Margin
	LI	Lines per Inch
	SS	Single Space
	DS	Double Space
	TS	Triple Space
Page Controls	NP	New Page
	GB	Group Begin
	GE	Group End
Page Calculation	HE	Page Header
	FO	Page Footer
	SK	Skip Lines
	PN	Page Number
Place Markers	PE	Pause Each Page
	PH	Pause Here
	SM	Set a Marker
Print Enhancements	BB	Boldface Begin
	BE	Boldface End
	+B	Superscript Begin
	+E	Superscript End
	−B	Subscript Begin
	−E	Subscript End
	UB	Underline Begin
	UE	Underline End

Table 2.1: *Printer option groups (continued).*

Group	Option	
Variable Text Entry	PP	Print Page number
	EK	Enter Keyboard
	MM	Mail Merge

If you simply want to replace a setting in a printer option, there is no need to delete the line first. Simply place the cursor on that line and repeat the selection process. The new selection overwrites the old.

Line Length and Print Density

Printing requires some mechanical understanding of where everything goes on a page. Spend some time watching the print head move across the paper. Where does it start and end? Is your paper running even with the left side of the platen? This is the kind of information that lets you print with predictable accuracy.

Tip: *You can adjust the margin settings to create visually equal margins.*

The platen width is the distance the print head travels across the printer roller. Most printers have a platen width of 8 inches, although standard paper is 8½ inches wide. Paper is usually aligned so that the left-most character just barely fits on the paper when the left margin is set at 0 inches.

When you enter the first line of text, you will see that the default margins leave space for only 60 characters. When printing with the default margins and the paper aligned as described above, the right margin will appear to be about three-quarters of an inch wider than the left margin. You can change the left and right margins to make them appear equal. For example, if the printer is set for ten characters per inch (the Word Processor default setting), left and right margins can be set to 0.8 and 0 inches respectively, allowing you to print 72 character spaces.

Why have we chosen such a narrow right margin? Given the platen width and paper location, the left margin is exactly 0.8 inches wide. The right margin is actually half an inch wide, because it includes the half inch beyond the platen width. The right margin will be uneven, with few characters extending to column 72, hence the actual half inch on the right is enough to balance 0.8 inches on the left.

Alternatively, you can center the paper on the 8-inch platen, so that the left-most character begins a quarter-inch from the left edge of the paper. In that case you can use a left margin of 0.5 inches and a right margin of 0.3 inches to get visually equal margins. Note that some tractor-feed mechanisms must be used this way with standard tractor-feed paper.

Caution: *The Word Processor uses 77-character lines.*

The screen shows 80 character columns per line, but even with no margins, the words will wrap at column 78. The maximum line length on the screen is 77 characters. You should know all this when you set wide margins.

Because the margins are set in tenths of inches rather than character spaces, only the 10 CI setting matches the screen to the printer. If the printer option settings allow more than 77 characters, the printer will not print the text exactly as you see it on the screen. Given the screen's effective 77-character width, margin settings of 0.3 on the left and 0 on the right will print the text as it appears on the screen (unless you have used print enhancements). The maximum margins for other print densities are problematic: there may be no perfect match, so it's best to use a conservative line length.

Tip: _You can print more than 77 characters on a line._

To print more than 77 characters on a line, select more characters per inch or change the platen width if your printer can accommodate this. The page calculations still work, though the lines will not break as shown on the screen. In fact, you may not see the first page break until beyond screen line 66.

Caution: _You can use only one character size per line._

Word processors use available printer font capabilities much more than most other programs, but the Word Processor in AppleWorks is limited in this respect. In general, you can use only one character size per line. If you want to know about the few exceptions to this rule, see the advanced printer techniques in Chapter 6.

Caution: _Proportional printing can produce unwanted results._

Proportional printing adjusts the amount of space between characters, depending on the width of each character. For example, an "i" requires less space than an "m" does. P1 and P2 were designed primarily for the Apple Dot Matrix Printer (DMP), although five other listed printers have one proportional mode. Proportional 1 prints on average about 15 characters per inch on the DMP, and it is probably the most attractive font on that printer. Some DMP users prefer to use it whenever possible. The Proportional 1 option can produce a couple of unwanted results, however.

For some reason, spaces are not considered to be characters of a fixed size. When paragraph indentations are created by tabs, some paragraphs may be printed with a greater indentation than others. Indentations created with spaces, even sticky spaces, are treated the same way. For the same reason, proportional printing does not work with aligned columns—the columns almost never remain aligned during printing. These problems effectively limit proportional printing to text with block paragraphs.

Text Positioning

You will sometimes want to center text and use other text positioning options. Read the following tips and cautions carefully, because these options can produce unwanted results.

Caution: *The indent option cannot indent the first line of a paragraph.*

The indent option indents everything but the first line of a paragraph, thereby creating what the AppleWorks Reference Manual calls hanging paragraphs. The indent option is functionally similar to increasing the left margin, except that indenting counts character spaces instead of tenths of an inch.

Tip: *Use the default setting for left-justified text.*

You will almost always use left-justification for letters and text. Left-justification is built in (the term "unjustified" in the default setting refers to the right margin). With typeset text, as in this book, adjustments are made to spaces between letters as well as spaces between words to produce an aligned (flush) right margin. In the Word Processor, however, right-justification and proportional printing work independently, and neither works very well.

Caution: *Right-justification can produce unwanted results.*

Right-justification is simply called justification in AppleWorks, because left-justification is built in. Justification aligns the right margin by adjusting spaces between words, whereas P1 and P2 adjust spaces between letters. Justification has the same problems as proportional printing with indentation and aligned columns, because spaces are adjustable characters.

If you use a long print line, 14–17 CI print, and few long words, justification can look good. If you use a short print line, 10–12 CI print, long words, aligned columns, or indented paragraphs, justification will make decisions about spacing that may disorient readers.

Tip: *Centering works between margins and favors the left margin.*

If you center titles, it is doubly important to adjust margin settings to create visually equal margins, so that the title also appears centered on the page. In a bound report, set margins to create visually equal margins on the part of the page you can see.

When there are an even number of characters in a line, and an odd number of characters in the title, the extra character goes left of center. Whatever the mismatch, AppleWorks favors the left side. This is a good design choice, because when the right margin is not justified, few lines extend to the last available character space.

Page Length and Line Density

This is one group of options that you can ignore most of the time. The default settings were wisely chosen for normal use. However, it may take some practice to insert double-spacing marks correctly.

Tip: *When you specify less than 11 inches for paper length, make certain your printer does not accept top-of-page commands.*

For 4 × 6-inch continuous post cards, you will need a paper length of 4 inches; with mailing labels you may need a paper length of 1 inch. On the Change a Printer menu, make certain that the response to option 2, for accepting top-of-page commands, is No.

Many printers allow you to enter control codes to change the paper (or form) length, but the Word Processor offers no option for entering special codes. The Data Base and Spreadsheet do have this special code (SC) option.

Tip: *The top and bottom margin settings really do make sense.*

Notice that the default margin settings are 0 for the top and 2 inches for the bottom. Most people prefer to insert paper in the printer up to the intended first line. This allows room to sight the paper and set the roller bar on friction-feed printers.

The default margins give you the flexibility to allocate actual top and bottom margins by adjusting the starting point on the paper up or down. For example, you may prefer a little more than an inch of margin for the top and a little less than an inch for the bottom.

Caution: *The spacing options can be inserted only in front of paragraphs.*

To begin double spacing, insert the DS code on the line before the line where you want it to take effect. (Note that an empty line does not count in this rule, although a line with nothing more than a sticky space does count.) You cannot change spacing in the middle of a paragraph; if you access the printer options in the middle of a paragraph, the DS will be placed in front of that paragraph. Remember all this well, because if you forget, double spacing will start sooner than you expect. The same rules apply to triple spacing, and to single spacing when you return from double or triple spacing.

Page Controls

The page controls are surprisingly dependent on the Word Processor rules for paragraph integrity. Pay special attention to the techniques for working around these rules.

Tip: *To use page control options effectively, learn the rules for text integrity.*

The Word Processor has an inherent respect for paragraph integrity. It will never print only one line of a paragraph on a page (if that paragraph has at least two lines), and it will not allow the new page option to break a paragraph in any way.

Any text group that ends with a carriage return is a paragraph so far as AppleWorks is concerned. Remember that rule and consider the implications. It means that a table can be divided between pages, because each line ends with a carriage return (to preserve column alignment). A section title can be printed all alone at the bottom of a page, because it is considered a one-line paragraph.

Given these rules, the trick is to designate text groups that cannot be divided between pages. Use the GB (group begin) and GE (group end) options to mark these groups. You can insert them as you write, preparing for any eventuality. Or you can wait until the end of your writing, calculate the pages (with Apple-K), and then insert group designations where you need them.

Tip: *Use carriage returns within paragraphs to accommodate page control options.*

If you are certain of margins and pitch settings and know that the text lines will be less than 77 characters wide, you can insert carriage returns where a line would normally wrap. This makes separate paragraphs in the AppleWorks sense, even though the text is still printed as a single paragraph. Once you insert a carriage return, you can insert NP, GB, GE, and DS where they would not otherwise be permitted.

Page Calculation

The Apple-K command calculates pages, but there are some minor calculation problems you should understand. Pay special attention to the following caution and the caution on printing from the cursor.

Caution: *Empty lines are generally not counted in page calculations.*

After page 1, when a calculated page begins with an empty line, that line is not included in the remaining calculation. This is rarely a problem, because in practice most return markers occur between single-spaced paragraphs. But how do you begin a page with enough empty lines to allow for a drawing to be pasted in later? Put a sticky space just in front of the first return marker you want counted.

Incidentally, AppleWorks correctly calculates empty lines when you use the printer option to skip lines (SK), but that option does not display the space on the screen.

Tip: *Printer options require lines of their own on the screen.*

A printer option such as Double Space requires a line of its own on the screen, but not on the printed page. The line is always counted on the screen, even when the option is hidden in normal display mode. Word Processor files often have several printer options stored at the beginning of the file. In normal display mode it is therefore common to see the first displayed line listed as line 5 or beyond.

Tip: *Page calculations may show partial lines at the end of each page, but those calculations are invariably correct.*

After calculating page breaks, you may see partial lines just before the page-dividing line. This is because 80-character columns may be available to the printer, but only 77-character columns are available on a screen line. The page break calculations are invariably correct. Figure 2.9 shows an example of a page break with a partial line preceding it, and Figure 2.10 shows how the lines appear when the document is printed.

Partial lines may also appear when printer option markers fill character spaces that are not actually printed. Again, the page-break calculations are invariably correct.

```
File: Word.Process.A            PRINT MENU          Escape: Review/Add/Change
=====|====================|====================|====================
so we can replace the space with a sticky space (Apple-Space bar) to keep
them together. You will often need to do this for words with associated
numbers.
     Sticky spaces can also be used independently to make the Word Processor
recognize an otherwise empty line. As we will later see, this can be
important for page calculations and double spacing.

A)WRITING LETTERS(A
     Business letters are generally less than one page long, with simple
formatting and printing requirements. You may want to use
- - - - - - - - - - - - - - End of Page 5 - - - - - - - - - - - - - - -
the same thought in
more than one letter, or produce a dozen or more letters of almost exactly
the same form. The following tips present useful information for those who
write business letters.

TIP: Left-justified letters are the easiest to format.
     Left-justification (or blocked style) is an efficient letter form for
both the word processor and the reader. There is no need to spend time
centering headings and closings (in fact, people who do so are now considered
------------------------------------------------------------------------
Print from?  Beginning  This page  Cursor
```

Figure 2.9: Partial lines in page calculations

```
A)WRITING LETTERS(A
        Business letters are generally less than one page long, with
simple formatting and printing requirements. You may want to use


Word Processor 2.5








        the same thought in more than one letter, or produce a dozen or
more letters of almost exactly the same form. The following tips
present useful information for those who write business letters.
```

Figure 2.10: *Printout showing the page break indicated in Figure 2.9*

Caution: *When you print from the cursor or from the page on which the cursor is positioned, use Apple-K first.*

Although AppleWorks calculates the pages after you request printing, that may not be good enough. You must calculate the pages yourself with Apple-K before entering the print command sequence with Apple-P. If you forget to do this on versions through 1.3, your printout may include text from the previous page.

Tip: *Consider the header and footer lines in planning pages.*

Page headers and footers take up lines on the screen only once, at the beginning of the file, but they take up space on every page during printing. Headers and footers are printed within the specified text depth, not out in the top or bottom margins.

A header or footer will use at least three lines per page. This means that if you use single spacing and the default top and bottom margins, you will have room for 51 lines per page aside from the header or footer.

Because headers and footers are usually brief lines, they can make a standard margin look too large. You may therefore want to decrease the bottom margin setting.

Caution: *You can get locked out of AppleWorks if you press Return at the wrong time while finding a page.*

If you are working with an AppleWorks version through 1.3, try making this mistake when you can afford to start over. The correct sequence for finding a page is listed below, followed by a note on the error.

1. Press Apple-K to calculate the pages.

2. Press Apple-F for the Find menu.

3. Press P to select the page option.

4. Enter a page number, and press Return.

The cursor moves to the bottom of the page selected. However, if you make the mistake of pressing Return *before* entering the page number, AppleWorks may lock you out and you will have to reboot with the Startup disk.

The error cannot occur unless the pages have been calculated, and there is no problem when you enter a Return incorrectly while attempting to find text or markers.

Caution: *If you calculate pages and then immediately delete the last page break line, you can get locked out of AppleWorks.*

This can occur in version 1.1 of AppleWorks. It is likely to happen only if you add carriage return markers to the end of a file to see how many more lines would fit on the last page. If you instinctively delete return markers after calculating pages, you may delete the page break line by mistake.

Tip: *Page numbering is controlled by three different options working together.*

The header or footer option controls the line location of the page number, the print page option (PP) controls the character location of the page number within the line, and the page number option (PN) controls the actual number printed.

The page number automatically increases by one with each new page, but you can begin numbering pages with any number up to 256 (the highest number you can print). For example, Section 2 of a report may be a separate file, but the first page of that section can be page 26.

The ^ symbol indicates the PP option, the specific character location for printing the page number. It is usually located in the header or footer. The actual page number 1 is designated with the PN option anywhere prior to the PP option, which means that footers allow more flexibility than headers.

Place Markers

The most important place markers are the pause markers used to control printing. With them you can print specific ranges of text. The set-a-marker option (SM) identifies fixed points, something that the AppleWorks Ruler cannot do.

Caution: *The pause here option (PH) cannot break a paragraph.*

As with the page control options, you may need to insert a carriage return in order to use PH within a paragraph. If you are using PH simply to stop at the end of a page, use PE (pause each page) instead, because it avoids the need to insert a carriage return.

Tip: *Pausing at the end of each page offers several advantages.*

The option to pause at the end of each page allows you to manually insert single sheets into a friction-feed printer. However, the PE option can also be used to control text loading into a printer.

AppleWorks provides no option to print just part of a document, such as the first four pages of a 25-page report. If you want to print only the first four pages, calculate the pages (with Apple-K), enter a PE anywhere on page 4, and print from the beginning. When the flashing cursor reappears on the screen, press Escape to return to the document.

You can use a similar technique to print a specific range of pages, such as pages 12 through 15 of a 25-page report. If you want to print only this range, calculate the pages, insert PE anywhere on page 15, move the cursor to page 12, and choose "This page" on the printer menu. When the flashing cursor reappears on the screen, press Escape. Or, if you want to continue printing, press the Space bar and release another page to the printer.

If you want to print just part of the last page of a specified range, insert PH in the appropriate place on that page. PH cannot be used within a paragraph, but you can enter a carriage return to create a paragraph in the AppleWorks sense.

You can also use pause options to control print flow whenever you try new techniques. For example, you can change to space-and-a-half printing (within a document) by selecting eight lines per inch double-spaced, but you may want to see it work before committing another page.

Print Enhancements

Boldfacing, superscripting, subscripting, and underlining are the most important print enhancements used in writing. Eight printer menu options provide these. Underlining and boldfacing can also be used with control commands. Italics are not listed on the Printer Options menu. If your printer can produce italics, see Chapter 6 for tips on accessing them.

Tip: *Character-control markers take up space on the screen but not on the printed page.*

The presence of character-control markers for such print enhancements as underlining and boldfacing can make a significant difference between what you see on the screen and what you get from the printer. For example, if you have six character-control markers on a line, that can be enough to push a five-letter word onto the next line on the screen, but not on the printed page.

Unfortunately, you cannot turn off the display of character-control markers to see how your text will appear on the printed page.

Caution: *Superscripts and subscripts may not print properly on some tractor-feed printers.*

Almost all printers have friction feeds that allow superscripts and subscripts to be printed correctly. But if you plan to use these options often in printing long reports, you will want to use a tractor feed so that you can walk away from the printer—just make certain the tractor is bidirectional.

A unidirectional tractor pulls the paper up over the roller but cannot pull it back down. This means that the print line will not return to the normal position after a superscript or subscript. Some printers avoid this problem by using a separate set of small script characters that require no tractor movement.

Tip: *Use Control-L for underlining and Control-B for boldfacing.*

Moving back and forth from the Printer Options menu can be time-consuming. Instead, you can begin and end underlining with

Control-L, and begin and end boldfacing with Control-B. The convenience of this method may tempt you to use it as well to access italics or alternate character sets. It can be done: the mechanics of installing additional character controls are explained in Chapter 6.

Caution: *Underlining and boldfacing turn off at the end of a paragraph.*

Most AppleWorks users expect underlining and boldfacing to keep going until reaching an end marker. However, both of these print enhancements end at the next carriage return marker. This has an advantage: you almost never need to add a second marker in a title line. However, you might want boldface to continue beyond a carriage return marker so that you need not individually mark each item in a list. Some people print whole documents in boldface. In either case, you can modify the connection between AppleWorks and the printer to achieve continuous print enhancement. Chapter 6 explains how this is done.

Tip: *You can underline spaces between words.*

The underlining command applies to characters only, not to spaces. To underline spaces, use the underline key (_) between words. It should be obvious, but try asking someone how to do it. Note that this technique makes the words joined by an underline into one word in the AppleWorks sense, so you may need to place a space after an underline character to allow a book title, for example, to wrap to the next text line.

Variable Text Entry

The Word Processor has two options for entering variable text. The page number option enters numbers, and the enter keyboard option allows you to enter text from the keyboard during printing.

Tip: *Make the most of the page number option.*

The page number option (PN) allows you to enter a different number on each page, and it has several additional uses that may surprise you.

The first page of Chapter 2 can be page 2.1, provided that 2.^ is entered in the header or footer. If you want to begin the numbering with 2.2 on the second page of a chapter, the header or footer should be moved to the second page. The actual page number 2 is then designated with the PN option anywhere on the second page prior to the header or footer.

The Word Processor displays page numbers to 512, but it does not print page numbers beyond 256. You can skip page numbers by inserting another PN option on another page. For example, you may want to jump from page 14 to page 18 to accommodate illustration pages.

The page number option can also be used to print sequential identification numbers for such things as invoices. The number can be entered more than once on a page. Figure 2.11 shows an interesting example.

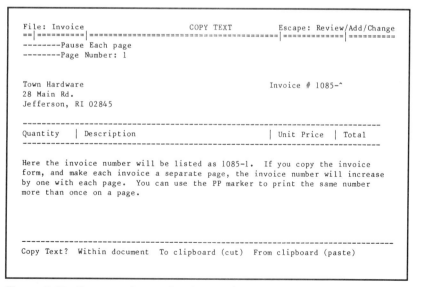

Figure 2.11: *Page number as invoice number*

Tip: *You can enter more than 50 characters with the EK option.*

To enter more than 50 characters of text from the keyboard while the printer pauses, select the EK option more than once, leaving no spaces between the marks. (You can provide any needed spacing in the text you enter.) For example, text with the EK option indicated by ^ ^ ^ ^ will accept up to 200 inserted characters.

MOVING AND COPYING TEXT

If you have used the Word Processor a great deal, you may already appreciate how much time you can save by taking advantage of its capabilities for moving and copying text. This section includes tips for using the copy command in ways that you might not have considered.

Tip: *It is faster to move text forward than backward within a file.*

When you use the clipboard, you may notice differences in the time it takes AppleWorks to move text within a file. If you move text from the beginning of the file to somewhere near the end of the file, it goes quickly. If you move text from the end of the file to somewhere near the beginning, it takes longer. The same is true when you use the clipboard to copy text.

Moving and copying using the "Within document" option takes about the same amount of time either way. It is generally slower than the clipboard route.

When you reorganize a file extensively, move text segments forward if you have the choice. Remember also that the smaller the file, the faster the Word Processor works.

Tip: *When moving or copying text, highlight the space or spaces following the last sentence.*

If your sentences usually end in a period followed by two spaces, include those two spaces when you highlight a block of text. This way, everything will fit perfectly when you insert the block of text later. When moving or copying text from the clipboard, place the cursor on the first character that will follow the inserted sentence.

Tip: *Use the copy command to repeatedly insert text.*

Copy a repeated phrase to the clipboard and then copy it from the clipboard as often as needed. The phrase remains on the clipboard until you replace it with another. Although you can have only one block of text on the clipboard at a time, it is easy to store several more blocks of text at the beginning or end of your working document. By using Apple-1 and Apple-9, you can retrieve and insert blocks of text quickly.

Tip: *Use the copy command to copy printer options.*

Zoom to the layout mode that shows printer options at the beginning of the file. Copy the options to the clipboard and copy from the clipboard as often as needed to any number of files. (Delete the existing options in those files first.) This works well when you use many printer options in one section of a report and want the other sections to match. Figure 2.12 shows a complete range of printer options waiting to be copied.

The same process works within a file. Instead of using Apple-O to access printer options each time you need to insert a new page marker, copy an existing new page marker to the clipboard. Then copy the marker from the clipboard wherever you need one.

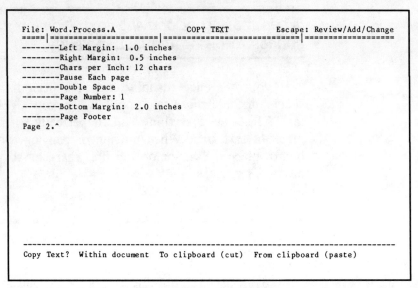

```
File: Word.Process.A              COPY TEXT           Escape: Review/Add/Change
=====|=====================|=============================|====================
--------Left Margin:  1.0 inches
--------Right Margin:  0.5 inches
--------Chars per Inch: 12 chars
--------Pause Each page
--------Double Space
--------Page Number: 1
--------Bottom Margin:  2.0 inches
--------Page Footer
Page 2.^




------------------------------------------------------------------------------
Copy Text?  Within document   To clipboard (cut)   From clipboard (paste)
```

Figure 2.12: *Printer options waiting to be copied*

Tip: *Move text to the clipboard to delete it.*

Sometimes you think you should delete a section of text, but you are uncertain, and you know the decision will be irreversible. (There is no Undo command in AppleWorks, as there is in some other word processors.)

If you have any doubts about deleting, move the text to the clipboard and attempt a rewrite. If that works, forget about the clipboard, because you will overwrite it whenever you copy or move to it again. If you still think you might need the copy later, move the text from the clipboard to the end of the file or to any file of text parts.

Tip: *Use the copy command to copy blank spaces.*

A specific number of blank spaces can be treated just as any other text. For example, suppose you want to insert 28 spaces into each of 12 lines in a table, between the first and second columns. Copy 28 spaces to the clipboard, then repeatedly copy the spaces from the clipboard.

In creating tables, you will want to do this when you forget a column. You can enter information into the new column using the overstrike cursor, so that nothing is misaligned.

The same general technique applies to characters used for borders, such as repeated hyphens or asterisks. It also applies to dotted and solid lines used in contracts.

Tip: *When you copy from a file to the clipboard, the file remains unchanged.*

If you load a file onto the Desktop for the single purpose of copying text to another file, copy to the clipboard rather than move. When you copy, the file remains unchanged, and you can remove it from the Desktop quickly, without having to respond to menu questions in the option for removing files from the Desktop.

FINDING AND REPLACING TEXT

It takes time and practice to discover the many uses of the powerful find and replace commands in the Word Processor. If you are new to using these commands, pay special attention to the tip on replacing words one at a time.

Tip: *The Word Processor has the most powerful find and replace commands in AppleWorks.*

Table 2.2 shows the differences between the find and replace commands in each AppleWorks program. The Word Processor alone has the ability to replace text and identify case-sensitive

Table 2.2: *Options available for find and replace functions*

Option	Word Processor	Data Base	Spreadsheet
Finds text	X	X	X
Finds case-sensitive text	X		
Finds numbers	X	X	as labels only
Finds page numbers	X		
Also finds	markers		coordinates
Searches from	cursor	beginning	cursor
Replaces one instance	X		
Replaces all instances	X		
Maximum number of characters	30	30	25

text. You can use Apple-R rather than Apple-F when you want to find only case-sensitive text—simply choose not to replace and then move on to the next instance.

The first entry in the normal replace command appears in uppercase letters, no matter how you enter it. The second entry appears as you entered it, with any capitalized letters you specified. Replacement words are always case-sensitive.

When finding text, AppleWorks always proposes the last text you used, unless you leave the file and then return. Simply pressing Apple-Q and Return willcreate a fresh slate. The other way is to use Apple-Y before entering any new text to be found or replaced.

Caution: *The find command has no wildcard option.*

Some word processors allow you to use wildcard characters to find words that might be spelled in different ways. For example, suppose you wanted to find all instances of *Ericson*. You could use a wildcard to spell *Eri∗son* in a way that finds all common spellings. The ∗ accepts any number of possible characters, including *c, cs, k, ks, ck,* and *cks.*

Because the AppleWorks Word Processor has no wildcard option, you have to plan searches carefully. In this case you might find and replace each of six possible spellings. Or you might find and replace the one correct spelling, and then just find other spellings. When a find is unlikely, use just the find command and plan on editing text if an instance occurs - don't bother with the replace command.

Try to find a word by isolating an uncommon stem, in this case a space followed by *Eri*. Use a case-sensitive search to eliminate other words whenever you can, even if no other words come to mind.

Tip: *Use the find command to improve your writing.*

Almost everyone who writes either overuses or misuses certain words and phrases. Buy a good paperback reference book such as Strunk and White's *The Elements of Style* (Macmillan, 1979) and read it carefully. Make a list of the problem phrases you tend to use. Whenever you write, go back and search for these phrases using the Word Processor find command. This command accepts up to thirty characters, including spaces.

You can search for problem words, such as the vague adverbs *quite, often, sometimes, rather,* and *very.* You can find all instances of *to* if you want to check for split infinitives, or all instances of *is* and *are* to substitute active verbs. Remember to include the leading space character with each word, because the letters occur within many other words.

There will be times when you need to write quickly in simple sentences without giving much thought to spelling or punctuation. When you know you have a problem, enter an ellipsis (...) within the text and find it later. If a fact needs to be verified, enter multiple question marks (???) and find them later.

Caution: *The find and replace commands search from the cursor for text, pages, and markers.*

If you want to search through a whole file, use Apple-1 first, to return to the beginning of the file. If you have a header or footer line, the cursor will return to that line. If you don't use Apple-1 first, you will be searching through only the part of the file that follows your current cursor position.

Tip: *When you replace words, replace them one at a time.*

You may be tempted to replace all instance of a word or phrase. Consider the word *I* about to be replaced by *you* in a report. Unless you specify case-sensitive text and include the preceding and trailing space, you can cause yourself much grief, because there is no neat way to convert unwanted *you* entries back to *I* entries.

When you replace characters, words, or phrases, replace them one at a time for the first twenty times you use the command. Keep notes on unexpected results and lessons learned. When you feel confident, start replacing all instances in routine cases. If you have any doubts whatsoever, replace one at a time.

If you replace misspelled words one at a time after your spelling checker lists them, you can see them in a larger context. This can improve your proofreading, because you may have made other mistakes in the same vicinity.

Tip: *There is a way to check spacing following sentence-ending periods.*

If you proofread a letter or brief report on the screen, it is difficult to make certain that exactly two spaces follow each sentence-ending period. The most common errors are three spaces or just one. There is a way to check this, however, that's a little easier on your eyes.

First, switch to the overstrike cursor, because it makes extra spaces stand out. Use Apple-R to replace all instances of a period followed by three spaces. Replace them one at a time with a period followed by two spaces. There will generally be few or no instances of a period followed by three spaces.

Next, use Apple-R again to replace all instances of a period followed by one space. Again, replace them one at a time with a period followed by two spaces. This will find every sentence-ending period, but each occurrence will then appear vividly as either one space or two. You can move through the file quickly by alternately pressing the N and Y keys as appropriate. You should be able to correct the spacing in a 10K file in less than a minute.

If you use one space after each sentence-ending period, life is much easier. Use Apple-R to replace all instances of a period followed by two spaces. Then do it again to find cases that had three spaces after a period when you did it the first time.

Tip: *There is a simple way to verify spacing between words on different lines.*

In the process of editing text, you may occasionally forget how many spaces there are between the last word of a line and the first letter of the following line. If that happens, put the cursor on that first letter, delete back until the two words meet, and then insert the space or spaces you need.

When a sentence ends with a period in the last usable character column, column 77, this technique can sometimes cause the following line to indent one space. If that happens, go back to the previous line, enter the two required spaces on that line, and then delete the indented space on the next line. Columns 78 and 79 will hold functional spaces, but not characters.

If you want to confirm that there are two spaces at the end of a line, you can place the cursor just before the end of that line and use Apple-F to find the next occurrence of two spaces.

Tip: *Use the find command to review text formatting.*

In all versions, the word processor find command can locate "Options for printer" in the text. It brings you to the Printer Options menu, but this time to specify a search. You can look for all right margin settings, but not a specific right margin inch setting. This limitation is an acceptable design choice, because you will normally want to step through the complete series of margin settings (or other print settings) within the file.

As with the text find command, the search proceeds from the cursor location to the end of the file. Unlike text, printer option choices will not stay loaded within the find command. You must start every request from scratch.

Beyond review of text formatting, this find option can locate markers that you have long forgotten. The most commonly forgotten printer options are Pause Here markers. The next most common are for New Page.

Tip: *The replace command can be used to expand macro codes.*

Some word processors insert a larger word or phrase at the time a designated character combination is typed. This is often called macro writing, and although AppleWorks does not have this capability, it can be simulated using the replace command.

For example, you can type *xx* everywhere *AppleWorks* is intended, then replace all occurrences of *xx* with *AppleWorks*. Although *aw* would also be a good substitute, the replacement instructions in that case would have to include the spaces before and after the *aw*. You do not want to replace an occurrence of *awesome* with *AppleWorksesome*.

Although no double letter occurs as rarely as xx, several others are at least improbable enough to use for additional words. These include hh, ii, jj, qq, uu, and yy. Double letters can be entered quickly, but you run the risk of accidentally entering triple letters. When you replace double letters, search for triples just in case. Note also that these are all lowercase letters—capitals simply take too long to enter.

Combinations of letters and numbers, such as a1 and a2, can be used to replace commonly used long words such as *application* and *architecture*. You can make a complete list of equivalents for your own writing purposes. Include commonly used phrases as well. Figure 2.13 shows a text screen with macro codes instead of complete words.

WRITING LONG REPORTS

If you write extended reports with complicated formatting, you need to know more about the Word Processor. Reports often extract information from other sources, including spreadsheets, databases, and information services such as CompuServe. In Chapter 5 we will discuss transfer methods; here we will deal with internal problems related to the length and complexity of Word Processor files.

Tip: *The Word Processor can handle up to 2,250 lines per file.*

The 2,250 lines amount to 40–45 pages of single-spaced text—normally enough for one section of a report. Sections tend to make

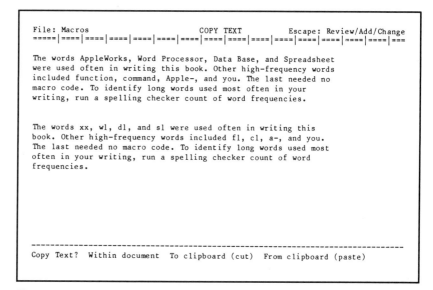

```
File: Macros                          COPY TEXT           Escape: Review/Add/Change
=====|====|====|====|====|====|====|====|====|====|====|====|====|====|====|===

The words AppleWorks, Word Processor, Data Base, and Spreadsheet
were used often in writing this book. Other high-frequency words
included function, command, Apple-, and you. The last needed no
macro code. To identify long words used most often in your
writing, run a spelling checker count of word frequencies.


The words xx, wl, dl, and sl were used often in writing this
book. Other high-frequency words included fl, cl, a-, and you.
The last needed no macro code. To identify long words used most
often in your writing, run a spelling checker count of word
frequencies.




------------------------------------------------------------------------------
Copy Text?  Within document  To clipboard (cut)  From clipboard (paste)
```

Figure 2.13: Macro codes instead of complete words

logical files, so there is rarely a need to chain files for printing purposes. Page numbering presents no problem, because the second section of your report can start at any designated number from 1 to 256.

The Super Desktop Expander software that comes with the RamWorks card can extend the Word Processor's capacity to more than 5,000 lines per file. That allows for 90–95 pages of single-spaced text, which can be useful for printing complete reports from one file.

Tip: *You can "chain" files for printing purposes.*

There is no facility for chaining files as such, but there is a way to have files print with consecutive numbers and keep all the pages full. Follow these steps:

1. Calculate page breaks using Apple-K.

2. Move the cursor to the last page.

3. Note the page number of the last complete page.

4. If the last page is incomplete, move that text to the clipboard.

5. Move the text from the clipboard to the beginning of the next file.

6. Use PN to specify the page number from which the next file should start printing.

Use this method for final drafts only, because insertions and deletions will change the page breaks.

Tip: *Use rules of thumb for approximate word counts.*

The Word Processor lacks character and word counts, but the lower-right corner of the screen shows the line and column numbers. Multiplying the line count by the line-ending column number gives an approximate character count, and dividing the character count by eight gives an approximate word count. In AppleWorks a Word Processor file occupying 10K on a disk will have about fifteen hundred words.

If you need accurate word counts, most spelling checkers can provide them. For example, Sensible Speller can tell you the total number of words, the number of unique words, and the frequency distribution for each unique word.

Tip: *When a Return takes too long to insert a blank line, your file is too long.*

When you become impatient waiting for a Return to take effect, that is a good indication that your file is too long. If you have more to write, consider dividing the file into two or more smaller files. You can merge the two files later for printing.

Tip: *Make a file of commonly used sentences and paragraphs for use in other documents.*

Every once in a while you read a report or article that explains a point better than you have ever been able to do it yourself. Rewrite the best paragraphs in your own style, and store them in a file called Writing. Review and rewrite them again from time to time.

If you like to quote Shakespeare or Homer, store your favorite lines in the Writing file. If you have standard contract text, store that in a Contract file. The idea is to have the necessary components on hand.

Tip: *Use temporary place markers to find your way home.*

Whenever you leave a Word Processor file to go to another AppleWorks file, you come back to the exact place you left.

When you leave for another part of the same file, you lose your place. This is one good reason to store text parts in separate files.

Within a text file, there are three ways to get back quickly. You can remember the line number you were on. This allows you to use Apple-1 through Apple-9 and full-screen cursor moves to get back quickly.

Alternatively, you can leave an unusual character string, such as @@, where your cursor was. A character string marker brings you back to an exact line-and-column position. Use the find command to return, and then erase the characters. Macros can make it work quickly (see Chapter 7).

You can also create a place marker with a specific number, and use the find command to return, because Apple-F includes an option for finding markers. Unfortunately, place markers must go between paragraphs, which limits their accuracy. Neverthless, they remain a good choice when you need to mark two or more places in a file at the same time. You can also use macros to make this a quick process.

Caution: *Word processors have increased the chances of tell-tale revisions.*

Sometimes the most embarrassing words get left behind: extra verb tenses, extra adjectives, and so forth. Word processors can work from templates and revise text quickly, which makes it simple to assemble text and test different constructions. In the process, it's easy to overlook details, and spelling checkers cannot identify the problem.

Here are some examples of the tell-tale revisions word processing can produce:

- A sentence begins "The good excellent report . . ."

- The date is September 12, 1987, but the date on the letter is January 1, 1987.

- A letter to Ellen Hayes includes two inappropriate paragraphs from a letter to someone else.

- A revised phrase reads "We would be are willing . . ."

Furthermore, we have had little experience proofreading these kinds of errors, and they remain largely outside our focus. Telltale revisions require preventative maintenance. When you complete a revision, reread it at that time with special attention to verbs and adjectives. If you write letters from a template, make the template changes right away. Above all, read anything you have assembled as if you had just written it.

Tip: *After writing a report outline, save the outline file.*

Once you have saved the outline file to disk, rename the file on screen and develop the report directly from the outline. If you need to see the outline itself again for an overview of the report structure, you can always add the original outline file to the Desktop.

Outlines begin as lists, and most have only two levels, except perhaps for selected sections where you have to go into greater detail. This book began as a list of tips and cautions entered in a Spreadsheet file. For more about this method of writing outlines, see Chapter 5.

Tip: *Always keep footnotes in a separate file.*

Whenever you enter a superscript to indicate a footnote in the report, copy that superscript to its proper place in a separate footnote file. Enter the footnote information then, while the connection remains clear in your mind.

The Word Processor cannot calculate footnote locations, and manual fitting is a trial-and-error process. Use footnotes as end notes whenever possible. That way you can copy the completed footnote file to the end of the report file for printing.

Tip: *If you make calculations for reports, keep a scientific calculator and note pad nearby.*

An inexpensive scientific calculator remains an indispensable tool. Keep one nearby for any back-of-the-envelope calculations you need to make while writing reports. Your scientific calculator may even include a reference manual of applied math formulas for everything from finance to engineering.

If you have added a memory card to your Apple and have loaded AppleWorks entirely into RAM, keep a Spreadsheet Calculator file on the Desktop. As you will see in Chapter 4, that worksheet can serve several additional purposes.

Tip: *You can print text in two columns.*

Some reports and most newsletters are easier to read when you print text in two columns. The general idea is to print one column, reset the paper, and print the second column. Our example will be for just one page, the simplest case.

Our example will also assume that the left edge of the eight-inch printer platen matches the left edge of the paper. Thus, if we set a margin of 0 at the right, the margin on the printed paper will be half an inch.

Assume that the printed page will have a half-inch margin at the left and right, two equal text columns of 3.6 inches, and an intercolumnar space of 0.3 inches.

In the Word Processor, use the margins you would normally use for writing text. When you finish writing, return the cursor to the beginning of the file and set the left margin to 0.5 inches. Set the temporary right margin to 3.9 inches (the sum of the intercolumnar space and right column widths — there is no need to set a right margin with this platen alignment).

Use Apple-K to calculate the pages. Right after the first page break, change the margins. Set the right margin to 0. Set the temporary left margin to 4.4 inches (the sum of the left margin, left column, and intercolumnar widths).

Return to the beginning of the file and enter the printer option PE to pause at the end of each page. Align the paper to be printed.

Print the first page (actually the first column). At the end of the column, nothing will happen until you press the Space bar again. Turn the printer off and move the paper back to the alignment point. Turn the printer back on and press the Space bar to release page 2 (the second column).

You can expand this method for other purposes. To print more than one page, reset the margin settings after each column. To print three columns of addresses, center the paper over the platen so that a quarter inch of paper extends beyond each end. Those are the only left and right margins you need. If you align everything correctly, you can photocopy the sheet onto peel-off label sheets. This works well when you need the same address labels repeatedly.

USING SPELLING CHECKERS

In this section several tips and techniques are provided for using spelling checkers with AppleWorks. Some tips demonstrate techniques for using the Pinpoint Document Checker with Word Processor files. These techniques generally apply to other spelling checkers commonly used with AppleWorks, such as Sensible Speller.

Tip: *Correct spelling adds to your credibility.*

Many competent people have great difficulty spelling words, and they frequently do not even know when they have erred. Others make typing mistakes, transposing letters when they know very well how to spell the words. Some of us omit letters in haste. These are three different problems, but each can be at least partly managed.

For problems with spelling, the best approach is to buy a good paperback dictionary and keep it on top of your monitor. When you start spelling words correctly the first time, copy is easier to proofread and correct no matter what tools you use.

For problems with typing errors, the find (Apple-F) or replace (Apple-R) commands can help. When you find an error, enter the same spelling to find additional occurrences, because such errors tend to recur. For example, if you find an occurrence of *spreadhseet* instead of *spreadsheet,* the chances are that you typed it incorrectly more than once—mistakes with transposed letters are predictable.

Tip: *Spelling checkers work efficiently and accurately.*

Checking spelling is part of proofreading, which also includes identifying mistakes in punctuation, capitalization errors, incorrect words, improper constructions, and editorial inconsistencies. These tasks require more time than most of us want to commit. People who never check like to assume that everything came out right. Those who proofread know otherwise—corrections always take more time than expected.

By using a spelling checker, you can save time. A spelling checker can narrow the focus for proofreading, and that improves your accuracy in finding nonspelling errors.

Pinpoint's Document Checker installs easily and works quickly with AppleWorks files. It processes files in batches, collecting the words, attempting to match them to a dictionary, and listing unmatched words to a text file. It can also process files interactively, so you can make corrections in context as errors are found.

Tip: *Add words to the dictionary.*

The most important option in any spelling checker is the one for adding specialized words (for example, product names such as VisiCalc). Add words carefully, because you can compromise your word list with mistakes. Your entries should come directly from published sources, including specialized dictionaries. You can write down your specialized words with the Word Processor and then run an interactive spelling check on that file. If Document Checker cannot find a match, you can ask it to "learn" the word (add it to the secondary word list).

The following example provides some understanding of how spelling checkers work. Document Checker spent 192 seconds processing a 1,800-word file about AppleWorks. It then sent 22 unmatched words to the printer. Of those words, 2 were indeed misspelled and 8 were specialized words. Another 9 were abbreviations and such things as Spreadsheet cell coordinates.

The main dictionary includes 80,000 entries in a 106K file (the data is compressed). The secondary word list is a text file, so you can review it with the Word Processor. Checking the text file takes extra time, so you trade time for accuracy. Although your professional field may have thousands of specialized words, you will probably use only about 200-400 often enough to justify adding them to a secondary word list.

Tip: *Use AppleWorks commands to correct misspelled words.*

Only two words were misspelled in the 1,800-word file, but Document Checker sent 22 unmatched words to the log file. That kind of ratio is common for people who spell reasonably well. Instead of using the spelling checker to display every word in context, read the printed list of unmatched words. Highlight the misspellings with a yellow marker, and make the corrections from AppleWorks.

Suppose you typed *spreadhseet* instead of *spreadsheet*. With Apple-F, you can find the first occurrence and answer No when the message asks if you want to find the next occurrence. That leaves the cursor on the word, where you can make the correction. When you press Apple-F again, AppleWorks proposes the last word you searched for, and you are back in the hunt.

Apple-R works best when you know that a word was spelled incorrectly in the same way several times.

Tip: *Learn and respect the limitations of your spelling checker.*

Spelling checkers cannot flag words such as *there* when *their* is intended. Also, most spelling checkers live in a world of upper-case letters (think of the complications if it were otherwise). That means they cannot tell the correct spelling of *AppleWorks* from the incorrect *Appleworks*. If you buy a spelling checker, read the manual and take advantage of any options that will mini-mize the number of suspect words. For example, Document Checker offers the option to find repeated words, such as *the the*. This is normally a proofreading task.

Spelling checkers cannot generally keep track of last names, many of which are often misspelled. However, you should add names that you use repeatedly to the dictionary. You should also enter place names and brand names that you use frequently.

Finally, you should understand that it takes time to run a spell-ing check. The great strength of the Document Checker is its abil-ity to check up to sixteen files in a batch, on its own, while you do something else. When you load dictionaries into a RAM disk in extended-memory, the Document Checker can even seem fast.

Tip: *Not everyone needs a spelling checker, at least not all the time.*

If you spell accurately, take proofreading seriously, recognize misspellings, and write fewer than four single-spaced pages at a time, a good paperback dictionary may be an adequate resource. The inexpensive Scribner-Bantam English dictionary contains 80,000 entries, including place names. It also includes essays on synonyms.

SUMMARY

This chapter has reviewed a broad range of options and problems in the Word Processor. You will be able to use many of the tips and techniques repeatedly.

Practice using the printer options and remember their logical groups. Keep track of carriage return markers and remember the AppleWorks definitions of a paragraph. Practice using the clipboard and experiment with the find and replace commands.

Above all, concentrate on writing well. Everyone uses a word processor differently, so develop your own techniques. AppleWorks can handle large and complicated projects, and it is fast when you use modular construction methods. Remember that spelling counts: keep a paperback dictionary close by.

As you understand more about the Word Processor, you will find that you can write and edit more efficiently. The next two chapters will draw upon what you have learned about printer options in this chapter. While exploring the Data Base and Spreadsheet, you will continue to change file names, copy to the clipboard, and use AppleWorks commands for unexpected purposes. You will continue building component parts that can be used again and again in many useful applications. In Chapter 5 some of those parts will be transferred back to the Word Processor.

3
The Data Base

any people first use the Data Base to make lists. With each list, they learn more about the Data Base's capabilities for selecting records, creating report formats, printing labels, and so on. Some of these things can also be done on the Spreadsheet, so there is additional information on database management in Chapter 4. Chapter 5 includes tips for using the Data Base and Spreadsheet together.

As database managers go, the AppleWorks Data Base is easy to learn and teach. You can see the records individually during data entry or in a table for an overview. Most people find the Data Base simple enough for them to begin entering information into existing files without much instruction. When you teach others, let them work with an existing file on their own. AppleWorks has good error-trapping routines and clearly marked escape routes, so it is difficult to get lost.

The Data Base offers convenient reporting options. These reports can also be edited on the Word Processor, and when the Data Base is used in conjunction with the Mail Merge option in AppleWorks version 2.0, it provides greatly extended reporting capabilities, including the ability to generate form letters. In fact, some experienced users think AppleWorks is the most efficient database manager available for common applications.

Additional memory capacity makes the Data Base unusually large and fast. Data Base files tend to need more memory than Word Processor files or modular Spreadsheet applications. Although it is possible to divide Data Base files by some category into A–M and N–Z sections, this compromises arranging and selection capabilities. Additional memory capacity allows you to undertake projects that can have more than 6,000 records. When you exceed the limits of the 128K Apple, simply add the memory you need.

This chapter provides tips for using the AppleWorks Data Base in thirteen sections. Everyone who uses the Data Base, or plans to, should read the first section of general tips.

The section on building lists includes basic information on designing templates for multiple purposes. It introduces tips on choosing categories and developing a simple database as a basic component for other databases. In the next three sections, tips are given for using the available options for finding, selecting, and arranging records. The topics have been divided in this way to focus on the logic of record-selection rules. Pay particular attention to the undocumented problems in these rules. Sections on creating report formats cover both labels-style and tables-style reports. The section on printing reports includes important information on techniques for working with small cards and labels.

Database applications require considerable attention to design. Three sections cover advanced techniques for designing and developing Data Base applications. The following section explains how to merge records from one file with those of another. The last section outlines the design and use of inventory and citation databases. All this taken together should make the Data Base easier to use for large applications.

GENERAL DATA BASE TIPS

The tips below apply throughout the Data Base, and include minor cautions. The Data Base requires attention to detail, and you should pay special attention to the need for documenting everything you do.

The Data Base encourages development of templates that can be modified for many different purposes. If you know when and how to change file names, you can develop applications more efficiently. If you appreciate the cost of acquiring data, you can develop applications within your budget.

Tip: *Print and annotate hard copies of the Data Base menus.*

You will need a hard copy of the Data Base menu and the Data Base Printer Options menu, as well as menus for the Apple-F, Apple-N, Apple-R, and Apple-P commands. If you have not yet done so, print copies of all these screens using Apple-H, and hang the copies on a note board near your Apple. Pencil in notes about when you use each option. A hard copy of the Data Base menu is shown in Figure 3.1.

Tip: *The cursor appears on the first record when you reload a file.*

A file with records is also always displayed in multiple-record layout when you reload it, regardless of whether you were previously using single-record layout.

While the file is on the Desktop, the cursor and the display mode always remain as you left them, which is exactly as it should be. Make a note of this, because when you make a quick change to another file, you will almost always need to come back to precisely the same place.

There is one exception to the above: if you leave the file from a report format, the cursor returns to multiple-record layout.

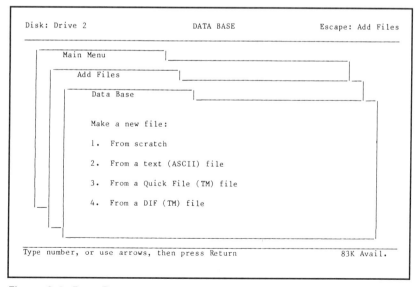

Figure 3.1: *Data Base menu*

Tip: *Use uppercase letters for Data Base category names.*

Many database managers distinguish category names from actual data with inverse video. AppleWorks does not, so use uppercase letters for category names, and the appropriate combination of upper- and lowercase letters for the data. (This is another case in which it is more important to differentiate between word groups than between letters. By the time you have entered the tenth record, you will probably know the category names by heart and in order.)

Tip: *Category and report format naming rules are more flexible than file naming rules.*

Category and report format names can begin with numbers and include symbols (such as # and *). In addition, a category name can be up to five characters longer than a ProDOS file name. A report format can have a name up to 19 characters long. It can also be exactly the same as an AppleWorks file name if you so choose. Table 3.1 shows the differences in the rules.

Table 3.1: Rules for file, report, and category names

Option	ProDOS Files	AppleWorks Files	Data Base Reports	Data Base Categories
Maximum characters	15	15	19	20
Lead numerals			X	X
Internal numbers	X	X	X	X
Lowercase letters	X	X	X	X
Symbols			X	X
Blank spaces		X	X	X

Tip: *Once you change the name of a Data Base file that has been saved, you can do almost anything with it.*

This is an important tip, and the concept will be adapted for specific purposes throughout this chapter. Once a file is saved to primary and backup disks, you can change the name on the Desktop and make any changes you like without changing the files on disk. You can copy, delete, replace, and rearrange data for any purpose. If you make a serious mistake, simply remove the file from the Desktop, load the original file again, and change its name on the Desktop once more.

Tip: *Data Base design can be done with pencil and paper.*

When two or more people use the same Apple, there will be times when one person wants to use AppleWorks and cannot. That is a good time to start working with pencil and paper. For example, you can design Data Base record layouts using graph paper. You can design report formats using a hard copy of a report format screen that includes all the categories. Print a hard copy of the Printer Options menu showing all the default values, like the one in Figure 3.2. Pencil in proposed changes for a specific report format.

Tip: *Document all your work.*

When you write a report on the Word Processor, you rarely need directions when you load it again several weeks later. When you develop a database application with several report formats, you may get lost later unless you have previously made notes.

The documentation you write should explain why you developed the application. It should include step-by-step instructions

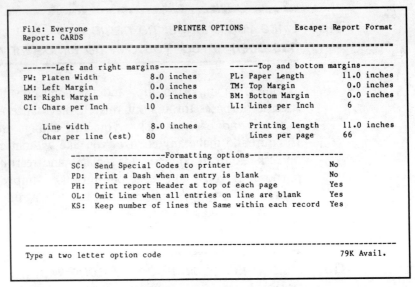

```
File: Everyone                 PRINTER OPTIONS              Escape: Report Format
Report: CARDS
================================================================================

-------Left and right margins--------          ------Top and bottom margins-------
PW: Platen Width              8.0 inches    PL: Paper Length          11.0 inches
LM: Left Margin               0.0 inches    TM: Top Margin             0.0 inches
RM: Right Margin              0.0 inches    BM: Bottom Margin          0.0 inches
CI: Chars per Inch            10            LI: Lines per Inch         6

    Line width                8.0 inches        Printing length       11.0 inches
    Char per line (est)   80                     Lines per page        66

         -------------------Formatting options--------------------
    SC:  Send Special Codes to printer                        No
    PD:  Print a Dash when an entry is blank                  No
    PH:  Print report Header at top of each page              Yes
    OL:  Omit Line when all entries on line are blank         Yes
    KS:  Keep number of lines the Same within each record     Yes


    -----------------------------------------------------------------------------
    Type a two letter option code                               79K Avail.
```

Figure 3.2: *Data Base Printer Options menu*

on how to load and use the Data Base file, and should note any problems encountered with the data. Your documentation should be filed along with hard copies of important screens and formats (a multiple-record display screen, a single-record display screen, a list of the report formats, each report format, and the respective printer option settings for each).

Every application should have its own manila file folder or something functionally equivalent. Print a tables-style report of all the data in the file.

Tip: *Data acquisition costs more than you think.*

Databases need specific information. Think of all the missing ZIP codes and all the misspelled last names in your rotary card file at work. What happens if you plan to enter these names and addresses into a database and generate mailing labels from it? You simply have to find the correct information before you begin.

The time spent on the simple application presented in the next section will give you some idea of how much data acquisition costs in large applications. In fact, the cost of obtaining, reviewing, entering, and updating data should be a primary consideration in the design of any AppleWorks application. Appendix C includes more on reference information and the costs of data acquisition. When you understand how to search for information, you can often save time and expense.

Tip: *Save your work to disk at least every 20 minutes.*

Press Apple-S at least every 20 minutes when you are entering data. Save to a backup disk as well on every second or third save. Remember that you can save small files faster. For initial data entry you can use small files of up to about 240 records. Later, use the clipboard to copy them into one large database.

BUILDING LISTS

If letters are the most common Word Processor files, lists are probably the most common Data Base files. Good planning and design can save considerable time in building and using databases. For this section I have constructed a LIST template (see Figure 3.3), from which I built an "Everyone" list as an example database (see Figures 3.4 and 3.5). From such a list you can create card files, mailing labels, form letter headings, and telephone lists. The Everyone list keeps information on the people and institutions you need to remember from day to day—it can be filled with the names and addresses in your current business card collection.

Tip: *Make a LIST template that contains at least 15 categories and two basic report formats.*

Name your basic Data Base template LIST. It should have at least 15 categories, a tables-style report, and a labels-style report.

Most applications use fewer than 15 categories, and most are lists of names and addresses. The first seven template categories can be named FIRST NAME, LAST NAME, PLACE, STREET,

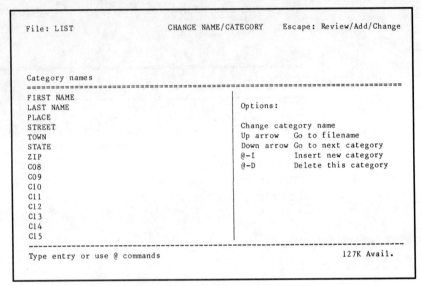

```
File: LIST                  CHANGE NAME/CATEGORY      Escape: Review/Add/Change



Category names
====================================================================================
FIRST NAME
LAST NAME                                     Options:
PLACE
STREET                                        Change category name
TOWN                                          Up arrow   Go to filename
STATE                                         Down arrow Go to next category
ZIP                                           @-I        Insert new category
C08                                           @-D        Delete this category
C09
C10
C11
C12
C13
C14
C15
------------------------------------------------------------------------------------
Type entry or use @ commands                                        127K Avail.
```

Figure 3.3: *LIST template showing category order*

```
File: Everyone                  MOVE RECORDS      Escape: Review/Add/Change

Selection: All records


FIRST NAME  LAST NAME   PLACE      STREET            TOWN        STATE ZIP
=========================================================================
Joanne      Martinelli  -         25 Brook Rd.      Jefferson   RI    02845
Robert      Smith       -         28 Bayberry Rd.   Esterly     CT    06414
Roberta     Miller      -         14 Brook Rd.      Jefferson   RI    02845
Edward      Joiner      -         19 Mill Rd.       Jefferson   RI    02845
Rob         Martin      -         22 Meadow Rd.     Jefferson   RI    02845
William     Venn        -         24 East Rd.       Jefferson   RI    02845
Robin       Jones       -         33 Field Rd.      Jefferson   RI    02845
Joan        Smith       -         72 Jefferson Pike Westbrook   MA    02731
Thomas      Farmer      -         12 Field Rd.      Jefferson   RI    02845
Susan       Smith       -         81 Main Rd.       Jefferson   RI    02845
Arnold      Wright      -         52 Field Rd.      Jefferson   RI    02845



------------------------------------------------------------------------------
Move records?  To clipboard (cut)  From clipboard (paste)
```

Figure 3.4: *Everyone list in multiple-record layout*

```
    File: Everyone                REVIEW/ADD/CHANGE              Escape: Main Menu

    Selection: All records


    Record 10 of 11
    ================================================================================
    FIRST NAME: Susan
    LAST NAME: Smith
    PLACE: -
    STREET: 81 Main Rd.
    TOWN: Jefferson
    STATE: RI
    ZIP: 02845
    PHONE: (401) 888-3311
    NOTE: Town Librarian
    CODE: Fl
    KEYWORD: SMITH
    R1: -
    R2: -
    R3: -
    R4: -
    --------------------------------------------------------------------------------
    Type entry or use @ commands                                   @-? for Help
```

Figure 3.5: Single-record layout from the Everyone list

TOWN, STATE, and ZIP. AppleWorks uses no precommitted category forms, so the name of any category can be changed and used for any kind of information.

Empty categories require little memory, so if you do not need all the categories in your template for a particular application, there is no need to delete the extra ones. Figure 3.3 shows the category-order screen for the LIST file.

If you have an extended memory card and want to expand on this technique, a later tip explains how to store an additional 15 categories and use them to advantage.

Tip: *Spend time thinking about the categories you will need.*

You can quickly convert the basic LIST template into an Everyone list. First, think about the additional categories you will need, based on the information you want to enter as records. The categories described below should suffice for most purposes. Figures 3.4 and 3.5 show the list in multiple- and single-record layouts.

I chose to have FIRST NAME as the first category because it is easier to create report formats—almost all labels-style reports have the first name first.

Some people prefer to enter the last name before the first name in the category order, because lists are often sorted by last name. However, it is probably more important to read names in the order you say them: first name first.

Some people like to use a separate category for the form of greeting. Such a category could be used to enter a preferred name, where a legal name appears in the FIRST NAME category. For example, someone named Mary Smith may prefer to be greeted by her middle name, Lynn. A form-of-greeting category could also be used for noting gender and professional credentials and titles. In the Everyone list, you can use the NOTE section to note gender and any discrepancies between legal and preferred names. Professional credentials and titles can be entered after the name in the LAST NAME category.

The PLACE category is for the name of the institution for which the address follows. You can sort records by this category when it is more appropriate for your needs. If you most often deal with similar types of institutions, you may want to rename this category COMPANY, for example.

The NOTE category can be used to store brief notes on what you need to remember, if anything. For example, "President?" might indicate that you are not certain whether the person is in fact the president of the firm.

It is sometimes necessary to include a separate category for institutional titles, for example, Dean, Associate Director of Finance, or whatever is appropriate. (Correct titles are sometimes difficult to track down.) If you have relatively few titles to worry about, there is no need for such a category. Simply enter titles in the NOTE category as needed.

The CODE category allows you to divide the people in the list into several groups (for example, clients, friends, relatives, and suppliers), for finding or selecting records later. (See a following tip on using this category effectively.)

The KEYWORD category will be used for either a duplicate last name, a duplicate company name, or a subject word that you can later use to select records from the database.

Tip: *Try to be accurate and consistent when you enter data.*

Consistent data entry rules make it easier to enter and find information in a database. Consistent rules also make it easier to proofread and edit records. Following are some commonly used rules; you will probably want to add some of your own.

FIRST NAME: Such as Ralph, Rolf, Dr. Bob, or R.J., as the person prefers. Include a middle initial only if the person uses one in a signature. In general, use the simplest form for first names.

LAST NAME: Such as Wright, Smith AIA, or other abbreviations for professional credentials and titles. Pay special attention to the spelling, because everyone deserves to have their name spelled correctly.

PLACE: Some institutions have names that are two lines long: for example, David Taylor Engineering Laboratory, Department of Mechanical Engineering. Shorten the name if such cases are rare on your list; otherwise use an extra category. You might shorten the name in this example to Taylor Lab, Mech. Engineering.

STREET: Use standard postal abbreviations for Boulevard, Avenue, Street, Road, Lane, Circle, Place, etc. This category is also for Post Office box numbers and rural delivery route box numbers.

TOWN: Use standard abbreviations for East, West, South, North, etc.

STATE: Use two-letter postal abbreviations, such as MI for Michigan. States that begin with A and M are the most difficult to remember. (Arizona is AZ, Arkansas is AR, and Alaska is AK. Missouri is MO, Montana is MT, and Mississippi is MS.)

ZIP CODE: Five digits (02881) or nine (02881-4356). The shorter form works better if you plan to transfer information with DIF files.

If the address is for a foreign country, include any postal code used in that country in the STATE category. Then enter the country name in the ZIP CODE category. When you arrange the ZIP codes using the A–Z option, all country names will be arranged in alphabetical order after any American addresses. When you enter country names, use consistent spelling.

PHONE: The form (401) 989-2714 covers most possibilities. The telephone company generally places the area code in parentheses. By a happy coincidence, that makes it easier to transfer telephone numbers in DIF files. This point is discussed in greater detail in Chapter 5.

The form x1234 can designate an extension number with one to four digits. Put the extension in a separate category or add it to the right of the phone number. The Data Base can arrange entries of variable length because it left-justifies them.

Tip: *Use the copy command to enter similar records.*

Copying saves time and it makes entered data more consistent. If two or more records include similar information, enter the first record and copy the rest. Use the multiple-record layout to see the results. Edit the copied records for any category entry that needs to be changed. If many records have the same entry in only one category, use Apple-V to make that entry a standard value.

Tip: *One CODE category can do the work of two or more.*

Suppose you have divided the people in your Everyone list into several groups, including clients, friends, relatives, and suppliers, and have chosen codes for each as follows:

- C (clients)

- F (friends)

- R (relatives)

- S (suppliers)

Suppose you have also classified each person according to frequency of contact, with these codes:

- 1 (weekly)

- 2 (monthly)

- 3 (quarterly)

- 4 (annually)

- 5 (less frequently)

By combining the two codes, you can make one category do the work of two. For example, R4 might include relatives in another country; S5 might include a parts supplier for equipment that has worked perfectly for years.

These codes allow for four variables with letters and five with numbers. The single-letter part of the code can represent as many as 26 variables. The single-number part of the code can represent up to 10 variables (if you include zero).

Only the first character of a combined code can be sorted effectively, so place the character of the code you would be most likely to sort by (for example, relationship or frequency of contact) first. This is a significant limitation in the Data Base. You will see in Chapter 4 that this limitation is not so significant in the Spreadsheet, where arranging can be done by rows within selected ranges.

Tip: *Limit the number of records in your lists.*

If you want to run your life without a secretary, 240 records is a reasonable limit for an Everyone list. If you have fewer records, good for you. If you have more, think about thinning out records.

Tip: *Develop consistent standards for thinning out records.*

The tedium of data entry will invariably encourage you to throw out records. Be careful, though, because it gets more boring as you go along. Give as much consideration to records near the end of the list as you did to those at the beginning. Or, to put it another way, set rigorous standards from the start.

Tip: *When you revise a single category entry in the Data Base, remember to press Return after completing the entry.*

Make it a habit to press Return after you make an entry, especially when you are in multiple-record layout. In that layout, you can press Escape without triggering a reminder beep, and your revisions will be lost.

Notice the message in the upper-right corner of the screen when you make a change:

Escape: Restore former entry

Even if you have replaced all the characters in an entry, pressing Escape restores the previous entry perfectly.

FINDING RECORDS

Sometimes you want to find a record to see if it is in the database, to see whether it is a duplicate record, to reassure yourself of its content, or to revise it. If you already know some of the text in the record, you can use Apple-F to find it. If you know the general area it is in, you may simply want to scan multiple-record layout in that area. If you are just plain lost and need to find a familiar record, such as the first or last, you can use Apple-1 or Apple-9.

The tips that follow cover the general process of finding records and finding your way around. You already know Apple-F from the Word Processor. It searches for anything that contains specified text. In this sense it can be considered as a record-selection rule that searches all categories at once. The Data Base has no replace command, but this section describes a useful replacement technique.

Apple-F and the record-selection rules often do similar things equally well. The record-selection rules appear in a separate section because they require an introduction to Boolean logic, and because they have some serious undocumented problems.

Caution: | *Returning from a file save can be confusing.*

If you save your file from single-record layout, the cursor may come back to some record preceding the one you had been working on. Although this can be disorienting, there is no need for concern.

Here is an example of what can happen. Suppose you want to enter new records at the end of an existing file. You load the file, select single-record layout, and attempt to move beyond record 222, the last current record. The message screen that appears in Figure 3.6 is a significant dividing line in the Data Base.

Suppose you answer Yes and subsequently enter a dozen new records. After you save the file while in record 234, the cursor returns to record 222, the last record in the file before you started the session. The Data Base does this consistently.

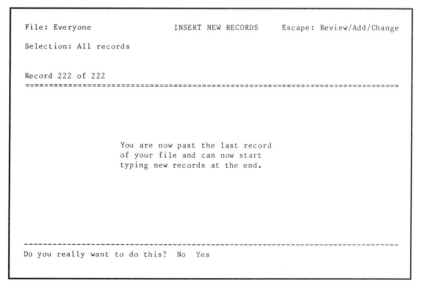

```
File: Everyone                INSERT NEW RECORDS      Escape: Review/Add/Change

Selection: All records


Record 222 of 222
===============================================================================




                        You are now past the last record
                        of your file and can now start
                        typing new records at the end.






            -------------------------------------------------------------------
Do you really want to do this?  No  Yes
```

Figure 3.6: *Message screen at the end of the database*

Apple-9 will take you back to record 234. If you save the file from somewhere other than the last record, remember the record number if you want to find it again. If you subsequently go beyond record 234, add a dozen more records, and save the file from record 246, the cursor will return to record 234.

Tip: *If you are in single-record layout and cannot get to the record you need, switch to multiple-record layout.*

This tip is related to the caution above. Suppose you want to enter new records at the end of an existing file. You load the file, select single-record layout, and attempt to move beyond record 222, the last current record. The message screen shown in Figure 3.6 appears. You answer Yes and then enter one record.

Next, you need to see an entry five records back, but in single-record layout you cannot step back into the previous file area. Use Apple-Z to zoom to multiple-record layout, find the record you need, and then change back to single-record layout with Apple-Z again.

Tip: *If you are in multiple-record layout and cannot see a category, use Apple-Z or Apple-L.*

Multiple-record layout shows only as many categories as will fit on the screen. (Many people find this hard to believe, because scrolling to the right is so simple in the Spreadsheet.) If you need to see only a few entries in a category that is not visible in multiple-record layout, switch to single-record layout. For example, multiple-record layout displays five categories, but not the NOTE category you want to see. If you need to see the NOTE entry for one record, place the cursor anywhere on that record and press Apple-Z to view the record in single-record layout.

If you need to see and compare NOTE entries for 80 records, press Apple-L to rearrange the categories. You can move the NOTE category onto the multiple-record screen and remove some other category. This can be tedious, and it explains why some people prefer to use the Spreadsheet, where you can scroll the screen to see all the information.

Tip: *Use Apple-F as an effective record-selection rule.*

Apple-F can be used to find records that contain specified text and numbers, and it searches through all categories at once. For most purposes it is the simplest way to find what you want. In some searches you will get exactly what you want; in other searches, at least a few extra records. For example, if you want to find a specific ZIP code, that five-digit number probably exists in no other category. Apple-F works neatly in that case.

If you search a database for all addresses in Vermont, you can use VT—it is unlikely that the letters VT will appear together otherwise. Apple-F would not work well with MO, the postal abbreviation for Missouri. The letters MO appear often in other words, such as Morris, mountain, and almond. You cannot specify MO with leading or trailing spaces to isolate the two characters, as you can in the Word Processor. (Although you can deliberately enter spaces in a category, that can cause many more problems than it solves.)

When two letters are likely to appear together often in a Data Base file, use the record-selection rules to confine the search to a single category.

With Apple-F you can gather records quickly, copy them to the clipboard, and use them for other purposes, including starting a new Data Base file.

Caution: *Apple-F is slower in AppleWorks version 2.0.*

Version 2.0 takes almost twice the time version 1.3 does to find an entry using Apple-F, and the difference can be frustrating. That's unfortunate, because most people prefer to use the find command rather than the record selection rules.

On the other hand, record selection with Apple-R in version 2.0 takes little more than half the time required by earlier versions. Delimited searches are inherently faster than unlimited searches anyway, so if you get used to record selection, you can work very quickly. It is true that Apple-R requires more thought than Apple-F; Chapter 7 explains how macros can partly automate this process.

Tip: *Apple-F searches the entire database, regardless of where the cursor is located when the search begins.*

Apple-F in the Data Base differs from Apple-F in the Word Processor and the Spreadsheet. Table 3.2 shows the differences in the find and replace commands within the three programs. You cannot search part of a database using only the find command.

Tip: *Use Apple-F from multiple-record layout.*

Even when you want to find one record, you may retrieve more than one, so it is helpful to see them displayed on the

Table 3.2: Options available for find and replace functions

Option	Word Processor	Data Base	Spreadsheet
Finds text	X	X	X
Finds case-sensitive text	X		
Finds numbers	X	X	as labels only
Finds page numbers	X		
Also finds	markers		coordinates
Searches from	cursor	beginning	cursor
Replaces one instance	X		
Replaces all instances	X		
Maximum number of characters	30	30	25

multiple-record screen. If you use Apple-F from single-record lay-out, only the first retrieved record is displayed. By using Apple-F from multiple-record layout, you can immediately scan up to 15 records at once. Pressing Escape will return you to all the records in multiple-record layout.

Caution: *The Apple-" command is actually Apple-'.*

The Reference Manual rightly calls this the ditto command, so it made sense to refer to it with ditto marks (otherwise known as quotation marks). However, to create the ditto marks you would also have to press Shift, which is not part of the command. So Apple simply added "do not press Shift" in their instructions. In this chapter I will write the command as Apple-'.

Tip: *Apple-' can substitute for the replace command lacking in the Data Base.*

The Word Processor has a replace command (Apple-R) but the Data Base does not, even though this is a commonly used feature in other database managers. However, there is a way to use Apple-' as a substitute:

1. In multiple-record layout, use Apple-F or the record-selection rules to retrieve all the records with the informa-tion you want to replace.

2. Enter the new information in the first retrieved record.

3. Place the cursor in the same category of the next record and hold down Apple-' to quickly change the information.

4. Move through the remaining records, using Apple-' to replace the old information with the new.

This method gathers the required records together before you make the changes, and allows you to see each change as you make it. Even if the Data Base did have a global replace command, it would be risky to replace information without seeing it in context.

SELECTING RECORDS

Most people select records just before printing, but record selection works equally well in the Review mode. That is where experienced users make decisions about what to report and print.

There are some serious problems in the AppleWorks record-selection rules prior to version 2.0. Every program has undocumented problems, but it hurts most to find problems with logical functions, because they are difficult enough to master anyway. If you have depended on the Data Base to track accounts receivable or send legal notices, some of the tips and cautions that follow may prompt you to review your previous work.

Tip: *Use the record-selection rules from multiple-record layout.*

Even when you want to select one record, you may retrieve more than one, so it is helpful to see them displayed on the multiple-record screen. If you use the rules from single-record layout, only one selected record is displayed. By using the record-selection rules from multiple-record layout, you can immediately scan up to 15 records at once. Press Apple-1 to begin the display with the first selected record.

Using Apple-R again will return you to all the records in multiple-record layout. Simply answer Yes to the question, "Select all records?"

Caution: *AppleWorks has problems discriminating numbers, especially zeros.*

This is a problem through AppleWorks version 2.0, and it has several dimensions. We will begin with the simplest case, a category with number entries. Here are the most common errors:

1. If you ask for all records in which that category is less than, say 4, you also get all records with no entry in that category. You can get around this problem by specifying entries that are less than 4 and not blank.

2. If you ask AppleWorks to select records in which that category equals 0, you also get all records with no entry in that category. You can get around this problem by specifying entries that end with 0 and begin with 0. (Either used alone could retrieve unwanted records.)

3. If you ask for all records in which that category is not equal to 0, you get everything except records with 0 or no entry. You broaden the retrieval to include records with no entry by specifying entries that are blank or not equal to zero.

The problems become far more complicated if a category accepts either a letter or a number. This is a complex case—avoid the situation if at all possible. (A code that includes both a letter and a number is different—AppleWorks has no problems there.)

We will repeat the first case above, but with the new complication. If you ask for all records in which that category is less than 4, you also get all records with no entry in that category, plus all records with letter entries in that category. You can get around the problem by specifying entries that are less than A, and less than 4, and not blank.

Caution: *The "equals" criterion in the record-selection rules may retrieve unwanted records.*

This problem occurs in AppleWorks versions prior to 2.0. The easiest way to describe it is with specific examples. Suppose your database includes two people with the first name of Roberta. You select all records in which the first name "equals" Roberta, but the records you retrieve also include everyone with the first name of Robert.

Suppose your database also includes one person named Rob and another named Robin. You select all records in which the first name "equals" Rob, but the records you receive also include everyone with the first name of Robert, but not Robin.

The Data Base appears to match six letters at a time. When the match word has fewer than six letters, it also takes six-letter words that begin with the match word. (But it will not take words of fewer than six letters that begin with the match word.) For match words with more than six letters but fewer than twelve, it seems to be satisfied with a match on the first six letters alone.

It is sometimes difficult to foresee the effects of this problem in specific applications. Suppose your database includes a last name of Martinelli. You select all records in which the last name "equals" Martinelli, but the records you receive also include someone with the last name of Martin. However, when you select Martin, Martinelli is not retrieved. Figures 3.7 and 3.8 illustrate this.

Although the Data Base will sometimes retrieve more than you want, it apparently does not retrieve less. There appears to be no problem matching numbers.

Tip: *The "contains" rule can sometimes get you around the "equals" problem in the record-selection rules.*

It helps to use the "contains" rule more often. For example, the rules will not select Martin when you specify last names that "contain" Martinelli, as shown in Figure 3.9. Note that this is a prudent choice anyway. There may be an occasion when some last name you thought equalled Smith was actually Smith with a mistaken empty space in front of it or Smith, AIA. The "contains" rule works accurately in either case.

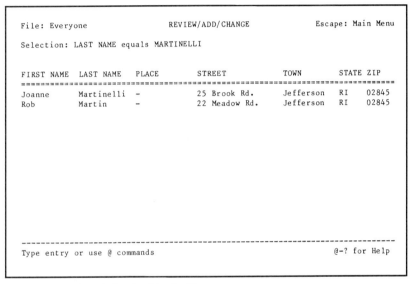

```
File: Everyone              REVIEW/ADD/CHANGE           Escape: Main Menu

Selection: LAST NAME equals MARTINELLI


FIRST NAME  LAST NAME  PLACE      STREET         TOWN       STATE ZIP
====================================================================
Joanne      Martinelli  -        25 Brook Rd.   Jefferson  RI    02845
Rob         Martin      -        22 Meadow Rd.  Jefferson  RI    02845




------------------------------------------------------------------
Type entry or use @ commands                        @-? for Help
```

Figure 3.7: *"Equals" rule: Martinelli*

```
File: Everyone              REVIEW/ADD/CHANGE           Escape: Main Menu

Selection: LAST NAME equals MARTIN


FIRST NAME  LAST NAME  PLACE      STREET         TOWN       STATE ZIP
====================================================================
Rob         Martin      -        22 Meadow Rd.  Jefferson  RI    02845




------------------------------------------------------------------
Type entry or use @ commands                        @-? for Help
```

Figure 3.8: *"Equals" rule: Martin*

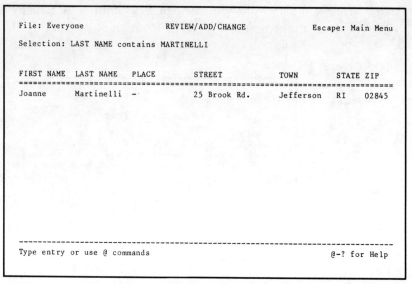

```
File: Everyone              REVIEW/ADD/CHANGE           Escape: Main Menu

Selection: LAST NAME contains MARTINELLI


FIRST NAME  LAST NAME  PLACE      STREET          TOWN        STATE ZIP
=======================================================================
Joanne      Martinelli  -·        25 Brook Rd.    Jefferson   RI   02845










----------------------------------------------------------------------
Type entry or use @ commands                               @-? for Help
```

Figure 3.9: *"Contains" rule: Martinelli*

Caution: *The "does not end with" rule does not work.*

This problem occurs in AppleWorks versions prior to 2.0. If you ask for any last name that "does not end with" S, the Data Base returns Anderson, Barnes, and Collins. The rule simply does not work: not for letters, not for numbers, not for punctuation marks. Figure 3.10 shows an example.

If you started using "does not end with" statements before learning that they are worthless, you may have developed serious doubts about your understanding of logic. Have faith in yourself—it was Apple's problem all along.

Caution: *The "ends with" rule can produce unwanted results.*

In AppleWorks version 1.1, the "ends with" criterion in the record-selection rules sometimes failed to retrieve requested records.

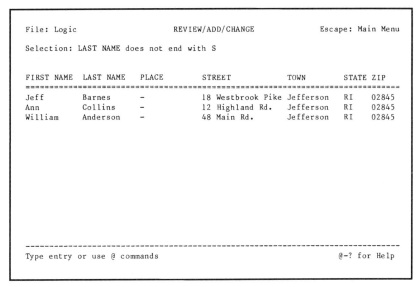

```
File: Logic                REVIEW/ADD/CHANGE          Escape: Main Menu

Selection: LAST NAME does not end with S


FIRST NAME  LAST NAME  PLACE      STREET            TOWN       STATE ZIP
=======================================================================
Jeff        Barnes     -          18 Westbrook Pike Jefferson  RI    02845
Ann         Collins    -          12 Highland Rd.   Jefferson  RI    02845
William     Anderson   -          48 Main Rd.       Jefferson  RI    02845




-----------------------------------------------------------------------
Type entry or use @ commands                          @-? for Help
```

Figure 3.10: *"Does not end with" rule*

Suppose you are working with the Everyone list (shown in Figure 3.4), which has two last names ending in the letter n. (One last name is Martin and one is Venn.) When you ask the Data Base to retrieve all last names ending in the letter n, you get Martin but not Venn (see Figure 3.11). When the character preceding the last character is the same as the last character, this record-selection rule ignores the record.

The problem includes numbers. For example, suppose you have made a CODE category for a two-digit number, hoping that it can do the work of two CODE categories. (A two-digit number in the form of 92 can indicate ten different cases that "begin with" 0–9, and ten more independent cases that "end with" 0–9.) However, the record-selection rule ignores the record if the preceding digit is identical. Thus, in order to select all cases that "end with" 1, you must also specify the criterion "or equal 11".

With AppleWorks it is preferable to use one letter and one number, as in an earlier tip; with a code in the form of C2, the problem cannot occur.

Although this problem does not occur after version 1.1, remember the people who never upgraded their AppleWorks disk.

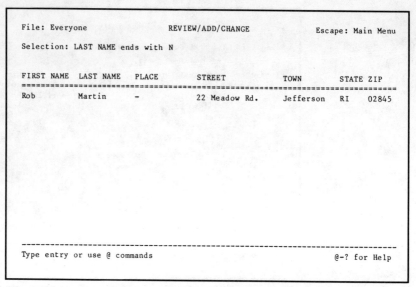

```
File: Everyone               REVIEW/ADD/CHANGE          Escape: Main Menu

Selection: LAST NAME ends with N


FIRST NAME  LAST NAME  PLACE       STREET         TOWN       STATE ZIP
===================================================================================
Rob         Martin     -           22 Meadow Rd.  Jefferson  RI    02845










------------------------------------------------------------------------------------
Type entry or use @ commands                                @-? for Help
```

Figure 3.11: *"Ends with" criterion in AppleWorks version 1.1*

If you have AppleWorks version 2.0, consider the possibility that your template may some day find its way to someone using an earlier version.

Tip: *When you use more than one positive record-selection rule, "or" increases the number of records selected.*

As you would therefore expect, "and" decreases the number of records selected. The logic of this is easy to understand.

Suppose you have three records with the respective last names of Anderson, Barnes, and Collins. If you ask for any last name that "begins with" A, the Data Base selects Anderson. If you ask for any last name that begins with A or B, you get Anderson and Barnes, as shown in Figure 3.12.

If you ask for any last name that begins with A and B, you get nothing, as shown in Figure 3.13, because a name cannot begin with both A and B at the same time.

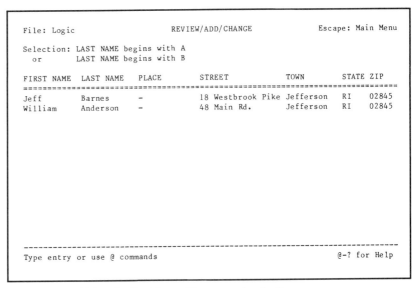

```
File: Logic                    REVIEW/ADD/CHANGE              Escape: Main Menu

Selection: LAST NAME begins with A
    or     LAST NAME begins with B

FIRST NAME  LAST NAME   PLACE       STREET            TOWN        STATE ZIP
===============================================================================
Jeff        Barnes      -           18 Westbrook Pike Jefferson    RI    02845
William     Anderson    -           48 Main Rd.       Jefferson    RI    02845





Type entry or use @ commands                                 @-? for Help
```

Figure 3.12: *Using "or" with positive record selection*

Tip: *When you use more than one negative record-selection rule, "or" increases the number of records selected.*

As you would expect from the above tip, "and" decreases the number of records selected. The logic of this requires some thought.

Suppose you have three records with the respective last names of Anderson, Barnes, and Collins. If you ask for any last name that "does not begin with" A, the Data Base selects Barnes and Collins. This is easy enough to understand.

If you ask for any last name that "does not begin with" A *or* "does not begin with" B, the Data Base retrieves all three names, as shown in Figure 3.14. Why? In this case Barnes and Collins fit the first rule because they do not begin with A, while Anderson and Collins fit the second rule because they do not begin with B.

The way to exclude both Anderson and Barnes is to ask for any last name that "does not begin with" A *and* any last name that "does not begin with" B, as shown in Figure 3.15.

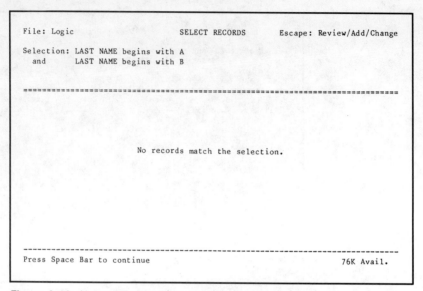

```
File: Logic                        SELECT RECORDS        Escape: Review/Add/Change

Selection: LAST NAME begins with A
   and      LAST NAME begins with B


===============================================================================




                   No records match the selection.






-------------------------------------------------------------------------------
Press Space Bar to continue                                          76K Avail.
```

Figure 3.13: Using "and" with positive record selection

Try the examples at least once yourself. Note that it is less confusing to use positive record-selection rules whenever you have a choice.

Tip: *Use the record-selection rules as multiple filters.*

To use multiple filtering, you must first understand that the record-selection rules are used in two different places.

The record-selection rules in the Review/Add/Change mode are separate from the record-selection rules in the report mode. If you specify selection rules in the Review/Add/Change mode and then use Apple-P to select a report format, the rules you have specified will not apply if the report format was previously saved with record-selection rules in effect.

You will normally enter record-selection rules for a report from within the report mode. You may initially see rules in effect when you select the report format, but they are from a previous report session.

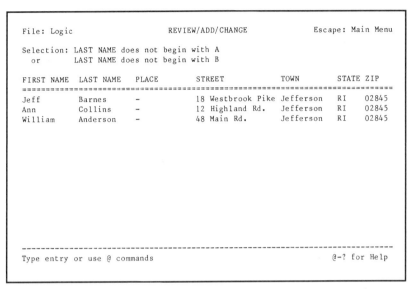

```
File: Logic                  REVIEW/ADD/CHANGE           Escape: Main Menu

Selection: LAST NAME does not begin with A
   or      LAST NAME does not begin with B

FIRST NAME  LAST NAME   PLACE        STREET           TOWN        STATE ZIP
==========================================================================
Jeff        Barnes      -        18 Westbrook Pike Jefferson     RI    02845
Ann         Collins     -        12 Highland Rd.   Jefferson     RI    02845
William     Anderson    -        48 Main Rd.       Jefferson     RI    02845




                                                                  

-------------------------------------------------------------------------
Type entry or use @ commands                             @-? for Help
```

Figure 3.14: *Using "or" with negative record selection*

The Data Base permits no more than three sets of selection rules to be applied at once. However, you can use the first selection in the Review/Add/Change mode as a filter for the second selection in the report mode. Here's how to do it:

1. From either single- or multiple-record display mode, press Apple-R and specify record-selection rules for records you do not want.

2. When the selected records appear, move them to the clipboard to get them out of the way temporarily.

3. Select a report format for printing the remaining records.

4. Specify record-selection rules within the report format.

5. Print to a printer, the clipboard, or disk.

6. Return to multiple-record layout and move the records on the clipboard back to the Data Base file.

Here the first selection in the Review/Add/Change mode filtered the records for the second selection in the report mode. If a

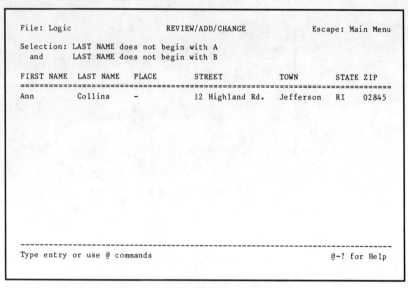

```
File: Logic                    REVIEW/ADD/CHANGE              Escape: Main Menu

Selection: LAST NAME does not begin with A
   and     LAST NAME does not begin with B

FIRST NAME  LAST NAME  PLACE       STREET          TOWN       STATE ZIP
==============================================================================
Ann         Collins      -         12 Highland Rd. Jefferson  RI    02845









------------------------------------------------------------------------------
Type entry or use @ commands                                  @-? for Help
```

Figure 3.15: *Using "and" with negative record selection*

first selection ever retrieves more than 250 records, you can move the records to another file temporarily. A tip on such temporary files appears later in this chapter.

ARRANGING RECORDS

The process of arranging records is also frequently referred to as sorting records. Although the Apple-A command is easy to use, there are some fine points to understand. AppleWorks uses a modified ASCII order for sorting, in which all letters are treated as uppercase letters. This section provides some useful insights on getting the most out of Apple-A.

Caution: *Alphabetical arranging follows a modified ASCII order.*

In the ASCII table, the digits 0–9 precede the letters A–Z, and capital letters precede lowercase letters. AppleWorks, however, treats all letters as capitals. If you arrange by last name, deRosa will appear before Zorn. Whenever you have doubts about order, consult the ASCII table in Appendix B.

Because the Data Base makes no distinction between values and labels, it left-justifies all entries. You can sort a category containing numbers with either the 0–9 or the A–Z option.

In versions through 1.3, if you sort a category using the A–Z option, numbers appear before letters. However, numbers are sorted by the leading digit, so that 18 comes before 2, for example. If you sort using the 0–9 option, the number entries appear between the word entries beginning with O and P. However, the numbers appear in correct numerical order: 2 comes before 18.

Version 2.0 handles the 0–9 option correctly: number entries appear before letter entries. All versions of AppleWorks also allow reverse sorting.

Tip: *Create a separate category for anything you want to sort.*

Think about what you will need. For example, you cannot sort by street name and street number if you combine the two in one category. Most people would not need do that kind of sorting anyway, but someone who makes deliveries might.

If you use separate categories for street name and street number, make certain that you spell street names consistently and with the same postal abbreviations. When you have Pole 24 instead of a road number, it will follow any pure number on that road when you sort using the 0–9 option.

In this example, you sort first by street number and then by street. The reason is logical: street number order makes sense only within each street.

Tip: *When you sort by more than one category, remember to sort by the most important category last.*

In determining the most important category, you are making a judgment only within the limited context of your needs for a specific report.

For example, suppose you want to sort the Everyone list by ZIP code in numerical order and by last name in alphabetical order *within* each ZIP code. In this context the ZIP code is more important than the last name. You would therefore sort by ZIP code last, as in Figure 3.16.

What if you simply want to generate a list by last name in alphabetical order, and there are three Smiths on the list. You decide to arrange the three Smiths in numerical order according to the ZIP code. In this context the last name is more important than the ZIP code, so you sort the last name last, as in Figure 3.17.

Caution: *Arranging selected records arranges all records.*

When you select records in multiple-record layout, you may want to arrange them by one or more categories. You can do that as you would the entire database. However, the entire database will be arranged by the same criteria at the same time, which may not be what you intended.

When you need to sort selected records, create a temporary file by changing the name of the Desktop file, adding one empty record, and deleting all the other records. Load the original file from the disk to the Desktop again and begin selecting records. Copy them to the clipboard, and then move them from the clipboard to the temporary file.

Tip: *Use unique identification numbers for each record to predict the order of arrangement.*

Suppose you sort records by last name only, and two people have the same last name, such as Smith. Susan Smith may or may not precede Robert Smith. There is no way to predict the relative order unless you know the order in which they were originally entered in the database or the last criterion for which they were

```
File: Everyone                REVIEW/ADD/CHANGE            Escape: Main Menu

Selection: All records


FIRST NAME  LAST NAME   PLACE        STREET            TOWN       STATE ZIP
==========================================================================
Joan        Smith       -         72 Jefferson Pike Westbrook    MA    02731
Thomas      Farmer      -         12 Field Rd.      Jefferson    RI    02845
Edward      Joiner      -         19 Mill Rd.       Jefferson    RI    02845
Robin       Jones       -         33 Field Rd.      Jefferson    RI    02845
Rob         Martin      -         22 Meadow Rd.     Jefferson    RI    02845
Joanne      Martinelli  -         25 Brook Rd.      Jefferson    RI    02845
Roberta     Miller      -         14 Brook Rd.      Jefferson    RI    02845
Susan       Smith       -         81 Main Rd.       Jefferson    RI    02845
William     Venn        -         24 East Rd.       Jefferson    RI    02845
Arnold      Wright      -         52 Field Rd.      Jefferson    RI    02845
Robert      Smith       -         28 Bayberry Rd.   Esterly      CT    06414



--------------------------------------------------------------------------
Type entry or use @ commands                              @-? for Help
```

Figure 3.16: *Records sorted by last name and then ZIP code*

```
File: Everyone                REVIEW/ADD/CHANGE            Escape: Main Menu

Selection: All records


FIRST NAME  LAST NAME   PLACE        STREET            TOWN       STATE ZIP
==========================================================================
Thomas      Farmer      -         12 Field Rd.      Jefferson    RI    02845
Edward      Joiner      -         19 Mill Rd.       Jefferson    RI    02845
Robin       Jones       -         33 Field Rd.      Jefferson    RI    02845
Rob         Martin      -         22 Meadow Rd.     Jefferson    RI    02845
Joanne      Martinelli  -         25 Brook Rd.      Jefferson    RI    02845
Roberta     Miller      -         14 Brook Rd.      Jefferson    RI    02845
Joan        Smith       -         72 Jefferson Pike Westbrook    MA    02731
Susan       Smith       -         81 Main Rd.       Jefferson    RI    02845
Robert      Smith       -         28 Bayberry Rd.   Esterly      CT    06414
William     Venn        -         24 East Rd.       Jefferson    RI    02845
Arnold      Wright      -         52 Field Rd.      Jefferson    RI    02845



--------------------------------------------------------------------------
Type entry or use @ commands                              @-? for Help
```

Figure 3.17: *Records sorted by ZIP code and then last name*

arranged. Here we could sort first by first name and then by last name. But what if we had two people named Susan Smith?

When each record has a unique identification number, it is much easier to predict order. You simply sort by the ID number first, and then by whatever criterion you choose.

There may be times when you will want to manage more than 30 categories of information in parallel Data Base files. In that case each related file absolutely must have corresponding categories with a unique ID number for each record.

Tip: *For people-related files, social security numbers can serve as unique identifiers.*

No two people have the same social security number, so the numbers can serve as unique identifiers. In fact, social security numbers are often used by insurance companies and colleges as ID numbers.

All social security numbers have nine digits, always in the form 044-21-3368, which makes them easy to sort. The only drawback to using social security numbers is that they do not fare well in DIF file transfers, as we will see in Chapter 5.

LABELS-STYLE REPORT FORMATS

Data Base reports come in two basic formats: labels-style reports and tables-style reports. When you design a format, you must specify exactly where on the paper each category should be printed. Sometimes you will want to have all the categories print out (for example, on Rolodex cards), and sometimes you will want only pertinent categories printed (for example, on mailing labels).

In this section, there are tips on designing labels-style report formats for printing Rolodex cards and mailing labels. There are also tips on dealing with blank categories and formatting for justification. Pay special attention to the tip on printing to the screen first.

In the next section tips will be given for designing tables-style reports, and in the section on printer options you will find tips for setting printer options for printing onto Rolodex cards and mailing labels.

Tip: *Apple-P will not access the printer until you have selected a report format.*

Obviously, you cannot select a report format until you have designed one. So the first time you use the print command you may still be a long way from actually printing. This confuses people more than any other feature of the Data Base.

Caution: *Beware of report formats with lines that begin with categories that are sometimes empty.*

AppleWorks version 1.1 had a problem adapting to blank categories. If the first of several categories on a line is blank and the next is left-justified, the line will begin with two blank spaces. You can generally design around this limitation, so think of those who never upgraded.

Tip: *Use left-justification for categories in mailing labels.*

The < mark means that category will be left-justified as indicated. For example, in the report format shown in Figure 3.18, the last name will be left-justified one space after the end of the first name.

Apple-J inserts or deletes left-justification when the cursor is on the first letter of the category name. Left-justification includes the number of spaces you specify. For example, if you want one category to follow the last character of the previous category by ten spaces, leave ten blank spaces. (The < mark does not count as a space.)

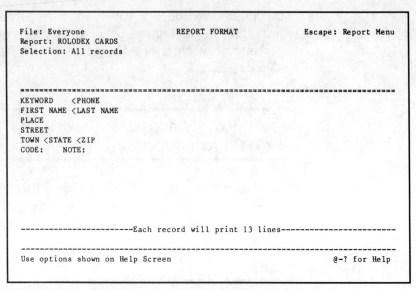

```
File: Everyone              REPORT FORMAT              Escape: Report Menu
Report: ROLODEX CARDS
Selection: All records



=======================================================================
KEYWORD     <PHONE
FIRST NAME <LAST NAME
PLACE
STREET
TOWN <STATE <ZIP
CODE:    NOTE:




------------------------Each record will print 13 lines------------------

-----------------------------------------------------------------------
Use options shown on Help Screen                        @-? for Help
```

Figure 3.18: *Report format for Rolodex cards*

Caution: *When you delete a category from a report format line that has left-justified categories, you lose the left-justification.*

This is not a significant problem, simply because you can see the < mark disappear if you are paying attention. Once you have deleted the unwanted category, use Apple-J again to replace the left-justification where needed.

Caution: *Apple-V does not work exactly as described in the AppleWorks manuals.*

With the cursor on the first letter of a category name, Apple-V inserts or deletes that category name in the printed report. However, if a category name has been left-justified, the cursor must be on the < mark preceding the name, not on the first letter.

When the category name has been inserted, you will see a colon following the category name.

Tip: *Use the report format options to the limit.*

You can use category names to add information to reports. For example, category names such as BILLED TO and SHIPPED TO can be included in a report format that produces invoices.

Reserved or empty categories can hold messages entered in new records as standard values. For example, an invoice report format might include a temporary message in an unused or reserved category. This information can be quickly changed with the Apple-' command in multiple-record layout.

You can add report titles to the top of each report page. Titles are entered using the Apple-N command from within a report format. Titles are generally more useful than page headers.

To illustrate this tip, create a labels-style report format to print Rolodex cards from the Everyone list. Follow these steps:

1. Press Apple-P and choose option 3 to create a new "labels" report.

2. Name the report ROLODEX CARDS.

3. Remembering the tips and cautions in this section, move the necessary categories into position as shown in Figure 3.18.

4. Use Apple-J where left-justification is necessary. Leave four spaces when you left-justify the PHONE category.

5. Use Apple-V to print the CODE and NOTE category names on the cards. Information in the first record appears on the screen, giving you a good idea of how things fit.

6. Delete the categories that will not be printed on the mailing label, and leave seven blank lines at the bottom of the label. The finished report format should have 13 lines. Compare it with the report format shown in Figure 3.18.

In the section of this chapter on printer options there is a tip on selecting the printer options for this report and printing it, first to the screen and then to Rolodex cards.

Tip: *You can create report formats from other formats.*

To illustrate this tip, create a labels-style report format to print mailing labels from the Everyone list. Use the ROLODEX CARDS format as a beginning, and follow these steps:

1. Press Apple-P and choose option 4 to duplicate an existing format.

2. Give the report a name, such as MAILING LABELS.

3. Remembering the tips and cautions in this section, delete the two categories in the first row, and then delete the resulting empty line.

4. Delete the two categories in the last row, and then delete all but two empty lines.

The finished report format should have six lines. Compare it with the report format shown in Figure 3.19.

In the section of this chapter on printer options, you will find tips on selecting the printer options for this report and printing it, first to the screen and then to mailing labels.

TABLES-STYLE REPORT FORMATS

The tables-style report format is sometimes the most appropriate way of presenting information. This is especially true for in-house record-keeping applications. In large management information systems, these are the reports that often come on green-bar paper more than 14 inches wide.

Tip: *Use tables-style report formats when you need to see a large array of information all at once.*

The tables-style report shown in Figure 3.20 includes only the first eight categories and one calculated category from a potentially large database of abandoned housing, many of which can

```
File: Everyone                    REPORT FORMAT              Escape: Report Menu
Report: MAILING LABELS
Selection: All records



===============================================================================
FIRST NAME <LAST NAME
PLACE
STREET
TOWN <STATE <ZIP


------------------------Each record will print  6 lines-----------------------




-------------------------------------------------------------------------------
Use options shown on Help Screen                                  @-? for Help
```

Figure 3.19: Report format for MAILING LABELS

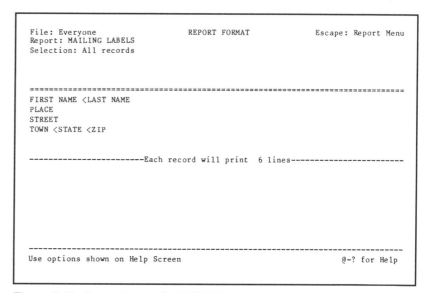

```
File:   Housing                                          Page  1
Report: Street.1
ST #   ST NAME      ZIP     FILE   UNIT  BACK TAX  SINCE   LIEN  COMBINED
-----  ------------ ------- ----   ----  --------  ------- ------ --------
   12  Elm St.      02884    45     1      3422     1980    890    4312
   21  Elm St.      02884    51     1      1234     1979   1278    2512
   26  Elm St.      02884    54     2       287     1982   4120    4407
  127  Elm St.      02884    61     1      1435     1978   2008    3443
   14  Jackson Pl.  02883    57     1      2130     1981   3890    6020
   26  Jackson Pl.  02883    58     2       612     1983   4875    5487
   31  Kendall Rd.  02885    39     2      1882     1982           1882
  134  Kendall Rd.  02885    49     1       120     1983            120
  148  Pine St.     02884    59     1       810     1980   5461    6271
   18  Taylor Ct.   02885    46     2      4559     1978   2488    7047
                                   14*    16491*           25010* 41501*
```

Figure 3.20: Printed tables-style report

be rehabilitated. The database is designed to match the right properties with the right people under the right conditions. Given those information requirements, this kind of database could logically have 10 to 30 categories. Figure 3.21 shows a single-record layout with 10 categories in use.

The report format name indicates that the street address (number and name) begins the table. Here the street names provide a logical basis for arranging the records in alphabetical order. In this database, you can arrange the records so that properties on the same street appear by street number in ascending order. In fact, this report could be arranged by any category column. It is important to document your choices: always circle the heading of an arranged category column or highlight it with a yellow marker.

What makes the tables-style report most appropriate in this case? The database has values that should be subtotaled and totaled, it has category values that should be combined, and there are several ways to arrange the records.

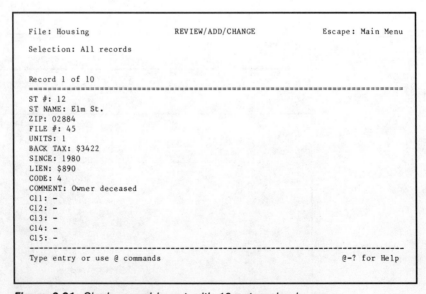

```
File: Housing                REVIEW/ADD/CHANGE            Escape: Main Menu

Selection: All records


Record 1 of 10
==============================================================================
ST #: 12
ST NAME: Elm St.
ZIP: 02884
FILE #: 45
UNITS: 1
BACK TAX: $3422
SINCE: 1980
LIEN: $890
CODE: 4
COMMENT: Owner deceased
C11: -
C12: -
C13: -
C14: -
C15: -
------------------------------------------------------------------------------
Type entry or use @ commands                                 @-? for Help
```

Figure 3.21: Single-record layout with 10 categories in use

Caution: *Totaling and combining columns can produce unexpected formatting results.*

Notice that the LIEN column in Figure 3.20 has a total marked with an asterisk. To total a column in a report format, place the cursor on the column to be totaled and press Apple-T. (In this report, we chose to print the total with no decimal places.)

The COMBINED column has the sum of BACK TAX and LIEN amounts for each record. In the Report Format process you place the cursor on the column to be calculated and press Apple-K. Here the formula F + H was entered, because the columns are also lettered from left to right, as they are in the Spreadsheet. Compare Figures 3.20 and 3.21: notice that the totaled and calculated columns lose their dollar signs, and $0 becomes a blank space.

Caution: *Calculated categories exist only within tables-style reports.*

The COMBINED category in Figure 3.20 exists only in tables-style reports. You cannot use the Data Base as a worksheet in which a column C in multiple-record layout contains the formula A + B, and everything recalculates on screen. You see Data Base calculations on the screen only when you print the appropriate tables-style report to the screen.

Remember that the Data Base hardly ever functions as the Spreadsheet would, even though they share commands. They are different programs and function differently.

Tip: *You can use empty categories in multiple-record layout to denote calculated categories.*

Figure 3.21 shows a record in single-record layout. You could include a dummy COMBINED category between LIEN and

CODE. These dummy categories can then be used in multiple-record layout as a form of documentation. They can be quickly deleted from the tables-style report and replaced by calculated categories.

Tip: *Good tables-style report formats are often difficult to read.*

When you total columns, create calculated categories, or right-justify entries, the column in the tables-style report format appears with nothing but nines. Because the most readable tables-style reports use those capabilities, their report formats are often difficult to read. Figure 3.22 shows the report format used to create the report shown in Figure 3.20.

Whenever you use such a tables-style report format, print records to the screen first. When you have seen enough to be certain the report meets your needs, press Escape to return to the report format.

```
File: Housing                      REPORT FORMAT              Escape: Report Menu
Report: Street.1
Selection: All records




=================================================================================
--> or <--  Move cursor                    @-J  Right justify this category
  >  @   <   Switch category positions      @-K  Define a calculated category
--> @  <--  Change column width             @-N  Change report name and/or title
@-A  Arrange (sort) on this category        @-O  Printer options
@-D  Delete this category                   @-P  Print the report
@-G  Add/remove group totals                @-R  Change record selection rules
@-I  Insert a prev. deleted category        @-T  Add/remove category totals
---------------------------------------------------------------------------------

ST #   ST NAME      ZIP    FILE   UNIT  BACK TAX SINCE    LIEN     COMBINED   L
-A---  -B---------- -C----- -D--   -E--  -F------ -G------ -H------ -I------   e
99999  Elm St.      02884  9999   9999  99999999 9999999  9999999  99999999   n
99999  Elm St.      02884  9999   9999  99999999 9999999  9999999  99999999   7
99999  Elm St.      02884  9999   9999  99999999 9999999  9999999  99999999   7
                                        ====  ========    ======= ========
---------------------------------------------------------------------------------
Use options shown above to change report format                    137K Avail.
```

Figure 3.22: *Tables-style report format*

Tip: *You can add titles, column headings, and group headings in several different ways.*

When you are creating a tables-style report format, Apple-N allows you to change the report name. If you press Apple-N and Return, the cursor goes to the title line, where you can enter up to 78 characters.

When you accept a report header in the printer options, the category names become the column headings. When you need different column headings, put those headings in the title line, and then use Apple-O to reach the printer options, where you can specify no report header.

You can also add a report title to the same line. Place it at the left over an empty category entered first to create an offset margin. That category can be used to enter group headings wherever needed within the same offset. Sort last by the category that controls group totals. Then add the group heading to the first record in each group.

Dummy record entries can also provide column headings and borders. If you begin each dummy record category with one or two spaces, they will usually sort to the beginning of the file, where you want them. Use Apple-M to move these records exactly where you need them before printing a report.

Finally, note the distinction between a report name, entered in the printer selection sequence when you include a page header, and a report title, entered in the report format. The former prints at the beginning of each page; the latter prints only at the beginning of the report.

Tip: *For printers with an 8-inch platen width, you can design similar report formats to print just the remaining categories.*

In the case of the report format in Figure 3.20, continuing columns can be called Street.2, to show that it is the second section of a series of tables beginning with the street address (number and street name). By carefully marking the starting point at the top of the page, you can print Street.1 on one half of a folded 11" x 17" page and Street.2 on the other half.

If this happened to be a 30-category database, there could conceivably be a Street.3 report format. Note that it is rarely necessary to print every database category in a report. However, it is prudent to keep a printed record of everything entered into the database.

Tip: *The "label table" is a hybrid form for report formats that include at least one relatively long narrative category.*

This type of report format begins as a labels-style report format. You can set the categories to occupy fixed widths, with no left-justification. So you're in fact setting up the report with a tabular format, just as with tables-style report formats. However, by using a labels-style report format you can give a long COMMENT category a second line all its own. The report then looks like a double-spaced table with occasional comment lines. Totals and calculations cannot be used in such a report format.

Figure 3.23 illustrates a label-table version of the Street report shown in Figure 3.20. If you need a long comment line in what would otherwise be a tables-style report, this is the kind of report format to use.

You can also wrap a standard tables-style report onto two lines. This takes careful calculation and a little practice: the printer must begin the second line with a new category, and the column headings should be slightly offset from one line to the next. You may want to change the order of categories in the report so that related categories appear above and below each other.

PRINTER OPTIONS

If you have mastered printing with the Word Processor, you are well prepared to work with the lesser number of Data Base printer

```
File:    Housing                                    Page  1
Report: Label.Table
ST #   ST NAME         ZIP    FILE # UNITS BACK TAX SINCE LIEN   CODE

 12    Elm St.         02884  45     1     $3422    1980  $890   4
       Owner deceased
 21    Elm St.         02884  51     1     $1234    1979  $1278  0
       -
 26    Elm St.         02884  54     2     $287     1982  $4120  4
       -
127    Elm St.         02884  61     1     $1435    1978  $2008  1
       -
 14    Jackson Pl.     02883  57     1     $2130    1981  $3890  2
       Minor fire damage on Apr 12 84
 26    Jackson Pl.     02883  58     2     $612     1983  $4875  3
       -
 31    Kendall Rd.     02885  39     2     $1882    1982  $0     4
       -
134    Kendall Rd.     02885  49     1     $120     1983  $0     3
       -
148    Pine St.        02884  59     1     $810     1980  $5461  2
       -
 18    Taylor Ct.      02885  46     2     $4559    1978  $2488  3
       Minor fire damage on Dec 28 83
```

Figure 3.23: *Printed label table*

options. There are a few important differences worth noting. In the Data Base you need to change platen width and paper length more often. Data Base applications use the smallest paper length (the page for a mailing label may be only one inch long), and the largest paper width (reports can be printed on very wide paper). The Data Base also takes a slightly different approach to page headers, and has some additional line adjustment options, as you will see in the tips that follow.

Tip: *Choose the paper that fits the application.*

Most Word Processor documents use standard 8½ x 11-inch blank white paper. Data Base applications typically use a broader range of paper stock: green-bar paper in several sizes, mailing labels, continuous index cards, and multipart forms. Determine what kind of layout would most suit your applications, and than choose paper that will meet your requirements.

This section explains how to print a labels-style report onto Rolodex cards. Rolodex makes continuous cards for tractor-feed printers. The perforated edges make the card feel slightly fuzzy at first, but over time the edges wear down. The $2^1/_6$ x 4-inch size is large enough to include the basic information you need for a file of this sort.

Most stationery stores can order a range of cards, forms, and paper if they are not already in stock. In addition, many mail-order firms specialize in paper for data processing.

Caution: *The Data Base lacks some useful printer options found in the Word Processor.*

Table 3.3 lists the Word Processor printer options, noting those that are also available in the Data Base and Spreadsheet. When you design Data Base applications, think about available printer options at the beginning. Depending on your formatting requirements, it may be necessary to print reports to the clipboard for further editing in the Word Processor. Or it may be necessary to use the Mail Merge option to extend reporting capabilities. For more on these subjects, see Chapter 5.

Table 3.3: Printer Options

Option	WP	DB	SS
Line Length, Print Density			
Platen width	X	X	X
Left margin	X	X	X
Right margin	X	X	X
Characters per inch	X	X	X
Proportional-1	X		
Proportional-2	X		
Text Positioning			
Indent	X		
Justified	X	X	X
Unjustified	X	X	X
Centered	X		X

Table 3.3: *Printer Options (continued)*

Option	WP	DB	SS
Page Length, Line Density			
Paper length	X	X	X
Top margin	X	X	X
Bottom margin	X	X	X
Lines per inch	X	X	X
Single space	X	X	X
Double space	X	X	X
Triple space	X	X	X
Page Controls			
New page	X		
Group markers	X		
Page Calculation			
Page header	X	X	X
Page footer	X		
Skip lines	X		
Page number	X		
Place Markers			
Pause each page	X		
Pause here	X		
Set a marker	X		
Print Enhancements			
Boldface	X		
Superscript	X		
Subscript	X		
Underline	X		
Variable Text Entry			
Print page number	X		
Enter keyboard	X		
Mail merge	X		

The Data Base and Spreadsheet have other specialized options, including the option to enter special codes for the printer. This option is primarily useful for changing form lengths and print densities. It can be used to begin boldfacing and underlining but cannot turn them off. This means the option cannot be used for selective underlining, as in bibliographical reports, for example.

Tip: *Use the special codes option to control form length on your printer.*

When you installed your printer, you probably answered Yes to option 2 on the Add a Printer menu. This option asks whether the printer accepts top-of-page commands, and assumes an 11-inch page length. In the Data Base you will often use much shorter pages (as short as one inch in the case of mailing labels). The SC option to enter special codes allows you to enter your printer's codes for shorter pages. Note that pages are often called forms in printer manuals. The mechanics of entering these codes are described in Chapter 6. Special codes modify the top-of-page commands and are saved with the report format.

If you are uncertain about your printer's codes for form length, return to the Add a Printer menu. Because you have already installed the printer, it will now be called the Change a Printer menu, but the menu options are the same. Answer No to option 2. This allows the Data Base printer options to work correctly. You must later return to the Change a Printer menu to re-enable the top-of-page command, but this is easy to do with a macro (see Chapter 7).

Tip: *Take out your ruler when you select Data Base printer options.*

Take out your ruler and a hard copy of the printer options screen, showing all the default settings. In most cases you will find that relatively few entries need to be changed. To set the printer options for the ROLODEX CARDS report format, change the platen width to 4.0 inches because the Rolodex card is exactly that wide. (Measure your cards, because there are several sizes available.) Set the left margin to 0.2 inches because you have no space to waste. Set the paper length to 2.2 inches—slightly longer than the 2^1/$_6$-inch card, but that is as close as you can get. All of the spacing has been built into the report format, so you will be printing with top and bottom margins of 0 inches. Everything should fit perfectly at six lines per inch.

All of the formatting options (SC, PD, PH, and OL) should indicate No on the screen (we will assume that the top-of-page command has been disabled). You could print a dash when a category contains no information, but we have chosen not to do that—a Rolodex card should have blank lines, so that you can pencil additional entries in the right places later. For the same reason, do not choose to omit a line when all entries on the line are blank. KS, a fifth option to keep the same number of lines in each record, does not appear because it can only be Yes when OL is Yes. For Rolodex cards, you will not need a report header. Figure 3.24 shows the Printer Options menu, with the settings for printing Rolodex Cards.

```
File: Everyone                  PRINTER OPTIONS          Escape: Report Format
Report: ROLODEX CARDS
==============================================================================

    -------Left and right margins--------     ------Top and bottom margins-------
PW: Platen Width              4.0 inches   PL: Paper Length         2.2 inches
LM: Left Margin               0.2 inches   TM: Top Margin           0.0 inches
RM: Right Margin              0.0 inches   BM: Bottom Margin        0.0 inches
CI: Chars per Inch           10            LI: Lines per Inch       6

    Line width                3.8 inches       Printing length      2.2 inches
    Char per line (est)      38                Lines per page       13

             -------------------Formatting options-------------------
         SC:  Send Special Codes to printer                      No
         PD:  Print a Dash when an entry is blank                No
         PH:  Print report Header at top of each page            No
         OL:  Omit Line when all entries on line are blank       No




    --------------------------------------------------------------------------
    Type a two letter option code                                37K Avail.
```

Figure 3.24: *Printer options set for Rolodex cards*

Tip: *Print reports to the screen first, then test print several records to paper.*

The Data Base is the only AppleWorks program that lets you print to the screen. Take advantage of this option and save paper, because you may need to make a few trial runs.

Save everything with Apple-S and print to the screen. If that works dependably, test print on plain paper. The trick is to get the left edge of the platen even with, or just inside, the left edge of the paper. Roll up the paper to exactly where the printing should begin. Remember that you are using no top margin. Then follow these steps:

1. Use the record-selection rules to select several records.

2. Press Apple-P, select your printer, and press Return.

3. Press Return again to print one copy of the report.

4. When all the card entries are printed, match the paper with the cards to see how they align.

5. Repeat the printing process with actual Rolodex cards.

6. When everything prints out correctly, as in Figure 3.25, document all the measurements and physical reference points you used.

Tip: *Use standard one-across mailing labels.*

The AppleWorks Data Base can print only one column of mailing labels per pass. Single-column labels are commonly called one-across labels. They come in narrow, easy-to-store boxes, and they are remarkably easy to load into printers. Move the tractor or pin on the right side, and leave the left side where it is for regular paper.

If you already have labels mounted two-across on tractor-feed paper, use it in two passes. Turn the sheets around after the first

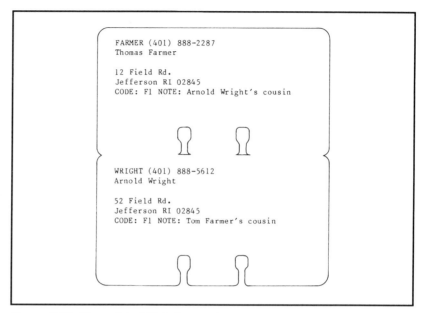

Figure 3.25: *Two printed Rolodex cards*

pass and come back with the remaining column on the left. If the labels are three-across, use three passes, with different margin and platen settings for the middle column.

Standard one-across mailing labels are 3.5 inches wide and exactly one inch from the top of one label to the top of the next. The label itself is $^{15}/_{16}$ of an inch. Look for labels that resist smudging, especially if you use a daisywheel printer. With some attention to alignment, you can print five lines on a standard label. Most mailing label reports use only four lines.

With standard labels, the MAILING LIST report format requires only three printer option entries. Change the platen width setting to 3.5 inches, the left margin setting to 0.2 inches, and the paper length to 1 inch.

The formatting options are the same as those for the ROLODEX CARDS report format, except that the responses for OL and KS are Yes. You need to omit lines when they are blank, but you also need to keep the same number of lines in each label, so that the printer stays aligned with the labels. Figure 3.26 shows how the labels should look when they are printed.

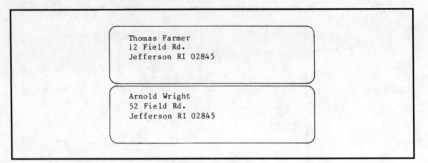

```
        Thomas Farmer
        12 Field Rd.
        Jefferson RI 02845



        Arnold Wright
        52 Field Rd.
        Jefferson RI 02845
```

Figure 3.26: Two printed mailing labels

Tip: *To generate more than nine copies of a record, copy records within the database.*

The print option allows up to nine copies. If you want to print 200 copies of a single return-address label, follow these steps:

1. Enter the address once in the database if you have not already done so.

2. Using Apple-C, copy the address 39 times.

3. Select the MAILING LABELS report format.

4. Select the record you want by last name.

5. Print 5 copies of the report.

You will get 200 labels because the record selected appeared 40 times in the database.

Tip: *Use continuous cards for mailing and for index cards.*

Many stationery supply stores offer continuous cards for tractor-feed printers. They come in 3 x 5-inch and 4 x 6-inch sizes, sometimes even in pale colors. They can be used as index cards, post cards, and even tags.

If you plan to use them for post cards, the larger ones are the more appropriate choice, simply because they can hold more information. Both card sizes take the same postage.

DESIGNING TEMPLATES

Good planning and design can save considerable time in the development and use of templates. By designing interchangeable parts you can build templates more efficiently. This section covers basic design details and offers some cautions.

Pay special attention to the difference between original category order and record layouts. As you will learn, original category order should influence many design decisions. In this section you will also find tips and cautions for record-layout options that allow you to enter records more efficiently.

Tip: *Learn the difference between original category order and record layouts.*

When you initially name categories, you name them on a category screen that determines original category order. This order generates one single-record layout and one multiple-record layout.

Many people simply use the single-record layout that follows original category order. If you use Apple-L to change the location of any category in single-record or multiple-record layout, you create a custom record layout. You will probably use Apple-L repeatedly to change multiple-record layout.

Adding or deleting categories causes the Data Base to lose all report formats and custom record layouts. This leaves you with the original single-record and multiple-record layouts generated by the original category order.

Remember the difference between original category order, record layouts, and custom record layouts, because this is the key to transferring records from file to file.

Tip: *When designing Data Base templates, think first about original category order.*

When the time comes to transfer information to related files, categories are transferred in their original order, defined when you first named the categories. Changes in single-record layout and multiple-record layout have no effect on transfers. For more tips on this, see the section on merging records later in this chapter.

Categories can be displayed in any order within a custom multiple-record layout, even if that order is completely different from the order of the single-record layout.

Tip: *Single-record layout often duplicates original category order, and for good reason.*

Records are almost always entered through single-record layout. Categories that require keyboard entry should be listed consecutively, in logical order, beginning with the first category. Categories with seldom-changed standard values should follow those that normally require keyboard entry. Unused or reserved categories belong at the end.

You will probably want to use the single-record layout that follows original category order. Although it is easy to change category order in a custom single-record layout, there is an important limitation. In files with more than 15 categories, you cannot create a custom single-record layout and then move the cursor from top to bottom, first down one column and then the other. You have only two choices: a left-to-right pattern moving from top to bottom, or the original order in which you defined categories. Figure 3.27 shows the menu options.

Tip: *Single-record layout is surprisingly flexible.*

The original LIST template (see Figure 3.3) had 15 categories, a tables-style report, and a labels-style report. Most applications

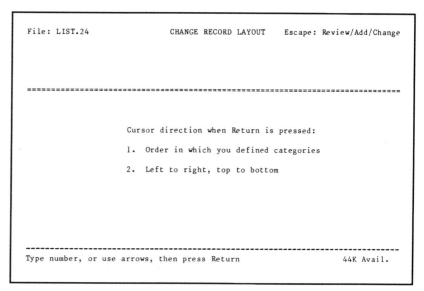

```
File: LIST.24                CHANGE RECORD LAYOUT     Escape: Review/Add/Change



======================================================================================


                    Cursor direction when Return is pressed:

                    1.  Order in which you defined categories

                    2.  Left to right, top to bottom







----------------------------------------------------------------------------------
Type number, or use arrows, then press Return                        44K Avail.
```

Figure 3.27: *Menu options for custom single-record layout*

use no more than 15 categories—an easy number to manage in single-record layout. However, with some imagination you can store additional categories in a way that has little effect on cursor movement. Figure 3.28 shows an example. Notice that the first seven categories have been individually indented. Categories 16–30 have the same name—a vertical bar (|). They appear at the far right border, out of the way. You can move them over to provide an end marker for any category, as shown with category 4 in Figure 3.28. This provides a practical guide for measuring information that you must later print onto narrow paper, such as index cards or labels.

Tip: *If your data comes from forms, make the single-record layout match the form.*

Your eye can scan a form faster when it matches the Data Base single-record layout. You may not be able to design both the form and the screen at the same time, but you can almost always design the screen to match the form. The category sequence should be

```
   File: LIST.30              REVIEW/ADD/CHANGE          Escape: Main Menu

   Selection: All records


   Record 10 of 11
   ========================================================================
   FIRST NAME: Susan                                              | : -
    LAST NAME: Smith                                              | : -
        PLACE: -                                                  | : -
       STREET: 81 Main Rd.                       | : -
         TOWN: Jefferson                                          | : -
        STATE: RI                                                 | : -
          ZIP: 02845                                              | : -
   C08: -                                                         | : -
   C09: -                                                         | : -
   C10: -                                                         | : -
   C11: -                                                         | : -
   C12: -                                                         | : -
   C13: -                                                         | : -
   C14: -                                                         | : -
   C15: -                                                         | : -
   ------------------------------------------------------------------------
   Type entry or use @ commands                          @-? for Help
```

Figure 3.28: LIST template with 30 categories

from left to right on a line, reading down the screen. If you later change forms, you can change the single-record layout.

When the form includes many more categories than you plan to enter, make a paper overlay for the form, so that you see only the entries you need. That saves time and minimizes data-entry errors.

Tip: *Avoid deleting categories.*

The memory cost of carrying extra categories is minimal, and you may need the categories some day. Carrying 21 empty categories requires about 5K per 500 records. If you delete categories, you lose all the report formats in the database and must reconstruct them. If you later have to add the categories, you lose all the report formats again.

Tip: *Rename categories to avoid deleting and inserting categories.*

Apple-N offers an important option within the Data Base, that of renaming categories. A file does not lose its report formats or custom record layouts unless you insert or delete categories. Therefore, if any existing file has report formats you can use and enough categories for the data at hand, save time by modifying the existing file.

Consider this example. The Everyone list created earlier in the chapter contains 11 named categories and four that are unused. Suppose you want to put a library association membership list onto an AppleWorks database. You can develop the application quickly by modifying the Everyone list. Use Apple-N to change the Desktop file name to Members.

The association list has no need for the KEYWORD category, so change the name to YEARS, a category indicating how long a person has been a member of the association. You can continue to change names and use the categories for slightly different purposes. You can also name the three formerly unused categories and use them for records of annual donations from each member.

The MAILING LABELS report format remains in use unchanged. The ROLODEX CARDS report format undergoes minor changes to become the INDEX CARD report format.

If you have no need for the records in the Everyone list, removing them is the easiest step of all. Place the cursor on the second record, press Apple-D, Apple-9, and Return. That leaves a single record, the minimum required. You can delete that record after you enter the first association member record. Figure 3.29 shows the transformed single-record layout.

Tip: *Use a COUNT category in each template.*

It is always good to know how many records a report includes. You can reserve one category for counting. Use Apple-V to give it a

```
File: Members                    INSERT NEW RECORDS        Escape: Review/Add/Change



Record 11 of 11
===================================================================================
FIRST NAME: -
LAST NAME: -
PLACE: -
STREET: -
TOWN: -
STATE: -
ZIP: -
PHONE: -
COMMITTEE: -
YEARS: -
1983: -
1984: -
1985: -
NOTES: -
RESERVED: -
-----------------------------------------------------------------------------------
Type entry or use @ commands                                          31K Avail.
```

Figure 3.29: *Single-record layout for the Members list*

standard value of 1. When you subtotal and total categories, include the COUNT as a totaled category at the right edge of the report. If you use dummy records for report titles or borders, make certain that those records have no entry in the COUNT category.

You can also count by borrowing any available category and entering the value 1 in the first record. Use Apple-' to copy that value of 1 from the beginning to the end of the file. Remember to enter 1 in the same category for records added later. You can even use a calculated category for counting: the "formula" can simply be a value of 1. It will then appear in all printed records when that calculated category is included in a tables-style report.

Tip: *Use a MARK category in each template.*

There will be times when you want to print specific records that you cannot select with rules. For example, suppose a bookseller has a Data Base file that includes authors, titles, and prices.

When he wants to find and mark ten titles for an invoice, he can find those titles and place a 1 in the MARK category.

For the report, he can select all records in which the MARK category equals 1. There is no need to include the MARK category in the report. When you use this method repeatedly, you can keep incrementing numbers (or letters). When you eventually need to clean out the MARK entries, display that category in multiple-record layout, sort by MARK, and use Apple-' to copy an empty cell and replace all entries in the column.

Tip: *Use generic report names.*

The Everyone list has the generic report format name MAILING LABELS. The name can serve equally well in an association's membership database. This list also has a more specific report format name—ROLODEX CARDS. If the report format was simply named CARDS, there would be no need to change the name. In this case, however, the cards differed in size and shape, so using specific names made sense.

Generic names and standard designs make component parts more readily interchangeable. That, in turn, makes AppleWorks even more useful. However, there will be times when specific names are more appropriate.

DEVELOPING APPLICATIONS

Design and development are closely linked. Sometimes the process of building a template will provide insights to better design. Make notes on what you found and use them to design other applications. This section covers techniques you can use in construction and revision.

AppleWorks presents some minor construction problems that you can work around. You have designed interchangeable components, and this is where you get to assemble them.

Tip: *When you must add categories, use Apple-H to mini-mize the time needed to reconstruct report formats.*

The ability to add categories to the Data Base is useful, even though you lose all the report formats and custom record layouts. Use Apple-H to print a hard copy of the screens showing the old report formats, custom record layouts, and printer options. It makes reconstruction much easier.

Tip: *Use short category names to make room for information in single-record layout.*

If you use a one-character category name, you still have room for another 76 characters of information on that line in single-record layout (assuming you have no more than 15 categories). Brief category names are even more important when you have more than 15 categories and available entry space in the single-record layout is limited.

Tip: *Consider category length when you use more than 15 categories.*

When a Data Base application uses only 15 categories, each category can have an entire screen line. When you use 16 to 30 categories, the default setting places them in a column on the right half of the single-record screen.

When two categories share one line, the available character space for each category decreases by more than half, to 36 characters. That may be inadequate for a long place name or a comment. When you use more than 15 categories, avoid blocking a category that needs more than 36 character spaces.

There is a way to cope with this problem. By carefully arranging the category name locations on the single-record layout screen, you can give long entries the space they need. To do this, arrange short categories side by side. For example, an Apple-Works date needs only 11 spaces (including the leading and trailing space required by all entries), so you can easily fit another category alongside it. From single-record layout, press Apple-L to change screen layouts.

Figure 3.30 illustrates one possible layout that makes maximum use of the space available. Notice that the original category order has not been changed, which means that the cursor can still move from top to bottom, first down one column and then the other.

Tip: *If you run out of entry space, you can still push the data in.*

No matter how carefully you design the single-record screen, you can still encounter an unexpectedly long entry. In that case you can fit it in with a "pushing" technique that makes the most of the insert cursor. Follow these steps:

1. Type in the right half of the long entry.

2. Go back to the first character you just entered.

3. Type in the left half of the entry, pushing the right half of the entry under the category name to the right.

You can actually store up to 79 characters this way, although the Data Base prints only 76 per category. The technique works equally well in multiple-record layout.

Caution: *The maximum record length may be less than 1,024 characters in specific applications.*

The AppleWorks Reference Manual lists the maximum record capacity as 1,024 characters. This limit does not include category names, nor does it include calculated categories.

```
File: CAT.30                  REVIEW/ADD/CHANGE              Escape: Main Menu

Selection: All records


Record 1 of 1
================================================================================
A: -                                        PHONE: (401) 888-2546
B: 123456789 123456789 123456789 123456     Q: -
C: -                                        R: -
DATE: Sep  1 87                             S: -
E: -                                        TIME:  5:30 PM
F: -                                        U: -
G: 123456789 123456789 123456789 123456     V: C2
H: -                                        W: -
     I: Indented                            X: -
J: -                                        Y: -
K: -                                        ZIP: 02674
L: -                                        1: -
M: -                                        2: -          3: -         4: -
N: -
O: 123456789 123456789 123456789 123456789 123456789 123456789 123456789 123456
--------------------------------------------------------------------------------
Type entry                                                  @-? for Help
```

Figure 3.30: *Single-record layout with 30 categories*

You can actually fit up to 1,140 characters on a single-record screen. Because category names can use up to 600 character spaces, an application can easily use every character space on the screen. However, even with brief category names, you may not be able to use 1,024 characters for data.

The single-record screen accepts everything you enter. If you go over the character limit, the Data Base quietly removes characters when you move to the next record. There is no warning message. When you come back, some of the most recently entered information may be missing. Unfortunately, the Data Base can begin removing information even before you reach a thousand characters.

There is a way to cope with the problem. When you design the single-record layout, enter a dummy record that uses all the available entry spaces you intend to use. If the Data Base accepts the record, you can probably count on the layout to work dependably.

Tip: *A Data Base file can have 33 categories.*

The three additional categories are calculated categories. They exist only within tables-style reports. You cannot use the Data

Base like a Spreadsheet, in which column A plus column B equals column C, and everything then recalculates on screen. You can see calculated results on the screen only by printing a report to the screen.

A calculated category can reference only cells to its left, and it can calculate with only the four basic arithmetic functions.

There is another limitation. For calculation purposes, the Data Base identifies categories with column letters, as the Spreadsheet does. However, there are no columns AA through AD for the last four possible categories. That means values in categories 27 through 30 cannot be calculated. Figure 3.31 shows the far limits of a file with 33 categories.

Tip: *A Data Base file needs only one record, and that record can be empty.*

This is the minimum compliance for the Data Base's one-record requirement. It is important for one reason: it is often prudent to change the name of an existing Data Base file and delete all of its

```
File: CAT.33              REPORT FORMAT            Escape: Report Menu
Report: Cat.33
Selection: All records



================================================================------========
--> or <--  Move cursor                   @-J  Right justify this category
  >  @   <     Switch category positions   @-K  Define a calculated category
--> @  <--   Change column width           @-N  Change report name and/or title
@-A  Arrange (sort) on this category       @-O  Printer options
@-D  Delete this category                  @-P  Print the report
@-G  Add/remove group totals               @-R  Change record selection rules
@-I  Insert a prev. deleted category       @-T  Add/remove category totals
-------------------------------------------------------------------------------

22  23  24  25  26  27  28  29  30  Calculated    Calculated    Calculated    L
-V- -W- -X- -Y- -Z- --- --- --- --- ----------    ----------    ----------    e
                                    9999999999     9999999999    9999999999    n
                                    9999999999     9999999999    9999999999    2
                                    9999999999     9999999999    9999999999    3
                                                                               2
<--- More -----------------------------------------------------------------------
Use options shown above to change report format                    33K Avail.
```

Figure 3.31: *Data Base report format with 33 categories*

files. This process effectively copies a database structure for other data that require a similar structure.

The last record left behind from the old file should have nothing but dashes. You can create that record in the following way: go just beyond the last record in a database, and the next record will appear with nothing but dashes. Press Return in any category, and the dashes become a confirmed record.

The empty record also makes a good marker in the database. Keep it at the end of the file. Copy or move it anywhere you need visual separation in multiple-record layout. If you want to collect all the empty records, sort on selected categories to bring them to the beginning of the file.

Tip: *Apple-' can be used to make vast temporary changes in records.*

There are times when you will want to copy a file with useful information, empty all but the categories you need, and use what remains for other purposes. This approach works well, but remember to change the name of the file before doing it.

If you want to remove all the information from a category without deleting the category, follow these steps:

1. In multiple-record layout, use the record-selection rules to retrieve all the records with the information you want to replace.

2. Use Apple-Y to delete everything from the category entry in the first record.

3. Place the cursor in the same category of the next record and hold down Apple-' to quickly empty all the remaining records.

You are then free to enter your new information. For example, by copying a return address into available categories while in multiple-record layout, you can create a labels-style report format that can print both a return address and a mailing address on a post card, as shown in Figure 3.32. Or you can use a category to print AIR MAIL on the mailing labels and post cards.

As long as you remember to change the file name to prevent damage caused by accidentally saving the file, you can write over any category that has no immediate utility. There are almost no limits to what you can do.

Tip: *You can copy a Data Base file for specialized purposes.*

Databases often contain information for several different specialized purposes. For example, the Members database tells us where members of the library association live. It also provides information for annual planning and budgeting.

The Data Base multiple-record layout cannot show you all the information in every category at once. However, you can change

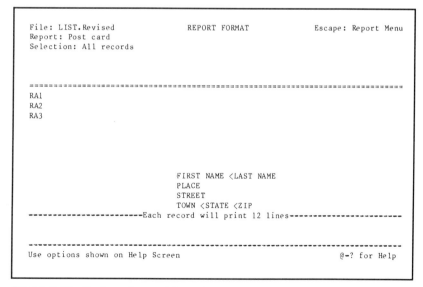

```
   File: LIST.Revised              REPORT FORMAT              Escape: Report Menu
   Report: Post card
   Selection: All records


   ================================================================================
   RA1
   RA2
   RA3




                            FIRST NAME <LAST NAME
                            PLACE
                            STREET
                            TOWN <STATE <ZIP
   -------------------------Each record will print 12 lines-----------------------


   --------------------------------------------------------------------------------
   Use options shown on Help Screen                                  @-? for Help
```

Figure 3.32: *Post card report format*

the name of the Members file to Members.Finance and design a multiple-record layout for budgeting purposes. It can have a calculated category to keep a record of each member's cumulative contributions over a three-year period. It can have totaled categories for total membership income in each of the three years. You can enter additional records for other sources of income. It is also possible to enter budget items, with negative numbers to represent expenditures against income. The totaled category then shows an expected net balance or deficit.

Figure 3.33 shows sample elements of a budget planning report for a library association. When you design applications, first use sample elements to test the concept. Here we have used ten of 530 members and two of 20 budget items.

It is common for associations to have many members and relatively few budget items. For such cases, the Data Base is a practical multipurpose tool. In most cases, however, the Spreadsheet is more appropriate for budgeting.

Copying a master file presents one complication. When you update records, do so on the master file only. Then copy any updated records to the clipboard, and move them to the specialized file. Before you actually make the transfer, delete the obsolete records from the specialized file.

```
File:    Members.Finance                                      Page  1
Report: Budget
FIRST NAME LAST NAME   1983    1984    1985   1983-85   PHONE
---------- ------------ -----   -----   -----  -------   --------------------
Thomas     Farmer         20      20      20       60   (401) 888-4864
Edward     Joiner                 15      30       45   (401) 888-9912
Robin      Jones          15      15      20       50   (401) 888-2276
Rob        Martin         15      15      20       50   (401) 888-3243
Joanne     Martinelli             50      50      100   (401) 888-1276
Roberta    Miller         15      15      20       50   (401) 888-1132
Susan      Smith          25      25      24       74   (401) 888-5784
Robert     Smith          15      15      20       50   (203) 358-3114
Joan       Smith          15      15      20       50   (617) 445-9082
           Smith Fund   1800    1800    2000     5600
Arnold     Wright         15      15      20       50   (401) 888-6674
                        1935    2000    2244     6179

---------- ------------ -----                           --------------------
           Painting     -210    -320    -580    -1110
           Repairs     -1680   -1620   -1750    -5050
                       -1890   -1940   -2330    -6160

                          45*     60*    -86*      19*
```

Figure 3.33: Budget planning report

AUDITING DATABASES

It is always a good idea to audit your own work, particularly in the design of database applications. As you learned with the record-selection rules, even the best designs fail in one way or another. This section contains several tips about designing databases to minimize problems with errors.

Caution: *The Data Base has no validation capabilities.*

Categories containing numbers often have acceptable ranges. For example, if you enter people's ages, the age values will all be between 1 and 120. There are no negative age values and no 200-year-old people. For all practical purposes you can assume that acceptable values will have only one or two digits.

Some database managers permit you to enter limits for specific categories. In this case, if someone then tried to enter an age value of 142, it would not be accepted. The AppleWorks Data Base, however, does not permit you to define limits for categories. As you will learn in Chapter 4, it is possible to write a limiting formula for Spreadsheet cells. Tips in Chapter 5 explain how to use the Spreadsheet to enter data for use in the Data Base.

Tip: *Set column widths to detect errors in data entry.*

You can enter critical data in multiple-record layout. The columns should be just wide enough to enter the largest number in the series. If a column of age values will be no wider than two digits, make the column two spaces wide. You will then be unable to enter three digits from left to right. Never worry about the column label—you can always widen it after the data has been entered.

The same general approach works for dollar values, ZIP codes, telephone numbers, two-letter state abbreviations, social security numbers, and many other kinds of label entries. They cannot be completely entered from left to right if there is insufficient room in a cell.

In some cases a one-digit error can create serious problems. For example, suppose a town's grand list of taxable property includes homes assessed at up to $280,000. An incorrect $2,800,000 entry will increase the grand list considerably, and taxes will therefore be apportioned incorrectly. The person who receives the wrong tax bill will get the mistake corrected, to be sure, but it is then too late to reapportion taxes.

These kinds of mistakes really do occur from time to time. With large values it also helps to use appropriate commas. The Data Base will accept comma entries, but then removes them from reports.

Tip: *Scan the multiple-record display for consistent patterns.*

Category entries can be right-justified in table reports, but they are left-justified in both record layouts. Whenever title widths permit, columns in the finished multiple-record display should be just wide enough to show the largest value or text entry with one empty character space on the right.

You may be surprised how easy it is to scan individual columns and detect errors. Correct each mistake as you find it, and look for the same kinds of mistakes to recur. This process of proof-reading and correcting will make you increasingly more accurate in data entry.

Tip: *The Data Base offers convenient forms of dates and times, which can also be entered from a clock.*

AppleWorks uses no precommitted category forms, so any category can be used for any kind of information. However, if you use the word DATE in a category name, AppleWorks enters the date in the form Sep 1 87, provided you enter a reasonable approximation of the date (such as 9.1.87). Note the gap between Sep and 1 in the AppleWorks form.

If you use the word TIME in a category name, AppleWorks enters the time in the form 7:00 AM, provided that you enter a reasonable approximation such as 7. In the USA versions of AppleWorks, every time value between 7 and 11:59 is assumed to be AM unless you specify otherwise by adding the letter P. Every time value between 12:00 and 6:59 is assumed to be PM unless you specify otherwise by adding the letter A.

If you use both DATE and TIME in a category name, DATE always takes precedence.

Applied Engineering offers software that enters dates and times directly from its clock card when you press @ in the respective DATE and TIME categories. These automated functions are useful where time records are important, as in shipping and receiving operations.

Tip: *Use two or more date categories to track updates.*

Few databases are built in a day, and almost none get updated all at once. Whenever you have available space, use a DATE1 category for the date of original entry and a DATE2 category to indicate the most recent update. This is another reason to use the automatic dating described in the previous tip.

You can select date records that contain just the month, such as Sep, or any consecutive part of a date. This can sometimes save time while entering selection rules. For years since 1932, there can be no confusion in the AppleWorks form between day of the month and year.

Caution: *AppleWorks dates have several problems.*

Without the clock, AppleWorks provides no method for trapping errors in the months of September, April, June, and November.

Any month can have 31 days. That gives you three chances to make a mistake in February.

There is no way to enter the year 2000, which may be of current interest to long-term investors. If you enter a month and day with no year, AppleWorks assumes 00, but that is always 1900 when you arrange dates chronologically.

Tip: *Consider using another date format for later calculations.*

You can use a different date format that may be more practical for transfer to the Spreadsheet (which has no chronological sort). Use one category for year, and the following category for month and day. If all or most entries are current, YEAR can be a standard value, such as 1988 or 88. The DAY category can be a decimal, such as 1.20 for January 20. You can arrange either category with the 0–9 option. If you later rename the DAY category DATE, AppleWorks will change the format to Jan 20 when you place the cursor at the beginning of the entry, press the Space bar, and then press Return.

Chapter 5 will explain how the Spreadsheet can perform calculations with dates in this format. You can continue to use the AppleWorks form for dates that require no calculations. If you have already used the AppleWorks date form and want to calculate dates, see Elna Tymes' *Mastering AppleWorks*, 2nd ed. (SYBEX, 1987) for a BASIC program to do that.

MERGING DATABASES

In many applications you will need to merge information from several different sources. This section provides tips for merging information from two similar or markedly different Data Base files. Surprisingly few AppleWorks users even know that this can be done.

Tip: *When you merge records from two different files, their original category orders must match.*

Focus all your attention on the original category orders. From the Review mode you can press Apple-N to see the original order. Print a copy of the category names screen of the source file, then load the destination file. Compare its category names screen with the hard copy you just printed.

Suppose both files have exactly the same original category order. To merge the information, follow these steps:

1. Change the name of the Desktop files, just to be safe. Name the files Source and Destination.

2. Using multiple-record layout, copy the records in the Source file to the clipboard, then from the clipboard to the Destination file.

3. Check the multiple-record layout in the Destination file to make certain that the category information is consistent.

Note that when the information is transferred, the categories appear in the order of the Destination file's single- and multiple-record layouts. In the multiple-record layout, the category widths are those of the Destination file.

You can ignore the single- and multiple-record layouts of the Source and Destination files until the final check. If they match, the original category orders may still differ. If their orders differ beforehand, the Destination file will evaluate everything in its original category order. Focus all your attention on the original category orders.

Tip: *Two Data Base files can be merged even if they have different numbers of categories.*

Decide what categories you need to transfer from the Source file to the Destination file. For example, Table 3.4 compares the original

Table 3.4: *Everyone list and Members list categories compared*

Origin File	Destination File
FIRST NAME	LAST NAME
LAST NAME	LAST NAME
PLACE	PLACE
STREET	STREET
TOWN	TOWN
STATE	STATE
ZIP	ZIP
PHONE	PHONE
NOTE	COMMITTEE
CODE	YEARS
KEYWORD	1986
R1	1987
R2	1988
R3	NOTES
R4	RESERVED

category orders of the Everyone list (the Source file) and the Members list (the Destination file). The categories are identical through the eighth category, PHONE. The remaining categories have no value to the Destination file, except for NOTE, which has information that belongs in the NOTES category in the Destination file.

You can proceed with the merge almost as in the last tip. Follow these steps:

1. Change the name of the Desktop files if you have not already done so. Name the files Source and Destination.

2. Delete all Source file categories after PHONE, except for NOTE. Don't worry about report formats, because you will never use this file again.

3. Insert five categories between PHONE and NOTE. Name them anything, and then return to the multiple-record layout.

4. Copy the records in the Source file to the clipboard, then from the clipboard to the Destination file.

5. Check the multiple-record layout in the Destination file to make certain that the category information is consistent.

Note that all the records from the Source file have gained the additional categories of the Destination file. However, the Source files have no information in those categories.

The rules for transferring are easy to remember. If the Source file has more categories than the Destination file, the additional categories will be lost in the merge. If the Source file has fewer categories, it will gain the additional categories of the Destination file, but they will contain no information.

Tip: *When the original category orders of two files do not match, print the records to an ASCII file.*

Suppose the Source file categories begin with LAST NAME and the Destination file categories begin with FIRST NAME. This presents a problem. In this case, proceed as follows:

1. Create a labels-style report format for the Source file in the original category order of the Destination file. Count and make a note of the number of categories in the report.

2. Select the records you want to print.

3. Print the report to an ASCII file.

4. Create a new Data Base file from the ASCII file. Enter the correct number of categories for the new file.

5. Using multiple-record layout, copy the records in the Source file to the clipboard, then from the clipboard to the Destination file.

6. Check the multiple-record layout in the Destination file to make certain that the category information is consistent.

Tip: *Merge files to find duplicate entries.*

If you have ever received two copies of a form letter or mistakenly sent two copies to the same person, you will appreciate this technique. It saves postage, paper, and embarrassment.

Suppose you have two mailing lists on separate files. By merging the records, you can find and delete duplicate entries. Create a multiple-record layout with FIRST NAME, LAST NAME, STREET, STATE, ZIP, and PLACE in that order. Arrange the records alphabetically by first name, then by last name. Scan the LAST NAME column for duplicate entries. The street address column is the next best reference point.

If the files are too large to merge, merge sections at a time. When you find obvious duplication, you may find slightly different spellings. One spelling of a name may be more plausible than the other, but such corrections are often matters of judgment.

INVENTORY AND CITATION DATABASES

Most of us store parts that we think we will need later. The Data Base can track those parts, reminding us of what we have, what we need, where to find them, and how much they cost. Inventory applications vary widely, but most require extensive arranging, record selection, and calculation. This section gives an example of an inventory that belongs in the Data Base rather than the Spreadsheet.

Like inventories, citation databases are specialized lists that depend heavily on Data Base arranging and record selection. In this section we will look at an example that uses keyword retrieval techniques.

Tip: *Plan calculated categories carefully, because the Data Base gives you only three.*

When the arithmetic is simple and the requirements for record selection are extensive, the application probably belongs on the

Data Base. However, you must plan within limitations: you get only three calculated categories, and each can take information only from a column to the left.

A project parts inventory is a good example of the kind of inventory the Data Base handles well. Suppose you want to build a greenhouse addition or plant a large vegetable garden. You have to know which tools, parts, and materials the project requires. You want to know what you need, what you have, what remains to be purchased, and what it will cost. In the budget planning report (Figure 3.33) you saw the results of calculated categories, column totals, and group totals. Here you will learn how to build a structurally similar application. Figure 3.34 shows a tables-style report for a project parts inventory. You can design this kind of table on a piece of graph paper.

Note that you need to total only one category. Calculated categories are shown with lowercase letters in the headings. Two of the three calculated categories permitted are used. The first calculated category simply subtracts the number of each part you have on hand from the total number needed for the project. The second, Total $, multiplies the number of units left to buy by the unit dollar price. It also multiplies that product by 1.06 to include sales tax.

```
File:    Greenhouse                                              Page  1
Report: Group
GROUP   PART                  UNIT   NEED HAVE Buy UNIT $ Total $ SUPPLIER
------  --------------------  ------ ---- ---- --- ------ ------- -----------
Finish 4'x8' sheetrock        sheet    5    1   4   6.89   29.21 Hart Lumber
Finish 3.5"x24" fiberglass    roll     2        2  14.80   31.38 Hart Lumber
Finish Door                   one      1        1 139.50  147.87 Hart Lumber
Finish 6"x24" fiberglass      roll     1        1  15.20   16.11 Hart Lumber
Finish 2'x8'x1" EPS foam      sheet    6    1   5   4.85   25.70 West Supply
                                                          250.28

Frame  2"x4"x8' stud          one     26   10  16   1.84   31.21 West Supply
Frame  2"x4"x10' stud         one      8        8   2.12   17.98 West Supply
                                                           49.18

Other  16d common nails       lb.      2        2    .68    1.44 RB Hardware
Other  12d common nails       lb.     10    2   8    .62    5.26 RB Hardware
                                                            6.70

Roof   Shingles               bundle   2        2  11.20   23.74 Hart Lumber
Roof   6" flashing            foot    50       50    .16    8.48 RB Hardware
Roof   4'x8'x5/8" plywood     sheet    2        2  14.80   31.38 West Supply
                                                           63.60

                                                          369.76*
```

Figure 3.34: Tables-style report for a greenhouse project

If you wanted to know the replacement value of parts on hand, you would require the third calculated category. Then you would not be able to combine the two totals. You can see how quickly the Data Base gives way to the Spreadsheet when calculations are needed.

Tip: *Use the group totals command for category subtotals and record counting.*

The group totals command (Apple-G) serves two different purposes. First, the group-total category controls subtotal locations for every other totaled category in a tables-style report. Whenever the category entry changes, the Data Base calculates a subtotal. It is therefore important to arrange by the group-total category before getting a report format.

In the greenhouse project inventory example, you can use the GROUP category to subdivide the project logically, each with its own subtotal, as in Figure 3.34. Notice that when the category entry changed from Finish to Framing, the Data Base entered a subtotal and skipped a line. Figure 3.35 shows the tables-style report format that created the subtotals. Notice the helpful reminder:

Group totals on: GROUP

You can equally well use group totals on the SUPPLIER category to generate shopping lists and estimated costs for each supplier. Here it would be most efficient to duplicate the existing tables-style report format and revise it.

Tip: *Citation databases are becoming essential tools in an increasing number of professions.*

Many of us own reference books and periodicals, but few of us buy everything we need. People in many professional fields depend on libraries and on-line information services. Databases

```
File: Greenhouse              REPORT FORMAT           Escape: Report Menu
Report: Group
Selection: All records


Group totals on: GROUP
=========================================================================
--> or <--  Move cursor                @-J  Right justify this category
  >  @  <    Switch category positions  @-K  Define a calculated category
--> @ <--   Change column width         @-N  Change report name and/or title
@-A  Arrange (sort) on this category    @-O  Printer options
@-D  Delete this category               @-P  Print the report
@-G  Add/remove group totals            @-R  Change record selection rules
@-I  Insert a prev. deleted category    @-T  Add/remove category totals
-------------------------------------------------------------------------

GROUP   PART                  UNIT   NEED HAVE Buy UNIT $ Total $ SUPPLIER    L
-A----  -B----------------    -C----  -D-- -E-- -F- -G---- -H----- -I--------- e
Finish  4'x8' sheetrock       sheet  9999 9999 999 999.99 9999.99 Hart Lumber n
Finish  3.5"x24" fiberglass   roll   9999 9999 999 999.99 9999.99 Hart Lumber 7
Finish  Door                  one    9999 9999 999 999.99 9999.99 Hart Lumber 5
                                                           =======
-------------------------------------------------------------------------
Use options shown above to change report format              227K Avail.
```

Figure 3.35: *Report format used to generate Figure 3.34*

can help you manage information, so that you can retrieve citations efficiently to find publications or generate bibliographies. For example, the bibliography in Appendix D came from a citation database.

Citation databases have long been essential tools for research, particularly in science, technology, and medicine. These databases are now being used in a steadily increasing number of professions. In fact, control of the literature has become so important that specialized database managers have been designed to download citations and abstracts from on-line information services, reformat the information, and generate bibliographies in any of several publication formats. The AppleWorks interface to one of these programs is discussed in Chapter 5.

Tip: *Citation databases inevitably generate bibliographies.*

It is therefore important to structure and punctuate the citation entries as you would for a bibliography. For example, the author's complete name goes in one category, last name first. The entry should end with a period.

Other information in the citation record helps to generate carefully defined bibliographies. Specific entries for records can vary in multipurpose notes categories: some records include catalog numbers from a university library; others may include a publisher's mailing address.

Tip: *Design bibliographical files to handle both books and periodicals.*

What kinds of categories should you include in a bibliography? The answer depends on how you plan to use the bibliography. In a multipurpose database manager you cannot handle all the forms of citation found in Kate Turabian's *A Manual for Writers* (University of Chicago Press, 1987). Nor can you include all the descriptive keywords you might want for retrieval purposes. What follows is a description of one reasonable and practical compromise that considers data entry time, memory capacity, and the limits of patience.

AUTHOR: Always try to remember a publication by the last name of the author, not the title. The author's last name comes first, because bibliographies are alphabetized that way. If a publication has two authors, both should be listed, as shown in Figure 3.36. For three or more authors, use the first author's name followed by "et al" instead of all the other names. For strict bibliographical purposes, middle initials should be included if they are given on the title page. Abbreviate editor as "ed." This category serves the same purpose for both books and articles.

TITLE: This category is for book titles, where all letters are capitalized or underlined. It serves equally well for titles of articles, printed in mixed-case lettering within quotes. Titles are supposed to define what the book or article is about, but not all titles do. For example, if a title in sociology alludes to Greek mythology, it tells us little about the content. A good title includes words that are keys for logical retrieval. In fact, keywords are so useful that they will be given an additional category all their own.

```
File:    Citations                                        Page   1
Report: File Cards
Selection: KEYWORDS contains /FINANCE
    or      KEYWORDS contains /GRAPHICS

Dooley, Thomas, and David Spiller.
FINANCIAL PLANNING IN TRANSIT.
Washington: U.S. Dept. of Transportation, 1983.

Flast, Robert.
54 VISICALC MODELS.
New York: Osborne/McGraw-Hill, 1983.

Tufte, Edward R.
THE VISUAL DISPLAY OF QUANTITATIVE INFORMATION.
Cheshire, CT: Graphics Press, 1983.




Press Space Bar to continue                          184K Avail.
```

Figure 3.36: *Bibliographical listing by author*

OTHER: This category handles the complications that often come after a book title. These complications are well documented in the Turabian book mentioned earlier. This is where you put such things as "2nd edition."

PUBLISHER: In the case of books, this is for the home city and name of the publisher. In the case of articles, it is for the name of the periodical (all letters capitalized or underlined). The NOTES category can be used for the address of book or magazine publishers, because they can be difficult to track down later. Always take information when you can get it.

YEAR: This is for the publication date. For books enter just the year. For articles enter the volume and number, followed by the month and year of publication. The month and year alone will do in a pinch.

Never name this category DATE, nor anything with that sequence of letters in it. If a category contains the word *date*, you cannot enter just the month and year in the preferred form, because AppleWorks converts anything in a DATE category to its own date form. That means Jun 83 instead of (June 1983).

PAGES: This category is for articles only. Use complete numbers to clarify the information (for example, "pp. 123–126" rather than "pp. 123–6"). Consider the paging to be consecutive if the article is broken only by advertisements (for example, "pp. 123–124, 126" is unnecessary if page 125 is just an ad.) This is a made-up rule, but you will appreciate it if you enter articles from journals such as *Byte*.

KEYWORDS: This category can be used to include selected keywords in a series separated by slash marks. When the citation records include keywords, you can retrieve information more accurately. If the literature in your field has standard keywords, use them. Some journals included suggested keywords with the articles. Figure 3.37 shows a record with several keywords. You can use "good" as a short keyword substitute for excellent, and thereby search for the best entries associated with any keyword.

NOTES: As already mentioned, this category serves many purposes, and it deserves a full entry line of 76 characters.

CODE: Codes can store much information in a small space. For example, a code in the form A2 can serve two purposes. The letter can represent a subject time period, and the number can indicate a library where the title can be found. For example, the code D2 might indicate a book about 19th-century botany in a specific university library.

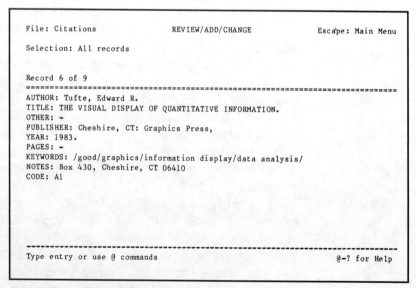

```
File: Citations                REVIEW/ADD/CHANGE           Escape: Main Menu

Selection: All records


Record 6 of 9
================================================================================
AUTHOR: Tufte, Edward R.
TITLE: THE VISUAL DISPLAY OF QUANTITATIVE INFORMATION.
OTHER: -
PUBLISHER: Cheshire, CT: Graphics Press,
YEAR: 1983.
PAGES: -
KEYWORDS: /good/graphics/information display/data analysis/
NOTES: Box 430, Cheshire, CT 06410
CODE: A1




------------------------------------------------------------------------------
Type entry or use @ commands                              @-? for Help
```

Figure 3.37: Citation record with keywords

Caution: *You cannot underline selectively in Data Base reports, so think ahead about how to handle titles.*

AppleWorks has specific limitations. Underlining (Control-L in the Word Processor) is not available in the Data Base, so you may want to capitalize book and periodical titles in your bibliography. For thesis writing it would be better to enter titles in mixed-case lettering, then insert underlining marks in the Word Processor.

Tip: *Use keywords for information retrieval.*

Keyword searching depends on the descriptive value of the title and additional information in a KEYWORDS category. The easiest way to search is with the find command (Apple-F), but that checks all categories. As with any other Data Base application, record-selection rules are more specific.

For example, suppose you want to find information on spreadsheet templates in a file of citations. Finding all entries containing *spreadsheet* would also retrieve spreadsheet review articles. Using the "contains" record-selection rule for KEYWORDS can better define the search. Here you would request all records in which the KEYWORDS category contains *spreadsheet* and *template*.

Sometimes a keyword such as *ship* can also be contained in longer words, as in *apprenticeship* and *shipping*. You can specify the keyword as */ship/* with the preceding and trailing slash marks included. If you use this technique, the last entry in the KEYWORD category must always be followed by a slash.

Tip: *Use consecutive categories for abstracts.*

An abstract is a precise summary of a publication. Sometimes the table of contents in a periodical will describe the contents of an article in one or two lines. Some journals specifically summarize dozens of publications in 200-to-500-word abstracts. This saves time for researchers tracking specific information.

You can write your own abstracts in citation records by reserving a number of 76-character lines. Name them A1, A2, and so on until you have enough room. There is no need to use every line for every record. For example, you may have a very limited and specific interest in an article. The abstract is for your own purposes and should reflect that fact.

SUMMARY

This chapter has reviewed a broad range of options and problems in the Data Base. You will find that you can use many of the tips and techniques repeatedly. As you understand more about the Data Base, you will be able to develop advanced applications more efficiently.

Practice using the tips for finding and arranging records, and experiment with the cautions for record selection. Practice changing file names and making changes. The Data Base encourages modular construction and fast renovation. Remember that if the project grows, you can always add memory for more record capacity.

Above all, concentrate on logical system design from the beginning, because that saves development. You can often adapt an existing template. When you need a report format, duplicate the existing format that comes closest to your needs and revise from there.

The next chapter will draw upon what you have learned in this chapter about printer options and the arranging command. You will continue to change file names, copy to the clipboard, and use AppleWorks commands for unexpected purposes. You will find more tips and techniques for building component parts that can be used again and again in many useful applications. In Chapter 5, some of those parts will be transferred back to the Word Processor and elsewhere.

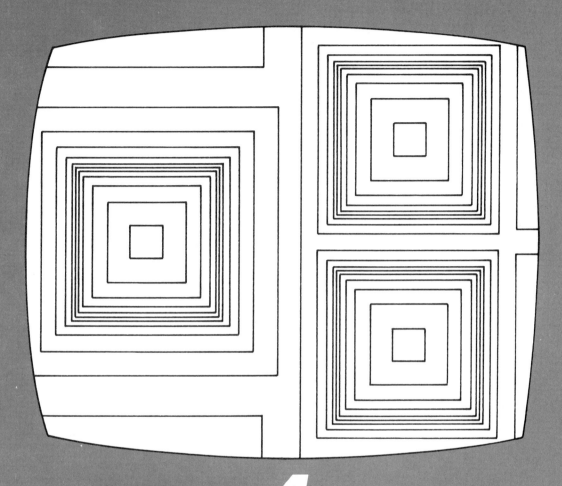

4

The Spreadsheet

*T*he VisiCalc spreadsheet was the first program to make people understand that the Apple II could be used effectively in a broad range of professional applications. VisiCalc quickly became a standard Apple program and many people still use the ProDOS standard or advanced version. It is fitting that the AppleWorks Spreadsheet uses similar notation and reads most VisiCalc files. However, as you will see, the AppleWorks Spreadsheet encourages some unique approaches to applications design.

AppleWorks has fewer functions than other spreadsheets: no trigonometric or logarithmic functions, no graphing capability, and few logic functions. The Spreadsheet does have a useful sorting function that others lack, as well as 999 rows and 127 columns for large worksheets. The AppleWorks Spreadsheet is fast when loading data, recalculating, and accepting data entries.

The AppleWorks Spreadsheet has several unusual features, including some difficult sequences for setting manual recalculation and changing column widths. The Spreadsheet cannot read all VisiCalc files, and it creates binary files that VisiCalc cannot read. Thus only Spreadsheet DIF files can be loaded into VisiCalc.

One of the Spreadsheet's greatest strengths is its file transfer capability. Experienced users can quickly copy formulas from other sources. This capability makes it possible to overlook how difficult it can sometimes be to construct formulas from such a limited number of functions.

You can build self-contained components in a PARTS file, copy them to the clipboard, move them into another worksheet, and fit them into a larger system. No other spreadsheet for the Apple can match this building-block facility. This program has been vastly underestimated, by Apple as much as by anyone.

This chapter provides tips in thirteen sections. It begins with the most generally useful tips for anyone using the Spreadsheet. A section on creating budgets includes useful information on designing worksheets for multiple purposes. The next two sections include tips that review worksheet recalculation and the available math functions. You should particularly note the functions that work in two different ways. The section on available printer options includes important information on managing worksheet width.

Spreadsheet applications require much attention to design. This chapter includes sections on designing and developing Spreadsheet templates. The tips in the following sections cover logical, financial, and other Spreadsheet functions. In each of these sections, small templates are provided to illustrate some of the special capabilities of AppleWorks. The next section outlines graphics options, including an important relationship to SuperCalc 3a. The following section examines the rules for transferring VisiCalc and DIF files to the Spreadsheet. Finally, the last section reviews techniques for using the Spreadsheet as a specialized database manager. All this taken together should make the Spreadsheet easier to use for large applications.

GENERAL SPREADSHEET TIPS

The tips that follow apply throughout the Spreadsheet. The Spreadsheet requires attention to detail, and you should pay special attention to the tip on documenting everything you do.

Tip: *Print and annotate hard copies of the Spreadsheet menus.*

You will need a hard copy of the Spreadsheet menu and the Spreadsheet Printer Options menu, as well as menus for the Apple-L, Apple-P, and Apple-V commands. If you have not yet done so, print copies of all these screens using Apple-H, and post the copies on a note board near your Apple. Pencil in notes about when you use each option. A hard copy of the Spreadsheet menu appears in Figure 4.1.

Tip: *No matter how you save a Spreadsheet file, it loads in a predictable way.*

No matter how you save a Spreadsheet file, the cursor always reappears where you left it, and in the normal display mode

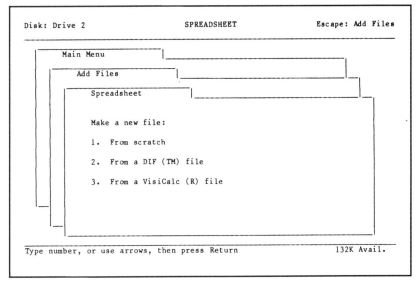

Figure 4.1: *Spreadsheet menu*

(rather than formula display mode). On the Desktop, the cursor also remains where you left it, and the display mode remains unchanged.

Note that the cursor location in the Spreadsheet differs from the convention used in the Word Processor and Data Base. In those programs the cursor returns to the beginning of the file when you reload the file.

Tip: *Use lowercase letters in worksheet titles and formula entries.*

When VisiCalc was first developed, the Apple II had only uppercase letters. Many of the printed templates for worksheets were therefore written entirely in capitals, but using both cases makes titles easier to read. The titles can always be set off with row borders made of repeated dashes or equal signs.

Formula entries accept lowercase letters. When the formula has been completed and entered, lowercase letters automatically convert to uppercase. However, if you have experience with VisiCalc, you may prefer to depress the Caps Lock key when writing formulas.

Tip: *Once you change the name of a Spreadsheet file that has been saved, you can do almost anything with it.*

This is an important tip, and the concept will be adapted for specific purposes throughout this chapter. Once a file is saved to primary and backup disks, you can change the name on the Desktop and make as many changes as you want without risk of damaging the previously saved files. You can copy, delete, replace, and rearrange data for any purpose. If you make a serious mistake, simply remove the file from the Desktop, load the original file again, and change its name on the Desktop once more.

Tip: *Spreadsheet design can be done with pencil and paper.*

When two or more people use the same Apple, there will be times when one person wants to use AppleWorks and cannot. That is a good time to start working with pencil and paper. For example, you can design worksheets using a grid form printed by the Spreadsheet itself. You can often design formulas on paper more efficiently than on screen. You can do preliminary calculations on the back of an envelope with an inexpensive scientific calculator. Use hard copies of related worksheets. Use a hard copy of the Printer Options menu that shows all the default values, as shown in Figure 4.2. Pencil in proposed changes for a specific report.

Tip: *Document all your work.*

When you write a report on the Word Processor, you rarely need directions when you load it again several weeks later. When

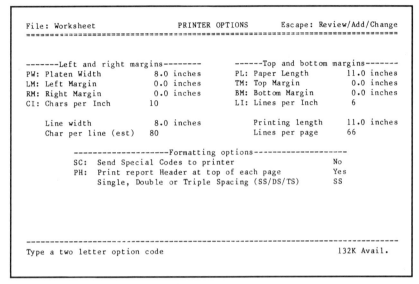

Figure 4.2: Spreadsheet Printer Options menu

you develop a Spreadsheet template, you may get lost later unless you have written yourself some directions.

The documentation you write should explain why you developed the application. It should include step-by-step instructions on how to load and use the Spreadsheet file. It should note any problems encountered with the data. It should include hard copies of important screens: key formulas, input values, and report formats along with their respective printer option settings.

Every application should have its own manila file folder or something functionally equivalent. Print a report with key formulas and all data used in the template.

Tip: *Save your work to disk at least every 20 minutes.*

Press Apple-S at least every 20 minutes to save what you have entered. Save it to a backup disk as well on every second or third save. You may want to save a file even more often if you happen to be writing difficult formulas. Note that AppleWorks saves Spreadsheet files faster than other files.

PLANNING BUDGETS

If letters are the most common Word Processor files, budgets are probably the most common Spreadsheet files. The tips in this section will help you to construct a budget template. From this starting point, you can use copying techniques to create more complex budget applications. The budget example in Figure 4.3 will provide a reference point for many tips in this chapter. Turn to this figure whenever necessary.

Tip: *When you teach others about the Spreadsheet, teach them first about structure.*

Worksheet rows are horizontal and numbered; columns are vertical and lettered. A cell is described by its column letter and row number, such as B4. Cells can contain values (12, −1.23, 3.14159) or labels (Cost, 1984 Losses, ------, Totals). Note that

```
File: Apple.Budget          REVIEW/ADD/CHANGE           Escape: Main Menu
==========A==========B========C========D========E=======F========G========H====
      1│Apple IIe System                              6%
      2│                           Base            Sales
      3│Item               Code    Cost  Shipping    Tax     Total
      4│-------------------------------------------------------------
      5│80-column 64K card    1   149.95    3.00    0.00    152.95
      6│Two disk drives       2   359.90    8.00    0.00    367.90
      7│Control card          3    49.00    2.00    0.00     51.00
      8│Dot matrix printer    4   359.95   20.00    0.00    379.95
      9│Buffered printer card 5   159.95    0.00    9.60    169.55
     10│Monochrome monitor    6    90.00    8.00    0.00     98.00
     11│-------------------------------------------------------------
     12│Totals                                             1219.35
     13│
     14│
     15│
     16│
     17│
     18│
       -------------------------------------------------------------
G12: (Value, Layout-F2) @SUM(G4...G11)

Type entry or use @ commands                            @-? for Help
```

Figure 4.3: Budget worksheet template

numerals can be used in labels or as labels by themselves. Just start the entry with a quotation mark (") so the Spreadsheet will recognize it as a label. (The quotation mark does not appear in the cell.) You must also use the quotation mark to enter a border of dashes (------) that would otherwise be interpreted as minus signs.

Tip: *Think about how your budget would look on paper, because it will look about the same on the Spreadsheet.*

You can transfer many useful applications from paper to worksheets almost directly. That goes for most budgets, like the sample budget worksheet shown in Figure 4.3. This budget supposes that a library association has received a classic 1983 Apple IIe, the kind with white key lettering. We need a budget for completing the system to use with AppleWorks. We have six lines of information to enter, and the number we ultimately care about will be on the bottom line in cell G12. (Notice that items shipped from out of state are not subject to sales tax.)

The budget would look the same on paper, with the exception of the Code heading for column C. This column is for arranging the rows in the spreadsheet back into their original order once they have been sorted according to another criterion. Arranging is a process that is difficult to do on paper but simple on a computer.

Tip: *Follow common practice in using dividing borders.*

Type in a dividing border of dashes (remember to begin by typing a quotation mark). The common practice is to enter a border in the row just below the column heading and another in the row just above the totals row. Some people use the equal-sign to make borders in other places. For example, if two or more different templates appear in the same file, an equal sign border is commonly used to separate them.

Tip: *Make just one border, then copy it to other rows.*

When you enter row borders across an entire screen, you have to do it in two sections because a repeating label accepts only 69 characters. The most efficient way to copy label rows is to and from the clipboard.

Tip: *Use code numbers to arrange rows back to their original order.*

The column of code numbers in Figure 4.3 can be used to arrange the rows back to their original order after they have been rearranged for some other purpose. You will sometimes list items in a logical order that AppleWorks cannot appreciate; in such cases you should also enter an original-order code. In Figure 4.3, related peripherals are grouped together. AppleWorks cannot appreciate this order, but it understands the ascending values used in the Code column.

A unique code or identification number for each record can make that record unique. As you may remember from Chapter 3, this is also a key to predicting arranged order in records.

RECALCULATING WORKSHEETS

Like most spreadsheets, the AppleWorks Spreadsheet offers the option for manual recalculation. After you choose this option, use Apple-K to recalculate (not the exclamation mark used in other spreadsheets). This section includes several tips and a caution for using Apple-K more efficiently.

Tip: *Use manual recalculation most of the time.*

Whenever you enter new values, the Spreadsheet automatically recalculates your worksheet. This may be helpful when you first start work on a template, but it eventually takes more time than it is worth. When you get impatient, set manual recalculation.

Tip: *Know when to use row calculation order.*

Most worksheets can be calculated in either column or row order. Column order is the default; you must specify row order when you want it. Look first at the calculation process. If any cell formula depends on a calculated cell above and to the right, use row order. If any cell formula depends on a calculated cell below and to the left, use column order. You cannot have both dependency cases in the same worksheet.

When order makes no difference in the calculation process, look at the shape of the template. If it has many calculated columns and few rows, use the row order of calculation, because it is slightly faster with that shape. If the template is long and narrow, use column order. ,

Tip: *Use Apple-U to recalculate individual cells.*

When you change a formula in one cell, there is no reason to recalculate the whole worksheet. When you edit that formula, it automatically recalculates, even if you have specified manual recalculation.

If you change a variable and want to see how it affects results in the next related formula, just make believe you are editing that formula. Use Apple-U, enter a space, and then delete the space. That qualifies as an edit, and the formula recalculates.

Tip: *The manual recalculation setting stays with the file.*

Once you select manual recalculation, that selection (or "standard value") stays with the file, just as it does in VisiCalc. Therefore, when you save the worksheet as a Spreadsheet file, it will return with the manual recalculation selection when you load it again. This is not true of all spreadsheet programs. In Multiplan, for example, the manual recalculation selection remains independent of a file and must be chosen each time you use the file.

Caution: *If the Spreadsheet has been set for manual recalculation, it will not automatically recalculate when saved.*

VisiCalc and Multiplan both automatically recalculate worksheets when they are saved, even under the manual recalculation setting. The AppleWorks Spreadsheet is consistent: it does not recalculate. This provides more flexibility and requires greater responsibility on your part.

Tip: *It is almost always a good idea to recalculate a worksheet before saving it as a Spreadsheet file.*

There are several good and bad consequences of having a Spreadsheet that does not automatically recalculate when you save it. For example, you might want to save a worksheet quickly just before going to lunch, knowing that you will soon get back to it. You can save it faster without recalculating. On the other hand, if something comes up and you cannot get back to it for another week, there is some chance that you will print out an incorrect report. It is therefore generally prudent to recalculate before saving.

MATH FUNCTIONS AND FORMULAS

If you can write formulas correctly, you can design and build a broad range of useful applications templates. This is where you have the most control over AppleWorks. Many people find spreadsheet design challenging and satisfying.

You will no doubt be surprised by some of the math functions available. Pay special attention to the tips for series calculations.

Tip: *Although a formula is limited to 69 characters as originally entered, you can add up to nine more by editing.*

AppleWorks is considerably more restrictive than other spreadsheets in formula length limitations. You will probably reach the 69-character limit from time to time. By going back to edit with Apple-U, you can add up to nine more characters to a formula. This may save you from having to continue the formula to another cell. Continued formulas can sometimes be difficult to interpret.

Tip: *Use @SUM to add continuing series, and mark the series with the cursor.*

In the budget example (Figure 4.3) the total cost for a given component is base cost plus the shipping plus the sales tax. For row 5, this can be written as

+ D5 + E5 + F5

meaning "the contents of cell D5 plus cell E5 plus cell F5." This kind of formula can be tedious, and if you begin a formula with a cell name and forget the + before the cell, you get an unwanted label.

And how do you total column G for a result in G12? You could write the formula +G5+G6 . . . , but that would be even more tedious. The Spreadsheet has a summation function that allows you to write

@SUM(G5. . .G10)

This means "sum (or add up) the series beginning with G5 and ending with G10." Named functions in the Spreadsheet all begin with the at symbol (@).

With the @SUM function, you can use the cursor to mark the beginning and ending cells of a series. To do so, follow these steps:

1. Move the cursor to the cell that will contain the formula.

2. Enter @SUM(in the cell.

3. Move the cursor to G5, the beginning cell in the series.

4. Enter . . . (three periods) in the cell. The cursor moves back to the formula cell.

5. Move the cursor to G10, the ending cell in the series.

6. Press) and the formula is complete.

By convention, the beginning cell is the left-most cell in a series, or the cell nearest row 1, so write your formulas that way. Note that if you enter only one period for the summation series, AppleWorks will add the other two.

Tip: *Include border rows in summation formulas.*

In the budget example (Figure 4.3) you can write @SUM(G4. . . G11) to avoid a pitfall. You include border rows that have no effect on the calculation, because someone else may later want to arrange (sort) rows 5 through 10 in ascending order of total cost. The value $152.95 and the rest of row 5 would end up in row 7. The value $98.00 and the rest of row 10 would end up in row 6. The formula @SUM(G5. . .G10) would then become @SUM(G7. . .G6). With the border rows included in the formula that cannot happen, because those rows are not being rearranged.

The border rows provide similar protection when you insert, delete, or move rows.

Tip: *Use empty columns one character wide to provide protection for row totals and related operations.*

In template design it is common to move certain columns several times while trying to decide how a report should look. By setting a border column one character wide, you can prevent unwanted changes to formulas for row totals.

Relatively few people have learned to do this, because until 1984 the standard VisiCalc program lacked the option to specify the width of an individual column. All columns had to have the same number of character spaces. With the ability to create one narrow column, the protection is easy to include and does not clutter the worksheet.

Tip: *Block operations can save you time.*

Like VisiCalc, AppleWorks can perform block operations. For example, in Figure 4.3 you can write a formula in F14 to sum three columns of entries all at once:

@SUM(D4...F11)

In other cases, you may want to perform calculations on discontinuous series. For example, in Figure 4.3 you can write a formula to sum all base costs and sales tax amounts:

@SUM(D4...D11,F4...F11)

As with other formulas, you can and should point with the cursor to enter the correct cell coordinates.

Caution: *The @AVG function works two different ways, depending on the formula structure used.*

Although @AVG(E1. . .E3) will ignore an empty cell at E3, the formula @AVG(E1,E2,E3) will count the empty cell. The two formulas will therefore produce two different averages. The same discrepancy holds for formulas using @COUNT, @MIN, and @MAX. For example, in the formula @MAX(E1,E2,E3) an empty cell is the maximum value if the other two cells contain negative values.

Tip: *Use the exponentiation function to its limits.*

Exponentiation uses the caret (^) mark. The Reference Manual makes little reference to this function, but it has great range. To begin with the simplest form, 3 ^ 2 is 3 squared, or 9. The power can be represented as a value in another cell, as with 23 ^ B5. If B5 contains no value, the power 0 is assumed, and the resulting value is 1.

The exponent can also be a decimal fraction, as in 3 ^ .5, an alternative to @SQRT(3) that saves four character spaces. For calculation, however, using the @SQRT function is several times faster than using the exponentiation formula.

Caution: *The Spreadsheet uses left-to-right order of operations, not the algebraic order of operations used in BASIC.*

Consider the difference between the two orders of operation. Suppose you want to evaluate (4 + A1)*(6 + 3). If A1 = 3, the formula is the same as 7*9. In the Spreadsheet and VisiCalc you can get the correct result, 63, by writing 4 + A1*(6 + 3). In an algebraic calculator, such a formula would be interpreted as 4 + 27, or 31.

Multiplan and SuperCalc 3a both use the algebraic order of operations. You can use enough parentheses in the Spreadsheet so everyone can understand the formulas. Many serious users always write formulas with parentheses throughout. Extra parentheses require more memory and take more time for recalculation, but in this case the differences are less than five percent, barely a matter of principle.

Tip: *Use parentheses consistently for documentation purposes.*

Whether you use extra parentheses or the minimum required, do it consistently. Someone else may have to review your work. Although most people can interpret minimal left-to-right notation, formulas with extra parentheses are easier to follow. It is very difficult to review formulas that use inconsistent notation.

Tip: *Relative formula references are more common than "no change" references.*

Return again to Figure 4.3 and note cell G5. Recall that the formula for that cell was + D5 + E5 + F5. Suppose you want to copy the formula in G5 to cells G6 through G10. When you copy formulas, you will see a message asking whether there is "no change" in D5 or whether it is "relative." Press R three times to indicate that all three cells are relative references.

You are saying, in effect, "Make the formula relate to the row it will be in. Use a D6 in the copy of the formula meant for row 6, not a D5." Most references in spreadsheets are relative. (A "no change" example appears later in this section.)

Tip: *Use RN notation to document formula design.*

Sometimes formulas must make absolute references to a value in one cell. For example, an interest rate used throughout a worksheet may be located in cell B6. Every formula that includes the interest rate must reference B6.

Because formulas can contain both relative and absolute references, it's helpful to use some kind of notation to keep track of which references are relative and which are absolute. When you copy formulas down columns, use a notation somewhere in the column to denote whether the cell references in the formula are relative (R) or absolute (N for no change). You can make the notation when you write the first formula. The notation belongs in a cell that will not be printed in reports. Figure 4.4 shows the notation below cell G12 in the budget template. When you copy formulas across rows, use a notation somewhere in the row, again in a cell that will not be printed.

```
File: Apple.Budget           REVIEW/ADD/CHANGE              Escape: Main Menu
==========A==========B=========C========D========E=======F========G=======H====
  1|Apple IIe System                                   6%
  2|                                        Base      Sales
  3|Item                           Code     Cost Shipping   Tax      Total
  4|-------------------------------------------------------------------
  5|80-column 64K card              1      149.95    3.00    0.00    152.95
  6|Two disk drives                 2      359.90    8.00    0.00    367.90
  7|Control card                    3       49.00    2.00    0.00     51.00
  8|Dot matrix printer              4      359.95   20.00    0.00    379.95
  9|Buffered printer card           5      159.95    0.00    9.60    169.55
 10|Monochrome monitor              6       90.00    8.00    0.00     98.00
 11|-------------------------------------------------------------------
 12|Totals                                                           1219.35
 13|
 14|                                                                   RRR
 15|
 16|
 17|
 18|
   -------------------------------------------------------------------
 G14: (Label, Layout-R) RRR

 Type entry or use @ commands                              @-? for Help
```

Figure 4.4: RN notation in the budget template

Tip: *You can copy formulas in any direction.*

In Figure 4.3, the appropriate formula for cell G12 is

@SUM(G4. . .G11).

Try copying the formula in G12 to cells F12 through D12. That sounds backwards, but it works. There will be many times when you can save time by copying from right to left, or bottom to top.

Caution: *Spreadsheet rows have undocumented capacity limits for formulas.*

Although 127 values can fit in one row, 127 summation formulas cannot. For example, if you attempt to copy a formula from cell Al through cell CZ1, you will probably get an unexpected warning that some cells were lost. Figure 4.5 shows the

```
File: ROW.LIMITS                    COPY          Escape: Review/Add/Change
========A========B========C========D========E========F========G========H====
    1|    256
    2|
    3|
    4|     16
    5|
    6|
    7|
    8|        When you press the Space Bar, AppleWorks will insert the
    9|        copied formulas as far as they go, in this case to cell CH4.
   10|
   11|
   12|
   13|
   14|
   15|
   16|
   17|
   18|
    -------------------- Some cells were lost from row 4 --------------------
A4: (Value) @SQRT(A1)
@SQRT(A1)
Press Space Bar to continue                                     84K Avail.
```

Figure 4.5: *Error message for formula copying*

error message. It means the requested copying could not go as far as you specified.

Whenever this happens, follow the row until you find the last column to which the formula was copied. Blank the last copied cell, move the cursor down one row, and continue with an appropriate revision of the original formula. If you save the worksheet shown in Figure 4.5 without blanking the last copied cell, AppleWorks may not be able to load the file again. Instead, you will see the error message in Figure 4.6.

Table 4.1 lists simple formulas, along with the last cell to which they can be copied from column A.

There is an important exception to this caution: AppleWorks version 2.0 running on a system with at least 256K RAM has a much larger capacity limit—five times that of earlier versions. It can therefore retrieve the problem worksheet files we just "lost." The larger limit can easily handle 127 columns of any formula in Table 4.1.

Tip: *The arithmetic operations in AppleWorks are accurate to at least 14 places.*

This accuracy means that trigonometric functions generated with Taylor series calculations can actually be more accurate on the AppleWorks Spreadsheet than on other spreadsheets. There are more tips on series calculations later in this chapter.

Although the Spreadsheet lacks scientific notation, precise values can be stored as multiples of ten to a specified power.

PRINTER OPTIONS

If you have mastered Word Processor printing, you are well prepared to work with the lesser number of Spreadsheet printer options. There are a few important differences worth noting. In the Spreadsheet you are generally most concerned with fitting all the needed columns onto the paper. The Spreadsheet also takes a slightly different approach to page headers, more like that in the Data Base program.

Table 4.1: *Sample formulas with copying limits*

Formula	Last Column through Which Formula Can Be Copied
1+A1	BI
+A1+1	BG
@SQRT(A1)	CH
+A1^.5	BG
@IF(A1>0,324,0)	AF
@NPV(.12,A1...C1)	AT
@SUM(A1...A11)	BO

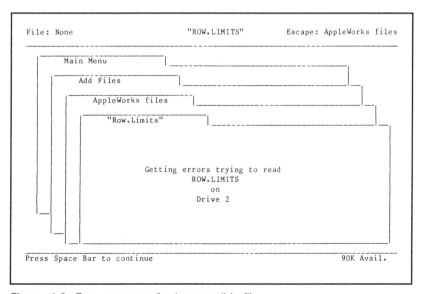

Figure 4.6: *Error message for inaccessible file*

Caution: *The Spreadsheet lacks some useful printer options found in the Word Processor.*

Table 4.2 shows which Word Processor printer options are also found in the Data Base and Spreadsheet. Each has other specialized options. The Data Base and Spreadsheet have the option to enter special codes for the printer. This option is primarily useful for telling the printer to recognize different form lengths. It can be used to begin boldfacing or underlining but cannot turn them off. Thus, you cannot boldface or underline selectively in the Spreadsheet.

Table 4.2: *Printer options*

Option	WP	DB	SS
Line Length, Print Density			
Platen width	X	X	X
Left margin	X	X	X
Right margin	X	X	X
Characters per inch	X	X	X
Proportional-1	X		
Proportional-2	X		
Text Positioning			
Indent	X		
Justified	X	X	X
Unjustified	X	X	X
Centered	X		X
Page Length, Line Density			
Paper length	X	X	X
Top margin	X	X	X
Bottom margin	X	X	X
Lines per inch	X	X	X
Single space	X	X	X
Double space	X	X	X
Triple space	X	X	X

Table 4.2: *Printer options (continued)*

Option	WP	DB	SS
Page Controls			
New page	X		
Group markers	X		
Page Calculation			
Page header	X	X	X
Page footer	X		
Skip lines	X		
Page number	X		
Place Markers			
Pause each page	X		
Pause here	X		
Set a marker	X		
Print Enhancements			
Boldface	X		
Superscript	X		
Subscript	X		
Underline	X		
Variable Text Entry			
Print page number	X		
Enter keyboard	X		
Mail merge	X		

When you design Spreadsheet applications, think about these limitations at the beginning. It may be necessary to print reports to the clipboard for further editing in the Word Processor. For more on this subject, see Chapter 5.

Tip: *Use small margins in standard template files.*

Provide just enough space for a small margin, something like 0.5 inches as a standard setting. Use no margin on the right. If the printer has an eight-inch platen width, you will often be faced with a tight fit. You may even need to set a 0-inch left margin and shift the paper to the left to use all of the available platen.

Tip: *Pay special attention to the estimate of characters per line.*

This estimate is almost always the critical measurement in printing worksheets. If the number of characters you want to print is greater than the number of characters the printer can physically fit between the margins, the printer will wrap the line onto a second line, and you have another sheet of paper for the recycling bin.

After setting the printer options, press Escape to return to the document. Press Apple-P to print. Note the options. "All" means the block bounded by cell A1, the last row with something in it, and the right-most column with anything in it. Use the "block" option whenever you are uncertain about dimensions, and outline the block by moving the cursor. Note how quickly Apple-9 highlights vertical space.

Press Return, then select the printer. This is the moment of truth when you find out if the number of characters you want to print is more than the printer can physically fit on its line. If you ever need to bail out at this point, simply press Escape and go back to widen the platen width, specify more characters per inch, or define a block with fewer columns.

Figure 4.7 shows the message you will get before you print a worksheet block that is too wide for the printer. In this case you should bail out.

Caution: *When you print a header, check the platen width first.*

This caution applies to printers with platen widths of more than eight inches. After printer selection, note that you have the option to enter a date. It is normally printed in the upper-right

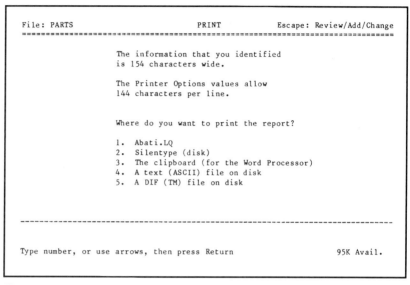

```
File: PARTS                         PRINT              Escape: Review/Add/Change
================================================================================
                          The information that you identified
                          is 154 characters wide.

                          The Printer Options values allow
                          144 characters per line.


                          Where do you want to print the report?

                          1.  Abati.LQ
                          2.  Silentype (disk)
                          3.  The clipboard (for the Word Processor)
                          4.  A text (ASCII) file on disk
                          5.  A DIF (TM) file on disk




        ------------------------------------------------------------------------

        Type number, or use arrows, then press Return              95K Avail.
```

Figure 4.7: *Worksheet block wider than printer capacity*

corner of the page, under the page number. However, both the date and page number will be at the far right of the platen setting, which may be beyond the right edge of the paper.

If you are using 8½-inch paper in a wide carriage, the print head can move beyond the paper, print on the roller, and rip into the paper on the return pass. Be certain to check the platen width setting first.

DESIGNING TEMPLATES

Good planning and design can save considerable time in the building and use of templates. By designing interchangeable parts you can build Spreadsheet templates efficiently. It is also always a good idea to audit your own work, particularly in the design of spreadsheet applications. This section covers many design details and several cautions about designing templates to minimize problems with errors.

Tip: *Learn to design and build templates yourself.*

You can buy ready-made templates on disk, and they have a place, but it is much easier to modify and maintain a template when you have assembled the component parts yourself. It takes relatively little time to learn efficient worksheet design, and AppleWorks makes it easy to use a building-block development strategy.

Experienced spreadsheet users do purchase templates on disk when those templates include significant amounts of entered data that they need. They may also purchase templates to see how a competent specialist approaches a difficult problem in some substantive field. Such templates tend to have complicated formulas and structures.

Tip: *For the most appropriate applications templates, consult sources in your own field.*

Journals and other reference sources in your own field can provide information on preferred calculation methods and reporting formats for specific applications. In some professional journals you can now find printouts of Lotus spreadsheet templates. More often, you will find a manual calculation method that can be converted as it appears on paper. Most applications developers simply need to see one common example of the way things are done. They can then write the appropriate spreadsheet formulas for almost any example.

Tip: *Write templates based on common examples you understand.*

The most useful kind of template is really just a worked example, preferably a common example that you thoroughly understand. To adapt this kind of template, you replace the existing information with your own information.

Tip: *Read VisiCalc and Lotus template examples.*

Many good template articles have been written for VisiCalc. VisiCalc notation remains widely used because other spreadsheets have followed its conventions. Many user groups offer templates at minimal cost, and you can develop a good utility collection this way.

Many good template articles have been written for Lotus-type spreadsheets. They use notation similar to that of VisiCalc but with the algebraic order of operations. Following are a few hints on how to make sense of the differences.

Ignore the macro instructions, because AppleWorks has no built-in macro facility. If a function looks completely different, there probably is no equivalent in AppleWorks. On the other hand, @ROUND is a Lotus function that appears in AppleWorks version 2.0. It takes the place of a rounding formula described in this chapter. @V,LOOKUP,1 looks something like @LOOKUP in AppleWorks. In Lotus notation you must specify whether the lookup table is vertical or horizontal. The 1 means that the second row in the table is one column farther away than it would be in AppleWorks. If the offset is 0, as in AppleWorks, you would simply see @V,LOOKUP.

You can often understand the gist of an application without reading the details of every formula. Look for the key formulas and highlight them with a yellow marker.

Tip: *Give yourself plenty of time in the design stage.*

Most spreadsheet applications require considerable thought in the design stage. What data do you really need? Where are you going to find the data? Remember that collecting information is usually the most time-consuming part of any application. Time spent in the design stage saves far more time later.

Tip: *Spreadsheet reports should include all assumptions.*

An assumption is a variable that is taken for granted. For example, you can assume that interest rates will remain at 10 percent throughout the life of a construction project. The Spreadsheet model may just include .10 in every relevant formula, with no provision to enter another variable except by editing each formula. Interest rates are almost never built in as assumptions.

Whenever there is a potential for disagreement about an assumption, make a provision to enter it as a variable along with other input data. When you do build in assumptions, make it easy for others to find the assumptions on which the calculations were based. It is surprising how many people either forget or neglect to do this.

If you read spreadsheet reports from other people, consider all of the assumptions carefully: they are probably wrong more often than the actual calculations.

Tip: *Put all the variables up front.*

A template works best when you can enter all the variable data in one place up front on the worksheet, preferably in one column and in logical order. The label explaining what to enter should be right-justified. Use two or three consecutive cells—whatever it takes to make everything clear.

Alternatively, you can left-justify the labels and use the equal sign and the right-arrow character to point to the proper cell. Above all, be consistent, so that you can return to a worksheet months later and still find the variables easily.

Tip: *Move the work area around to make concise reports.*

Sometimes a necessary work area will separate the input data from the results. It is generally not a good idea to clutter a report with unnecessary information and intermediate results.

What do you do with an intrusive work area? In models calculated by columns, you can drop the working formulas and intermediate results far down into lower rows by inserting rows. The formula references will be automatically adjusted.

If you make the work-area columns one or two characters wide, they will virtually disappear. The distance between input data and results in the report will then be minimal. You can find the formula cells by looking for the pound sign (#), which simply indicates that the values were too narrow to display the values. Figures 4.8 and 4.9 provide a simple example of how the technique works. In many cases the work area will be more than 10 columns wide.

In models calculated by rows, you can move the working formulas and intermediate results to the right into other columns.

Caution: *Value entries can only be right-justified, and some formats have no buffer space to the right.*

In the Spreadsheet most right-justified values really are right-justified, without the one-character buffer space found in VisiCalc

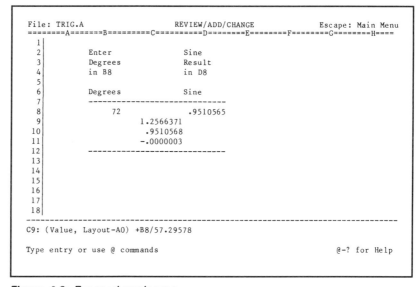

```
File: TRIG.A                    REVIEW/ADD/CHANGE              Escape: Main Menu
========A=======B=========C=========D========E========F========G========H====
  1|
  2|        Enter              Sine
  3|        Degrees            Result
  4|        in B8              in D8
  5|
  6|        Degrees            Sine
  7|        ----------------------------
  8|          72              .9510565
  9|                 1.2566371
 10|                  .9510568
 11|                 -.0000003
 12|        ----------------------------
 13|
 14|
 15|
 16|
 17|
 18|
  ------------------------------------------------------------------------
C9: (Value, Layout-A0) +B8/57.29578

Type entry or use @ commands                               @-? for Help
```

Figure 4.8: *Exposed work area*

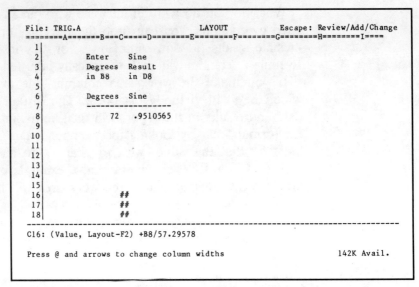

```
File: TRIG.A                          LAYOUT          Escape: Review/Add/Change
========A=======B===C=====D========E========F========G========H========I====
  1|
  2|        Enter    Sine
  3|        Degrees  Result
  4|        in B8    in D8
  5|
  6|        Degrees  Sine
  7|        ------------------
  8|             72  .9510565
  9|
 10|
 11|
 12|
 13|
 14|
 15|
 16|             ##
 17|             ##
 18|             ##
-------------------------------------------------------------------------------
C16: (Value, Layout-F2) +B8/57.29578

Press @ and arrows to change column widths                      142K Avail.
```

Figure 4.9: *Hidden work area*

and Multiplan. Therefore, there is no space between those values and flush-left labels in the next column to the right. To make the worksheet readable, you should begin each label entry with a space or insert a buffer column one space wide.

Caution: *Value entries in the dollar and comma formats do include the buffer space to the right.*

Financial reports generally use comma or dollar formats. These formats are identical except for the dollar sign. The buffer space is needed for closed parentheses that designate negative values (other formats simply use the minus sign). If you use dollar or comma formats in the same column with other value formats, the column will appear ragged on the right. Pay special attention to choices when you format value cells by blocks: use comma formats consistently within columns. Figure 4.10 shows differences in value formats.

```
File: Formats                REVIEW/ADD/CHANGE              Escape: Main Menu
========A=========B=====C=====D=========E=========F=========G=========H====
 1|
 2|                   Value   Layout
 3|                 -----------------------------------------------------------
 4|               -1840.1   Appropriate, Negative
 5|
 6|                  1840    Fixed: 0 decimal places
 7|
 8|              1,840.10    Commas, Fixed: 2 decimal places
 9|
10|             $1,840.10    Dollars, Fixed: 2 decimal places
11|
12|           ($1,840.10)    Dollars, Negative, Fixed: 2 decimal places
13|
14|                 .254    Appropriate
15|
16|                25.4%    Percent, Fixed: 1 decimal place
17|                 -----------------------------------------------------------
18|
---------------------------------------------------------------------------
B12: (Value, Layout-D2) -1840.1

Type entry or use @ commands                              @-? for Help
```

Figure 4.10: *Differences in value formats*

Tip: *There are three kinds of dates appropriate to Apple-Works, and each has a particular advantage.*

The form 10/23/87 is used to set dates for ProDOS files. In the Data Base, this form is automatically converted to the form Oct 23 87 in categories that have "date" in their name. These dates can then be arranged by chronology or reverse chronology. In the Spreadsheet, however, such dates are recognized simply as labels.

Spreadsheet dates in the form 9.04 can be arranged by ascending or descending values within a year. Years in the form 1987 can also be arranged as values. First arrange the month.day column, and then the year column. Later in this chapter, you will learn how to calculate the number of days between dates that use this format.

Spreadsheet dates in the form 8709.04 can be entered as values fixed to two decimal places and arranged in 0-9 order. However, the form is unwieldy, and you are more likely to make mistakes this way.

Tip: *Use whole numbers for percentage entries.*

The Spreadsheet allows you to enter .12 into a cell that uses the percent format. The entry then appears as 12%. When someone else enters a replacement value, they might enter it in a form such as 12.4, which then appears as 1240%.

It is generally safer to avoid the percent format. Use a whole number, enter *percent* or *%* in an adjacent label cell, and divide the value by 100 in formulas where .12 or .124 are needed.

VALIDATING DATA AND FORMULAS

Studies of worksheets have shown that more than a quarter contain data and formula errors that make calculated results unreliable. You can minimize this risk by following the tips in this section. The Spreadsheet can then serve as a highly-controlled entry place for data used in other applications, including the Data Base (see Chapter 5).

Tip: *You can use tests to validate data entered in worksheets.*

Categories containing numbers often have acceptable ranges. For example, if you enter people's ages, the age values will all be between 1 and 120. There are no negative age values and no 200-year-old people. For all practical purposes we can assume that acceptable values will have either one or two digits.

You can test entries for specific categories by writing a limiting formula. For example, suppose you designate B4 as a cell for entering age values. You can then have cell C4 test whether to accept or reject the value. This requires the following conditional formula:

@IF(B4<100,B4,@ERROR)

If someone enters 142 or 100 in cell B4, cell C4 will display the word ERROR. This may not be very friendly, but NA is the only other message you can use. The formula above does not allow for the possibility of someone entering a 0 or negative number. To catch such an entry, you would have to include another condition in the formula.

When you use this kind of validation, all subsequent operation on the input data must reference the validation cell, in this case C4. Remember that cell B4 will accept anything. Figure 4.11 shows two examples of the application. The formulas in cells C5. . .C8 are copied from C4, with all references relative.

The second example accepts only those age values from 21 through 99, and the formula is more complicated. The section on logic functions later in this chapter explains how formulas with two conditions are written.

Tip: *Set column widths to detect errors in data entry.*

This is an alternate way of detecting errors in entered values. In most cases, columns should be just wide enough to show the

```
File:  Input.Tests              REVIEW/ADD/CHANGE           Escape: Main Menu
========A========B========C========D========E========F========G========H=====
 1|
 2|  Enter Ages Below
 3|  ----------------
 4|              ˙12        12    @IF(B4<100,B4,@ERROR)
 5|               99        99
 6|                8         8
 7|              142     ERROR
 8|               23        23
 9|
10|
11|  Enter Ages Below
12|  ----------------
13|               12     ERROR    @IF(B13<100,@IF(B13>20,B13,@ERROR),@ERROR)
14|               99        99
15|                8     ERROR
16|              142     ERROR
17|               23        23
18|
   -------------------------------------------------------------------------
C4: (Value) @IF(B4<100,B4,@ERROR)

Type entry or use @ commands                          @-? for Help
```

Figure 4.11: Testing input values

largest number. If a column of age values will be no wider than two digits, make the column two spaces wide. Any mistaken entry of three digits will appear as *##*. Never worry about a column label: you can always accommodate it with an empty column to the left or right.

If the dollar total of a column will be no more than 99,999, use commas format and make the column seven character spaces wide. (Remember that commas format has a buffer space on the right.) Any mistaken entry above 99,999 will be easy to recognize as you scan the column, because it will appear as *#######*. If you plan to total the column, widen it to accommodate the total after you make all the entries.

A slightly different approach works for ZIP codes, telephone numbers, two-letter state abbreviations, social security numbers, and many other kinds of label entries of fixed length. They will spill over if there is insufficient room in a cell and thereby become conspicuous. By carefully setting column widths, you can scan patterns in columns and correct errors. Figure 4.12 shows some examples.

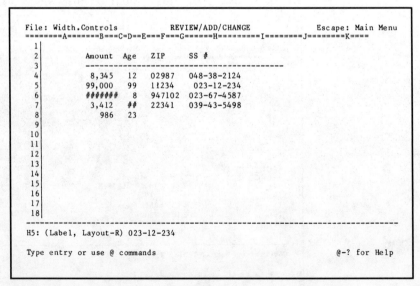

Figure 4.12: Using column widths and formatting to find errors

Tip: *Use a cross-checking formula to validate column totals.*

In practice, people often total columns and forget about whether the row total gives the same result. If one of the summation formulas uses an incomplete cell series, there could be a significant discrepancy. Figure 4.13 illustrates a case in which it is prudent to check the row total against the column total. The formula in G14 is

@SUM(D12. . .F12)

The discrepancy is caused by an incorrect formula in G8.

Some people prefer a longer formula that does the checking and totaling entirely within one cell, in which case this would be the formula in G12:

@IF(@SUM(D12. . .F12) = @SUM(G4. . .G11),
@SUM(G4. . .G11),@ERROR)

```
File: Apple.Budget          REVIEW/ADD/CHANGE              Escape: Main Menu
=========A=========B========C========D========E=======F========G========H====
   1│Apple IIe System                            6%
   2│                                  Base     Sales
   3│Item                      Code    Cost Shipping  Tax    Total
   4│ - - - - - - - - - - - - - - - - - - - - - - - - - - - - - - - - - -
   5│80-column 64K card          1   149.95    3.00  0.00   152.95
   6│Two disk drives             2   359.90    8.00  0.00   367.90
   7│Control card                3    49.00    2.00  0.00    51.00
   8│Dot matrix printer          4   359.95   20.00  0.00   359.95
   9│Buffered printer card       5   159.95    0.00  9.60   169.55
  10│Monochrome monitor          6    90.00    8.00  0.00    98.00
  11│ - - - - - - - - - - - - - - - - - - - - - - - - - - - - - - - - - -
  12│Totals                         1168.75   41.00  9.60  1199.35
  13│
  14│                                                      1219.35
  15│
  16│
  17│
  18│
     - - - - - - - - - - - - - - - - - - - - - - - - - - - - - - - - - - - -
G8: (Value, Layout-F2) +D8+F8

Type entry or use @ commands                          @-? for Help
```

Figure 4.13: *Column total summation error*

If the sums do not match, you can expect to find ERROR in cell G12. Unfortunately, AppleWorks sometimes generates ERROR when none exists. The problem is caused by the underlying representation of decimal values. We will discuss a similar problem in the section on financial analysis and rounding.

Tip: *Use cell protection to keep from writing over formulas.*

Appleworks permits cell protection when you use Apple-V to select the protection option. Thereafter, you can set conditions about what can be entered in a given cell: values only, labels only, nothing, or anything. In day-to-day use, it is easy to destroy a formula by entering a value into a formula cell, so allow nothing in completed formula cells. In cells where input values are entered, allow values only. AppleWorks will not permit you to make illegal entries in protected cells until you remove the protection. When you use Apple-V to edit a protected cell, however, AppleWorks will not warn you that the cell is protected, so always check the protection status displayed in the layout prefix.

Tip: *Use Apple-H to print out key formulas.*

Zoom to the formula display mode. Widen the columns enough to show the complete formulas. The Apple-H command can then print a group of formulas with row and column borders. Values are left-justified in the formula display mode, but that is a minor inconvenience.

If you need to proofread or document just one formula, use the normal display mode. When the cursor is on the key cell, the formula, format, and location for that cell will appear at the bottom of the screen that Apple-H prints. This method is particularly useful for long formulas, where it would otherwise be necessary to greatly increase the width of a column. It is the only way to document formulas longer than 69 characters.

DEVELOPING TEMPLATES

Efficient template development depends on many small time-saving techniques. It is important to know significant limitations and options that were not documented in the AppleWorks Reference Manuals.

Tip: *Make a PARTS file for formulas and template components.*

A utility file can be used as a warehouse for component parts. The idea is to group together the modules you use regularly in worksheet design. One obvious example is storage space for the letter and number borders. The Spreadsheet uses letters to designate columns and numbers to designate rows, and these references enable users to identify cell locations. Unfortunately, you have to add the borders into the worksheet if you want to see them in a printout. Hence B2 is the first cell you can use for labels, values, or formulas in an artificially bordered worksheet.

Copying the border row from the utility file is simple enough, because the copy function handles rows very well. The row number border is a different matter, because you can only copy entire rows, not isolated columns. You can generate the numbers by copying a relative reference formula $(1+A2)$, where cell A2 contains the entered value 2. However, when you zoom in (Apple-Z) to the formula display mode, the generated border numbers appear as their formulas.

You can alternatively store actual values (2 through at least 100) below everything else in the utility file, where the rows are clear. Copy them into clear rows on other Spreadsheet documents, and then into exact locations within the document when the template is complete. These borders are often essential for documentation of applications that are both large and complex.

The sample file in Figure 4.14 includes border letters, monthly column headings, summation formulas, and a small template for

```
File: PARTS                    REVIEW/ADD/CHANGE              Escape: Main Menu
========A========B========C========D========E========F========G========H====
 1|
 2|Worksheet Parts:
 3|
 4| A        B        C        D        E        F        G        H
 5|=============================================================================
 6|         Jan      Feb      Mar      Apr      May      Jun      Jul
 7|---------------------------------------------------------------------------
 8|         0.00
 9|         1.11
10|---------------------------------------------------------------------------
11|Totals   1.11     0.00     0.00     0.00     0.00     0.00     0.00
12|
13|
14|Formulas:
15|
16|           Pi    Radius     Area    Height    Volume
17|          3.14     2.10     13.85    2.74      37.96
18|
---------------------------------------------------------------------------
B11: (Value, Layout-C2) @SUM(B7...B10)

Type entry or use @ commands                              @-? for Help
```

Figure 4.14: PARTS file

calculating the volume of a cylinder. The formula for D17 is $C17 \wedge 2*B17$. A file might hold dozens of formulas, each self-contained within one or more rows. These formulas and sample data are the most basic building blocks.

Caution: *It is difficult to edit labels that cross cell boundaries.*

Although labels that are wider than a cell's width will automatically continue into other cells, subsequent editing is done cell by cell. If you must add or delete letters, it is usually easier to start the original entry over again. Repeated border labels will also continue into other cells, but they cannot be edited.

Tip: *To reach cell A1, use Apple-F and the "last selection" option.*

There are no direct commands for moving to the beginning (upper-left) and end (lower-right) cells. Apple-1 through Apple-9 move the cursor to the beginning and end of the column in which it is located. Apple-← or Apple-→ will move the cursor through a row one screen at a time.

Apple-F will propose the last selection as a default, and if that happens to be cell coordinate A1, it gets you back there quickly. Recalculation will erase the last selection, however, so you would have to specify cell A1 again.

Caution: *Not all empty cells are blank cells.*

You can press Apple-B, Return to blank a cell. That produces a truly blank cell. You can press ", Space bar, Return to empty a cell, but that actually creates a label cell with one space character.

Does it make a difference? In most cases one works as well as the other. However, the AppleWorks ruler (divider) will recognize an empty label cell below the intended worksheet area, and Apple-9 can then take the cursor where you never intended it to go. An empty cell outside the worksheet area can also use additional memory.

On the other hand, you can selectively protect an empty label cell. Properly placed, it can make the ruler into a true ruler with fixed points, even as the worksheet grows. In short, the empty label cell is a small-but-useful tool.

Tip: *Insert a column whenever that is faster than changing a column's width.*

When you insert a column, it will be the same width as the column to the right of it. It is sometimes easier to insert and move columns of a desired width than to use the layout sequence.

Tip: *When constructing template sections, use catercorner layout.*

Suppose you want to make another budget template similar to the Apple IIe System budget in Figure 4.3, and you want to store it in the same file. The existing template ends in cell G14 if you include the RN notation. The next template should begin in cell H15, or any other cell below it and farther to the right.

Using this kind of catercorner layout allows you to change column widths without affecting the worksheet section above. It also allows you to copy rows to the clipboard without affecting the worksheet section to the left.

To make a quick catercorner copy of the budget template, follow these steps:

1. Insert seven columns to the left of column A.

2. Copy rows 1 through 14 to the clipboard.

3. Delete the seven empty columns you just inserted.

4. Move the cursor to row 15 and move from the clipboard.

The process varies from case to case only in the number of columns inserted and the number of rows copied. From the catercorner layout a template section can be quickly and neatly transferred almost anywhere.

Caution: *When you set value and label formats, the row and column options have no effect on subsequent entries.*

The row and column options format only those values and labels that have already been entered in the worksheet. They have no effect on future entries into cells that are currently empty.

The AppleWorks Reference Manual explains this limitation as it applies to cell protection, but not to cell formats. It was a wise design choice, because there is no need to allocate memory to a complete row or column when you need only a defined area. The following tip shows a simple way around the problem created by this design choice.

Tip: *You can use the block option to set value and label formats in blank areas.*

The block option formats values and labels that have already been entered in the worksheet, as well as future entries into cells that are currently empty. The block option works dependably even if you define one row or column as a block.

Incidentally, the block option works the same way for cell protection, although the AppleWorks Reference Manual does not point that out.

Tip: *Use Apple-W and Apple-T together to partition areas on the screen.*

Apple-W creates windows that are either side by side or on the top and bottom of the screen. Apple-W always adds a row or column border. Apple-J will jump across the border.

Apple-T fixes the location of rows above the cursor, columns to the left of the cursor, or both. Apple-T is called the title command because it is commonly used for title rows and columns, but this does not have to be the case. Apple-T can simply set off any fixed area. It never adds a row or column border, and Apple-J will not jump to the fixed part of the screen.

The two commands can complement each other. If you want to show four different areas, for example, use Apple-W to set windows side by side. Then use Apple-T to set titles first in the left window, then in the right to create a horizontal separation in addition to the vertical partition created by Apple-W. To move from the lower-right area to the lower-left area, use Apple-J to jump across the column border. To move the cursor to the upper-left or upper-right area, you must remove one of the titles. Figure 4.15 shows an example of a screen divided into four areas.

```
File: Apple.Budget            REVIEW/ADD/CHANGE            Escape: Main Menu
==========A==========B==========D========E=======F=======G========H=====
    1│Apple IIe System      1               6%
    2│                      2        Base   Sales
    3│Item                  3        Cost Shipping  Tax    Total
    4│--------------------- 4 ---------------------------------------
    5│80-column 64K card    5       149.95   3.00   0.00   152.95
    6│Two disk drives       6       359.90   8.00   0.00   367.90
    7│Control card          7        49.00   2.00   0.00    51.00
    8│Dot matrix printer    8       359.95  20.00   0.00   379.95
    9│Buffered printer card 9       159.95   0.00   9.60   169.55
   10│Monochrome monitor   10        90.00   8.00   0.00    98.00
   11│--------------------- 11 ---------------------------------------
   12│Totals               12      1168.75  41.00   9.60  1219.35
   94│--------------------- 994 --------------------------------------
   95│                     995
   96│   Row 96            996     Row 996
   97│                     997
   98│                     998
   99│                     999
---------------------------------------------------------------------
H999

Type entry or use @ commands                              @-? for Help
```

Figure 4.15: *Four display areas in one worksheet*

When you press Apple-T to remove one of the titles, the lone menu option says None. This means that if you choose that option, you will have no fixed title areas within that window. The other title partition will remain in effect until you use Apple-T with the cursor in the other window.

Caution: *Some Spreadsheet blocks are limited.*

The copy command allows you to copy whole rows, whole columns, or blocks within the document. Unlike the blocks used for printing, these blocks can include part of only one row or column. The move command within the document moves only whole rows and columns. Given these limitations, these are the guidelines to follow when you need to move a block between files:

1. Copy the block into open rows, below the last row currently being used.

2. Move or copy the isolated block to the clipboard.

3. Move or copy from the clipboard into open rows in the new document.

4. Copy within the document to maneuver the block to where you want it.

All moving and copying must be completed without recalculating. Moving or copying a row from the clipboard will push subsequent rows down. Moving a column will push subsequent columns to the right. Copying a block within a worksheet will overwrite any existing unprotected cells in its way.

LOGIC FUNCTIONS

Mathematical formulas tell the Spreadsheet what operations to perform on cell values. Logic statements define the conditions under which those operations should be performed. Logic statements add another dimension to templates. Most AppleWorks users would benefit from using logic functions more often. We have reviewed logical statements in the Data Base record-selection rules, but in the Spreadsheet they work almost perfectly. This section decribes some interesting and useful approaches. You will learn how to use flags to control formulas, how to use @COUNT in logical statements, and several other techniques that may well surprise you.

Caution: *The Spreadsheet does not let data "pop through" as VisiCalc does.*

Many spreadsheet applications involve large amounts of data and relatively simple processing. When you run out of space or memory, how do you transfer subtotals from one sheet to another? In VisiCalc DIF files the data from other worksheets can "pop through" into blank cells. The AppleWorks Spreadsheet does not let that happen. Nor does the Spreadsheet have the Visi-Calc pound function (#) to turn the results of a formula into a pure value entry, which would make it easy to transfer formula results through the clipboard.

To use a DIF file in AppleWorks, you must first create a new Spreadsheet file from that DIF file, and then move or copy the information from the new file to the intended destination. Compared to the VisiCalc method, this is a slow process. However, there are two ways around this limitation. They are presented in the two following tips.

Tip: *AppleWorks version 2.0 can transfer rows between worksheets.*

Version 2.0 can move and copy rows in a special way. If those rows include cells with formulas, you can choose to transfer either values-with-formulas or values-only from the clipboard. The Spreadsheet automatically offers you the choice. Thus, although you cannot "pound" values directly within a worksheet, you can move or copy to the clipboard and then back to the same worksheet.

There are minimal requirements for using this option. You must include at least two rows in the move or copy. At least one row must contain a formula, and the second must contain at least a value or repeating label. You can transfer the rows directly from one worksheet to another.

Suppose you have four worksheets, each representing a geographical area: East, West, North, South. You can quickly consolidate their totals in a file named Combined. To do that, follow these steps:

1. In the East worksheet, copy the repeating border and totals line to the clipboard.

2. Using Apple-Q, select the Combined worksheet.

3. Move the rows from the clipboard using values-only.

4. Repeat the process for the West, North, and South worksheets, stacking the rows neatly in the Combined worksheet.

5. Total the Combined worksheet.

This process leaves the area worksheets unchanged. If you need to repeat the same consolidation from week to week, consider using a macro to automate everything (see Chapter 7).

Tip: *Logic functions can also transfer data efficiently.*

There is another transfer technique that works equally well, and you can use it with any version of AppleWorks. Suppose you are looking at the bottom line of the East worksheet described in the previous tip. The idea is to turn values generated by formulas into pure value entries. Figure 4.16 shows an example.

```
File: East                        REVIEW/ADD/CHANGE              Escape: Main Menu
=========A===============B===============C============D========E====
171|     Item A-155        11,789.12      121,876.89
172|     Item A-156         3,897.09       33,276.54
173|------------------------------------------------------------------------
174|     Item R-001         2,897.23        4,578.14
175|     Item R-002        11,897.23       25,467.12
176|     Item R-003        12,324.78        7,658.67
177|     Item R-004         4,767.12       12,123.32
178|------------------------------------------------------------------------
179|     Item D-160        12,657.23        5,218.67
180|     Item D-161         8,789.12       12,312.98
181|     Item D-162        23,189.09       18,128.87
182|     Item D-163        12,568.63       34,886.02
183|------------------------------------------------------------------------
184|        Total       2,204,776.64     2,475,527.22              99
185|
186|        Total       2,204,776.64     2,475,527.22
187|
188|
    ------------------------------------------------------------------------
B186: (Value, Layout-C2) @IF(E184=99,B184,B186)

Type entry or use @ or  cmds                            @-? for Help
```

Figure 4.16: *Flagging a worksheet for data transfer*

The formula for cell B184 might be @SUM(B8...B183). You can enter the value 99 in E184 and add another formula in B186. Both entries are outside the printed worksheet area. The formula reads:

@IF(E184 = 99,B184,B186)

If E184 has anything other than the value 99 in it, the formula is disabled and the value itself is returned. The formula says, in effect, "If cell E184 has a value of 99 in it, use the result in B184. Otherwise, enter the value already in E186." This technique is called *flagging,* and 99 is the flag. Those who believe in Murphy's Law use more improbable flags, such as -1.618, while the fearless use 1. Note that when you put the flag in row 184, the transfer effectively removes the flag.

Tip: *Use logic functions to post accounts.*

Posting is a basic task in accounting. The task here is to enter amounts in the correct column, indicated by a code number at the top of the column. (These numbers are sometimes called object codes.) Posting is easy if you learn how to use conditional statements. Figure 4.17 shows an example. The formula for cell G4 is

@IF(E4 = 1,D4,0)

That part is easy enough. If you need more than one condition in a logic statement, read further.

AppleWorks through version 1.3 lacks the VisiCalc @AND and @OR functions, which are very useful for stating multiple conditions. However, you can create "and" conditions by nesting @IF functions properly. There are three parts to the above formula within the parentheses:

1.   The "if" condition

2.   The "then" result

```
File: Posting.Accts              REVIEW/ADD/CHANGE              Escape: Main Menu
======A=======B========C=========D=======E=======F========G========H====
  1|  Entry   Order                                  Date
  2| Number   Date      Item    Amount   Code        Paid       1        2
  3|----------------------------------------------------------------------
  4|    14    3.12      Paper    51.12     1          4.11     51.12     0.00
  5|    15    3.18     Pencils   18.96     2          4.18      0.00    18.96
  6|                    Pens     24.84     2                    0.00     0.00
  7|                             0.00                           0.00     0.00
  8|                             0.00                           0.00     0.00
  9|                             0.00                           0.00     0.00
 10|----------------------------------------------------------------------
 11|                            94.92                          51.12    18.96
 12|
 13|
 14|
 15|
 16|
 17|
 18|
   ----------------------------------------------------------------------
   G7: (Value, Layout-F2) @IF(E7=1,@IF(F7>0,D7,0),0)

   Type entry or use @ commands                              @-? for Help
```

Figure 4.17: Posting to numbered account columns

3. The "otherwise" result

If you wanted to post only the items paid, this is the formula you would use:

@IF(E4 = 1,@IF(F4>0,D4,0),0)

This means, "If E4 equals 1 and F4 is greater than 0, take the value in D4." As you can see, there are two ways to get a 0 in this formula, but only one way to get D4. The second part of the original formula has been expanded. The "or" condition is nested differently:

@IF(E4 = 1,D4,@IF(F4>0,D4,0))

This formula has two ways to get D4 and one way to get 0. The third part of the original formula has been expanded. It would be pointless to use an "or" condition in this particular application, but there are times when it can be useful. The point to remember is this: in multiple-condition statements you must define the branching very carefully.

Caution: *AppleWorks version 2.0 has a different @IF function.*

The @IF function in version 2.0 can work with two new functions: @AND and @OR. With the additional functions, you can rewrite the two posting formulas in the previous tip in forms that are easier to understand. The first uses @AND:

@IF(@AND(E4 = 1,F4 >0),D4,0)

The second uses @OR:

@IF(@OR(E4 = 1,F4 >0),D4,0)

You can use up to six test conditions following @AND or

@OR. You can also use multiple tests on one cell.

The @IF function in version 2.0 has new limitations, much like like those of Advanced VisiCalc: when you use two or more values in an equation, they must be to the left of the equal sign or within parentheses. In AppleWorks through version 1.3, the following formula works perfectly:

@IF(N5 = G4 + H4,1,0)

AppleWorks version 2.0 will evaluate that formula incorrectly unless you rewrite it as

@IF(N5 = (G4 + H4),1,0)

or

@IF(G4 + H4 = N5,1,0)

Advanced VisiCalc informs you of the error; AppleWorks version 2.0 quietly generates the wrong answer. This is a significant change that many people are likely to overlook. Check the @IF statements in any templates you have transferred to version 2.0 from an earlier version.

Tip: *Use the @LOOKUP function in place of complex logical tests.*

Suppose you use many specific object codes. You might post accounts to groups of those codes. Consider a group that includes object codes 18, 34, and 56. Figure 4.18 shows an example. Here you need a conditional formula that will mean, "If the object code is 18, 34, or 56, enter it in column G." This can be done with the @LOOKUP function. Enter the values −1, 18, 34, and 56 in cells I4. . .L4, and then again in cells I5. . .L5. We could use this formula in cell G4:

$$@IF(@LOOKUP(E4,I4. . .L4) = E4,D4,0)$$

It means, "If you look up the value of E4 in cells I4 through L4, and the value selected equals E4, enter the value of D4 in cell G4." The value 56 would retrieve a perfect match, but a value of 42 or 72 would not. The −1 value handles possible object code values of less than 18 that would otherwise generate the NA result. The formula in the lower-left corner in Figure 4.18 is used to post only the items paid.

Tip: *Keep at least two rows with zeroed entries at the bottom of an accounts sheet.*

The process described in the next paragraph will spare you the tedium of entering formulas from scratch or copying them column by column each time you need additional rows for new entries.

Keep at least two extra rows containing formulas used for cells in columns G and H and any following columns to which you must post. If the entries for cells in columns A–F are blank, the related formulas in columns G and H will generate 0.00. When you need more rows, copy the two zeroed rows to the clipboard, and then repeatedly copy from the clipboard until you have more

```
File: More.Posting              REVIEW/ADD/CHANGE              Escape: Main Menu
======A=======B=======C========D=======E=======F=========G===========H=====
   1| Entry     Order                             Date
   2| Number    Date      Item    Amount    Code   Paid    18,34,56        72
   3|------------------------------------------------------------------------
   4|    14     3.12    Paper      51.12     18    4.11      51.12        0.00
   5|    15     3.18    Pencils    18.96     72    4.18       0.00       18.96
   6|                   Pens       24.84     72               0.00        0.00
   7|                               0.00                      0.00        0.00
   8|      .                        0.00                      0.00        0.00
   9|                               0.00                      0.00        0.00
  10|------------------------------------------------------------------------
  11|                              94.92                     51.12       18.96
  12|
======I=====J=====K=====L=====M=====N====================O==================
   1|
   2| Lookup tables
   3|-----------------------------   ----------
   4|   -1    18    34    56    -1    72
   5|   -1    18    34    56    -1    72
    -------------------------------------------------------------------------
H7: (Value, Layout-F2) @IF(@LOOKUP(E7,M4...N4)=E7,@IF(F7>0,D7,0),0)

Type entry or use @ commands                                 @-? for Help
```

Figure 4.18: *Posting to account columns with several numbers*

than enough rows for the new entries. Figures 4.17 and 4.18 show extra rows with 0.00 entries for Amount (column D) and calculated values of 0.00 in columns G and H. In both figures, the formulas shown in the lower-left corner are from those extra rows.

Tip: *Use logic functions to keep running totals.*

The time record template in Figure 4.19 demonstrates another use of flagging. In this case, it matters whether the flag 99 has been removed from cell F4. It is removed only at the end of each week and reentered at the beginning of each week.

The formula for the weekly total in I8 is

$$@SUM(C8. . .H8)$$

To find the cumulative hours for the entire year ending this week, you add the week total to the cumulated total (Last Total). The formula for the cumulated new total in K8 is

$$@IF(F4 = 99,K8,I8 + J8)$$

```
    ====B========C===D===E===F===G===H====I======J=======K=========
3   Hours Allocated
4   Project B                      99 Flag
5                                            Week   Last    New
6   Person        Mon Tue Wed Thu Fri Sat    Total  Total   Total
7   ------------------------------------------------------------
8   Smith          4   3   5   2   7   0      21     141     162
9   Brown          2   2   2   4   5   2      17     129     146
10  Wright         3   4   1   2   0   2      12     114     126
11  ------------------------------------------------------------
12                 9   9   8   8  12   4      50     384     434
```

Figure 4.19: *Template using running totals*

This means, "If cell F4 equals 99, take the value already in this cell (K8); otherwise add together the values of I8 and J8." Only at the end of the week will a new total appear in column K.

Once you have the new total, how do you get it into the Last Total column? Next week is, after all, another week. The formula for the last cumulated total in J8 is

@IF(F4 = 99,K8,J8)

This means, "If cell F4 equals 99, take the value in cell K8; otherwise take the value already in this cell (J8)." When you remove 99, the value in this cell will not change. When you restore 99, the value in New Total will come in to take its place during the next recalculation.

So all week long 99 stays in cell F4, keeping columns J and K under control. Just before going home on Saturday, you blank out F4 and recalculate (with Apple-K). On Monday morning, you put 99 back in F4, recalculate, and start another week.

Spend some time with this example, because the concept is useful in many different circumstances. Many things are counted with daily, weekly, and year-to-date totals. In this sense, there is little structural difference between tracking hardware sales and wildlife migrations.

Tip: *Use logic functions and iteration to generate and store results for a range of "what-if" cases.*

Here logical flagging is used to control iteration. Some spreadsheet programs have automated iteration functions. With the

AppleWorks Spreadsheet, you can create a practical manually controlled model. This is a difficult model to describe, because it has several moving parts. You may want to read about the model once, and then enter the formulas to see it work.

Suppose you want to generate a series of annual mortgage payment calculations based on a change in one variable, the interest rate (see Figure 4.20). You start at .11 (or 11 percent), and add one percentage point with each recalculation. You also keep a record of the results at the bottom of the worksheet.

Cells F10 and F11 contain the mortgage formula in two parts (convenient for later calculation of interest and principal). The first part is contained in cell F11:

$$1 + F8 \char`^ F9$$

The second part is in cell F10:

$$+ F10*F8*F11/(F11 - 1)$$

If you use mortgage formulas, you now have one for future reference. (The two cells can equally well be considered a black box, appropriate for processing many kinds of formulas.)

```
File: Iteration              REVIEW/ADD/CHANGE              Escape: Main Menu
======A=====B=====C=======D=========E=========F=========G=========H=========I====
  1 |   Iteration
  2 | --------------------------------------------------------------------------
  3 |   99 Flag
  4 |             0 Counter Seed
  5 |             4 Counter
  6 |           .01 Variable Increment
  7 |           .11 Variable Seed
  8 |                                  .15 Interest Rate
  9 |                                   10 Years
 10 |                              1178.00 Amount  (1000s)
 11 |                            4.0455577 (1+I)^N
 12 |                               234.72 Annual Payment (1000s)
 13 |
 14 |
 15 |                                  .12   208.49 (1000s)
 16 |                                  .13   217.09
 17 |                                  .14   225.84
 18 |                                  .15   234.72
----------------------------------------------------------------------------------
F18: (Value, Layout-F2) @IF(C5=4,F8,F18)

Type entry or use @ commands                               @-? for Help
```

Figure 4.20: *Iteration model*

The formula for cell C5 is

@IF(A3 = 0,C4,C5 + 1)

This means, "If cell A3 equals 0, take the value in C4 (here a 0); otherwise add 1 to the value already in this cell (C5)." The formulas in cells F15 through G18 reference the counter in cell C4 to determine where the results of the calculations will be recorded. Looking at the most recent iteration first, the formula for cell F18 is

@IF(C5 = 4,F8,F18)

This means, "If C5 equals 4, take the value of F8; otherwise leave the value already here (in cell F18)." Cell F17 directly above has a similar formula:

@IF(C5 = 3,F8,F17)

Cell F17 was calculated on the previous iteration; from now on it will remain the same.

While the effective interest rate for each iteration goes into column F, the annual mortgage payment result goes into column G. The formula for G18 is

@IF(C5 = 4,F12,G18)

This means, "If C5 equals 4, send down the result of the calculation; otherwise leave what is already here."

The formula for cell F8 is

@IF(A3 = 0,C7,F8 + C6)

This formula determines the interest rate. When A3 equals 0, the interest rate is the seed number in C7; otherwise the number in F8 is incremented by .01 (one percentage point). You can see that this series began at .11 and has reached .15 on this iteration.

When 99 (or anything other than 0) is in A3, the iteration mechanism works each time you recalculate the worksheet. When A3 contains 0, it is time to load in the values for the next series.

Tip: *Pressing Apple-K twice initiates two recalculations.*

This is a useful option for iterative applications. For example, with a large model that uses the structural approach of the example in Figure 4.19, you can press Apple-K twice and take a longer lunch.

This technique is probably most useful for worksheets containing recursive formulas. For example, an invoice form may require a total in the upper-left corner. But if cell A4 depends on the results of a summation formula in cell E42, the total can only be known to cell A4 on the second recalculation.

Caution: *The Spreadsheet lacks some of VisiCalc's logic functions.*

VisiCalc includes the logic functions @AND, @OR, @ISNA, @ISERROR, @TRUE, and @FALSE. These serve a number of purposes. In AppleWorks version 2.0, the @AND and @OR functions allow you to clearly specify multiple conditions in logic statements. In other versions of AppleWorks it is more difficult to use multiple conditions.

The @ISNA function allows you to check for the value NA in a cell and act on the finding. The @ISERROR function allows the same options with ERROR. The AppleWorks Spreadsheet can enter NA and ERROR but cannot check for the values. Hence it cannot act on a finding.

The @TRUE and @FALSE functions are probably the least-used VisiCalc logic functions. They provide an alternate path for managing multiple conditions in logic statements.

Tip: *The @COUNT function can be used in place of the @ISNA function.*

The @NA function enters NA in an AppleWorks or VisiCalc cell, designating the cell as a value cell with no available value.

The @ISNA function allows VisiCalc users to check for NA in a cell and act upon that finding. For example, if the @ISNA formula finds NA, that cell has a special status and will not be considered to have a value of 0. AppleWorks lacks the @ISNA function, so NA in a cell simply produces the result NA in any formula that references that cell.

There is a way to make @COUNT replace the @ISNA (and @NA) function in AppleWorks. You may recall from a previous tip that the @AVG function works in two different ways, depending on the formula structure used. Although @AVG(E1. . .E3) will ignore a cell with no value entered at E3, the formula @AVG(E1 + E2 + E3) will count the cell. The two formulas therefore produce two different averages.

@COUNT also works in two different ways. Although @COUNT(E1. . .E3) will ignore a cell with no value entered at E3, the formula @COUNT(E1 + E2 + E3) will count the cell. This rule holds even for one cell: COUNT(E1. . .E1) will likewise ignore an empty value cell or any label cell. You can therefore use @COUNT to replace VisiCalc's @ISNA function.

Suppose you use @NA in VisiCalc to enter NA (not available) in cell B6 to designate no entry. You would like to use a conditional statement in cell B8 that says, "if the value NA appears in cell B6, enter 0 in B8, otherwise enter 1." In VisiCalc the formula would be written as follows:

@IF(@ISNA(B6),0,1)

This formula allows you to make a distinction between no entry and an entered value of zero.

In the AppleWorks Spreadsheet you can substitute a structurally similar formula that uses @COUNT. First enter the label

na

in B6. Use lowercase letters to remind yourself that this entry must be a label, not the result of a formula containing @NA. The formula for B8 would then be

@IF(@COUNT(B6. . .B6) = 0,0,1)

Figure 4.21 shows the application of the formula to four entries (the formula has been copied with relative references for each entry). Note that letters other than na will also serve our purposes. For example, xx is often used to denote cells reserved for input values. Figure 4.21 shows both xx and na serving the same purpose.

FINANCIAL ANALYSIS AND ROUNDING FORMULAS

Spreadsheets are probably most often used for financial analysis. The only financial function the AppleWorks Spreadsheet includes is @NPV, which means you have to write your own formulas for financial functions found in other spreadsheets, most notably a formula for internal rate of return. In this section you should pay special attention to the caution on using the @NPV function. If you are an accountant, note the problem with a commonly used rounding formula.

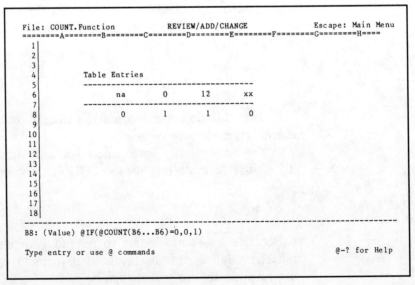

```
File: COUNT.Function           REVIEW/ADD/CHANGE           Escape: Main Menu
========A========B========C========D========E========F========G========H====
  1|
  2|
  3|
  4|       Table Entries
  5|       -------------------------------------
  6|            na       0       12      xx
  7|       -------------------------------------
  8|            0        1        1       0
  9|
 10|
 11|
 12|
 13|
 14|
 15|
 16|
 17|
 18|
------------------------------------------------------------------------------
B8: (Value) @IF(@COUNT(B6...B6)=0,0,1)

Type entry or use @ commands                          @-? for Help
```

Figure 4.21: Using @COUNT as a logic function

Caution: *The @NPV function is slightly different from the @NPV function in VisiCalc.*

Financial statements must consider the present value of earnings in future years. Money earns interest, hence an amount placed in the bank today will become a much larger sum in five years. The Spreadsheet has a net present value function; it is used in the worksheet shown in Figure 4.22.

The formula for cell F7 in this example is

@NPV(C7,B4. . .F4)

This means, "find the net present value for the series from year 1 to year 5, assuming .10 is the discount rate." The amount of $236.48 would be divided by 1.10 (1 plus the discount rate). The amount of $456.36 would be divided by $1.10 \char94 2$ (equal to 1.21), and so on. Add the adjusted amounts and you have the net present value. This is what the @NPV function does automatically.

The Spreadsheet's @NPV function always considers the cell nearest to cell A1 in a series to be year 1. In the formula

@NPV(C7,F4. . .C4)

C4 is considered year 1. In VisiCalc, however, F4 is considered year 1 in this formula. If you use such a formula in a VisiCalc application, then create a Spreadsheet directly from the VisiCalc file, the Spreadsheet gives a completely different result, according to its own rules.

```
    ===A==============B=======C=======D=======E=======F======G=========
  1
  2   Project Year:    1       2       3       4       5
  3   -----------------------------------------------------------------
  4   Earnings:      236.48  456.36  781.54  654.91  218.56
  5   -----------------------------------------------------------------
  6
  7          Discount Rate:    .10              NPV: 1762.34
```

Figure 4.22: *Calculating net present value*

The VisiCalc approach is preferable, because it allows you to quickly understand the structure of a cash flow. Some projects are back-loaded, paying relatively larger amounts in the later years. In such cases, the NPV calculated from right to left is much higher than ther NPV calculated from left to right. The extent of difference can be measured as a ratio of one NPV to the other.

Tip: *Although the Spreadsheet has no @IRR function, you can use an efficient template model for calculating internal rates of return.*

The Spreadsheet has no internal rate of return (@IRR) function, but you can construct a multiple-pass IRR template. The multiple-pass method demonstrates an interesting use of the @LOOKUP function.

Begin with ten years of net cash flow. There are generally at least half a dozen rows of revenue, depreciation, taxes, and so on above this line, but in this example the bottom line will be a given. (See Figure 4.23.)

First, you should know that this template is being calculated by rows. Most financial analysis models enter years (or months or quarters) in a row, and the row-order mode of calculation is usually the more efficient for this kind of application.

```
     ==C=====D====E====F====G====H====I====J====K====L====M====N

  5  Year    0    1    2    3    4    5    6    7    8    9   10
  6  -----------------------------------------------------------------
  7  Flow  -696  142  180  196  222  246  174  210  245  290  322
  8  -----------------------------------------------------------------
  9          1.1   1   .9   .8   .7   .6   .5   .4   .3   .2   .1
 10  P1     -545 -528 -507 -481 -447 -401 -337 -243  -97  149  601
 11          1.1   1   .9   .8   .7   .6   .5   .4   .3   .2   .1
 12
 13          .3  .29  .28  .27  .26  .25  .24  .23  .22  .21   .2
 14  P2      -97  -78  -58  -37  -15    9   34   60   88  117  149
 15          .3  .29  .28  .27  .26  .25  .24  .23  .22  .21   .2
 16  -----------------------------------------------------------------
 17  IRR    25%
```

Figure 4.23: *Internal rate of return template*

The net cash flow is given in thousands of dollars. In this case, there is a net $696,000 investment in year 0. Years 1 through 10 have positive cash flows, although negative flows in any given years can be evaluated as well. This is a reasonably good project, with an IRR of 25%. But how do you find that out? An interesting multiple-pass approach is used. Row 9 lists possible internal rates of return from 110% to 10%, in decimal form. The value in D9 is 1.1. The formula for E9 is +D9−.1 (easily copied across the row, with +D9 being relative).

Row 10 is a sequence of net present value formulas, because at some point you will cross over from a negative to positive NPV. The formula in D10 is

@NPV(D9,E7. . .N7)+D7

D7 gets added on at the end because the @NPV function never evaluates year 0. When copying this formula across the row, D9 is the only relative reference, while the other cells are absolute references requiring no change.

Row 11 is identical to row 9. We need to repeat the possible internal rates of return for the @LOOKUP formula in cell D13:

@LOOKUP(0,D10. . .N10)

In this case the formula takes the value in the cell just below L10, the last cell with a value less than or equal to 0. That means the value .3 will begin the next list of possible internal rates of return in row 13, and the series will end with .2 in column N.

The possibilities have narrowed: the IRR will certainly fall between .3 and .2 (30% and 20%). The formula for E13 is +D13−.01 (easily copied across the row, with +D13 being relative). Note that each cell is now reduced by .01 (rather than .1).

Row 14 is similar to row 10. In this case, you cross over from a negative to a positive NPV between .26 and .25, hence the IRR will be more than 25% and less than 26%. Row 15 is identical to row 13, to allow for the @LOOKUP formula in cell D17:

@LOOKUP(0,D14. . .N14)−.01

In this case the formula finds the value in the cell below H14, the last cell with a value less than or equal to 0. You can therefore safely say that the IRR is at least .26 − .01 (equal to .25). The D17 cell is in percent format, hence the resulting 25%.

For greater accuracy, you can use another pass to find another significant digit, or you can interpolate, but for most purposes the solution given is adequate.

Experienced spreadsheet users might wonder why row 9 ends with the value .1 rather than 0. Remember that the model is looking for an upper limit to begin row 13, not a lower limit. If the IRR had been negative, D17 would have shown an ERROR message. If the IRR had been greater than 110%, D17 would have shown the NA (not available) message. You can experiment with several different cash flows to test the limits of the template.

You have a few design options with this model. The NPV can run for any number of years (20 is common). The cash flow for a 20-year model would run to column X, but the multiple-pass work area would still end in column N. The only formula change would be to the NPV formula:

@NPV (D9,E7. . .N7) + D7

would become

@NPV(D9,E7. . .X7) + D7

You can also use a 20-year model for less than 20 years. Just remember to fill the unused years with zeros.

Caution: *There is a problem with the @INT function, and it affects a rounding formula used by accountants.*

When you work with dollars and cents, you enter dollars and cents, and there is no need for further rounding. When you start multiplying and dividing these entries, you can generate decimal fractions to three or more places. For example, if a simple sales tax multiplication generates such values as 18.246 and 24.784, the column total might eventually differ from conventional rounding practice by a few pennies. Whenever a value in the third decimal place is 5 or more, round up to the next penny. Figure 4.24

shows sales tax values to three decimal places in column C, manual rounding of those values in column F, and rounding with an equivalent accounting formula in column G. Notice the discrepancy between cells E12 and F12. What you see in cell E7 has been rounded to 2 digits for display purposes only, and the display is not the reality. The reality is 18.246.

Accountants need to round the reality as well. The formula in cell G7 does that during multiplication:

@INT(B7*.05*100+.5)/100

Think about how this works. The value is processed through the following sequence: 18.246, 1824.6, 1825.1, 1825 (the integer), and 18.25. The sequence for cell E9 has a different outcome: 24.784, 2478.4, 2478.9, 2478 (the integer), and 24.78.

The underlying numerical evaluation routine in AppleWorks uses binary code to represent decimal fractions. This works perfectly for fractions with denominators that are powers of two, but everything else is a very close approximation.

For most practical purposes the binary code system works well enough. In accounting, however, you must round each thousandth

```
File: Rounding                REVIEW/ADD/CHANGE              Escape: Main Menu
======A=======B========C=====D=========E===========F=========G==========H====
   1|
   2|
   3|
   4|                                Fixed with 2    Manual      Formula
   5|           Amount   5% Tax   Decimal Places  Rounding     Rounding
   6|          ---------------    ----------------------------------------
   7|           364.92  18.246            18.25     18.25        18.25
   8|           153.90   7.695             7.70      7.70         7.70
   9|           495.68  24.784            24.78     24.78        24.78
  10|           223.92  11.196            11.20     11.20        11.20
  11|          ---------------    ----------------------------------------
  12|          1238.42  61.921            61.92     61.93        61.93
  13|
  14|
  15|
  16|
  17|
  18|
          --------------------------------------------------------------------
          G7: (Value, Layout-F2) @INT(B7*.05*100+.5)/100

          Type entry or use @ commands                       @-? for Help
```

Figure 4.24: Example for the rounding formula

to the nearest hundredth. For example, .005 becomes .01, and .995 becomes an even dollar. In AppleWorks the 5 in the thousandths place can only be a very close approximation.

Consider the following discount formula in which B22 has a value of 3.99:

@INT(B22*.5*100 + .5)/100

The result is a correct 2.00, because half of 3.99 is 1.995, which should be rounded upward. Substitute 1.99 for 3.99 in the formula and the result should be 1.00, because half of 1.99 is .995, which should also be rounded upward. However, the Spreadsheet gives an incorrect result of .99. If you use such a formula in a VisiCalc application, it gives the correct 1.00 answer. If you then create a Spreadsheet directly from the VisiCalc file, the Spreadsheet still gives an incorrect .99 result.

You can handle a case of 1.99 with an unorthodox variation of the essential formula:

@INT(B22*.5*100 + .5000001)/100

The modified formula then produces the correct result of 1.00. This formula correctly handles the many cases of .5, leaving you vulnerable only to the decidedly remote case of .4999999 (which almost no one cares about anyway). In fact, for practical accounting purposes, you can use .5001 in the formula.

Caution: *In AppleWorks version 2.0, @ROUND also has rounding problems.*

You can use @ROUND in a brief formula that replaces the standard rounding formula in the previous caution. Assuming a value of 1.99 in cell B22, we have

@ROUND(B22*.5,2)

You must enter the number of decimal places, even if 0. In this case we used 2 to round the result to hundredths. Unfortunately, this formula generates the same .99 result that we saw in the previous caution.

There is yet another complication. When a decimal fraction ends in .5, the AppleWorks @ROUND function is designed to round up when the integer part of the value is odd. Thus 1.995 rounded to the nearest hundredth becomes 2, because the integer 1 is odd. It rounds down when the integer is even, so 0.995 becomes .99 (which is consistent with the unwanted results of our standard rounding formulas).

But even this convention fails: add five entries of 20.001 and round the result to two places. According to the AppleWorks convention, the sum of 100.005 should round down to 100.00, but it rounds to 100.01 instead (because accumulated binary approximation errors bring the actual value just over .05).

This odd/even rounding convention is highly unorthodox for spreadsheets—other spreadsheet programs consistently round up. If you use @ROUND in Advanced VisiCalc and then use that file to create a Spreadsheet file, rounding results will change for values with even integers.

You can make @ROUND consistently round up decimal fractions ending in 5 by using a variation of the method described in the previous caution. Simply add .0000001 to every value rounded. This is the modified formula:

@ROUND(B22 + .0000001 * .5,2)

For practical accounting purposes, you can use .0001 in the formula.

Tip: *@ROUND can also round off values to the left of the decimal point.*

AppleWorks version 2.0 rounds off from zero to seven decimal places. You enter negative values to round off up to seven places to the left of the decimal. For example, to round the value 122 in B22 to 120, use the following formula:

@ROUND(B22,-1)

In the case of 115, a slightly different odd/even rounding rule applies. Because all integers ending in 5 are odd, the next digit to the left is the one that counts. You can make @ROUND consistently round up integers ending in 5 by adding .0000001 to every formula, as shown below:

@ROUND(B22 + .0000001,-1)

OTHER FUNCTIONS

Tip: *Use the 14-place accuracy in AppleWorks to calculate logarithms.*

To find the natural logarithm for a given value, you use the smallest exponent available. In the following formula, assume that cell A5 contains the value for which we want to find the log:

((A5 ^ .00000001)-1)/.00000001

Figure 4.25 shows results for the series from 3.0 through 4.0. Notice that AppleWorks cannot display the complete decimal fraction on the formula line, but it works perfectly. (Just don't try to edit the formula later—the decimal fractions will turn to zeros.)

The antilog is simply the value of *e* taken to the log value. Assuming the log value is stored in B5, use the following formula with the value of *e* rounded to seven decimal places:

2.7182818 ^ B5

The common (base 10) log is equivalent to the natural log divided by 2.3025851 (again, a value rounded to seven decimal places). The common antilog is simply 10 taken to the common log value.

```
File: SS.LOGS                REVIEW/ADD/CHANGE              Escape: Main Menu
===========A=================B================C===========D========E========F====
  1
  2
  3           Value                 Log      Antilog
  4        -----------------------------------------------------
  5             3.0          1.0986123        3.000
  6             3.1          1.1314021        3.100
  7             3.2          1.1631508        3.200
  8             3.3          1.1939225        3.300
  9             3.4          1.2237754        3.400
 10             3.5          1.2527630        3.500
 11             3.6          1.2809339        3.600
 12             3.7          1.3083328        3.700
 13             3.8          1.3350011        3.800
 14             3.9          1.3609766        3.900
 15             4.0          1.3862944        4.000
 16        ---------------------------------------------------------
 17
 18
       ------------------------------------------------------------------------
       B5: (Value, Layout-F7) ((+A5^.0000000)-1)/.0000000

       Type entry or use @ commands                          @-? for Help
```

Figure 4.25: *Calculating Logarithms*

Tip: *Use series calculations for trigonometric functions.*

The Spreadsheet lacks trigonometric functions, but you can use a Taylor series calculation for the sine calculation. (Many applied math and engineering textbooks explain Taylor series in detail, listing many related series calculations as well.)

Suppose you need to find the sine of 72 degrees. You must first convert the degrees to radians. There are 180/pi radians in a circle. Each radian equals 57.29578 degrees. Therefore, divide 72 by 57.29578 to convert degrees to radians.

The standard sine formula uses factorials, indicated by exclamation marks. The formula follows the algebraic order of operations:

$$X - X^3/3! + X^5/5! - X^7/7! + \ldots$$

The cosine formula follows an equally obvious pattern:

$$1 - X^2/2! + X^4/4! - X^6/6! \ldots$$

Figure 4.26 shows a template for trigonometric functions. The Spreadsheet adaptation of the sine formula begins in cell B6:

$$+ B5 - (B5 \wedge 3/6) + (B5 \wedge 5/120) - (B5 \wedge 7/5040) + (B5 \wedge 9/362880)$$

The formula for B7 adds a little more accuracy:

$$- (B5 \wedge 11/39916800) + (B5 \wedge 13/6227020800)$$

The formula in C4 adds B5 and B6 together. The summation could have been handled just as well in B6. Because the Spreadsheet accepts only 69 characters in a formula entry, this series requires two cells. Note, however, that the second cell adds little to accuracy, so you can generally use a one-cell version of the formula.

The cosine formula is similar. The formula for B13 is

$$1 - (B12 \wedge 2/2) + (B12 \wedge 4/24) - (B12 \wedge 6/720) + (B12 \wedge 8/40320)$$

```
File: TRIG.Functions          REVIEW/ADD/CHANGE          Escape: Main Menu
========A========B========C========D========E========F========G========H====
  1|   ------------------------
  2|   Degrees          Sine
  3|   ------------------------
  4|      72          .9510565
  5|            1.26                  Enter degrees in A4.
  6|          .9510568                Press Apple-K to calculate
  7|         -.0000003                sine, cosine, and tangent.
  8|   ------------------------
  9|   Degrees          Cosine
 10|   ------------------------
 11|      72          .309017
 12|            1.26
 13|          .3090197
 14|         -.0000027
 15|   ------------------------
 16|   Degrees          Tangent
 17|   ------------------------
 18|      72          3.0776834
---------------------------------------------------------------------------
B6: (Value) +B5-(B5^3/6)+(B5^5/120)-(B5^7/5040)+(B5^9/362880)

Type entry or use @ commands                              @-? for Help
```

Figure 4.26: *Template for generating trigonometric functions*

The formula for B14 adds a little more accuracy:

$$-(B12\,\hat{}\,10/3628800)+(B12\,\hat{}\,12/479001600)$$

The tangent is equal to the sine divided by the cosine.

In applied math and engineering textbooks you can find additional series calculations used to generate other functions. Some series converge very slowly, or not at all beyond specified boundaries.

Tip: *For statistical functions and data analysis techniques, read VisiCalc template articles.*

The A.P.P.L.E. Co-op has published a remarkable data analysis series by Jeffrey Jacques. It appeared in 11 parts from December 1983 through May 1985. Table 4.3 lists the topics and dates.

The templates in this series were actually written for THE Spreadsheet, which is similar to VisiCalc. Many of the templates

Table 4.3: Data analysis series in *CALL-A.P.P.L.E.* journal

Issue Date	Pages	Part #	Subject
Dec 83	21–26	1	Introduction
Jan 84	37–39, 42	2	Frequency distributions
Feb 84	28–31	3	Contingency tables
Mar 84	37–39, 42–43	4	Measures of association
Apr 84	21–24	5	Linear regression
May 84	56–59	6	Chi-square
Jun 84	38–39, 42–46	7	Chi-square
Aug 84	34–38	8	F-test
Feb 85	32–38	9	Analysis of variance
Mar 85	25–29	10	Analysis of variance
May 85	21–23, 26, 28–29	11	Multiple regression

use @ROUND, which always rounds up in THE Spreadsheet. Many of the templates also use @ISNA to good advantage, but in its place you can use the @COUNT technique described in a previous tip.

Deane Arganbright has chapters on statistics and probability in *Mathematical Applications of Electronic Spreadsheets* (McGraw-Hill, 1985). The book uses VisiCalc notation, and introduces many other mathematical functions and operations.

GRAPHICS

Business graphics are generally used to make quantitative information easy to understand. If you already understand, don't bother with the graphics. If you want to present information to others, data tables may serve your purpose. In this section we will look at several options.

AppleWorks has no component data graphing program. The Spreadsheet does not have the VisiCalc graph format that uses asterisks. It also lacks the ability to leave a cell blank as one result of a conditional statement (a surprisingly important graphics option). But there are ways to produce useful graphics.

SuperCalc 3a, an advanced spreadsheet, has business graphics capabilities that should meet the needs of most AppleWorks users, and it can translate files from the Spreadsheet.

Tip: *VisiCalc has some limited graphics capabilities.*

You can use the graph format in VisiCalc, save the horizontal bar graph as a text file, and use that in the AppleWorks Word Processor. Advanced VisiCalc offers additional graphics options through its @LABEL function. If this option meets your needs, and you aleady have VisiCalc, use it. Figure 4.27 shows an example of such a transfer.

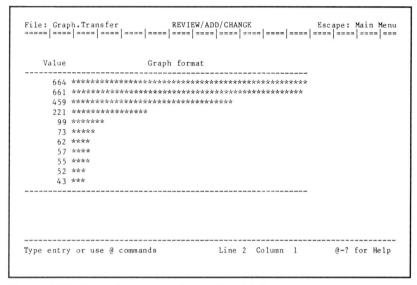

Figure 4.27: Graph format transferred from VisiCalc

Tip: *Use data tables to do the work of conventional business graphics.*

The Spreadsheet's arrange function can generate effective data tables. Edward Tufte's *The Visual Display of Quantitative Information* (Graphics Press, 1983) includes a section on the utility of such tables. The most instructive example in Tufte's book presents voting preferences in the 1980 presidential election using a super-table containing 410 percentage values neatly grouped in an ordered series of smaller data tables.

Sometimes the range and distribution of numbers make tables particularly effective. Consider the data in Figure 4.28 on the main agricultural crops in Sweden from 1977–81 (columns A–D), adapted from a Swedish Institute publication. The changes included arranging the crops in descending order of acreage, and adding a total.

The table works well because there are only 22 data points, and the three-digit numbers stand out. A hectare equals about 2.47

```
      =====A===========B========C=======D==    ===F=========G=======H====
  2         Arable Acreage  Yield in
  3         in Thousands    Metric Tons        Percent   Units  Degrees
  4   Crop       of Hectares per Hectare          100      50      360
  5   -------------------------------------    -------------------------
  6   Hay            664      4.3                 27.1    50.0     97.7
  7   Barley         661      3.4                 27.0    49.8     97.3
  8   Oats           459      3.4                 18.8    34.6     67.6
  9   Autumn wheat   221      4.5                  9.0    16.6     32.5
 10   Spring rape     99      1.7                  4.0     7.5     14.6
 11   Rye             73      3.4                  3.0     5.5     10.7
 12   Spring wheat    62      3.9                  2.5     4.7      9.1
 13   Mixed grain     57      2.9                  2.3     4.3      8.4
 14   Autumn rape     55      2.4                  2.2     4.1      8.1
 15   Sugar beet      52     44.0                  2.1     3.9      7.7
 16   Potatoes        43     28.7                  1.8     3.2      6.3
 17   -------------------------------------    -------------------------
 18   Total         2446                         100.0            360.0
```

Figure 4.28: Spreadsheet data table

acres, so the visual pattern would change if acres were the units of measurement. If yield were the significant variable under discussion, you would arrange the rows by yield, again altering the visual pattern.

Tip: *Data-table formulas can help you design graphics.*

If you need graphics only once in a great while, consider drawing them, particularly if you need large graphics. Hand-drawn graphics generally look friendlier than printed or plotted graphics.

The work area in columns F through H can provide insights to other ways of presenting the acreage information. For example, the percentage column may tell us all we additionally need to know about distribution of acreage. You can include the percentages in the data table, to the right of column B, and that may well eliminate the need for a graphic. The formula for cell F5 is

+B6/B18*F4

You can calculate bar lengths and draw a chart, but note that it will have some short bars. If the vertical axis has 50 units, the highest bar has 50, and the other bars are proportionately shorter.

The formula in cell G6 does the necessary calculations:

+ B6/@MAX(B5. . .B17)*G4

Caution: *Think twice before using pie charts.*

There are many understandable reasons for misgivings about pie charts. In perspective view, partly rotated, with irrelevant surfaces in the third dimension, they distort the basic perception of comparative surface area that you need in order to make judgments. With the crop data some of the slices would be too thin.

However, if you want to create a pie chart, the method for calculating degrees is similar to that for finding percentages. The formula for H6 is

B18/B6*H4

Flat pie charts sometimes make sense for metaphorical reasons, such as illustrating how a budget pie is being sliced. You can buy a circular (360-degree) protractor, mark off the slice angles, and draw the pie to any size you want. In any case, a pie should have no more than six slices.

When rectangular pixels on the screen make curved or angled lines, the choppy effect is called aliasing. Because printers faithfully reproduce that aliasing, hand-drawn circles always look better.

Tip: *AppleWorks can generate basic bar graphs.*

You can create a basic bar graph with columns that are three characters wide, as shown in Figure 4.29. In this example we will continue to use the crop data. Place the incremented hectare values in column A. To save space on the screen, we can remove a range of values from the vertical axis.

Place the hectare data for each crop at the bottom of each bar column. These are the controlling values. The formula for C3 is

@IF(A3< = C18,1000,-1)

This formula says "If the value in A3 is less than or equal to the value in C18 (at the bottom of the bar column), enter the value 1000; otherwise enter -1." The value 1000 will be too wide for the column and the cell will show ###. For each formula in that column, the first reference is relative to the column A value in its row, but C18 does not change.

Why do we use -1? It is easy to distinguish from the denser ###, and it will almost never occur elsewhere in the graph. That means you can print the graph to the clipboard, copy it from the clipboard to a Word Processor file, and replace all instances of -1 with two character spaces. See Chapter 5 for an explanation of the transfer method.

This template works equally well for other bar graphs. You can delete the middle row with the dotted line and enter new values on the vertical axis to create continuous increments. You can copy or delete columns to match the number of cases.

Tip: *The Spreadsheet has other graphics capabilities.*

You can create many kinds of graphics from characters, just as AppleWorks itself does. You can use underlining, minus signs, vertical bars, slashes, asterisks, and arrow characters for many practical purposes. You can create organization charts, time lines, graph paper, invoice forms, and even large letters for banners.

Whatever you attempt, use modular parts and copy them. For example, you need to create only one box to make an organization chart. Copy down a column, copy columns within the worksheet, and blank out any extra boxes. The column-insert techniques used to set catercorner templates work equally well with graphics.

Tip: *Use SuperCalc 3a if you need graphics and more spreadsheet functions.*

SuperCalc 3a includes good business graphics options, and it can translate AppleWorks files. To use SuperCalc 3a, you need an

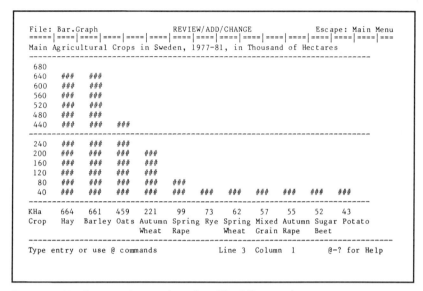

Figure 4.29: *Bar graph transferred to Word Processor*

Apple IIc, Enhanced IIe, or a standard Apple IIe upgraded with the Enhancement Kit (a set of four new chips that include a 65C02 processor).

SuperCalc 3a comes on three disks. The Tools disk contains a program to convert AppleWorks Spreadsheet files to SuperCalc files. Once the AppleWorks file is converted, you can create business graphics in several forms: bar chart, stacked bar chart, pie chart, line chart, and so on.

Caution: *SuperCalc 3a has some transfer limitations.*

The remarkably thorough SuperCalc 3a manual explicitly notes the limitations. The most important limitations include the following items that cannot be converted:

- Data in cells beyond column BK or row 254

- Formulas containing @NPV

- Formulas containing @CHOOSE

You should also know that SuperCalc 3a uses Super Data Interchange, a superset of the Data Interchange Format (DIF). We will look at this in some detail in Chapter 5.

CONVERTING VISICALC AND DIF FILES

There is nothing more satisfying than watching AppleWorks convert a classic VisiCalc template. Conversion saves considerable time in applications development, and you can find almost any kind of template imaginable. However, there are potential problems with conversion, and you should learn to work around them. The tips and cautions in this section will help you do that.

Tip: *If you plan to use VisiCalc and Advanced VisiCalc often, use the ProDOS versions.*

If you have a DOS 3.3 version of VisiCalc, review the procedures in Chapter 5 for converting to ProDOS. If you have the newer ProDOS version of VisiCalc, your files are already in the right format. In either case, you must cope with limitations to formula transfers that were not documented in the Reference Manual.

Caution: *If a VisiCalc formula contains more than 74 characters, you lose the formula during the attempted transfer.*

The formula disappears without a trace. You may not even realize that it is missing. However, if other cells depend on the results of that formula, they will have the expected reference problems.

Caution:	*The Spreadsheet lacks some of VisiCalc's functions.*

The Spreadsheet does not include trigonometric functions, logarithmic functions, and some important logic functions. Table 4.4 compares key functions in several spreadsheets. If a VisiCalc formula contains any of the functions missing from the AppleWorks Spreadsheet, you lose the entire formula. The affected cell typically contains a zero, and the cell formula will be @ERROR. If other cells depend on the results of that formula they will have the expected reference problems.

Table 4.4: Key functions affecting file translations

Function	SuperCalc 3a	VisiCalc	THE Spreadsheet	AppleWorks version 2.0
AND	X	X	X	X
ACOS	X	X		
ASIN	X	X		
ATAN	X	X		
CHOOSE		X	X	X
COL			X	
COS	X	X		
COUNT	X	X	X	X
EXP	X	X	X	
FALSE	X	X	X	
ISERROR	X	X	X	
ISNA	X	X	X	
LN	X	X	X	
LOG	X	X	X	
NOT	X	X	X	
NPV	X	X	X	
OR	X	X	X	X
PI	X	X	X	
ROUND			X	X
ROW			X	
SIN	X	X		
TAN	X	X		
TRUE	X	X	X	

Figure 4.30 shows some examples of attempted transfers for AppleWorks versions through 1.3. AppleWorks version 2.0 has the @OR function, so it returns the correct result of 2 for the second formula on the list.

Tip: *Rewrite VisiCalc formulas that cannot be transferred.*

You can cope with the 74-character limit by using additional cells to rewrite long VisiCalc formulas before transfer. You can sometimes rewrite VisiCalc formulas using only the functions available to the Spreadsheet, but that is considerably more difficult. The VisiCalc pound function (#) can change the results of "unacceptable" formulas into pure value entries. This capability allows the ProDOS version of advanced VisiCalc to complement the Spreadsheet by accepting data in DIF files, processing it with advanced functions, and returning intact worksheets. The column showing VisiCalc results in Figure 4.30 was created by copying each formula from column B and then using the pound function on the results.

```
File: VC.Transfer              REVIEW/ADD/CHANGE              Escape: Main Menu
===============A===============B=====C====D=====E========F========G====
 3|
 4| Formula                     AppleWorks VisiCalc
 5| ------------------------------------------------
 6| +A1+B1+C1                         6        6
 7| @IF(@OR(A1=1,B1=3),2,4)           0        2    Note: The following values
 8| @IF(@ISNA(D1),2,0)                0        2    are used: A1=1, B1=2, C1=3,
 9|                                                 D1=NA.
10| @SIN(.4)                          0     .3894   VisiCalc values shown were
11| @PI*A1                            0    3.1416   preserved with the pound
12| @LN(3.1)                          0    1.1314   (#) function in VisiCalc.
13| @EXP(1.131402)                    0    3.1000
14|
15| @INT(1.99/2*100+.5)/100         .99        1
16| @NPV(.12,A1...C1)            4.6226   4.6226
17| @NPV(.12,C1...A1)            4.6226   4.9847
18|
19| 79-character formula                  120016
20|
--------------------------------------------------------------
B8: (Value, Layout-A0) @ERROR

Type entry or use @ commands                               @-? for Help
```

Figure 4.30: *Examples of VisiCalc file transfer limitations*

Tip: *You can edit in up to four more characters to complete a VisiCalc formula after transfer to the Spreadsheet.*

With the Apple-U edit feature, you can add up to four more characters to a 74-character formula after transfer to the Spreadsheet. If you find a VisiCalc formula that is a close fit, abridge the formula before transfer, then add the missing section after transfer.

Tip: *Adjust the column widths in AppleWorks after transferring a VisiCalc file.*

VisiCalc has always offered the option to change column widths. Newer versions of standard VisiCalc offer the option to change one column width individually. Advanced VisiCalc has always offered this option.

Suppose you have a VisiCalc file with column A 9 characters wide, column B 4 characters wide, and column C 24 characters wide. When you create an AppleWorks Spreadsheet file from a VisiCalc file, the default column-width settings for the Spreadsheet will prevail. Column A will be just the right width, column B will be too wide for the data, and column C will show only part of the data. Use Apple-L to widen column C until all the data shows. Then make column B narrower.

Tip: *AppleWorks can convert files from spreadsheets that are similar to VisiCalc.*

THE Spreadsheet creates files that are largely interchangeable with VisiCalc. IACcalc and MagiCalc are copy-protected versions of THE Spreadsheet. They include additional functions that AppleWorks cannot convert (see Table 4.4).These spreadsheets use DOS 3.3, so read Chapter 5 for the mechanics of converting these files to ProDOS.

Caution: *VisiCalc cannot translate Spreadsheet files.*

The Spreadsheet creates binary files that VisiCalc cannot translate, but you can generate DIF files to send data to VisiCalc or other programs that use the Data Interchange Format. This presents an interesting dilemma: would you rather send DIF files out to VisiCalc for processing and receive VisiCalc files back, or would you rather send AppleWorks files to SuperCalc 3a for processing and receive DIF files back from that spreadsheet program? There is no right or wrong answer to that question, but it is a point to consider in the development of any advanced application that requires supplemental processing outside AppleWorks.

USING THE SPREADSHEET
FOR DATABASE MANAGEMENT

A surprising number of people use the Spreadsheet for database management. If you use the Spreadsheet often, it can be a matter of convenience.

Consider the significant differences between the Data Base and the Spreadsheet. The Data Base dimensions are 1,350 records by 30 categories of up to 75 characters each, expandable to more than 5,000 records. The Spreadsheet dimensions are effectively 999 records by 127 categories of up to 70 characters each. The additional categories make all the difference. With these complementing capabilities you can, in theory, manage more than 5,000 records with 127 categories. See Chapter 5 for additional information on the subject.

Tip: *Some database applications work better on the Spreadsheet.*

A database application is not necessarily a Data Base application. You may realize that when you are well into a project. There are ways to evaluate your options before you develop the application, however.

If data-related calculations are important, use the Spreadsheet. Calculations in the Data Base are limited to column totals, three row calculations, four math functions, and 30 characters per formula. You may sometimes know that there is a good chance you will exceed the calculation limits and no chance that you will exceed 999 records.

If you need to see a large array all at once, use the Spreadsheet. You can scroll across the entire worksheet to view all the categories. If you know that there is a good chance you will need more than 30 categories, use the Spreadsheet.

Tip: *Some database applications work equally well on the Spreadsheet and Data Base.*

If it makes no difference where a database goes, use the program you personally prefer. Many AppleWorks users seem to prefer the Spreadsheet to the Data Base.

Figure 4.31 shows part of a list of 109 records that includes telephone area codes, the major city within the area code, the first three ZIP code digits for the city, state names, and two-letter

```
File: Area.Code                   REVIEW/ADD/CHANGE           Escape: Main Menu
======A========B========C===D===E========F===========G=======H=======I====
   7|                 Postal Area  Key            ZIP
   8|    State  Abbreviation Code   City           Digits
   9|    ------------------------------------------------------------
  84|    North Dakota   ND   701    Bismarck       585
  85|    Ohio           OH   216    Cleveland      441
  86|    Ohio           OH   419    Toledo         436
  87|    Ohio           OH   513    Cincinnati     452
  88|    Ohio           OH   614    Columbus       432
  89|    Oklahoma       OK   405    Oklahoma City  731
  90|    Oklahoma       OK   918    Tulsa          741
  91|    Oregon         OR   503    Salem          973
  92|    Pennsylvania   PA   215    Philadelphia   191
  93|    Pennsylvania   PA   412    Pittsburgh     152
  94|    Pennsylvania   PA   717    Harrisburg     171
  95|    Pennsylvania   PA   814    Altoona        166
  96|    Rhode Island   RI   401    Providence     029
  97|    South Carolina SC   803    Columbia       292
  98|    South Dakota   SD   605    Pierre         575
     ------------------------------------------------------------
G84: (Label) 585

Type entry or use @ commands                              @-? for Help
```

Figure 4.31: Database on the Spreadsheet

state abbreviations. It can be arranged by any category, with each arrangement printed as a report. It requires no calculation, no record selections, and no labels-style report format. All five categories can be displayed at once in the Data Base multiple-record layout. This application is a good example of one that works equally well on the Data Base and Spreadsheet.

The most important limiting factors in the Spreadsheet are its lack of record-selection rules and labels-style report formats. If you print only tables-style reports of all records, use the Spreadsheet.

Tip: *Some database applications require both the Spreadsheet and the Data Base.*

The obvious candidates in this class have one or more of these characteristics:

- More than 999 records and 30 categories

- Many calculation and record-selection requirements

- Many calculation and labels-style reporting requirements

In Chapter 5 we will examine such options as downloading selected Data Base categories and records for extensive calculations on the Spreadsheet. As extended memory becomes more common, this may become the most important complement in AppleWorks.

Tip: *Sometimes numbers should be entered as labels rather than as values.*

There are many reasons to enter numbers as labels. ZIP codes must be entered as labels because Spreadsheet values do not display leading zeros, and ZIP codes begin with zero in several states. Social security numbers must be entered as labels because they contain two dashes. Apple-F will not find numbers in

Spreadsheet values, but Apple-F can find these numbers, and that makes database management possible.

In some cases there is an option. For example, let's say you want to store the names of people and their respective ages in a worksheet you are designing. The ages can be entered either as values or as labels. As labels they cannot be summed, but they can be found with Apple-F. As Spreadsheet values they can be summed but not found. The preferred form of entry depends on what you intend to do with the information. Table 4.5 compares the find command in each program.

Caution: *Alphabetical arranging follows the order of characters in the ASCII table.*

In the ASCII table, the digits 0–9 precede the letters A–Z. When you arrange rows, empty cells come first, then digits, then letters. (AppleWorks treats all letters as capitals.) Figure 4.32 shows an ASCII arrangement with selected examples. If you ever have specific questions about order, consult the ASCII table in Appendix B.

Table 4.5: Options available for find and replace functions

Option	Word Processor	Data Base	Spreadsheet
Finds text	X	X	X
Finds case-sensitive text	X		
Finds numbers	X	X	as labels only
Finds page numbers	X		
Also finds	markers		coordinates
Searches from	cursor	beginning	cursor
Replaces one instance	X		
Replaces all instances	X		
Maximum number of characters	30	30	25

```
File: ASCII.Sort              REVIEW/ADD/CHANGE              Escape: Main Menu
========A========B========C========D========E========F========G========H====
    1|
    2|
    3|            ***       42      Column C shows ASCII decimal
    4|       ----------     45      values for the beginning
    5|            .618      46      character of each label in
    6|              0       48      column B.
    7|          1,200       49
    8|           1000       49      AppleWorks treats lowercase
    9|        286-1234      50      letters as uppercase for all
   10|        323-3112      51      arranging.  The d in B12 is
   11|       =========      61      ASCII character 100, here
   12|         deRosa      100      treated as character 68.
   13|          Eaton       69
   14|           Zorn       90
   15|       [bracket]      91
   16|
   17|
   18|
----------------------------------------------------------------------------
B7: (Label, Layout-R) 1,200

Type entry or use @ commands                              @-? for Help
```

Figure 4.32: ASCII order in arranging labels

Tip: *You can arrange labels alphabetically even if they include nothing but numbers.*

ZIP codes and telephone numbers must be labels rather than values in the Spreadsheet, but you can still arrange them in ascending or descending ASCII order by arranging from A to Z.

There are some cautions that go with this. Keep the same format and numbers of digits for each entry in a given column, otherwise you can have serious problems. For example, consider the case of .618 and 0 in the same column. The decimal point comes before 0 on the ASCII table, so a label with .618 will precede 0 when AppleWorks arranges from A to Z. Likewise, 1,000 with a comma will precede 1000 because the comma precedes 0 in the ASCII table. Figure 4.32 shows some selected examples.

Although it is generally not a good idea, you can arrange worksheet rows from A to Z even if they include both labels and values. The values come first, then the labels beginning with numbers, and finally the labels beginning with letters. When you arrange from 0 to 9, the labels beginning with numbers come first, then the labels beginning with letters, and finally the values.

Tip: *The Spreadsheet can calculate dates quickly.*

Among the types of dates appropriate to AppleWorks, the month.day form of 1.01 is the most practical for worksheets. You can put the year in an adjoining column.

Date calculations use serial numbers assigned to consecutive days of the Julian calendar. If we set January 1, 1987 as day 1, January 1, 1988 would be day 366, and so on. Serial numbers are easy to transfer in DIF files.

Figure 4.33 shows the essential format. The month/day entry is in column A; the year in column B. The serial number calculation in cell B8 requires a long formula:

$$(@LOOKUP(B8,E13...G13)) + (@LOOKUP(A8,E8...P8)) + (A8-@INT(A8)*100)$$

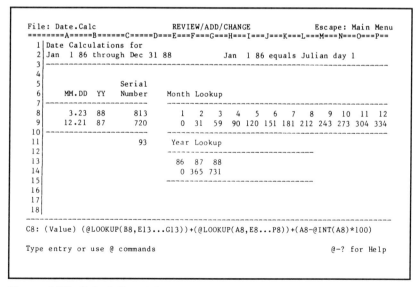

Figure 4.33: Calculating dates

The formula first looks up the year to see how many years' worth of days have passed since the base year. It then looks up the months to see how many months' worth of days to add on. Finally, it drops the integer in the month/day entry and multiplies the remaining decimal fraction by 100. That returns the days of the month.

The formula in B9 does the same thing for the date entries in row 9. The formula in C11 performs a simple subtraction. Figure 4.33 shows 93 days between dates. March 23, 1988 is the 94th day since December 21, 1987.

What about leap years, when February has 29 days? The practical solution is simple: add the extra day to the lookup entry for the leap year (here 1988). A calculated result will then be one day more than it should be only when the more recent date in the calculation falls in January or February of the leap year. That's good enough for most applications. (There is a way to avoid the problem by cycling years from March 1, but you would never be able to explain it to anyone.)

You can use this basic method in many different configurations. You can add more years to the lookup table. By changing the @LOOKUP references in the formula, you can put the lookup tables almost anywhere, preferably outside the area to be printed. For aging calculations, you can enter the present date and calculated serial number once at the top of the worksheet.

SUMMARY

This chapter has reviewed a broad range of options and problems in the Spreadsheet, and provided many tips and techniques that you can use repeatedly.

In many ways, this is the most challenging chapter in the book, because the Spreadsheet offers so many options and you need to build so many component parts. We have already done the most difficult work. Remember that you can find good models for applications development. Apple provides some useful examples on the sample files disk that comes with AppleWorks.

Practice working with the component parts from this chapter. Highlight the cautions with a yellow marker. Begin by writing small applications that use limited amounts of data. Build on them gradually and test everything thoroughly. Look for the simple, neat solutions to problems.

As you understand more about the Spreadsheet, you can develop advanced applications more efficiently. This is where most people do their best and most interesting work.

In the next chapter we will be drawing upon what we have learned in the first four chapters. We will continue to change file names, copy to the clipboard, and use AppleWorks commands for unexpected purposes. You will learn to use the clipboard, ASCII files, and DIF files to move component parts between AppleWorks programs, as well as to and from AppleWorks. In Chapter 5 some of the parts assembled here will be transferred back to the Word Processor and elsewhere.

5
Transferring Information

ppleWorks is an integrated package. The term *integration* generally means that the component programs use the same command logic, that you can transfer data easily from one program in the package to another, and that the data in one program's file can interact with the data in another program's file. AppleWorks offers reasonably complete integration in a practical and easy-to-learn form.

First, AppleWorks offers a good example of unified command logic. Most of the Apple commands have the same or similar functions in all three programs.

Second, the process of transferring information between files of the different programs is almost as easy as transferring information between files of the same program. Transfers from the Spreadsheet and Data Base to the Word Processor use the clipboard, though in a slightly different way than we have used it previously. Data transfers between the Spreadsheet and the Data Base, however, depend on the use of ASCII and DIF files.

Finally, AppleWorks version 2.0 has automated data interaction capabilities in the Mail Merge option, and the AppleWorks Mailing Program can work with earlier versions of AppleWorks. Each time you enter an AppleWorks command sequence you must enter it from the keyboard, but AppleWorks' fast highlighting capabilities make this process easier. Highlighting is used extensively in this chapter.

This chapter provides tips and techniques for transferring information between AppleWorks programs and between AppleWorks and other programs. The chapter is divided into ten sections, beginning with the most general tips. A section on transfer methods introduces techniques used throughout the chapter. The third section provides tips for transferring information between the Word Processor and the Spreadsheet. The next three sections cover transfers between the Word Processor and the Data Base, including use of the AppleWorks Mailing Program and the Mail Merge option. Following that, tips are provided for transferring data between the Data Base and the Spreadsheet.

In the eighth section, tips are provided on file conversions between ProDOS and DOS 3.3 formats. Pay special attention to the limitations of the Convert program. The following section presents some case studies in transferring information to and from AppleWorks for special purposes. The final section provides tips for using the Word Processor to write Applesoft BASIC programs, and it presents some programs you can use to complement the capabilities AppleWorks provides.

GENERAL TRANSFER TIPS

This section contains general insights about managing information transfers. The general tips below apply throughout the chapter, and they include minor cautions. Transferring information requires attention to detail; you should pay special attention to the need for documenting everything you do here.

Tip: *Learn each program thoroughly before working with two at once.*

You will usually begin with information in files from two different programs. It is important that you understand the operation of the two programs you are using, especially when you work with the Spreadsheet and Data Base. Pay attention to details about line length and data formats within a program, especially when using ASCII and DIF files.

Tip: *Print and annotate hard copies of all transfer menus.*

You will need copies of the Desktop menus for making new files from ASCII files and DIF files, along with the Spreadsheet and Data Base menus for printing to the clipboard. If you have not yet done so, print copies of all these screens using Apple-H, and hang the copies on a note board near your Apple. Pencil in notes about when you use each option.

Tip: *Document all your work.*

Write a Word Processor template that lists the basic steps for transferring data. When an application requires you to transfer information, start with the basic steps and add specific documentation for that application.

The documentation should explain why you need to transfer the information. It should note any problems encountered with various forms of the data, particularly in DIF transfers. It should include hard copies of important data screens. File the transfer documentation in the same manila folder that you use for the other documentation pertaining to that application.

Tip: *Plan your information transfers with pencil and paper.*

When two or more people use the same Apple, there will be times when one person wants to use AppleWorks and cannot. This is a good time to start working with pencil and paper. For example, you can sketch out information transfers on graph paper. Once you decide where information should be transferred, read your documentation for the generic steps in the transfers. The idea is to master the mechanics of transfer for the sake of your objectives.

TRANSFER METHODS

This section introduces the three basic transfer methods in AppleWorks—using the clipboard, using DIF files, and using ASCII files. Most transfers within AppleWorks are performed by copying, moving, or printing to the clipboard. Transfers between the Data Base and Spreadsheet normally use Data Interchange Format (DIF) files. For these transfers, it is important that you understand the implementation of DIF in AppleWorks. Transfers from the Word Processor to the Data Base normally use ASCII files. Some specialized transfers from the Spreadsheet to the Data Base and from the Data Base to the Word Processor also use ASCII files. Two kinds of ASCII files are discussed: unformatted and formatted. Formatted text files can be generated by a dummy Silentype printer, which works simply and effectively. See Chapter 6 for information on selecting the Silentype as one of your available printers. Since the Silentype merely simulates an actual printer, you don't have to own one.

Tip: *Use the clipboard whenever possible, because it is the simplest route.*

Most data transfers will use the clipboard. To transfer information between files of the same program, you move or copy lines to the clipboard. To move information from the Data Base or Spreadsheet to the Word Processor, you print to the clipboard. When you press Apple-P, the print menu will ask where you want to print the report. Choose "The clipboard (for the Word Processor)". Printing to the clipboard is functionally equivalent to copying, because the lines also remain in the source file. You can then either move or copy the information from the clipboard.

When you print to the clipboard, make certain that you have turned off the Spreadsheet or Data Base option to print a report header at the top of each page. (A header would be just one more thing to edit from your Word Processor file.)

Table 5.1 shows the most common routes for data transfer within AppleWorks. The clipboard is used for five of the eight direct transfers. The route from the Word Processor to the Spreadsheet is indirect, requiring an intermediate stop at the Data Base.

Table 5.1: Common routes for transferring data within AppleWorks

From	To Word Processor	To Data Base	To Spreadsheet
Word Processor	Copy to clipboard	Print to ASCII file	Through Data Base
Data Base	Print to clipboard	Copy to clipboard	Print to DIF file
Spreadsheet	Print to clipboard	Print to DIF file	Copy to clipboard

---

Tip: *The Data Interchange Format has been well documented.*

AppleWorks uses standard tools for data transfers, including DIF files. There are two outstanding books on the subject of DIF files: Donald Beil has written *The DIF File* (Reston, 1983), a book with good graphic illustrations and many useful case studies. Elna Tymes' *Mastering AppleWorks*, 2nd ed. (SYBEX, 1987) contains practical BASIC programs for creating and processing DIF files.

The Data Interchange Format was created by Software Arts in 1979 to transfer VisiCalc spreadsheet information to and from other programs. DIF has since become an industry standard. AppleWorks is one of many programs that can send and receive DIF files.

DIF files are text files with a defined structure. VisiCalc information can normally be defined in two dimensions—the worksheets are so many columns wide by so many rows long. The DIF technique places a header on the file to define the dimensions of the rectangle. When the file is saved it will be cataloged by ProDOS as a text file.

Tip: *Understand the AppleWorks implementation of DIF.*

The AppleWorks implementation of DIF can produce some unexpected surprises. The Spreadsheet can generate DIF files in row order or in column order, but it always receives files in column order. Row order converts existing columns into rows, in effect rotating them 90 degrees, but maintaining correct relative positions. Figure 5.1 shows the same data in column order (cells C4 to D9) and row order (cells B12 to G13). Notice how DIF transfers the repeated label in C5 to cell C12. The Data Base sends and receives DIF files in column order only.

The Spreadsheet explicitly defines values and labels, so labels in the Spreadsheet will always be treated as labels by the DIF file. The DIF file does not contain formulas, however—only the cell

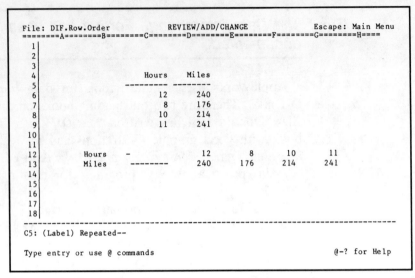

```
File: DIF.Row.Order              REVIEW/ADD/CHANGE            Escape: Main Menu
========A========B========C========D========E========F========G========H====
   1|
   2|
   3|
   4|                    Hours    Miles
   5|                    --------- ---------
   6|                      12      240
   7|                       8      176
   8|                      10      214
   9|                      11      241
  10|
  11|
  12|      Hours     -              12        8        10        11
  13|      Miles     --------      240      176       214       241
  14|
  15|
  16|
  17|
  18|
------------------------------------------------------------------------------
C5: (Label) Repeated--

Type entry or use @ commands                              @-? for Help
```

Figure 5.1: Spreadsheet file in column order and row order

values generated by the formulas. The DIF file contains neither layout nor protection attributes. Values are right justified; labels are left-justified. Figure 5.2 shows a column of entries originally made in the Spreadsheet (column B), along with the transformations those entries underwent through various transfers (columns D, F, and H). Column D contains the results of the original Spreadsheet file, copied to a DIF file and then back to a Spreadsheet file. Notice how the labels are now left-justified because of the DIF file transfer.

The Data Base does not explicitly define values and labels, so you must know the AppleWorks rules for deciding which entries become values. Column F in Figure 5.2 shows the end result of the original Spreadsheet file printed in column order to a DIF file, made into a Data Base file, printed again to a DIF file, and finally converted back into a Spreadsheet file. As expected, the labels and values lost their layout attributes. The label entry #234 became a value on the DIF trip from the Data Base, as did the 02678 ZIP code, the single dash (–), and the 042-67-4581 social security number. Only one Spreadsheet label in this group remained a label: the telephone number was protected by the parentheses around the area code. If it had been written in the

```
File: DIF.Changes                    REVIEW/ADD/CHANGE              Escape: Main Menu
========A===========B=======C=======D=======E========F========G========H=======
    1 DIF.Changes
    2
    3 SS Layout        SS Entry            SS-SS           SS-DB-SS            DB-SS
    4 --------------------------------------------------------------------------------
    5 Value              $97.40             97.4              97.4               97.4
    6
    7 Value            1,234.56           1234.56          1234.36           1234.56
    8
    9 Label               #234   #234                         234               234
   10
   11 Label              02678   02678                       2678              2678
   12
   13 Label                  -   -                              0
   14
   15 Label         042-67-4581   042-67-4581            42674581          42674581
   16
   17 Label       (401) 888-2345 (401) 888-2345    (401) 888-2345    (401) 888-2345
   18

    --------------------------------------------------------------------------------
    B5: (Value, Layout-D2) 97.4

    Type entry or use @ commands                              @-? for Help
```

Figure 5.2: *Data transferred through DIF files*

form 401-888-2345, the telephone number would have suffered the same fate as the social security number. On the other hand, a social security number in the form SS 042-67-4581 would have remained a label.

In summary, whenever you plan to transfer data back and forth between the Data Base and Spreadsheet, you should enter data in a form that will survive DIF transfers. If you have any doubts about whether data in a specific form will survive, make some test transfers with just a few records.

Caution: *Empty Data Base records are omitted from DIF files.*

In Figure 5.2, the empty cells in column B (even-numbered rows 6–16) became empty records when transferred to the Data Base file. On the return trip, these empty records were omitted from the DIF file: the empty cells you see in column F had to be reinserted before the final move into position within the worksheet.

There is one morc twist. Figure 5.2 also shows the results of a third test case. The original column B entries were entered directly into a Data Base file and printed to a DIF file. Column H contains the actual results copied from a Spreadsheet file that was made from that DIF file. Here the single dash disappeared instead of becoming a zero. Because the record contained only a single dash in the Data Base, the record was considered empty and was therefore removed on the DIF trip to the Spreadsheet. The empty cells you see in column H, including H13, were reinserted before the final move into position within the worksheet.

In summary, whenever you plan to transfer data back and forth between the Data Base and Spreadsheet, insert the characters xx or something similar in at least one category of otherwise empty records.

Tip: *ASCII files come in two basic forms.*

In AppleWorks through version 1.3, the Word Processor can create unformatted ASCII files with the print option for printing text files to disk. The information in unformatted files occupies the entire 80-character screen, with no word wrapping. Unformatted ASCII files have carriage returns where you entered them: at the ends of paragraphs and any other lines that you deliberately terminate. When you make a Word Processor file from an ASCII file, the Word Processor default margins give the text a defined shape, complete with word wrapping.

In Appleworks through version 2.0, the Data Base and Spreadsheet can also create unformatted ASCII files. These files have carriage returns where you entered them: at the end of each category or cell. Note that continuing label cells are treated as individual cells.

You can create formatted ASCII files by adding a special printer (the Silentype) to print files to disk. These files preserve the Word Processor line length by entering carriage returns at the end of each line. In the Data Base, formatted ASCII files place carriage returns at the end of each report line (not at the end of each category). In the Spreadsheet, formatted ASCII files enter carriage returns at the end of each row in the specified print block (not at the end of each cell).

As you will see, both kinds of ASCII files have advantages for specific applications.

Caution: *The Word Processor in AppleWorks version 2.0 prints formatted text files.*

In AppleWorks version 2.0, the Word Processor prints text files with carriage returns at the end of each line whenever you select the print option to print a text file to disk. This may come as a surprise to many people, if only because the version 2.0 User Manual includes a brief explanation of how to use the Silentype printer to print formatted text files from the Word Processor.

The Data Base and Spreadsheet in version 2.0 continue to print unformatted text files, but there is no longer a way to do that from the Word Processor.

Tip: *Use a dummy Silentype printer to print formatted ASCII files to disk.*

Chapter 6 describes the mechanics of adding the Silentype printer as one of your three printers, but you don't need an actual Silentype printer to print formatted ASCII files to disk. You use the Silentype simply because it is the only listed printer that recognizes none of the printer options for character enhancement. This means that no matter what character enhancements you use, the Silentype will ignore them and print a formatted ASCII file to disk, placing carriage return markers at the end of each printed line.

The actual Silentype always prints at ten characters per inch (10 CI), but the dummy can also print to disk at 12 CI and 17 CI. The actual Silentype has a 7.3-inch platen width, but the dummy can print to disk with much wider platen widths.

With carriage return markers at the end of each line, you can easily send files from the Word Processor to the Spreadsheet and to on-line information services, such as CompuServe. The carriage return markers also permit other interesting transfers that will be described later in this chapter.

To test the Silentype printing process, follow these steps:

1. Enter text in the Word Processor with the default margin settings. Figure 5.3 shows an example.

2. Print the file to disk as a formatted ASCII file using the Silentype printer.

3. Make a Word Processor file from the ASCII file created by the Silentype.

4. Reset the left margin to 0 inches.

Figure 5.4 shows the resulting text format (without showing the carriage return markers).

Notice that the Silentype incorporates margin settings: it prints the spaces required for the left margin, just as if the disk were paper. You can avoid this and still maintain the same line length by setting the left margin to 0 inches and the right margin to 2 inches *before* you print from the original Word Processor file. Figure 5.5 shows the format created by this revision (without showing carriage return markers). Silentype also prints top and bottom margins as empty lines, so set those to zero if you want continuous text.

In fact, the Silentype will accept most of the printer options used for text formatting. For example, if you want to skip lines in the Word Processor file, you can use SK. The Silentype will

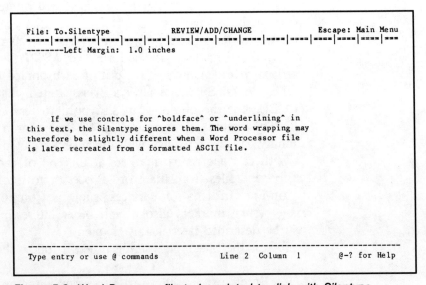

```
File: To.Silentype          REVIEW/ADD/CHANGE          Escape: Main Menu
====|====|====|====]====|====|====|====|====|====|====|====|====|====|===
--------Left Margin: 1.0 inches




        If we use controls for ^boldface^ or ^underlining^ in
this text, the Silentype ignores them. The word wrapping may
therefore be slightly different when a Word Processor file
is later recreated from a formatted ASCII file.







----------------------------------------------------------------------
Type entry or use @ commands        Line 2  Column  1      @-? for Help
```

Figure 5.3: Word Processor file to be printed to disk with Silentype

then add the specified number of blank lines to the ASCII file. In contrast, when you use the version 2.0 Word Processor print option to print a text file to disk, the program ignores SK and most other printer options.

```
File: From.Silentype            REVIEW/ADD/CHANGE            Escape: Main Menu
=====|====|====|====|====|====|====|====|====|====|====|====|====|====|===
--------Left Margin:  0.0 inches




            If we use controls for boldface or underlining in this
        text, the Silentype ignores them. The word wrapping may
        therefore be slightly different when a Word Processor file
        is later recreated from a formatted ASCII file.









        --------------------------------------------------------------------
Type entry or use @ commands              Line 2  Column  1        @-? for Help
```

Figure 5.4: *Word Processor file from formatted ASCII file*

```
File: From.Revised              REVIEW/ADD/CHANGE            Escape: Main Menu
=====|====|====|====|====|====|====|====|====|====|====|====|====|====|===
--------Left Margin:  1.0 inches



            If we use controls for boldface or underlining in this
        text, the Silentype ignores them. The word wrapping may
        therefore be slightly different when a Word Processor file
        is later recreated from a formatted ASCII file.








        --------------------------------------------------------------------
Type entry or use @ commands              Line 2  Column  1        @-? for Help
```

Figure 5.5: *Word Processor file from revised formatted ASCII file*

Tip: *It takes much longer to print an ASCII file to disk than to save an AppleWorks file, but the process is very dependable.*

It takes less than 40 seconds to save a 40K Word Processor file, but it may take two minutes to print the file to disk as an ASCII file. Be patient, because the process works dependably. In fact, if you should ever experience difficulty saving a Word Processor file to disk, you may still be able to print it to disk as an ASCII file.

WORD PROCESSOR AND SPREADSHEET

This is one of several sections on transfers for specific purposes. In AppleWorks, you will often transfer financial reports and data tables from the Spreadsheet to the Word Processor. This section provides information on "build-and-transfer" techniques for doing that. Occasionally, you will need to transfer text from the Word Processor to the Spreadsheet. Although the AppleWorks Reference Manual does not address the subject, the method is surprisingly easy.

Tip: *You can print single Spreadsheet cells to the clipboard.*

In the Spreadsheet you can move and copy complete rows to the clipboard, but not single cells. However, you can print single cells (and large blocks) to the clipboard for the Word Processor. The Word Processor is then the only place it can go, and the block can be no more than 75 characters wide. Anything beyond the 75th character is truncated.

Incidentally, try copying from the clipboard back to the Spreadsheet and read the error message. Is there a better choice of words?

Tip: *Use the Spreadsheet for lists and outlines.*

Because the Spreadsheet can print to the clipboard quickly, you can construct lists and outlines on worksheets for later transfer to the Word Processor. Lists grow unevenly: entries are added here and there. The Spreadsheet allows you to insert up to nine rows at a time. If you need to arrange the list in alphabetical order, use Apple-A. If you need to number the list, use the formula for generating row numbers. If cell A1 is 1, the formula for A2 will be $1+A1$. Copy this formula down the worksheet list as far as Apple-9 will take you. Remember that A1 is a relative reference.

Outlines are more complicated, but here again you often need to insert rows. There is really no reason to use Roman-numeral headings, capital-letter subheadings, and so forth, because indents alone will serve the same structural purpose. Make columns A, B, and C two or three character spaces wide. Begin main headings in column B, second-level headings in C, and third-level headings in D. Reserve column A as empty space between the outline and the row numbers. Figure 5.6 shows the basic outline for the beginning of this chapter.

When you finish the outline, print a block to the clipboard. The block should not include column A unless you want everything

```
File: C5.Outline              REVIEW/ADD/CHANGE              Escape: Main Menu
=====A==B==C=============D=======================E=================F======
  1 |=A==B==C=============D=======================E============
  2 |
  3 |    Chapter 5: Integration
  4 |       Overview
  5 |    General Transfer Tips
  6 |          Print and annotate hard copies
  7 |          Document all work
  8 |          Plan information transfers on paper
  9 |    Transfer Methods
 10 |          Use clipboard whenever possible
 11 |          DIF has been well documented
 12 |
 13 |
 14 |
 15 |
 16 |
 17 |
 18 |
------------------------------------------------------------------------
C6

Type entry or use @ commands                              @-? for Help
```

Figure 5.6: Outline in the Spreadsheet

indented in the Word Processor. If you do want everything indented, include column A and change its width to the number of character spaces you need. Incidentally, this is the only way to indent: printing to the clipboard ignores any margin settings.

Tip: *Use the Spreadsheet to construct and store large tables for the Word Processor.*

Use the overstrike cursor in the Word Processor to construct small tables. With simple data tables up to four columns wide and a dozen rows long, you generally get it right on the first lay-out. With larger, more complicated tables, you rarely get it right the first time. Your initial design attempt often provides a better understanding of the problem, leading to new insights and significant revisions. When you have to copy long vertical borders, calculate results, and align many columns, nothing matches the versatility of the Spreadsheet.

When you construct a table, use the PARTS template shown in Figure 4.14 for borders and other small parts. When you finish the table, print it to the clipboard. Make certain it is no longer than the Word Processor line or 75 characters. If the table is longer than the Word Processor line, the table lines will wrap. If the table is longer than 75 characters, the extra characters will be truncated when you print to the clipboard.

If you send a narrow table to the Word Processor, you can use column A to include a left margin. You can then use the overstrike cursor to enter a label from the Word Processor. Figure 5.7 shows an example.

Tip: *Expand the Spreadsheet PARTS file to serve as a note pad and calculator for the Word Processor.*

This is most useful when you have enough memory to load the AppleWorks program entirely into RAM, which allows Apple-Works to change instantly from one program to another.

```
File: Data.Table                    REVIEW/ADD/CHANGE              Escape: Main Menu
=====|====|====|====|====|====|====|====|====|====|====|====|====|====|====|===

Exhibit 28a:                   Arable Acreage   Yield in
                                in Thousands    Metric Tons
                        Crop    of Hectares     per Hectare
                       ---------------------------------------
                        Hay            664       4.3
                        Barley         661       3.4
                        Oats           459       3.4
                        Autumn wheat   221       4.5
                        Spring rape     99       1.7
                        Rye             73       3.4
                        Spring wheat    62       3.9
                        Mixed grain     57       2.9
                        Autumn rape     55       2.4
                        Sugar beet      52      44.0
                        Potatoes        43      28.7
                       ---------------------------------------
                        Total         2446


---------------------------------------------------------------------------
Type entry or use @ commands              Line 2  Column  1      @-? for Help
```

Figure 5.7: *Spreadsheet table edited on the Word Processor*

The expanded PARTS file can be divided into five sections: calculations, notes, template parts, commonly used formulas, and reference data (see Figure 5.8). The first ten rows are for calculations, the next ten for notes, the next twenty for parts, and so on. If you enter the label Last Cell in row 81, you can move the cursor to the beginning of each section by using Apple-1 through Apple-6. Using row 81 simply controls the dividing points, so change the location according to your space needs.

You can leave calculations on the worksheet for future reference. The PARTS file should be locked, so that you cannot save it by that name. However, you can still save the file as Calculator or some other appropriate name. If the calculations support a Word Processor file named Farm.Report, you can name the Spreadsheet file C.Farm.Report, using just a prefix.

Tip: *You can convert addresses in Spreadsheet rows to mailing labels in the Word Processor.*

The Spreadsheet is often used as a database manager, but it has no facility for creating labels-style report formats. Nevertheless,

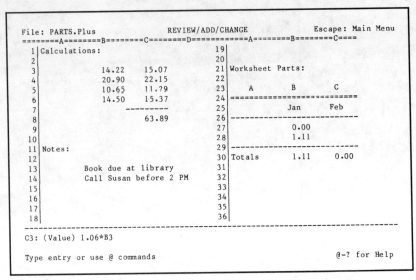

```
File: PARTS.Plus              REVIEW/ADD/CHANGE           Escape: Main Menu
========A========B========C========D===========A========B========C====
  1│Calculations:                    19
  2│                                  20
  3│           14.22    15.07         21│Worksheet Parts:
  4│           20.90    22.15         22
  5│           10.65    11.?9         23│   A        B        C
  6│           14.50    15.37         24│==========================
  7│                 ----------       25│         Jan      Feb
  8│                    63.89         26│--------------------------
  9│                                  27│         0.00
 10│                                  28│         1.11
 11│Notes:                           29│--------------------------
 12│                                  30│Totals   1.11     0.00
 13│       Book due at library        31
 14│       Call Susan before 2 PM     32
 15│                                  33
 16│                                  34
 17│                                  35
 18│                                  36
     ---------------------------------------------------------------------
C3: (Value) 1.06*B3

Type entry or use @ commands                              @-? for Help
```

Figure 5.8: *Expanded PARTS file*

you can produce mailing labels by printing an unformatted ASCII file to disk and then making a Word Processor file from the ASCII file. The worksheet cells will be transferred in stacked form, with each cell ending in a carriage return marker.

If you plan to create mailing labels this way, use one worksheet cell for each complete address line. Figure 5.9 shows the Spreadsheet format, and Figure 5.10 shows the Word Processor result. Notice that the transfer included empty worksheet column E to place empty lines between addresses in the Word Processor. The same general approach works with other kinds of lists in Spreadsheet rows.

Note that printing to the clipboard does not accomplish the same thing: it prints the formatted block as it appears on the worksheet. Printing to the disk with Silentype also prints the whole formatted block, and it includes any margins specified in the printer options.

Tip: *Use the Spreadsheet to print multicolumn text.*

There is a way to move information from the Word Processor to the Spreadsheet, and it has several practical uses. For example, if you want to create a wide stand-alone table with several columns, paragraphs of text, and calculated values, you probably want to begin by writing the text in the Word Processor.

```
File: Members                           PRINT              Escape: Review/Add/Change
=====A=========B===============C===============D=========E=======F=======
  1|
  2|
  3|
  4|
  5|
  6|   Name              Street         Town, State, ZIP       Phone
  7|   ----------------------------------------------------     --------------
  8|   Thomas Farmer     12 Field Rd.   Jefferson RI 02845     (401)  888-6674
  9|   Susan Smith       81 Main Rd.    Jefferson RI 02845     (401)  888-5784
 10|   Arnold Wright     52 Field Rd.   Jefferson RI 02845     (401)  888-4864
 11|
 12|
 13|
 14|
 15|
 16|
 17|
 18|
    ---------------------------------------------------------------------------
  E10

  Use cursor moves to highlight Block, then press Return            122K Avail.
```

Figure 5.9: *Spreadsheet file with addresses*

```
File: Members.Stack                 REVIEW/ADD/CHANGE              Escape: Main Menu
=====| ====| ====| ====| ====| ====| ====| ====| ====| ====| ====| ====| ====| ===
Thomas Farmer
12 Field Rd.
Jefferson RI 02845

Susan Smith
81 Main Rd.
Jefferson RI 02845

Arnold Wright
52 Field Rd.
Jefferson RI 02845




    ---------------------------------------------------------------------------
  Type entry or use @ commands           Line 1  Column  1        @-? for Help
```

Figure 5.10: *Word Processor file from unformatted ASCII file*

You can then transfer the text from the Word Processor to the Spreadsheet. This also allows you to move columns around to change the layout. Start by opening a Word Processor file and proceed as follows:

1. Write the text. You may prefer to do this within the default margins or within the margin settings that you normally use.

2. Set the left margin to 0 inches. Use the right margin setting to create the line length you need for one column of a multicolumn layout.

3. Insert the characters xx into each of any blank lines in your file to preserve those lines in a DIF file. Figure 5.11 shows the file just before printing.

4. Using the Silentype, print the file to disk.

Because a Spreadsheet cannot be created from an ASCII file, the formatted ASCII file must first be converted to a Data Base file. To do this, follow these steps:

5. Return to the Main Menu, and make a new Data Base file from an ASCII file. The Data Base should have only one category, and you will see only the beginning of each line. Figure 5.12 shows the Data Base file in multiple-record layout.

6. Create a tables-style report format. Accept what is shown, even though you still see only the beginning of each line.

7. Print the report to a DIF file on the disk.

Finally, the DIF file must be converted to a Spreadsheet file, as follows:

8. Return to the Main Menu and make a new Spreadsheet file from the DIF file.

9. Widen the column you will be using.

Figure 5.13 shows the completed transfer. This is the starting point for using the Spreadsheet as a layout surface for multicolumn text. It took some concentration to get here, but in Chapter 7 we will automate the transfer by writing a macro.

```
File: To.Spreadsheet              REVIEW/ADD/CHANGE           Escape: Main Menu
=====|=====|=====|=====|=====|=====|=====|=====|=====|=====|=====|=====|=====|===
--------Right Margin:  3.5 inches
--------Left Margin:   0.0 inches
     SHIP TO: Spreadsheet

     FROM: Word Processor

     If we use controls for ^boldface^ or
^underlining^ in this text, the Silentype
ignores them. The word wrapping may therefore
be slightly different when a Word Processor
file is later recreated from a formatted
ASCII file.
xx
     Empty lines will be eliminated when the
text becomes a DIF file. To preserve them,
enter xx or some symbol that is easy to find
and blank out.



------------------------------------------------------------------------
Type entry or use @ commands              Line 3  Column  1      @-? for Help
```

Figure 5.11: *Text to be printed to disk with Silentype*

```
File: Temp                        REVIEW/ADD/CHANGE           Escape: Main Menu

Selection: All records


Category 01
=================================================================================
     SHIP TO: S
-
     FROM: Word
-
     If we use
underlining in
ignores them. T
be slightly dif
file is later r
ASCII file.
xx
     Empty line
text becomes a
enter xx or som
and blank out.
------------------------------------------------------------------------
Type entry or use @ commands                                    @-? for Help
```

Figure 5.12: *Text in a one-category Data Base file*

```
File: Shipped                    REVIEW/ADD/CHANGE              Escape: Main Menu
===========================A===========================B========C========D====
    1|     SHIP TO: Spreadsheet
    2|     FROM: Word Processor
    3|     If we use controls for boldface or
    4|underlining in this text, the Silentype
    5|ignores them. The word wrapping may therefore
    6|be slightly different when a Word Processor
    7|file is later recreated from a formatted
    8|ASCII file.
    9|xx
   10|     Empty lines will be eliminated when the
   11|text becomes a DIF file. To preserve them,
   12|enter xx or some symbol that is easy to find
   13|and blank out.
   14|
   15|
   16|
   17|
   18|
---------------------------------------------------------------------------
A9: (Label) xx

Type entry or use @ commands                              @-? for Help
```

Figure 5.13: *Text in the Spreadsheet*

Tip: *Use the worksheet as a layout surface for a newsletter.*

Think of the worksheet as a large layout surface, something like a drafting table. Suppose you have transferred a column of text that is 90 rows long. Once that single column of text is on the worksheet, you can quickly copy sections of it to any place on the layout surface (leaving column space wherever any illustrations will be inserted). You can then blank the original text location whenever you want.

Given enough memory, a worksheet can hold up to 999 rows in a column and normally up to about 30 columns of 45-character lines (fewer columns if the lines are longer). Remember from Chapter 4 that rows have capacity limits, and they apply to text as well. With AppleWorks version 2.0 running on a system with at least 256K RAM, the row capacity increases five-fold.

There is a basic technique for using the worksheet as a layout surface. Recall that the copy command allows you to copy whole rows, whole columns, or blocks within the document. Unlike the blocks used for printing, these blocks can include part of only one row or column. The move command within the document moves only whole rows and columns.

To move text from rows 80–90 in column A to rows 10–20 in column B, copy within the worksheet. Follow these steps:

1. Press Apple-C to begin the sequence.

2. Press W for within.

3. Use the arrow keys to highlight the source block.

4. Press Return.

5. Move the cursor to cell B10, the first cell of the destination block.

6. Press Return again.

7. Blank cells B80 to B90 if they are no longer needed.

Notice that you did not have to specifically indicate the beginning and end of the destination block: there is only one way for a self-contained block to fall into place. A block of text has no references to any cells beyond its boundaries.

Caution: *In the Spreadsheet, proportional printing works with one column only.*

You can use proportional printing by entering the appropriate printer control codes under SC in the printer options. It will work as long as you have only one column of text in block paragraph form, within the limits described in Chapter 2.

Proportional printing will not work for multicolumn printing. If one column line fills only part of the available line space, characters in the next column to the right will shift over to fill some of that space.

Tip: *Use the Word Processor to document Spreadsheet templates, then copy the documentation to another Spreadsheet file.*

This is useful when you have not loaded the AppleWorks program entirely into RAM. The reason for putting Spreadsheet template documentation on another worksheet is simple: AppleWorks can change between Spreadsheet files faster than between files of two different programs.

When a Spreadsheet template requires considerable documentation, write the documentation on the Word Processor. Using the same procedures described in the tip on printing multicolumn text, send the text to a Spreadsheet file. Make column A narrow, and place the text in a wide column B. If the application is named BUDGET, the documentation file should be named BUDGET.DOC.

WORD PROCESSOR AND DATA BASE

The Word Processor and the Data Base can complement one another well, but few people use this capability to advantage. The AppleWorks Mailing Program and Mail Merge option provide the most useful techniques—tips on using this program are provided in the next two sections.

In AppleWorks, you will often transfer mailing lists from the Data Base to the Word Processor. This section provides some efficient techniques for doing this. You will sometimes need to transfer mailing lists from the Word Processor to the Data Base. After a few transfers you should feel confident about using ASCII files. Then you can use the same techniques with information other than mailing lists.

Tip: *Use the Word Processor to complete the editing of Data Base reports.*

You may find that you need to underline book and periodical titles in a Data Base report used for citations. In a financial report, you may want to add dollar signs or boldface print. You may want to replace selected words or numbers with new information. In short, you can use the Word Processor for what it does best.

In this kind of transfer, you print to the clipboard from a report format. Note that the report can also include category names with this method.

Tip: *You can convert Word Processor mailing lists to Data Base files.*

A list of mailing addresses in the Word Processor will normally appear as shown in Figure 5.14. By entering carriage returns after first name, town, and State, you can create the format shown in Figure 5.15, which the Data Base can then easily interpret when you make a new Data Base file from an ASCII file.

Notice the slash mark (/) in Figure 5.15. It indicates the end of a record, so you will know that it was an intentional entry, not a blank line entered by mistake. Another mark will do, provided you

```
File: Members.List                 REVIEW/ADD/CHANGE            Escape: Main Menu
=====|====|====|====|====|====|====|====|====|====|====|====|====|====|====|===
Thomas Farmer
12 Field Rd.
Jefferson RI 02845

Susan Smith
81 Main Rd.
Jefferson RI 02845

Arnold Wright
52 Field Rd.
Jefferson RI 02845




-------------------------------------------------------------------------------
Type entry or use @ commands              Line 1  Column  1          @-? for Help
```

Figure 5.14: Address list in the Word Processor

```
File: Members.List.2            REVIEW/ADD/CHANGE            Escape: Main Menu
=====|====|====|====|====|====|====|====|====|====|====|====|====|====|===
Thomas
Farmer
12 Field Rd.
Jefferson
RI
02845
/
Susan
Smith
81 Main Rd.
Jefferson
RI
02845
 /
Arnold
Wright
52 Field Rd.
Jefferson
RI
02845
-----------------------------------------------------------------------
Type entry or use @ commands            Line 1  Column  1        @-? for Help
```

Figure 5.15: Revised format of Figure 5.14 for transfer to the Data Base

use it for this purpose only. The pound sign (#) would not be a good choice, because it is commonly used in addresses with rural routes, box numbers, apartment numbers, and so on. It helps to see a consistent pattern of six lines and a standard mark. You can remove the marks quickly with Apple-' in multiple-record layout once everything has been transferred to the Data Base.

Caution: *Several things can go wrong during ASCII file conversions.*

First, count the number of categories in your mailing list. In Figure 5.15 there are seven, including the / category. Make a note of the number. If you enter the wrong number, the categories will be filled incorrectly.

Second, remember to calculate pages (with Apple-K) before printing from the line containing the cursor. If you print from the cursor line without calculating pages first, AppleWorks prior to version 2.0 may print text from the previous page. Use Apple-K first to ensure accurate printing.

Enter a pause here marker (PH) right after the mailing list, and print from the cursor line. In this case you can print to either a formatted or unformatted ASCII file. Begin printing, and when the flashing cursor reappears on the print menu, press Escape—you want to stop at the end of the mailing list rather than print to the end of the file.

Tip: *You can add mailing lists created in the Word Processor to existing Data Base files.*

This is a useful extension of the tip for converting a Word Processor mailing list to the Data Base. Once you create a new Data Base file from an ASCII file, the records can be copied to another Data Base file. As we learned in Chapter 3, the original category order of the Data Base source file must match the original category order of the destination file, at least for the categories in question. Consult Chapter 3 for the necessary details.

Tip: *The Word Processor can be used to separate combined Data Base categories.*

Suppose you have entered the town name, state postal abbreviation, and ZIP code in the same Data Base category, as in Jefferson RI 02881. In some cases that may be a wise allocation of categories and data entry time; in other cases it can be a design error, especially if you need to sort by ZIP code to take advantage of lower mailing rates.

How do you separate combined categories? You create a new database by following these steps:

1. Print copies of the single- and multiple-record layout screens and any other screens you will need to reconstruct the Data Base file.

2. Create a tables-style report format with all the categories in the order you want them.

3. Print the report to an unformatted text (ASCII) file on disk.

4. Create a Word Processor file from the ASCII file.

5. Separate the combined records by pressing the Return key each time you want a new category.

6. Print the edited text to either a formatted or unformatted ASCII file.

7. Make a new Data Base from the ASCII file.

8. Reconstruct the report formats and custom record layouts.

Notice that this procedure is similar to the one that was used in Figures 5.14 and 5.15. After you have separated combined categories once, you will learn to design record layouts with a sharp eye to future needs.

Tip: *Use the Word Processor to document Data Base templates, then copy the documentation to another Data Base file.*

This is useful when you have not loaded the AppleWorks program entirely into RAM. The reason for putting Data Base template documentation on another database is simple: AppleWorks can change between Data Base files faster than between files of two different programs.

When a Data Base template requires considerable documentation, write the documentation on the Word Processor. Using the same procedures described in the tip on printing multicolumn text, send the text to a Data Base file. Remember that the text requires only one category. Widen the first and only category in multiple-record layout. If the application is named LIST, the documentation file should be named LIST.DOC.

USING THE APPLEWORKS MAILING PROGRAM

The inexpensive AppleWorks Mailing Program (AMP) from International Apple Core generates form letters. Although it has been marketed for that purpose, it has at least as much value for extended Data Base reporting. If you use AppleWorks version 1.3 or earlier, AMP can substitute for the Mail Merge option in version 2.0.

In addition, AMP provides a model for writing Applesoft BASIC programs that are compatible with AppleWorks. The disk contains two versions of the program. The first version includes complete remark (REM) statements. The second, which you normally use, does not.

Tip: *Edit the AMP instruction files before you print them.*

The AppleWorks Mailing Program comes on a single disk in a plastic mailer. To get a copy of the instructions, you simply print the three AppleWorks Word Processor files on the disk. Use Apple-Z to review the formatting instructions and delete those that are inappropriate for your needs. For example, the CI settings are variously 4, 10, 12, and 15 (pointless if you have a daisy-wheel printer or prefer simplicity).

Tip: *AMP is easy to modify.*

The instructions provided with the program explain how to change one line in the program to adapt AMP for printer interface cards other than the Apple parallel card. Although the program was written in Applesoft BASIC, it runs fast enough for most mail-merge purposes. Because the disk includes a version of the program with complete remarks, you can make your own modifications. Anyone interested in using AppleWorks screen design conventions in Applesoft BASIC programs will want to study this listing.

Caution: *To use AMP, you must add another printer for printing to disk.*

AMP requires Word Processor files that have been printed to disk using your standard printer, normally assigned to slot 1. The process is similar to printing formatted ASCII files to disk, except that AMP permits the file to include any AppleWorks character enhancements and other printer options you have used. If you don't use (or want) character enhancements, the Silentype printer described in a previous tip will do the printing just as well.

The only way you can get a printer to print to disk is to specify that this is how the printer will be accessed. Surprisingly, there is no way to change the printer access option, as you can with other options. Therefore, you must add another printer to AppleWorks.

If your standard printer is listed, add the same listed printer again, with one difference: on the menu for adding a printer, specify that the printer will be accessed by printing onto disk.

If your standard printer is a custom printer, you must make another copy of the AppleWorks Program disk, delete the custom printer, and then add a custom printer dedicated to printing to disk. On the menu for adding a printer, specify that the printer will be accessed by printing onto disk.

Tip: *AMP uses standard Data Base report formats.*

Some mail-merge programs require report formats with special characters (such as dollar signs) beginning each report category. AMP lets you use your existing report formats to print unformatted text (ASCII) files to disk.

Form letters for AMP must be written with data-merge indicators, such as [MERGE1], to identify places where AMP must enter information. The mailing label report format in Chapter 3 can be used to supply the form letter heading shown in Figure 5.16. Notice that the letter uses a first-name greeting. The asterisk in [MERGE3*] means that the line space will be omitted if that category has no information. AMP sets up each letter individually, typically every six to ten seconds if you use a printer buffer. Otherwise it waits for the printer.

If you need the telephone number category in the letter, you can add that category at the bottom of the mailing labels report. Use Apple-L from within the report format. Any or all of the database categories can be added this way, and AMP will count them from left to right, top to bottom in the report format.

AMP's simple approach has another advantage: it can also use Spreadsheet data printed to an unformatted ASCII file. Each row is treated as a record, each column as a category. To create special reports, you can move columns, arrange records, and define the worksheet block to be printed.

```
File: AMP.Merge              REVIEW/ADD/CHANGE           Escape: Main Menu
=====|====|====|====|====|====|====|====|====|====|====|====|====|====|===

December 8, 1987

[MERGE1] [MERGE2]
[MERGE3*]
[MERGE4*]
[MERGE5] [MERGE6] [MERGE7]

Dear [MERGE1]:

      The letter area can also include merged information from
each Data Base record.  For example, if you want the reader to
verify information about record entries, you can list the
remaining categories in the following form:

Telephone: [MERGE 8]


------------------------------------------------------------------------
Type entry or use @ commands          Line 4  Column  1      @-? for Help
```

Figure 5.16: *Form letter for AppleWorks Mailing Program*

Tip: *Use AMP for extended Data Base reporting.*

There will be times when the reports you need will require more than the Data Base can provide. For example, you may want to write narrative reports with information from records inserted within sentences, or in tables between paragraphs.

Although AMP is called a mailing program, it can manage all 30 fields for this kind of extended Data Base reporting. The housing example used in Chapter 3 (Figure 3.20) might well use AMP to advantage. Suppose you want a standard narrative report on each of several properties. This report resembles a common form letter, except that the merges occur within the report text rather than in the heading. Each report is intended for someone interested in acquiring the property.

You could begin with a paragraph that provides a context for the specific information. The second paragraph might include the following:

The property at [MERGE1] [MERGE2] includes a [MERGE3]-family house. The recorded back taxes amount to [MERGE4], and the recorded lien on the property is [MERGE5].

Caution: *You must design applications around AMP's specific limitations.*

The limitations are well documented. AMP can handle from one to six merges per line, but it cannot make adjustments for lines that are shortened or extended by merged information. It will not print category names when they are specified in the report format. Sometimes you will have to plan carefully to allow for these limitations.

USING THE MAIL MERGE OPTION

Tip: *The version 2.0 Mail Merge option is convenient.*

The new built-in Mail Merge option is well designed for the kind of merging most people need. Everything happens within AppleWorks, so you will probably use the option even for limited tasks.

If you have not already used Mail Merge, this is how you provide the data from the Data Base for the Word Processor:

1. Go to the Data Base file that has the information you need.

2. Create a simple tables-style report format. It can include all the categories.

3. Select the records to be printed.

4. Print to the second clipboard option, which is reserved for Mail Merge.

5. Open a Word Processor file and begin writing the text.

6. When you need to specify a merge, press Apple-O and enter MM.

7. When you see the Data Base categories listed, select one to merge.

8. Specify whether you want the line space removed if there is no data in a record.

9. Continue writing and merging until the text is complete.

10. Print the text, specifying that you want to merge Data Base items with the document.

Figure 5.17 shows a form letter that was created with Mail Merge.

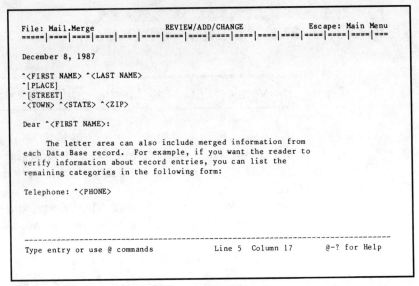

```
File: Mail.Merge              REVIEW/ADD/CHANGE          Escape: Main Menu
=====|=====|=====|=====|=====|=====|=====|=====|=====|=====|=====|=====|=====|=====|=====|===

December 8, 1987

^<FIRST NAME> ^<LAST NAME>
^[PLACE]
^[STREET]
^<TOWN> ^<STATE> ^<ZIP>

Dear ^<FIRST NAME>:

     The letter area can also include merged information from
each Data Base record.  For example, if you want the reader to
verify information about record entries, you can list the
remaining categories in the following form:

Telephone: ^<PHONE>



-----------------------------------------------------------------------------
Type entry or use @ commands         Line 5  Column 17      @-? for Help
```

Figure 5.17: *Form letter using Mail Merge*

The Mail Merge option uses angled brackets (< >) around merged category names, and a caret before each set of brackets to indicate that the brackets themselves should not be printed. Standard brackets ([ ]) mean that there will be no line space if a record has no data in that category. For purposes of documentation, you have the option to print the Word Processor document without merging anything.

Tip: *Use a simple report format for the Mail Merge clipboard.*

To print Data Base information to the Mail Merge clipboard, you must use a tables-style report. However, this is not a tables-style report in the normal sense. There is no need to set printer options, category display widths, or even category order. When you create a tables report format from scratch, all the categories are there, and that is all you need.

Caution: *The clipboard may not be able to hold all the records you want to merge.*

The clipboard normally accepts 250 lines; from the Data Base it accepts 253 records. For the sake of efficiency in smaller tasks, using the clipboard is a good design choice. Even so, some people will need more capacity. With the utility software included with their memory boards, Applied Engineering can take the Data Base clipboard to 2042 lines. In either case, you can use the clipboard again for additional sets of records.

Tip: *Load all merges into the Word Processor at the same time.*

If you know the order that merged categories will appear in the document, select all of them in that order when you first use the Printer Options menu.

Enter text with the cursor in insert mode—you would normally do that anyway—and the merge entries get pushed ahead. When you need the next merge entry, it's right there. You can add or delete spaces wherever necessary. Mail Merge always leaves one space after each entry, so a series of successive merges will be correctly spaced.

Tip: *Use the Mail Merge option for extended Data Base reporting.*

There will be times when the reports you need will require more than the Data Base can provide. For example, you may want to write narrative reports with information from records inserted within sentences, or in tables between paragraphs.

The technique here is essentially the same as with AMP, but there are minor changes. You can report Spreadsheet data only if you first send it to the Data Base. If you use the clipboard more than once to transfer records from a Data Base file, keep track of the break points so that you neither duplicate nor omit records.

DATA BASE AND SPREADSHEET

It is sometimes difficult to know whether an application belongs in the Data Base or in the Spreadsheet. Large advanced applications often begin in the Data Base and then transfer data to the Spreadsheet for specialized calculations.

In general, you should use the program you know best. Some people prefer to use the Spreadsheet because they can move the cursor to any piece of information quickly. Others prefer the Data Base because of the single-record entry screen. Sometimes you simply understand one program better than the other and can make it do more.

Tip: *Develop your own rules of thumb about when to transfer information.*

Recall the Apple IIe system budget we developed in Chapter 4 (Figure 4.3). Suppose you want to list everything related to the system: current prices, suppliers, and so on. You would soon have a large block of information. Should that information be a database? In this case, my advice would be to keep it as a worksheet unless there happened to be some need for a labels-style report format. The Spreadsheet can otherwise provide enough functions for this purpose, including arranging (sorting) by rows and finding text entries.

Adding other information, such as supplier addresses, might tip the balance toward the Data Base. Or suppose you want to use a complicated record-selection rule. With the worksheet on the screen, you can make a Data Base file as follows:

1. Press Apple-P and then B to print a block of information.

2. Use the arrow keys to highlight the block and press Return.

3. Select the option to print to a DIF file and press Return.

4. Press 2 for the column option. Enter a brief path name and press Return.

5. When the file has been saved, return to the Main Menu.

6. Create a Data Base file from the DIF file. Enter the path name and press Return.

7. Enter a name for the Data Base file and press Return.

8. Name each of the numbered categories you intend to use.

Tip: *Use the Spreadsheet to validate entries for the Data Base.*

As you learned in Chapter 3, the Data Base has almost no capabilities for validating data. As you learned in Chapter 4, Spreadsheet formulas can do a good job trapping potential errors.

Recall Figure 4.11 in Chapter 4, where we tested ages within limits. When the data entry exceeded the limits, the next column showed ERROR instead of the entry. After making corrections, you can delete the test column, leaving just the data.

Remember that the Spreadsheet makes a distinction between labels and values, so DIF file transfers take data from the Spreadsheet to the Data Base more predictably than those going the other way. Also remember that you can make the transfer with an unformatted ASCII file.

Tip: *Use the Spreadsheet to analyze quantitative information from the Data Base.*

Report formats and record-selection rules permit transfer of data subsets from the Data Base to the Spreadsheet for such things as statistical analysis and applications requiring many calculations, which only the Spreadsheet can handle.

In some cases it is better to analyze quantitative data in the Spreadsheet first, and then send only the results to the Data Base. In other cases the Data Base may have just enough power to complete a task. Note, however, the DIF files cannot transfer calculated categories, so you should not begin calculations in the Data Base and expect to complete them in the Spreadsheet.

For those who must transfer calculated categories, there is a way. Send them from the Data Base to the clipboard for the Word Processor. From the Word Processor they can be returned to the Data Base as real categories, and from there a DIF file can take them to the Spreadsheet.

Tip: *Use the Spreadsheet and Data Base capacity limits to complement one another.*

If you need to manage a database with fewer than 999 records but more than 30 categories, the Spreadsheet is a logical choice. For example, suppose you have 100 records with 50 categories. Even though each record may have fewer than 1,024 characters, a single Data Base file cannot accommodate them.

If you need to manage a database with fewer than 999 records but more than 1,024 characters, the Spreadsheet is again a logical choice. For example, suppose you have 100 records with up to 1,500 characters each. Even though the file may have only 30 categories, a single Data Base file cannot accommodate them.

If you need to manage a database with more than 999 records, the Data Base is the logical choice. But what happens if you have more than 30 categories or 1,024 characters? There are three choices: parallel Data Base files, parallel Spreadsheet files, or both.

A description of the third option effectively describes the first two as well. Suppose you have a file of 1,200 records with 36 categories. Ten categories are descriptive text, such as name, address, and so on. The other 26 categories are values, many of which will be used in calculations. Follow these steps to set up parallel files:

1. Make a Data Base file from a template (such as the LIST template described in Chapter 3).

2. Give each record a unique identification number, preferably values from 1 to 1,200.

3. Enter data into the first ten information categories.

4. Make another parallel Data Base file and assign corresponding identification numbers to the records.

5. Enter data into the remaining 26 information categories.

6. From the second Data Base, print 600 records to one DIF file and 600 records to another.

7. Make two new Spreadsheet files from the DIF files.

Now there are two Data Base files and two Spreadsheet files. The categories most often used with record-selection rules should be in the first Data Base file. The categories most often calculated should be in the Spreadsheet files. The Data Base files are the master files. Any revised information goes into the master file, from which new DIF and Spreadsheet files are generated.

Parallel files can remain forever separated, linked only by shared identification numbers for respective records. Parallel files can also trade categories if necessary. For example, you can print one Data Base category to a column-order DIF file as follows:

1. Arrange all files by ascending identification numbers.

2. Create a tables-style report format for just the selected category.

3. Select the first 250 identification numbers and print to a DIF file.

4. Create a new Spreadsheet file from the DIF file.

5. Copy the 250 rows to empty rows (such as 700 through 950) in the destination Spreadsheet file.

6. Copy the blocks within the destination file, then delete rows 700 through 950.

7. Repeat the process until the category entries have been added to all the records in the Spreadsheet files.

After following this complicated process, you can understand the importance of designing applications to avoid unnecessary transfers.

Tip: *When you move data back and forth between the Data Base and Spreadsheet, use the column-order option.*

The DIF column-order option means that a Spreadsheet column will become a Data Base category. Column-order is the only option available in the Data Base. In the Spreadsheet you must be careful to specifically select column order, because row order is the default selection.

Caution: *In transfers from the Spreadsheet to the Data Base, the order of the origin and destination files must match.*

When you use DIF files to transfer data from the Spreadsheet to the Data Base, the Spreadsheet column order must match the Data Base original category order.

These DIF data transfers are never direct: going from the Spreadsheet you must make a new Data Base file from the DIF file, copy records to the clipboard, and then move the records from the clipboard to the destination file. In this kind of transfer it is best to first move columns on the source worksheet to match the Data Base original category order.

When you use DIF files to transfer data from the Data Base to the Spreadsheet, the Data Base report format order need not match the Spreadsheet column order. Going from the Data Base you must make a new Spreadsheet file from the DIF file, copy records to the clipboard, and then move the records from the clipboard to the destination file. Before copying to the clipboard, you can move columns to match the column order of the destination worksheet.

Tip: *You can also use ASCII files to transfer data from the Spreadsheet to the Data Base.*

Using ASCII files has an advantage: it maintains the number of decimal places specified for value cells on the origin worksheet.

Transfer data from the Spreadsheet to the Data Base by printing a selected block of cells to an unformatted text (ASCII) file on disk. Create a new Data Base from the ASCII file, copy the records to the clipboard, and then move the records from the clipboard to the destination file. In this kind of transfer it is best to first move columns on the origin worksheet to match the Data Base original category order.

You cannot transfer data by ASCII file from the Data Base to the Spreadsheet, because the Spreadsheet cannot accept these files.

Caution: *Earlier versions of AppleWorks have trouble recognizing DIF files.*

When you attempt to create a Spreadsheet file from a DIF file, AppleWorks version 1.1 may respond incorrectly, repeatedly asking for the path name of the DIF file. If you first have the Data Base find the DIF file, the Spreadsheet program will respond correctly. Here's how to make the Data Base find the file without actually creating a Data Base:

1. Return to the Main Menu, and choose option 1 to add files to the Desktop.

2. Select the option to create a Data Base file from a DIF file.

3. Specify from 1 to 30 categories for the file.

4. Specify the path name of the DIF file.

5. When asked to enter a name for the Data Base file, escape to the Main Menu.

6.   Begin the process again, this time to make a new Spread-sheet file from a DIF file.

If you repeatedly transfer data between the Data Base and Spreadsheet, you should use a later version of AppleWorks.

Tip: *Data takes up a little less memory in the Data Base.*

There is a small advantage to using the Data Base over the Spreadsheet: the same data uses less memory space. For example, an 80K database in the Spreadsheet may require only 70K in the Data Base. For applications near the limits of your Apple system's memory, this may be a significant factor when you decide which program to use. The Data Base can also arrange more records—1,350 (and potentially more than 6,000) compared with a maximum of 999 for the Spreadsheet. In short, although database applications tend to be large, the Data Base uses memory very efficiently.

PRODOS AND DOS 3.3

AppleWorks teaches you about some of the things you can do with ASCII files, and the lesson continues beyond AppleWorks to other software. In transferring files, you will sometimes need to convert from DOS 3.3 format to ProDOS format. It takes enough time to make you think twice about commuting along that route every day.

If you have an Apple IIe, you probably have the ProDOS User's Disk Utilities. If you have an Apple IIc, you have a disk called the ProDOS System Utilities. These are the disks you need for transferring files between ProDOS and DOS 3.3.

Tip: *Learn the differences between DOS 3.3 and ProDOS files.*

DOS 3.3 and ProDOS files differ in many ways, but one difference is particularly important: a disk formatted for ProDOS has a volume name preceded by a slash mark (/). The volume name is separated from any file name by another slash. The name can be brief, such as the /P used throughout this book. ProDOS volume names can be no more than 15 characters long. The same rule applies to ProDOS file names. Volume names commonly precede file names, as in /P/Filename. Together they are called the path name.

Tip: *Think of a ProDOS volume as a disk.*

For most AppleWorks purposes, a ProDOS volume is the same as a standard 136K floppy disk. Although a ProDOS volume can have subdirectories, there is really no need to use them with a 5¼-inch system. An AppleWorks data disk seldom has more than about 20 AppleWorks files, so there is rarely any confusion. If you have a hard disk or a high-capacity floppy disk, however, subdirectories provide branching paths for finding your way through many files.

Caution: *The ProDOS utilities have limitations when converting ASCII files from ProDOS to DOS 3.3.*

The CONVERT program correctly converts text files up to about 30K. The equivalent Apple IIc program for changing disk formats is even more limited—to about 11K. The bottom line is that the path from ProDOS to DOS 3.3 is far more difficult than the route the other way. Appendix C includes information on a useful ProDOS text-file splitter that enables you to limit the size of your files so the CONVERT program can handle them. Central Point's Copy II Plus utility disk (version 6.0 or higher) can convert large files correctly.

The CONVERT program that comes with ProDOS 1.1.1 shows mouse characters instead of file names on the Apple IIc and Enhanced Apple IIe. You can patch the program to correct the display. Use a copy of your original ProDOS Filer disk. Unlock the CONVERT file and then go to Applesoft BASIC. When the right bracket character (]) appears, enter the following:

```
BLOAD CONVERT,TSYS,A$2000
POKE 26523,14 : POKE 26711,63
BSAVE CONVERT,TSYS,A$2000,L20481
```

Test the patched CONVERT before you really need it again.

TO AND FROM APPLEWORKS

In most cases, AppleWorks will meet all your needs. But occasionally you will need to find a program that does something AppleWorks cannot do. Consider overall efficiency when deciding which program to use for a given application. In engineering or navigation, where trigonometrical functions are used extensively, you may be better off using SuperCalc 3a or advanced VisiCalc rather than the AppleWorks Spreadsheet. You can always transfer information back to AppleWorks later. In this section we will look at some representative applications.

File transfers between ProDOS programs can be efficient enough for consistent use. File transfers between DOS 3.3 and ProDOS programs are more likely to be once-and-for-all transfers to the latter.

Tip: *Many word processors create ASCII files that you can easily convert to the AppleWorks Word Processor.*

Many AppleWorks users have some DOS 3.3 word processor files that they want to convert to ProDOS. Load the file in the original word processor, and have it save or print an ASCII file to disk if it can. From the ASCII file, the conversion proceeds as follows:

1. Insert the ProDOS utilities disk in drive 1 and turn on your Apple.

2. Press C to select the file-conversion utility. On the Convert menu, note that the arrow path is going the way you want—from DOS 3.3 in drive 2 to ProDOS in drive 1.

3. Insert the DOS 3.3 disk in drive 2.

4. Insert a formatted ProDOS disk in drive 1 and press P to set the ProDOS prefix (the name of the disk).

5. Press S to select the "slot and number" option, then press Return three times. The disk (ProDOS volume) will enter its own name.

6. Press T to transfer the file from DOS 3.3 to ProDOS.

When the disk drive stops running, you will have a ProDOS file.

Now you can load AppleWorks and go to the Main Menu. Then proceed as follows:

7. Begin a Word Processor file from an ASCII file.

8. Enter the path name for the ASCII file and press Return.

9. Enter a Word Processor file name and press Return.

When the disk drive stops running, you will have a usable Apple-Works Word Processor file. At worst, it will have carriage return markers at the end of each line, and you will have to remove these markers if you want to use different margins.

Tip: *If a database manager can generate ASCII files, use that route to the AppleWorks Data Base.*

General Manager is a respected DOS 3.3 database manager capable of managing more than 60,000 records per file on a hard disk. It can generate reports that serve as address files for mail merging in other word processors, and those reports can include every field (category) in the record. General Manager accepts up to 99 fields on a parent screen, but the AppleWorks Data Base handles only 30, so there are obvious transfer limitations.

Suppose you have selected entries in 29 categories in a General Manager database that you want to transfer to an AppleWorks Data Base. Generate an address file in General Manager. Convert that file to an ASCII file, and create a Data Base file from that ASCII file. Every record ends with a line containing only a slash (/) (used to signal a word processor). If you have 29 categories, you must count the line with the slash as category 30. This keeps the data transfer working correctly. Once you have named the new Data Base file and entered the appropriate category names, the transfer is complete.

Caution: *If you use DIF files to transfer information to the Data Base, make certain that the file is in column order.*

The Data Base will accept row-order DIF files, but the results may not be what you had in mind. For example, categories will then become records and vice versa. When in doubt, load DIF files first into the Spreadsheet, which can then generate a DIF file in the same order or rotated 90 degrees.

Tip: *Use specialized ProDOS database managers to complement AppleWorks.*

Though AppleWorks has a good multipurpose database manager, the Bookends Extended program from Sensible Software is a good specialized database manager that can be used to complement the AppleWorks Word Processor. Bookends Extended has special capabilities for managing citations, including the ability to store and select two forms of journal titles (which are often abbreviated in published articles). It has special capabilities for bibliographical information. For example, it can format reports for footnotes or bibliographies in any one of several styles, inserting the correct punctuation for each. As you may recall, the citation database in Chapter 3 was punctuated for one form of bibliography only.

Suppose you want to transfer a complete set of footnotes from Bookends to the AppleWorks Word Processor for use in a research paper. Bookends uses the ProDOS operating system, so you simply print a text (ASCII) file to disk and create a new Word Processor file from that file. Note, however, that with an ASCII file you must add your own underlining in the Word Processor.

Tip: *Use specialized ProDOS spreadsheets to complement AppleWorks.*

SuperCalc 3a and the ProDOS version of Advanced VisiCalc have many functions that the AppleWorks Spreadsheet lacks. These include date-calculation functions used in accounting, trigonometric functions for engineering, and the option to retrieve text as the result of a formula.

AppleWorks will translate VisiCalc files quickly, within the limitations documented in Chapter 4. SuperCalc 3a will translate AppleWorks Spreadsheet files, albeit slowly, within the limitations documented in the remarkably thorough SuperCalc manual. Both SuperCalc 3a and advanced VisiCalc accept and receive DIF files created by AppleWorks.

Tip: *You can transfer information from files of many other programs.*

Many other programs, including most spreadsheets, can print text files to disk. You can convert these ASCII files from DOS 3.3 to ProDOS, and then begin a Word Processor file from the ASCII file. Once you have the data in AppleWorks, you can think about how it must be edited for transfers to the Data Base or Spreadsheet. The carriage return is a surprisingly useful tool in such cases.

One classic transfer example involves the graph format in standard VisiCalc. In that program you can specify the display of a number as an equivalent number of asterisks. With formulas, you can equate any number of units with each asterisk. However, there is no way to transfer the graph format to the AppleWorks Spreadsheet, which lacks that function. The pound function (#) in VisiCalc will preserve only the value, not the asterisks.

VisiCalc can print a text file to disk, and that allows you to transfer that graph format to the Word Processor. Chapter 4 includes an example (Figure 4.26). Notice that this is a formatted text file.

Caution: *The Word Processor default margins can make transferred spreadsheet print files look scrambled.*

The Word Processor one-inch left and right margins, along with the default setting for 10 characters per inch, limit intact transfers to 60-character lines rather than 77-character lines. That may make some spreadsheet print files look scrambled. Once the information is in the Word Processor file, resetting the margins to 0 inches should make most print files readable.

APPLESOFT BASIC PROGRAMS

Many AppleWorks users want to write Applesoft BASIC programs or modify existing programs for specific purposes. You may even want to develop programs that add capabilities to AppleWorks by processing ASCII or DIF files. The Word Processor can be a big help here. The program example in this section generates natural logarithms. You will remember, of course, that neither the Data Base nor Spreadsheet have built-in logarithmic functions. You can compare the results here with the Spreadsheet formula in Chapter 4.

Tip: *The Word Processor is a useful Applesoft BASIC editor.*

AppleWorks can help you write and edit programs in Applesoft BASIC. The Word Processor provides many advantages for developing programs, such as the find and replace commands.

When working in BASIC, use uppercase letters, even where you might not in AppleWorks. The Apple IIc, enhanced IIe, and IIGS can interpret lowercase letters in Applesoft BASIC programs, but earlier Apple IIs cannot.

To work with the following example, begin a Word Processor file from scratch, depress the Caps Lock key, and begin entering the numbered lines of code listed below. This program will generate natural logarithms in the form of an ASCII file that can then be loaded into the Data Base.

```
10   REM THIS PROGRAM PRINTS A LIST
20   REM OF VALUES AND THEIR LOGS
30   REM TO A DESIGNATED TEXT FILE
40   D$ = CHR$ (4)
50   INPUT "FILE:";XX$
60   PRINT D$;"OPEN";XX$
70   PRINT D$;"WRITE";XX$
80   FOR X = 3 TO 4 STEP 0.1
90   PRINT X
100  PRINT LOG (X)
110  NEXT X
120  PRINT D$;"CLOSE";XX$
130  END
```

When you have typed in the program, follow these steps to convert the Word Processor file into a working Applesoft BASIC program:

1. Print from the beginning of the file to either a formatted or unformatted text (ASCII) file on disk. Enter the path name /P/LN.

2. Leave AppleWorks and load ProDOS in drive 1. When the menu appears, press B for BASIC. Note that the data disk can remain in drive 2.

3. Catalog the disk by entering CAT,S6,D2 and check to see that LN is there.

4. Enter EXEC LN to convert the text file to a BASIC file. Here you will see a series of right brackets (]).

5. Enter LIST to see the program.

6. Type SAVE LN2 to save the file as a BASIC program under a different file name.

7. Enter RUN to make it run. The program first asks you to name the file of logarithms it will be creating.

8. Enter the name LOGS in response to this prompt.

What is the program doing? Look at line 80 first. This program finds natural logarithms for specified values of X, in this case from 3 to 4, in increments of 0.1. The program will print a range of values and their natural logs to a text file (LOGS). The list will be 22 lines long in a single column, beginning as follows:

```
3
1.09861229
3.1
1.13140211
```

Notice that the values and natural logs alternate in a single column. This is an important feature, because you will be using the information in the Data Base. Now follow these steps:

1. Reload AppleWorks and start making a new Data Base file from a text (ASCII) file.

2. Specify two categories for the Data Base file, because each record is composed of a value and its natural log.

3. Designate the file with the proper path name, here /P/LOGS.

4. Give the new Data Base file a name.

Notice that the values and their respective natural logarithms are now in parallel columns, as shown in Figure 5.18. As you will remember from other examples in this chapter, this data can be transferred from the Data Base to the Spreadsheet in a DIF file.

This tip has provided a simple demonstration of an important concept. You can use Applesoft BASIC programs to perform special processing beyond the capabilities of AppleWorks, and the results can then be transferred to AppleWorks for editing and reporting. The program calculations, here confined to lines 80 through 110, could have been far more complex. Instead of having LN2 print to an ASCII file, you could have programmed it to print to a DIF file. For more on BASIC routines for creating DIF files, see Elna Tymes' *Mastering AppleWorks*, 2nd ed., (SYBEX, 1987).

There are additional things to know. Save at least one copy of the original Word Processor file, so that you can use it to make necessary program revisions later. You can also write the program with no line numbers for the remark (REM) lines. When you run EXEC to convert the ASCII file into a BASIC program, those lines will be excluded from the program, making it run faster.

```
File: DB.LOGS              REVIEW/ADD/CHANGE           Escape: Main Menu

   Selection: All records


   Category 01    Category 02
   ===============================================================================
   3              1.09861229
   3.1            1.13140211
   3.2            1.16315081
   3.3            1.19392247
   3.4            1.22377543
   3.5            1.25276297
   3.6            1.28093385
   3.7            1.30833282
   3.8            1.33500107
   3.9            1.36097655
   4              1.38629436




   -------------------------------------------------------------------------------
   Type entry or use @ commands                              @-? for Help
```

Figure 5.18: *Values and logarithms in the Data Base*

Tip: *You can convert an Applesoft BASIC program back into an ASCII file.*

Suppose you want to revise a program that came on a disk. Or suppose you forgot to save a Word Processor version of your last program. Following is a short subroutine that will convert an Applesoft BASIC program back into a text file.

Begin a Word Processor file from scratch, depress the Caps Lock key, and enter these lines:

```
63500   D$ = CHR$(4)
63506   INPUT "FILE:";XX$
63508   PRINT D$;"OPEN";XX$
63510   PRINT D$;"WRITE";XX$
63512   LIST 1,63499
63514   PRINT D$;"CLOSE";XX$
63516   END
```

The unusual numbering in this program allows you to append it to virtually any Applesoft BASIC program ever written. The program is reprinted from page 163 of *The ProDOS Handbook,* by Timothy and Karen Rice (SYBEX, 1985), where additional notes on the utility of this program are included. Note how it resembles the structure of the LN2 program. Where LN2 calculates, this program simply lists. In fact, you could have entered it by editing the Word Processor file from which LN2 was created.

You can use this subroutine to make the BASIC file LN2 into a text file once again, in this case simply to demonstrate how you can use AppleWorks to edit it. Follow these steps:

1. Print from the beginning of the Word Processor file to a text (ASCII) file on disk. Enter the path name /P/ REVERSE.

2. Leave AppleWorks and load ProDOS in drive 1. When the menu appears, press B for BASIC. Note that the data disk can remain in drive 2.

3. Catalog the disk by entering CAT,S6 and check to see that LN2 and REVERSE are there.

4. Enter LOAD LN2.

5. Enter EXEC REVERSE.

6. Enter LIST to see the two programs merged.

7. Enter RUN 63500.

8. When requested, enter a file name such as LNX, because you may still have the original LN text file on the disk.

Now all you have to do is reload AppleWorks, make a new Word Processor file from the ASCII file named LNX, and the cycle is complete.

SUMMARY

This chapter has examined many techniques for transferring information within AppleWorks, as well as to and from AppleWorks. Some of the techniques are simple, some necessarily complicated. When you look through the chapter again, use a yellow marker to identify the tips that will help you most. You will probably want to create a PARTS file and sample tables to transfer from the Spreadsheet to the Word Processor. You can experiment with the BASIC program even if you have never written a program.

In the next chapter you will find some additional printing techniques that can be used with each of the three AppleWorks programs. In Chapter 7 we will automate many of the techniques discussed in the first six chapters.

If you are interested in additional possibilities for applications development and information transfer, Appendix A looks at the potential for AppleWorks over the next few years.

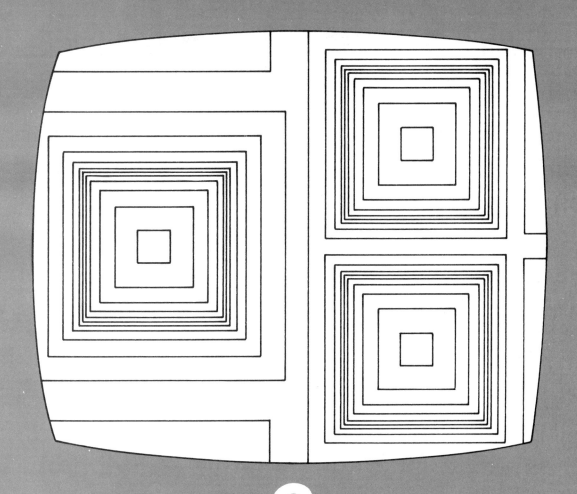

6
Installing Printers

*T*his chapter discusses the mechanics of installing printers, interface cards, and buffers. If you are having problems with your printer, read this chapter first. Printer problems include such curious things as an "80N" printed at the beginning of a Word Processor file, too many spaces between lines, and similarly frustrating anomalies. You can generally tell when a printing problem is a printer problem, because it occurs with the simplest text formatting.

Once you have configured your printer correctly, you can use the standard printing options described in the first five chapters of this book. This chapter also includes advanced printing options that require an understanding of your printer's specific control codes. You may or may not be able to use all the techniques described in this chapter. If you discover some options that are important to you and your printer does not have them, make a check list to use whenever you buy another printer.

Information on printing appears in the AppleWorks Reference Manual. Read that first if you have a printer listed there. If your printer is not listed there, read your printer manual. Consult this chapter if your printer is not working as you had expected.

This chapter provides tips and techniques for installing printers in seven sections. It begins with the most general tips, then moves on to tips on using interface cards. The following section provides techniques for using printers included on the AppleWorks list of available printers. Following that is a section on custom printers, providing important information on installing printers that Apple-Works has not included on its list. You will also learn why some listed printers should also be added as custom printers as well. A section on control codes includes several advanced methods for substituting and "piggybacking" codes. (Note that control codes are sometimes called command codes in printer manuals.)

In the section on printing techniques, you should pay particular attention to the cautions about differences between tenths of an inch and other fractions, particularly if you regularly print onto forms. The last section contains reference information on using printer buffers, one of the most cost-effective investments you can make.

GENERAL PRINTER TIPS

The following tips provide the most basic information about using printers with AppleWorks. If you are looking for a printer, pay special attention to considerations in choosing a printer. If you already have a good printer, take out your manual and read up on the things you will need to know for this chapter.

Tip: *Consider the printing speed, print quality, and level of noise when you choose a printer.*

Objective information on printers is surprisingly difficult to find. *PC Magazine* conducts thorough, independent comparative tests of decibel ratings, printing speed, and print quality. These measurements sometimes differ markedly from manufacturers' claims. Check your library for back issues.

Note that some dot-matrix printers are very fast, but only in draft fonts you may not find easy to read. Some fonts are easy to read but different from daisy-wheel print. If you really need true letter-quality print for letters and reports, there are some good, small daisy-wheel printers.

Listen to the printer run in an otherwise quiet place. Sit as near to it as you would in normal use. If the sound irritates you, consider choosing another printer. For example, a letter-quality printer running at less than 15 characters per second may sound enough like a human typist to be familiar and quite tolerable. That may be a more important consideration than marginally greater speed or a slightly lower decibel rating.

Tip: *You can minimize printer noise in several ways.*

Printer noise can be annoying, especially during extended print runs. Here is a list of ways to minimize that noise:

- Keep all the housing parts on the printer. These parts may get in the way when you need to adjust paper, but they do control noise.

- Place the printer on a firm shock-absorbing pad. Make certain that air can still enter through slots in the bottom of the printer.

- Use a sound enclosure (you can make one from cardboard and acoustic foam). It should cover at least three sides and the top of the printer, but with space for air circulation. The partly open end should face away from you.

- Wear ear plugs or listen to music through earphones.

- If you trust the tractor feed system, leave the room and close the door behind you.

Caution: *Before you buy a printer, find out whether the tractors are unidirectional or bidirectional.*

This caution is particularly important for those who use superscripts and subscripts, which require paper movement in both directions on most printers. Almost any printer can do this in the friction-feed mode, but some cannot do it with their pin- and tractor-feed mechanisms. If you print long papers with footnotes, for example, you need a bidirectional tractor. Friction feed is never quite good enough, because the paper slowly drifts on the roller, just a little to the right or left with each page. Note that some printers avoid this tractor problem by using a separate set of small script characters.

Tip: *Keep your printer manual nearby.*

Of all the manuals you own, your printer manual is the one you will use most often. Make photocopies of the pages that list control codes, and insert the copies in your AppleWorks notebook. Use a yellow marker to highlight important information, and add tabs to key pages. Consult the manual when you enter special printer codes in the Data Base and Spreadsheet.

Tip: *Printers are listed in the order you added them.*

When you first tell AppleWorks you want to print, the proposed printer is always the one at the top of the list. To have your printer there you must configure it first, even if that means removing the Imagewriter and any other printer that Apple has already added. It helps to have your standard printer on top, so you can use Return to step through the printing menu sequence.

INTERFACE CARDS

Earlier versions of AppleWorks made no provision for changing interface card control codes. Version 1.2 finally makes it easy to install non-Apple interfaces, many of which offer remarkable performance at reasonable prices. You can also find Apple-compatible parallel interface cards for less than $50.

Tip: *If your printer prints incorrectly, check the interface card configuration first.*

Even if you have a listed printer, your interface card may not respond to the default control codes entered for Apple interface cards. AppleWorks versions 1.2 and later allow you to change the control codes yourself, as shown in Figure 6.1. Control-I 80N is the default setting, but if you have installed a Grappler card, for example, Control-I 0N (zero N) is what you need.

AppleWorks version 1.1 assumes that you have an Apple interface card, so it does not provide any other configuration options. Many people with earlier versions of AppleWorks and Grappler cards find 80N printed at the beginning of every Word Processor file. If this is your problem, upgrade to version 2.0 and change the interface card control code. Then if you change interface cards at some point in the future, you can change the control codes easily.

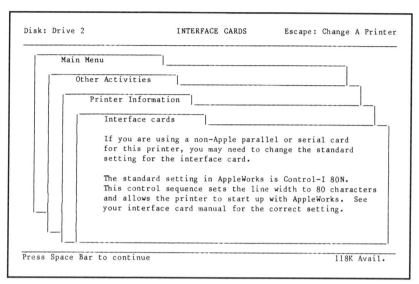

```
Disk: Drive 2              INTERFACE CARDS      Escape: Change A Printer
_____
    Main Menu                |_____
      Other Activities          |_____
        Printer Information        |_____
          Interface cards             |_____
            If you are using a non-Apple parallel or serial card
            for this printer, you may need to change the standard
            setting for the interface card.

            The standard setting in AppleWorks is Control-I 80N.
            This control sequence sets the line width to 80 characters
            and allows the printer to start up with AppleWorks.  See
            your interface card manual for the correct setting.



_____
Press Space Bar to continue                              118K Avail.
```

Figure 6.1: *The interface card option in AppleWorks version 1.2*

Tip: *If you must use AppleWorks version 1.1, there is a patch for non-Apple interface cards.*

Apple once distributed a free program for version 1.1 called the AppleWorks Interface Card Configuration Utility. You can capture it as a text file through CompuServe from the Micronetworked Apple Users Group (MAUG) mentioned in Appendix C.

With this Configuration Utility, you can modify a copy of the AppleWorks Startup disk so that it supports the Grappler card. When you have the Startup disk of version 1.1 modified for the Grappler card, the first screen will say "V1.1G USA". Note, however, that almost everyone would be wiser simply to upgrade from an earlier version to version 2.0.

APPLEWORKS PRINTERS

AppleWorks allows you to install three printers, one of which can be a custom printer. A fourth "printer" is already installed for printing ASCII files to disk. (When AppleWorks prints to disk, it has to pretend that it's accessing a printer.) In this section we will cover the mechanics of installing the first three printers.

Tip: *Install your standard printer first.*

Suppose you want to install a Qume Sprint 5 daisy-wheel printer as your standard printer. This printer is option 9 on the Add a Printer menu shown in Figure 6.2. Install it as the first printer by removing any existing printers and then selecting option 2 on the Printer Information menu. Give the printer a name such as Qume.5 and specify that it will be accessed from slot 1. If you have an Apple or an Apple-compatible parallel interface card, there is no need to change the interface control code. If you have another type of card, use the control code suggested in the interface card instructions. With the Grappler interface card, for example, the code would be Control-I 0N (zero N). Figure 6.3 shows one printer installed.

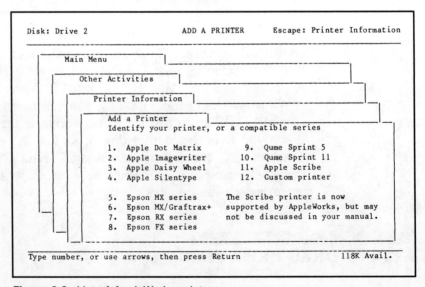

```
Disk: Drive 2              ADD A PRINTER      Escape: Printer Information
----------------------------------------------------------------------------
  ┌── Main Menu ──────────┐ ┌──────────────────────────────────────────┐
  │ ┌── Other Activities ──┐ ┌──────────────────────────────────┐
  │ │ ┌── Printer Information ──┐ ┌────────────────────────────┐
  │ │ │ ┌── Add a Printer ──────┐ ┌──────────────────────── ─┐
  │ │ │ │ Identify your printer, or a compatible series
  │ │ │ │
  │ │ │ │    1.  Apple Dot Matrix      9.   Qume Sprint 5
  │ │ │ │    2.  Apple Imagewriter    10.   Qume Sprint 11
  │ │ │ │    3.  Apple Daisy Wheel    11.   Apple Scribe
  │ │ │ │    4.  Apple Silentype      12.   Custom printer
  │ │ │ │
  │ │ │ │    5.  Epson MX series       The Scribe printer is now
  │ │ │ │    6.  Epson MX/Graftrax+    supported by AppleWorks, but may
  │ │ │ │    7.  Epson RX series       not be discussed in your manual.
  │ │ │ │    8.  Epson FX series
----------------------------------------------------------------------------
Type number, or use arrows, then press Return              118K Avail.
```

Figure 6.2: List of AppleWorks printers

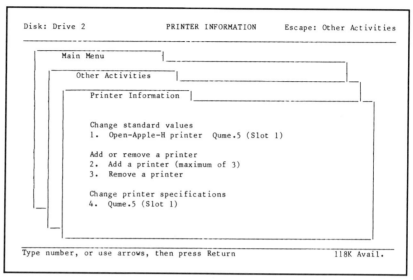

```
Disk: Drive 2                PRINTER INFORMATION        Escape: Other Activities
--------------------------------------------------------------------------------
      Main Menu          |_____
         Other Activities    |_____
            Printer Information |_____

            Change standard values
            1.  Open-Apple-H printer   Qume.5 (Slot 1)

            Add or remove a printer
            2.  Add a printer (maximum of 3)
            3.  Remove a printer

            Change printer specifications
            4.  Qume.5 (Slot 1)


--------------------------------------------------------------------------------
Type number, or use arrows, then press Return                      118K Avail.
```

Figure 6.3: *One printer installed*

Suppose you want to install an Abati LQ-20 daisy-wheel printer as your standard printer. Any printer not listed on the Add a Printer menu is considered a custom printer. A custom printer is option 12 on the Add a Printer menu's list of printers. Install it as you would the first printer by selecting option 2 on the Printer Information menu. Give it a name such as Abati.LQ. Configure the interface card if you have a non-Apple card.

Unless otherwise specified, the first printer on your list will be the designated printer for producing hard copies of the screen with the Apple-H command. In this example case, our other two printers will be printing to disk, and that disqualifies them from being designated as Apple-H printers.

Tip: *Test your printer before you really need it.*

When you install a listed printer, you want to make certain that AppleWorks has the correct control codes. You cannot go back to review the codes as you can with a custom printer. However, you can create and print a test file that includes at least one example of everything you want to test, such as underline, boldface, subscript, and superscript.

Type text lines made up of the lowercase and uppercase alphabets followed by all the other characters on the keyboard. Notice how your printer prints each character.

Copy the test lines at least 15 times. Before each set of lines, enter the printer option for a different CI setting. Start with 18 characters per inch and descend to 4 characters per inch. Use 10 CI as the setting at the top of the file. When you print the file, you can then determine when each CI setting takes effect. For example, if your printer prints 16.5 characters per inch, it makes a difference whether that takes effect at 17 or 16 CI.

You can incorporate other related techniques in this chapter within the same file. Once you finish it, you can use it with any printer, so make copies for friends.

Tip: *Install a wildcard printer.*

The second printer position can be used as a wildcard. What you install depends on what you need. Here we will consider two of many possibilities.

If your standard printer is a listed printer, install it again, but this time answer No to option 2: Accepts top-of-page commands. You can print nonstandard page lengths without having to change print settings or send special codes. Tips in Chapters 2, 4, and 7 cover this subject from several perspectives. A later tip in this chapter explains when you should install a listed printer as a custom printer.

If you use AppleWorks version 1.3 or earlier, you may want to use the AppleWorks Mailing Program. You will need Word Processor files that have been printed to disk using your standard printer, normally assigned to slot 1. The process is similar to printing formatted ASCII files to disk, except that the file includes any AppleWorks character enhancements and other printer options you have used.

The only way you can get a printer to print to disk is to specify that this is how the printer will be accessed. Surprisingly, there is no way to change the printer access option, as you can with other options. Therefore, you must add another printer to AppleWorks.

If your standard printer is listed, add the same listed printer again, with one difference: on the menu for adding a printer, specify that the printer will be accessed by printing onto disk.

If your standard printer is a custom printer, you can make another copy of the AppleWorks Program disk, delete the custom printer, and then add a custom printer dedicated to printing to disk.

Tip: *Install a dummy Silentype printer.*

Apple no longer sells the Silentype printer, but it is listed in AppleWorks as option 4 on the Add a Printer menu. It is a basic thermal printer, quieter than most. In this case, basic means that the Silentype default settings are ten characters per inch and six lines per inch, with no character enhancements available (not even underlining). In AppleWorks these settings make the Silentype a useful dummy for printing formatted text files to disk.

Install the Silentype as the third printer by selecting option 2 on the Printer Information menu. Name the printer Silentype and specify that it will print to disk. You can change the platen-width setting to 8 inches for the sake of conformity, but the Silentype will accept much wider platen widths no matter what the setting. Configure the interface card as you did for your standard printer. Figure 6.4 shows that we now have three installed printers.

Although the actual Silentype prints only ten characters per inch on paper, the dummy will also print to disk at other CI settings, such as 12 and 17. If you have any character enhancements entered in Word Processor text, the Silentype will completely ignore both the enhancements and their markers.

If you have AppleWorks version 2.0, you can print formatted text files without a dummy Silentype printer. However, you may still want to use a dummy Silentype because it can incorporate Apple-Works margin settings as space characters within formatted text files.

Alternatively, you can add the Silentype to print from slot 1, just as you would any other listed printer. When you do that, the Silentype will drive almost any printer at 10 characters per inch, ignoring all character enhancements.

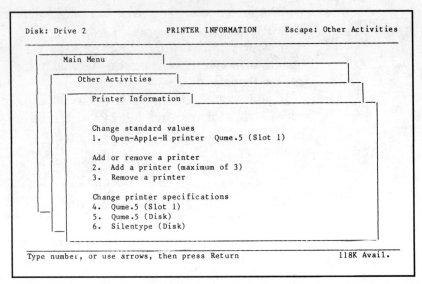

Figure 6.4: *Three printers installed*

Tip: *The printer for text (ASCII) files has no name.*

One useful option offered on the print menu in each program represents a dummy printer. In AppleWorks through version 1.3, it is just as important as the dummy Silentype because it can print unformatted ASCII files. Think of it as a printer, even though it has no name, and remember the distinctions between formatted and unformatted text files noted in Chapter 5. In Figure 6.5 this "no-name" printer is option 6. In AppleWorks version 2.0, this printer prints only formatted text files, something you can already do with Silentype.

Tip: *Although the Apple IIc uses a serial interface, it has a similar approach to installing printers.*

When you install a standard printer for the Apple IIc, Apple-Works offers a choice of two serial ports (rather than six slots). Serial connections transfer bits of data in single-file sequence,

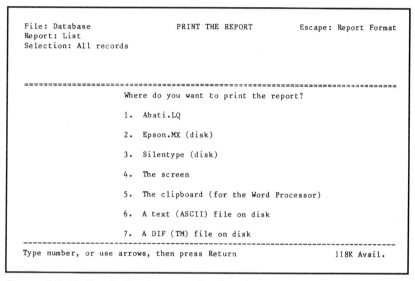

Figure 6.5: *Option 6: the "no name" printer in version 1.3*

rather than in eight parallel paths. The AppleWorks serial interface configuration includes options to set the baud rate, data format, and parity, all of which are explained in the AppleWorks Reference Manual.

Note that the Apple IIe can use a serial interface card and serial printers. Serial-to-parallel conversion devices allow the Apple IIc to use parallel printers. Many printers come in both parallel and serial versions, but few come with both connections on one version.

CUSTOM PRINTERS

Most people will eventually read Appendix B of the Apple-Works Reference Manual for two reasons. First, neither the widely used Okidata 92 dot matrix nor the widely emulated Diablo 630 daisy wheel are listed printers. Second, even if your printer is listed, there are significant advantages to entering a custom version of the same printer: a listed printer may have more capabilities that you can access from codes entered in the listing.

Tip: *Your printer may be compatible with a listed printer.*

Before you enter your printer as a custom printer, notice that the menu says "Identify your printer, or a compatible series." For example, because the Epson MX series has been so popular for so long, some other printers use Epson-compatible control codes. Check your printer manual to see if your printer uses the same codes as one of the other listed printers. This applies to newer Epson printers. For example, the LQ-800 can use the Epson MX/Graftrax+ location.

Tip: *Before you install your custom printer, find the list of control codes for it.*

The instructions for preparing a custom printer are easy enough to understand. The only difficulty is determining which codes to enter. A good printer manual will usually contain a table of ASCII printer control codes written as keystroke sequences or combinations, such as Escape D or Control-H. Some manuals provide only the ASCII decimal values (such 29 or 31). Conversions from ASCII values to keystroke sequences are provided in Appendix B. Some of the conversions requiring the Control key are listed in Table 6.1. The ASCII values 1–26 are the letters in alphabetical order. (Note that in some printer manuals the Control key may be signified by CTRL or by a caret (^).)

Control-[is equivalent to simply pressing Escape. Thus, an ASCII decimal value listed as 27 56 is the same as the keystrokes Escape 8. Everything else is easy once you have the list of ASCII codes. We will refer to them throughout this chapter.

Tip: *A listed printer can also be a custom printer.*

Some printers have more options than AppleWorks can hold in the space allocated to one printer. For instance, some printers

---

Table 6.1: *Selected Control-key ASCII conversions*

ASCII Value	Keystroke Combination
0	Control-@
1	Control-A
26	Control-Z
27	Control-[
28	Control-\
29	Control-]
30	Control- ^
31	Control-_

---

have two different fonts available at ten characters per inch or some other density. The Epson MX series (with optional Graftrax) provides an example. These printers are very reliable, and are often used in combination with a Grappler card. This remains a dependable system for draft printing and graphics, and almost all software includes a printer driver for this Epson.

An MX-80 can be entered as a listed printer under option 5, the Epson MX series. We can name it Epson.MX in this case. It can also be entered as a custom printer under a different name, such as Custom.MX.

When you enter the custom printer codes, type Escape E in the space for 10 characters per inch. The custom MX will then print entirely in emphasized mode, which is identical to the boldface option on the Printer Options menu. It is true that you can use Control-B to select emphasized mode for the listed printer, but the emphasized print continues only for the remainder of that paragraph. If you wanted to print in emphasized mode continuously, you would normally have to use Control-B at the beginning of each paragraph. By installing a custom MX on the same Program disk, you can solve that problem.

You can also enter "piggyback" codes (two or more independent codes merged in one entry) on the interface card control sequence, which means you can get the same effect without having to use the custom printer option. AppleWorks allows you to use up to three different interface cards—one for each printer. Hence you can add the listed Epson MX-80 twice and add Escape E to one interface card setting.

Tip: *The Okidata 92 really does work with AppleWorks.*

The Okidata 92 is widely used with the buffered Grappler + interface card. Together they make for an unusually fast and dependable system. The correspondence quality print on the Okidata 92 is attractive and readable. Unfortunately, many people believe that the Okidata 92 will not work with AppleWorks.

The Okidata 92 and 93 printer series, as well as the newer 192 and 193, all work perfectly with AppleWorks since version 1.2. In fact, all the drafts of this book were written with AppleWorks and printed on an Okidata 92. The most commonly used font control codes for the Okidata printer series are given in Table 6.2.

Escape 1 turns on near-letter-quality (NLQ) print, and Escape 0 turns it off. Escape 0 must be included in draft-quality codes to clear any previous NLQ setting. There is no NLQ font for 17 characters per inch, but you must include Escape 0 to access 17 CI after using any NLQ font. (It actually prints at 17.1 CI.) Other important control codes are given in Table 6.3.

Table 6.2: *Font control codes for the Okidata printer series*

Pitch	Keystroke Sequence
Draft quality print	
10 CI	Escape 0 Control- ^
12 CI	Escape 0 Control-\
17 CI	Escape 0 Control-]
Near-letter-quality print	
10 CI	Escape 1 Control- ^
12 CI	Escape 1 Control-\

Table 6.3: Print setting codes for the Okidata printer series

Print Setting	Keystroke Sequence
Six lines per inch	Escape 6
Eight lines per inch	Escape 8
Boldface on	Escape T
Boldface off	Escape I
Subscript on	Escape L
Subscript off	Escape M
Superscript on	Escape J
Superscript off	Escape K
Underlining on	Escape C
Underlining off	Escape D

Note that this printer uses start and stop underlining commands—option 2 on the Underlining configuration menu.

Caution: *You may need two or more Program disks to use all the options on your custom printer.*

The Okidata 92 has a problem similar to that of the Epson MX with 10 CI print. Entering Escape 1 for 10 characters per inch produces near-letter-quality print. Because you can list only one custom printer per Program disk, as shown in Figure 6.6, you will need to configure a second disk to access 10 CI in draft quality.

In practice, you may want to reserve 10 CI for fast printing of drafts and 12 CI for near-letter-quality printing. That makes it possible to work with just one Program disk. (Note that the printer configuration is loaded into memory when you first load AppleWorks, so you cannot just put another Program disk in the drive to change fonts.)

There is a technique for accessing both draft quality and near-letter quality from one 10 CI setting. Enter 10 CI as Control-^ and 12 CI as Escape 1 Control-\. The 10 CI will then print in draft quality after you use 17 CI, and in NLQ mode after you use 12 CI.

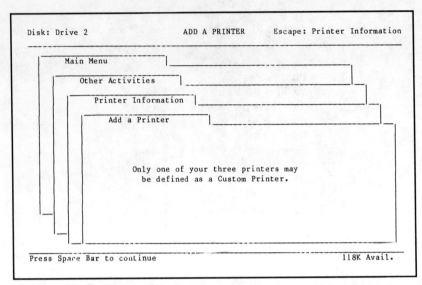

```
Disk: Drive 2              ADD A PRINTER       Escape: Printer Information
-------------------------------------------------------------------------
     ┌── Main Menu ──────────────┐
     │  ┌── Other Activities ──────┐
     │  │  ┌── Printer Information ──────┐
     │  │  │  ┌── Add a Printer ──────────┐
     │  │  │  │
     │  │  │  │
     │  │  │  │      Only one of your three printers may
     │  │  │  │        be defined as a Custom Printer.
     │  │  │  │
     │  │  │  │
     │  │  │  │
-------------------------------------------------------------------------
Press Space Bar to continue                               118K Avail.
```

Figure 6.6: Only one custom printer permitted

Caution: *Some of the installed codes for listed Epson printers are incorrect.*

In AppleWorks version 1.1, the Epson MX series printer with Graftrax+ has the most problems. Once started, the underlining will not stop until the end of a paragraph. If you want to underline, you must enter a custom version of the same printer using codes from the Epson manual.

Before version 2.0, the 16.5 CI font appears to have been entered as 17 characters per inch, with complications described in the following tip.

Tip: *If your printer has a fractional characters-per-inch font, enter that setting rounded down.*

For example, if you want to configure an Epson custom printer for 16.5 characters per inch (Escape F Control-O), enter 16 rather than 17 on both the Add a Printer menu and the Printer Options menu in each program. The 16 CI setting will always leave you with enough platen width (a maximum of 128 characters of 132 possible with an 8-inch platen width), but 17 CI can cause a short extra line when the characters go beyond the platen width (136 characters attempted when only 132 are possible). When you enter 16, you can still include all 132 characters by setting an 8.3-inch platen width. AppleWorks will be fooled, but the printer will work correctly.

Tip: *Many good letter-quality printers emulate Diablo 630 commands.*

The Juki 6100 is one of several inexpensive daisy-wheel printers that emulate Diablo 630 printer codes. The print enhancement codes for the Diablo 630 are given in Table 6.4.

On printers emulating the Diablo 630, Escape D and Escape U are used in one order for superscripts and in the opposite order for subscripts. Escape U causes the paper to feed up a half line, so the character ends up striking below the normal print line. Esc D then feeds the paper back down a half line to the normal printing position.

Other printers emulate the Diablo 630 in part. For example, the Abati LQ-20 uses Qume daisy wheels and ribbon cartridges, but its codes are similar to those of the Diablo 630: Escape Q and Escape & turn boldface on and off. Escape D and Escape U

Table 6.4: Print enhancement codes for the Diablo 630

Print Enhancement	Keystroke Sequence
Boldface on	Escape O
Boldface off	Escape &
Subscript on	Escape U
Subscript off	Escape D
Superscript on	Escape D
Superscript off	Escape U
Underlining on	Escape E
Underlining off	Escape R

turn superscript on and off. Escape _ and Escape R start and stop underlining.

Tip: *There are many more custom printer tips.*

As you have seen, many printers, including listed printers, can use the custom printer option to considerable advantage. You will undoubtedly find many variations and extensions of the techniques described in this chapter. Members of the Micronetworked Apple Users Group have even documented locations within AppleWorks for listed printer settings that can be changed to permit new listed printers.

For more on custom printer tips, read David Simerly's *Advanced AppleWorks* (SYBEX, 1988). It contains complete instructions for creating a Macintosh custom printer in Apple-Works to transfer text to a Macintosh word processor. In fact, he used that connection extensively to illustrate the book.

Chapter 7 has the most important custom printer tip of all: use macros. They allow you to change printers and codes quickly and automatically.

CONTROL CODES

This section provides additional techniques for using printer control codes, as well as tips for using boldfacing and underlining codes in ways you may never have considered. If your printer is not discussed in this section, take out your list of control codes for reference while you read the tips below.

Tip: *Use control codes as soft switches whenever you can.*

Some of the settings you may want to change on your printer are controlled by dip switches. Because these switches are so small, you may have trouble switching just one without disturbing the others unless you use a very small screwdriver. Sometimes these switches are hidden away inside the printer. You can often avoid using them by using control codes instead.

For example, the Apple DMP has dip switches to select character sets for different languages—French, German, Italian, Spanish, and Swedish. Suppose you want to write a letter in French at 10 CI. Suppose you also want the zero printed with a slash through it, so that no one will mistake it for a capital O. You can do all this at once by entering Escape N Escape D61 in the printer configuration option for 10 characters per inch, as shown in Figure 6.7.

When you finish the letter, change the entry back to the default Escape N for 10 CI. This technique saves the time and trouble of opening up the DMP to access its dip switches.

Tip: *Use "piggyback" codes for specific purposes.*

The Apple DMP example given in the previous tip uses what is sometimes called a "piggyback" code: two or more independent

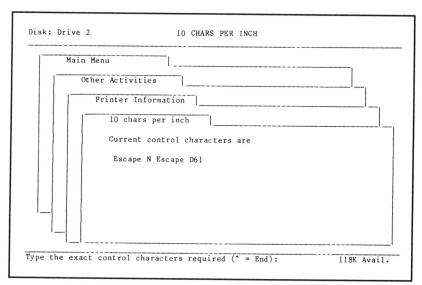

Figure 6.7: Using merged (or "piggyback") codes

codes merged in one entry. AppleWorks can accept up to 38 characters in a single merged code (13 in the Data Base and Spreadsheet special codes option). Empty spaces, Escape, and Control count as one character each in printer control code entries, so the example in Figure 6.7 used only six character spaces.

Tip: *You can exchange control codes.*

Suppose you will eventually print the final draft of a long report at 12 CI on a letter-quality printer. Your letter-quality printer runs at 14 characters per second, while your dot-matrix printer runs at 90 characters per second. You want to proofread the whole report and see the lines as they will break when you later print the final draft. You can print the report at 17 CI on the dot-matrix printer with the exact 12 CI line breaks of the letter-quality printer by entering the wrong control codes.

For simulating 12 characters-per-inch layout with 17 CI dot-matrix print, select the 12 CI option in printer configuration and insert the code for 17 CI. The printout also leaves you plenty of white space for editing marks and comments.

Tip: *You can change boldfacing or underlining control codes to print superscripts.*

Suppose that you use underlining and superscripts (for footnotes) frequently, but you don't use boldfacing. When specifying the printer configuration, enter the control code for superscript begin under "boldface begin". Enter the code for superscript end under "boldface end". This allows you to use Control-B to turn superscript on and off in the Word Processor, without having to enter the Printer Options menu.

If other people use your Apple and AppleWorks, of course, you'll have to tell them what you did. Better yet, keep your modified Program disk to yourself. And remember, when you trick AppleWorks, it can trick you in return if you forget about the modification.

> **Tip:** *You can change boldfacing or underlining control codes to print more than one character size per line.*

Suppose you want to use an 8.5 CI font in part of a title line. In printer configuration, enter the control code for 8.5 characters per inch under "boldface begin". Enter the code for the normal font under "boldface end". This allows you to use Control-B to turn 8.5 CI on and off quickly. Because the CI menu option works only for whole lines, this is the only way to mix character sizes on the same line. Furthermore, AppleWorks will not count these characters accurately, so use a carriage return at the end of the line.

> **Tip:** *You can change boldfacing and underlining control codes to call up alternate character sets.*

Alternate character sets include italics, scientific symbols, and foreign character sets. Use the same technique described in the previous tip, this time to access an alternate character set. In each case the screen will show the standard keyboard input, but the printer will print the substitute you designated for that character.

Remember that Control-B and Control-L remain in effect only to the end of a paragraph. (In AppleWorks, a paragraph ends when a line ends in a carriage return.) Italics, scientific symbols, and foreign character sets used for limited purposes can be accessed with this technique. For longer text applications, use the "piggyback" method previously described.

PRINTING TECHNIQUES

The mechanics of printing can be tedious. You have to spend time making certain that the paper fits just right, not too high or too far left. It takes a while to work accurately with sixths, tenths, and twelfths of an inch if you have already spent years using eighths and sixteenths. When you make everything fit, however, you waste considerably less paper and time.

Tip: *Learn the dimensions of the print head, platen, and roller on your printer.*

The platen width is the distance the print head travels across the printer roller. Most printers have a platen width of 8 inches, although standard paper is 8½ inches wide. Paper is usually aligned so that the left-most character just barely fits on the paper when the left margin is set at 0 inches.

For layout purposes, the most important things to know about a printer are where the platen begins on the roller and where the characters are printed in relation to the top of the print head.

Printers that use a fixed pin-feed system with an 8-inch platen may set quarter-inch margins on each side as a matter of course. You have to consider this in any additional margins you specify. For example, if you want an inch margin on the left, you can use a 0.7 or 0.8 setting and get very close to what you want.

Tip: *Maximum platen-width settings vary considerably within AppleWorks.*

The maximum platen width you can specify on the Add a Printer menu is 16.0 inches; Figure 6.8 shows that it can indeed be entered. In the Word Processor, however, the maximum platen width you can specify on the Printer Options menu is 13.2 inches, while the Data Base and Spreadsheet Printer Option limits are 25.5 inches. These settings override any settings on the Add a Printer menu. The Data Base and Spreadsheet platen limits make it easy to print formatted text files to disk for special purposes, even though few printers used with the Apple have platen widths wider than 13.2 inches.

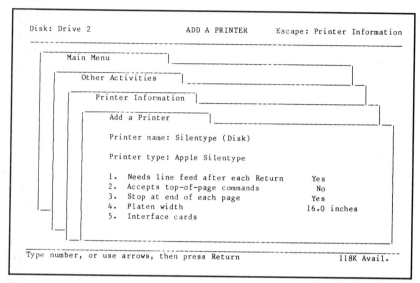

```
Disk: Drive 2              ADD A PRINTER    Escape: Printer Information
-----------------------------------------------------------------------
  | Main Menu                      |
    | Other Activities             |
      | Printer Information         |
        | Add a Printer            |

          Printer name: Silentype (Disk)

          Printer type: Apple Silentype

          1.  Needs line feed after each Return      Yes
          2.  Accepts top-of-page commands           No
          3.  Stop at end of each page               Yes
          4.  Platen width                           16.0 inches
          5.  Interface cards

-----------------------------------------------------------------------
Type number, or use arrows, then press Return            118K Avail.
```

Figure 6.8: *Maximum platen width in option 4*

Caution: *The top-of-page command can produce unwanted results.*

If your printer feeds too much paper between blank cards or labels, return to the Main Menu and then go to the printer information section of the Other Activities menu. You probably need a "no" response to option 2: "Accepts top-of-page commands". In general, if a page length differs from the standard 11 inches, turn off the top-of-page command.

The Data Base and Spreadsheet printer options allow you to enter special codes to control page length, which means that your printer can continue to accept top-of-page commands. Note, however, that the control range on your printer may be limited.

Caution: *Sixths and tenths of an inch rarely match up.*

Most printing is done at six lines per inch (6 LI), in which a top margin of 0.5 inches equals 3 lines. Tenths and sixths are otherwise poorly matched. In Data Base report formats, use multiples of 0.5 for top and bottom margins, and an empty report line or two for the leftover sixths.

Table 6.5 shows how the number of lines decreases as you change from a bottom margin of 1 inch to a bottom margin of 2 inches on standard 11-inch paper. A top margin of 0 is assumed in each case. Notice that in some cases two different settings can provide the same number of lines per page.

Caution: *Twelfths and tenths of an inch rarely match up.*

Most printing is done at ten characters per inch (10 CI), in which one tenth of an inch is equal to one character. Most printers offer additional choices for 12, 15, or other numbers of characters per inch. Let's take a closer look at the relationships between tenths of an inch and character spaces as the print pitch increases.

Table 6.6 shows how the number of characters per line decreases in various print pitches as you increase the right margin

Table 6.5: Lines printed per page with various bottom margin settings

Bottom Margin in Inches	Number of Lines per Page	
	6 LI	8 LI
1.0	60	80
1.1	59	79
1.2	58	78
1.3	58	77
1.4	57	76
1.5	57	76
1.6	56	75
1.7	55	74
1.8	55	73
1.9	54	72
2.0	54	72

from 0 to 1 inch on a standard 8-inch platen width. A left margin of 1 inch is assumed in each case. Notice that you cannot print some line lengths, such as 77 characters in 12 CI and 92 characters in 15 CI.

Tip: *You can create your own tables for margins and characters per line.*

Because there are many different character pitches available on different printers, this tip offers a method for creating your own tables. Follow the steps listed below:

1. In a new Word Processor document, type in 60 characters of the continuing series 123456789.123456789. within the default margins.

2. Copy the line to the clipboard, then from the clipboard twice, to the next two lines.

3. Remove the carriage return markers from the first two lines.

Table 6.6: *Characters printed per line with various right margin settings*

Right Margin in Inches	Characters per Line		
	10 CI	**12 CI**	**15 CI**
0.0	70	84	105
0.1	69	82	103
0.2	68	81	102
0.3	67	80	100
0.4	66	79	99
0.5	65	78	97
0.6	64	76	96
0.7	63	75	94
0.8	62	74	93
0.9	61	73	91
1.0	60	72	90

4. Copy the three-line section to the clipboard, then from the clipboard ten times, leaving a blank line between each section.

5. Press Apple-1 and select the number of characters per inch that you intend to use for the test.

6. Before each section, set a new right margin that is a tenth of an inch larger than the previous setting, as shown in Figure 6.9.

7. Print the test pattern to paper and count the characters per line for each margin width. Because the lines are numbered, the counting is easy.

Remember that some printers have pitches measured in fractional numbers of characters per inch. That is why the Data Base and Spreadsheet Printer Options menus show estimated (est) characters per line. AppleWorks neither accepts nor calculates fractional CI settings. All three AppleWorks programs correctly calculate the line lengths for all whole-number CI settings between 4 CI and 24 CI.

```
File: Margin.Copy              REVIEW/ADD/CHANGE              Escape: Main Menu
=====|====|====|====|====|====|====|====|====|====|====|====|====|====|====|===
--------Chars per Inch: 15 chars
--------Left Margin:  1.0 inches
--------Right Margin:  0.0 inches
123456789.123456789.123456789.123456789.123456789.123456789.123456789.1234567
89.123456789.123456789.123456789.123456789.123456789.123456789.123456789.1234
56789.123456789.123456789.

--------Right Margin:  0.1 inches
123456789.123456789.123456789.123456789.123456789.123456789.123456789.1234567
89.123456789.123456789.123456789.123456789.123456789.123456789.123456789.1234
56789.123456789.123456789.

--------Right Margin:  0.2 inches
123456789.123456789.123456789.123456789.123456789.123456789.123456789.1234567
89.123456789.123456789.123456789.123456789.123456789.123456789.123456789.1234
56789.123456789.123456789.

--------Right Margin:  0.3 inches
123456789.123456789.123456789.123456789.123456789.123456789.123456789.1234567
89.123456789.123456789.123456789.123456789.123456789.123456789.123456789.1234
-----------------------------------------------------------------------------
Type entry or use @ commands          Line 1  Column 1       @-? for Help
```

Figure 6.9: Copy for testing print lines at various margin widths

Caution: *The Word Processor screen uses 77-character lines.*

The screen shows 80 character columns per line, but even with no margins, the words will wrap at column 78. The maximum line length on the screen is 77 characters. You should know all this when you set wide margins.

Because the margins are set in tenths of inches rather than character spaces, only the 10 CI setting matches the screen to the printer. If the printer option settings allow more than 77 characters, the printer will not print the text exactly as you see it on the screen. Given the screen's effective 77-character width, margin settings of 0.3 on the left and 0 on the right will print the text as it appears on the screen. The appropriate margins for other print pitches are problematic: see the previous tips on margin widths and characters per line.

Tip: *You may be able to produce any line length by tricking AppleWorks with hard switches.*

As Table 6.6 shows, you cannot normally print 77 characters per line at 12 CI. However, there is sometimes a way around this limitation. Many printers use both hard and soft switches. Although soft switches generally override hard switches, most printers can respond to either alone. For example, the Abati LQ-20 has dip-switch controls for 10, 12, and 15 characters per inch. If the Printer Options menu and the printer dip switches are set for 12 CI, but no CI codes have been entered for printer configuration, AppleWorks calculates in 10 CI.

The reason for this is simple: AppleWorks defaults to 10 CI calculations in the absence of all the information it needs. Therefore, when the Abati dip switches are set for 12 CI, you can simply change the platen width setting in the Printer Options menu to a setting of 9.7 inches. With the default left and right margins in effect, the printer will then print a 77-character line at 12 characters per inch.

There are other uses for this technique. In this book, for example, all the screen copies were printed at 12 CI by using hard switches with no CI control codes installed in AppleWorks.

Tip: *Print a ruler to measure characters per inch.*

Many data processing suppliers offer rulers that measure characters at 10, 12, or 15 characters per inch. If you need to measure forms infrequently, print your own from a template. Figure 6.10 shows two ruler templates: one for 10 CI with a caret every five characters and one for 12CI with a caret every six characters. The two rulers are the same length on the screen, but the 12 CI version will be shorter when printed.

You can print any ruler of any length in the number of characters for which it will be used. Make long rulers in the Spreadsheet. When you use the ruler, align the first vertical bar points with the mid-point of the first letter. In this sense it is slightly different from a common wooden ruler.

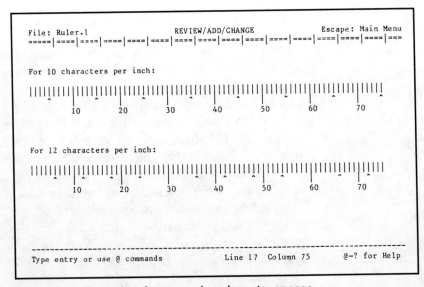

Figure 6.10: *Two rulers for measuring character spaces*

Caution: *Many daisy print wheels include non-ASCII characters.*

Non-ASCII characters are typically substituted for ASCII decimal numbers 92, 94, 96, and 123–126. Two of these characters are particularly important for AppleWorks: print wheels may substitute the copyright symbol in place of the caret, and the paragraph symbol in place of the vertical bar.

This means that you will have no vertical bar when printing hard copies of the screens and no caret when printing Spreadsheet formulas. Some mail-order suppliers offer daisy print wheels with the correct ASCII sequence of characters: these wheels are generally labeled ASCII 96.

Prestige Elite is one of the few fonts available in both word processor and ASCII 96 sequence. With timely wheel changes you can then have all the characters of both. Figure 6.11 compares the ASCII characters to the substitute characters. The copy was made by taking the printer off line to change daisy wheels after the ASCII 96 characters were printed.

PRINT BUFFERS

The efficiency of AppleWorks makes printing seem inefficient, but print buffers can minimize the time spent waiting to get back to AppleWorks. Most printers come with small internal buffers

	92	94	96	123	124	125	126
ASCII 96	\	^	`	{	|	}	~
Prestige Elite	®	©	°	§	¶	†	™

Figure 6.11: Characters typically substituted in the ASCII sequence

(2K or less). Printers commonly used with the Apple IIe print from 12 to 100 characters per second. By using larger buffers (8K–64K), you can regain use of the Apple within seconds after using the print command. For example, AppleWorks can send a 12K file to a buffer in about 14 seconds, and about 1K per second for anything beyond that size.

Tip: *Expand the buffer in your printer if you can.*

Some printers can hold more memory chips. For example, the standard 2K buffer within the Juki 6100 can be expanded to 8K. That is still not quite enough for most reports, but you need not send an entire file at once. Remember also that a Spreadsheet printout uses less memory than the worksheet from which it is derived.

You can clear the buffer by turning off the printer, without affecting the program running in AppleWorks. For example, suppose you print four pages of single-spaced text. It goes to the buffer in the printer in several seconds, about the time it takes to realize that your margins are wrong. If the Word Processor has returned to the text and the cursor is flashing, you can simply turn off the printer, empty the buffer instantly, reset the margins, and start over again.

Tip: *A buffered interface card may require more thought than a buffered printer.*

Consider the buffered Grappler + card for the Apple IIe. It comes with 16K memory, expandable to 32K or 64K. It was designed so that you can use Control-Open-Apple-Reset to boot another program without disturbing the buffer. To clear the buffer you must depress Control-Reset for two seconds, which takes you out of the AppleWorks program. If you want to continue with AppleWorks, you must reboot with the Startup disk or use the

Monitor routine described in Chapter 1. If you use the macro program described in Chapter 7, you can use Control-Reset routinely. You must clear any buffer in the printer as well, even if it is a small one.

To minimize the inconvenience of starting over whenever you make a formatting mistake, place a pause marker early in a document. If anything is wrong, you can press Escape from the print menu to get back to the program without committing everything to the buffer. On the other hand, if the document is printing correctly, just press the Space bar to keep loading. Other internal print buffers require less thought. For example, Applied Engineering has a buffer option for its memory cards. You can empty this buffer by pressing Control-Open-Apple-C, which has no effect on AppleWorks.

Tip: *If you have a buffered Grappler + card, install more 64K dynamic RAM chips.*

You can add 4164 DRAM chips to the buffered Grappler + card just as you would add RAM chips to an 80-character extended memory card. The 4164 DRAM chips cost about two dollars each, and the Grappler manual explains how to install them. Adding two chips doubles the original 16K buffer, and may be one of the best productivity investments available for an Apple IIe system. The 32K should be adequate for about 90 percent of your printing. Adding four chips beyond that increases the capacity to 64K.

SUMMARY

In this chapter we have reviewed solutions to the most difficult printer installation problems. We have discussed some techniques for tricking AppleWorks into providing more options. At this point you can return to Chapters 2 through 5 to try out these options. Make notes on how each technique works, and keep the information in your AppleWorks notebook.

Chapter 7 includes information on using macro programs to install and change printer control codes quickly. Macros can also minimize the time and thought required for other tasks, including setting text formats for printing. Appendix A includes a discussion of prospects for AppleWorks and the Apple II during coming years, including developments in printer interfacing.

The all-important ASCII table appears in Appendix B. Keep it near at hand, along with your printer manual. You may even want to write your own one-page manual for the Silentype.

7

Using Macros

acros can significantly increase the value of AppleWorks by eliminating much of the tedium in repetitive operations and much of the time required for manual keyboard entry. In this chapter we will discuss Super MacroWorks from Beagle Bros for AppleWorks version 2.0, because it includes the macro capabilities of other add-on macro programs such as MacroWorks and AutoWorks, and because it introduces extended programming capabilities.

Everything you have learned in previous chapters will be useful here, because automation requires precise understanding of efficient techniques and undocumented problems. To create macros you simply record the sequence of keystrokes you use to perform a task. The command language of AppleWorks is the language of macros.

There are potential pitfalls in macros, to be sure. You will not have a direct overview of your work. For example, there may have been a time when you decided not to print a Data Base report because something seemed out of place, and it turned out that many things were wrong. Before you depend on a macro, make certain that the manual operation works precisely as you had intended.

When using macros, you must make a distinction between the Open-Apple and Solid-Apple keys. Super MacroWorks and similar programs use the Solid-Apple key in combination with another key to call each macro. That means you need to think about such things as whether to give up Solid-Apple-E for switching between the insert and overstrike keys.

As with AppleWorks, we will discuss techniques that program reference manuals tend to overlook. As in Chapter 1, the tips and cautions in this chapter address the problems that tend to slow people down most often: design choices and uncertainties about what to do next when a macro goes awry. The overall performance of Super MacroWorks is impressive, and it is a valuable extension of ProDOS and the Desktop. Even if you decide not to work with macros, this chapter can reinforce your understanding of AppleWorks.

Figure 7.1 is the most important reference point in this chapter. It includes 38 basic macros—the ones I use most often. They appear in Super MacroWorks notation, but you can quickly convert them to MacroWorks notation using only the find and replace commands in AppleWorks. Because these macros contain only AppleWorks commands, you can rewrite them for other macro systems, including AutoWorks.

```
Macros                                          Remarks
--------------------------------------------------------------------------
START
<esc>:<all><oa-Q><esc>!                         Escape to Desktop from file
<left>:<awp><oa-tab><sa-left>!                  Move cursor to left margin
<right>:<awp><sa-left><down><left><left>!       Move cursor to end of line
<up>:<all><up><up><up><up>!                     Move cursor up 4 lines
<down>:<all><down><down><down><down>!           Move cursor down 4 lines

<spc>:<all><spc><spc><spc><spc>!                Insert 4 spaces
<tab>:<awp><tab><sa-tab>!                        Move cursor to right margin
-:<all>------------!                            Enter 12 dashes
`:<awp><sa-left><oa-M>T<sa-tab><rtn>!           "Delete" line to clipboard

A:<all><oa-Q><esc><rtn><rtn>!                   Add files to Desktop
B:<asp><oa-B>E<right>!                           Blank cell entry, move right
C:<asp><oa-L>C<rtn>C!                             Set a column width
D:<awp><right><oa-left><oa-M>T<oa-right><left><rtn>!  "Delete" word

E:<all><oa-E>!                                   Change editing cursor
F:<all><oa-1><oa-F>T<oa-Y>!                       Find new text from beginning
G:<awp><oa-F>MO<rtn>N<oa-D><rtn>!                 Go to marker 0 and delete it
H:<asp><oa-F>C<oa-Y>A1<rtn>!                      Home to cell A1 of Spreadsheet
I:<all>??? !                                      Insert 3 question marks

J:<all><right><right><right><right><right><right>!   Jump 6 spaces right
K:<asp><oa-U><spc><del><rtn>!                     Recalculate just one cell
L:<asp><oa-L><rtn>LR!                             Label right justified
M:<all><oa-O>SM<rtn>0<rtn><esc>!                  Set marker 0
N:<all><oa-N>a<rtn>!                              Change file name
O:<all><oa-O>LM<rtn>.5<rtn>RM<rtn>.3<rtn>BM<rtn>1.5<rtn>CI<rtn>10<rtn><esc>!
                                                  Set options for text pages

P:<all><oa-P><rtn>1<rtn><rtn>!                    Print file with first printer
Q:<all><oa-Q><rtn>!                               Quick change back to file
R:<all><oa-1><oa-Q><rtn><oa-R>T!                  Replace new text from beginning
S:<all><oa-S>!                                    Save

T:<all>AppleWorks !                               Text
U:<all><oa-C>F!                                   Undo: copy from clipboard
V:<asp><oa-V>RFM<oa-V>PY!                          Set manual recalc, protection
W:<all><oa-O>LM<rtn>0<rtn>RM<rtn>0<rtn>BM<rtn>1<rtn>CI<rtn>16<rtn><esc>!
                                                  Wide worksheet options

X:<all><oa-Q><down><rtn>!                         Change to next Desktop file
Y:<all><oa-D><sa-left><rtn>!                      Delete line to left of cursor
Z:<all>3<rtn>Y!                                   Zap changed file

[:<all><oa-Q><esc>5<rtn>1<rtn>1<rtn><oa-Q><rtn>!  Set to drive 1
]:<all><oa-Q><esc>5<rtn>1<rtn>2<rtn><oa-Q><rtn>!  Set to drive 2
\:<all><oa-Q><esc>5<rtn>7<rtn>4<rtn>2<rtn>Y<oa-Q><rtn>!
                                                  Toggle top-of-page setting

END
--------------------------------------------------------------------------
```

Figure 7.1: Set of basic macros

Many tips explain the reasoning behind design choices for these basic macros. In each case the text refers to Figure 7.1 for the specific notation. Where Super MacroWorks offers an additional command to create an alternative version of the macro, the revised notation appears within the tip.

This chapter is divided into 11 sections. The first section introduces tips on installing macro programs. The next section covers macro design tips that apply throughout AppleWorks. The third section explains how to write several macros that are particularly useful for the Desktop.

The following three sections describe macros written for individual programs: the Word Processor, Data Base, and Spreadsheet. By limiting the scope of individual macros, Super MacroWorks can store three macros for each key combination. The following two sections provide tips for using macros for transferring data and managing printers.

The ninth section reviews additional Super MacroWorks options for modifying AppleWorks. These include changing the beep, replacing help messages, and using Control-Reset. The last two sections discuss advanced applications and control programs. These sections are the most challenging, providing tips that suggest the great potential of AppleWorks. A summary concludes the chapter.

INSTALLING MACRO PROGRAMS

Installing Super MacroWorks requires much forethought. You can save time by reading this section before starting with Super MacroWorks or any macro program. Once installed, Super MacroWorks is surprisingly convenient to use, particularly if you need to use several sets of macros.

Tip: *You can minimize conflicts if you think ahead about installing macro programs.*

Patches and programs that modify AppleWorks can create problems. As noted in Chapter 1, you have to think ahead if you use more than one program at a time. The first rules to remember are to always use a copy of AppleWorks, not the original, and to archive at least one extra copy of the original.

If you want to add Super MacroWorks to versions of Apple-Works modified by programs used for memory expansion cards, you cannot do it. Super MacroWorks has a pre-expander patch that must be installed first. That means you have to start from scratch with copies of the original AppleWorks version 2.0 disks. See Chapter 1 for a tip on the order of installation. See the next tip for an additional complication.

Tip: *Macro programs come with their own macros.*

Super MacroWorks comes with an extensive collection of macros in several Word Processor files. In this chapter we will mention three types of macros:

- Built-in macros: Macro programs often include a few macros that you cannot change. The Super MacroWorks manual includes a complete listing of its own built-in macros. You will probably use most of them and ignore a few. Super MacroWorks offers an unusual option to reassign its Solid-Apple-<down> macro to another set of keys. In the next section, we will discuss the advantages of doing that. If you plan to reassign this built-in macro, you must do it before installing Super MacroWorks on AppleWorks.

- Basic macros: This is the set of macros that Super Macro-Works installs as the default file. These macros load when AppleWorks loads, but you can revise and replace them, and almost everyone does that. In Super MacroWorks the file is called Macros.Super, and you can read it as a Word Processor file. It resembles Figure 7.1 except for the actual macros. Figure 7.1 lists my choices for basic macros. If you want to install them as your basic macros, you need the Super MacroWorks program to install that file.

- Standard macros: Some macros are so logical that all macro programs should have them, and everyone should use them. In a following tip we will discuss Super Macro-Works macros that deserve to be standard macros. Basic macros usually include many standard macros.

Tip: *A macro is a record of keystrokes used to perform a task.*

The command language of AppleWorks is the language of macros. Most macro programs allow you to write the command sequence as text in a Word Processor file. Figure 7.1 shows a list of macros as it would appear in text. The list begins with START and ends with END. The actual macros begin in the left column, and documentation remarks begin in the right column. Even without translating the notation, you can understand the structure of macro writing.

The best way to start is with someone else's set of macros—the ones in Figure 7.1 or the ones that come with Super MacroWorks. You can revise or replace existing macros and write additional new macros. When you make a change, press Open-Apple-= to compile the complete list of macros.

In short, if you know how to complete a task manually, you can write a macro for it. Of course, you want to make certain that each macro will behave predictably wherever you use it, and you will learn how to do that in this chapter.

Tip: *There is a simple way to create and compile macros.*

When you attempt to write long macros, you may not be able to remember the exact command sequence. Fortunately, Super MacroWorks allows you to record the macro while you perform the task. A macro begins within AppleWorks when you press

Open-Apple-X. A message asks you to assign a key for use in conjunction with the Solid-Apple key. Once you assign the key, modified AppleWorks records the macro. You press Control-@ to end the macro. After that, the macro works automatically.

In most cases, you will want to add the recorded macro to your existing Word Processor list of macros. AppleWorks automatically lists all macros in effect when you press Open-Apple-$. It does not list the remarks associated with them, but there is a way around this limitation.

When AppleWorks prints the macros, delete the old ones and keep the one you just recorded. Move it into a logical place on the existing list of macros, somewhere between the words START and END. You can then add remarks to explain what it does. Use Open-Apple-= to recompile the list, just to make certain that you moved the macro intact.

Tip: *A completed macro has four parts.*

Every macro has a *label* to indicate which keys call it, *tokens* to represent keystrokes used within it, an *end marker* to indicate its end point, and *remarks* to note its purpose. The first three parts are absolutely necessary; the remarks are strongly recommended. A set or list of macros begins with the word START and ends with the word END (you can use uppercase or lowercase, but make certain that carriage returns immediately follow those words). Those are the basics of structure. Figure 7.1 shows a list of examples, and we will review the parts in more detail.

In Super MacroWorks, the label always appears at the beginning as a character followed by a colon (as in A:). Certain keys use labels with angle brackets:

<left>	←
<right>	→
<up>	↑
<down>	↓
<del>	Delete
<esc>	Escape

\<rtn\>	Return
\<spc\>	Space bar
\<tab\>	Tab

Super MacroWorks also recognizes a press on the Space bar as a space if you prefer not to use \<spc\>. You can spell tokens with uppercase or lowercase letters.

Tokens that represent function keys and commands appear within angle brackets. Tokens for the function keys listed above are the same as the labels.

In Super MacroWorks the first token after the label and colon tells where the macro applies:

- \<awp\> means only in the Word Processor

- \<adb\> means only in the Data Base

- \<asp\> means only in the Spreadsheet

- \<all\> means throughout AppleWorks

This allows you to assign up to four macros for each key. You can write a macro for one program without having to worry about unwanted results in the other programs. You must list limited macros before an all-inclusive macro. If you use Solid-Apple-K for two macros, one with \<awp\> and one with \<all\>, the latter works only in the Data Base, Spreadsheet, and Desktop menus.

Here are three examples of macro tokens for AppleWorks commands:

\<oa-Q\>	Open-Apple-Q, the Desktop Index command
\<oa-S\>	Open-Apple-S, the save command
\<ctrl-Y\>	Remove line to the right of the cursor

Once you understand the pattern, you can interpret tokens quickly.

The keystroke sequences show letters as you would enter them for printer options, and numbers as you would enter them from other menus. For example, consider the following sequence taken from the Solid-Apple-W macro in Figure 7.1:

<oa-O>LM<rtn>0<rtn> <esc>

This macro sequence goes to the Printer Options menu, specifies a left margin of 0, and returns to the the text line. It works equally well from a Data Base report format or Spreadsheet.

The macro end marker is an exclamation point. If you forget it, Super MacroWorks compiles everything up to the next exclamation point. The character does not otherwise appear in a macro, except within angle brackets or other specific marks used to delimit messages.

A remark should follow the end marker. It explains what the macro does. For more on macro remarks, see a following tip on documentation.

Tip: *Super MacroWorks adds useful commands to AppleWorks.*

Super Macroworks includes certain macros that you cannot change. They can therefore be considered as standard Super MacroWorks macros. The following list includes the most useful built-in macros:

- Open-Apple-Delete is the much needed command for deleting the character under the cursor. You will probably use it often. Solid-Apple-Delete does the same thing.

- Solid-Apple-Return moves the cursor to the next carriage return (the end of a paragraph in the AppleWorks sense). Among other uses, it lets you write macros to strip carriage returns from formatted text files.

- Solid-Apple- ^ finds the next print enhancement marker, but it searches more slowly than Apple-F. If you know the marker is somewhere nearby, this is the command to use. You can stop the search by pressing Escape.

- Open-Apple-; changes uppercase letters to lowercase. This is particularly useful for titles and headings. Open-Apple-: changes lowercase letters to uppercase.

- Open-Apple-+ prints a hard copy of whatever line the cursor is on. It is a controlled version of Apple-H, and it is usually more efficient than printing a complete screen of 24 lines. You can repeat the command for the next line.

- Solid-Apple-" enters the date in the format 1/14/88. This is particularly useful in the Data Base. Solid-Apple-' enters the date in the format January 14, 1988, which is more appropriate for writing letters.

Tip: *The Super MacroWorks manual makes macros appear more complicated than they are.*

Beyond macros, Super MacroWorks offers a set of commands that can perform logical tests, store the results, and proceed in different ways based on those results. The Beagle Bros manual draws no line between macros and control programs. This makes macros appear to be more complicated than they really are.

In this chapter, we will discuss control programs only in the last section, because basic macros are more immediately useful to most people. When you feel comfortable with macros, you will enjoy working with the programming language.

GENERAL MACRO TIPS

The following tips are useful for using and designing macros for AppleWorks. The techniques will help you use the available options more efficiently. If you have used macros in other programs, you may be surprised to learn that Super MacroWorks is also a programming language.

Caution: *There are no standard macros.*

Different macro programs provide different sets of default macros. The key assigned to a macro in one program may be assigned to a completely different macro in another program. Figure 7.1 is my list of basic macros based on common needs, which may be different from yours. You can use the list as a starting point.

If several people use the same Apple II, you will probably want to establish standards within the group. One person can read this chapter and write a proposed set of basic macros. The others can then suggest changes.

Tip: *Certain basic macros should remain as standards.*

Super MacroWorks includes a file of basic macros, any of which can be replaced. However, the following key assignments are so logical that they should remain on everyone's list of standard macros:

- Solid-Apple-← brings the cursor to the left margin of a Word Processor line. Solid-Apple-→ brings the cursor to the column immediately following the last character in the line (a good position for editing). These macros are easy to use with the index and middle fingers of the right hand.

- Solid-Apple-A adds files to the Desktop. It uses Apple-Q to reach the Desktop Index from any point in AppleWorks, then Escape to reach the Main Menu. You will probably come to appreciate this macro more than any other.

- Solid-Apple-D deletes a whole word in the Word Processor. The cursor can be anywhere on that word. The word is moved to the clipboard. If you like to keep text on the clipboard for long periods of time, you can revise the macro and make the deletion final. Solid-Apple-D can also remove printer option lines.

Tip: *Think about the procedures you use in your work.*

In designing a set of macros, think first about making the keyboard interface more efficient. Each macro should save time, so you need to think about how you spend your time at the keyboard. Make a list of the multiple-keystroke sequences you use often. In developing macros, the idea is to begin with the macro that saves you the most work in terms of thought and keystroke time.

After you make the list, number the entries according to the amount of time (and thought) they will save overall—time saved per operation multiplied by the number of operations per session. For example, a macro that replaces a four-key sequence 20 times in a typical AppleWorks session is worth more than one that replaces a 24-key sequence twice.

Tip: *Write the most useful macros first.*

The most useful macros are the ones you will use most frequently. You will want to remember these easily. They deserve mnemonic priority when you allocate letters and other characters to macros. You must also consider keyboard layout: because the Solid-Apple key is on the right, the most desirable keys for commonly used macros are those on the left.

The best mnemonics reinforce existing AppleWorks commands. For example, if Open-Apple-Y is the command to delete a line from the cursor to the right margin, Solid-Apple-Y can be the macro to delete a line from the cursor to the left margin. Fortunately, the Y key is near the middle of the keyboard.

The best development path is to create a basic set of macros, use them for a while, think about possible improvements, and then create a revised set. Figure 7.1 provides a ready-made basic set of macros that you can quickly adapt to almost any macro program.

You will eventually want to create specialized macro sets for the Word Processor, Data Base, and Spreadsheet. Each specialized set should include many macros from the basic set. You may even want to create specialized macro sets for specific integrated projects.

Caution: *Keep the Solid-Apple option for certain existing Apple-Works commands.*

When you use the Solid-Apple key for a macro, only the Open-Apple key works for an AppleWorks command that uses the same letter. Thus, if you use Solid-Apple-P for a macro, you cannot use it for the AppleWorks print command. Because the letter E is directly above the Open-Apple key, it is easier to use Solid-Apple-E during editing, so you will not want to give up E to a macro. Once you assign macros, Super MacroWorks limits the standard AppleWorks commands to the Open-Apple key. However, you can write a macro that simply replicates an Open-Apple command (see the entry for E in Figure 7.1).

On the other hand, after you use Apple-S, you have to wait for at least ten seconds anyway, so you may not consider it necessary to retain use of the Solid-Apple key for that command. These are simply examples from a range of possibilities—you will decide what works best for you.

Tip: *Document macros thoroughly.*

When you write a report on the Word Processor, you rarely need directions when you load it again several weeks later. When you write macros, or have Super MacroWorks write them for you, you need to add remarks about what each one does. A brief remark normally fits on the same line with the macro, following the exclamation point. If it includes a technique requiring further comment, place an asterisk after the remark and write additional information after the END mark.

You could also explain in the remarks why you chose to allocate a key for one purpose rather than another. This thought process will make you reconsider many choices and make a few changes.

Tip: *Install three printers.*

In Chapter 6 you learned how to install three printers in AppleWorks. There we wanted to get the most printing capability possible. Here we want to ensure that the macro sees the same Print Menu every time, so that option 4 in the Word Processor will always be the one to print a text (ASCII) file on disk, for example.

In this chapter, every macro that includes printing assumes that you are working with AppleWorks version 2.0 and three printers installed. Remember that, compared to earlier versions of Apple-Works, version 2.0 has one additional print option in the Data Base when you print a tables-style report. That option is for printing to the Mail Merge clipboard, and it does not appear when you use a labels-style report.

Tip: *Use numbers to select menu options.*

In manual operation, many people use the arrow keys to move the highlight bar on the Desktop Index or menu. This method often saves time and thought when you want the next item, and it provides a measure of visual certainty. When the highlight bar is already on the menu option you want, you normally just press Return.

Remember, however, that AppleWorks menus have numbered positions. Using numbers in macros guarantees that the program will make the correct selections, and the macros often take less space. Numbers also make macros easier to interpret, because you have a better idea where you are.

Tip: *Write macros for intermediate cursor controls.*

AppleWorks commands can move the cursor up or down one line at a time, or a whole screen at a time. When you add intermediate-range macros, start with four lines at a time. This provides a good scrolling speed without disorienting the viewer.

AppleWorks commands can move the cursor left or right one character space at a time, or a tab setting at a time in the Word Processor. In the Data Base and Spreadsheet, the Tab key moves the cursor a category or cell at a time. The Word Processor can also move a word at a time to the left or right. The most useful additional move is six characters to the right in Data Base categories and Spreadsheet cells.

As previously noted, Super MacroWorks comes with macros for whole-line moves in the Word Processor. Figure 7.1 includes my notations for macros that move the cursor.

Tip: *Add word and line deletions.*

The AppleWorks Open-Apple-Y command can delete the remainder of a line in the Word Processor; the remainder of an entry in a Data Base category; and the remainder of a label, value, or formula in a Spreadsheet cell. This is a powerful command, and completely final.

In the Word Processor, many people also want to delete a word at a time, a complete line from any point, or from the left of the cursor. Figure 7.1 provides macros that can do this, and the following tip discusses the relative advantages and disadvantages of making deletions final.

Tip: *Macros can combine moves and deletions.*

AppleWorks has no command for undoing deletions, but macros that delete text can send it to the clipboard (or even to another file). When you use macros to delete words or lines, consider using Open-Apple-M rather than Open-Apple-D within the macro. Here are two versions of a macro for deleting a word.

The first deletes a word, whereas the second moves it to the clipboard:

D:<awp><right><oa-left><oa-D><oa-right>
<left><Rtn>!
D:<awp><right><oa-left><oa-M>T<oa-right>
<left><Rtn>!

The second version appears in Figure 7.1. Deciding which to use is a matter of judgment. There is only one clipboard, and you may want to have text on it even while deleting other text. The ability to undo a deletion provides the most benefit when you delete a word with thoughts of placing it somewhere else in the sentence. However, the AppleWorks Open-Apple-D and Open-Apple-Y commands are final, and when you start mixing final deletions with undoable deletions, you must remember which is which.

One resolution to the dilemma is to keep a Solid-Apple-` macro in reserve. The grave accent key is out of the way at the lower left of the keyboard. The example in Figure 7.1 removes the complete Word Processor line no matter where the cursor is on that line. Even if you have no macros that delete to the clipboard, the Solid-Apple-U macro in Figure 7.1 provides a quick method for copying from the clipboard.

Tip: *A macro can change file names quickly.*

No matter how careful you are, you will occasionally experiment with a file without changing its name. In one of those cases you will save the altered file. You can use a macro to minimize the chance of that happening.

In this macro, you simply use Open-Apple-N, add a lowercase *a* to the beginning of the file name, and return to the file. This is the notation for Super MacroWorks:

N:<all><oa-N>a<rtn>!

If you save the file by mistake, the file name will appear near the top of its file type, and the initial lowercase *a* makes it easy to find and delete.

Caution: *Never use a macro to erase a file on screen.*

Zap is a good mnemonic for a Solid-Apple-Z macro that wipes out a line or even a paragraph, but never use it to wipe out a file. If you use it by accident, you can lose what you have not yet saved. If someone else uses it by accident, you have additional problems.

It takes only three keystrokes to remove a file anyway: Apple-1, Apple-D, Apple-9, Return. It is a perfect example of a case in which a macro can be far more trouble than it is worth.

Tip: *A macro can delete files quickly.*

The idea here is to take AppleWorks right to the point where you can select files to be deleted. It can work with any standard data disk location. The macro should do the following:

1. Use Apple-Q and Escape to go to the Main Menu.

2. Select option 5 and press Return to reach the Other Activities menu.

3. Select option 4 to delete files from the data disk. (AppleWorks then automatically lists the catalog for the data disk.)

The macro for deleting files can use Solid-Apple->. The angle bracket is the mark for specifying files to be deleted, and you are unlikely to press that key by mistake, because it requires the Shift key. This is the notation for Super MacroWorks:

>:<all><oa-Q><esc>5<rtn>4<rtn>!

After you select the files for deletion, the trip back uses Open-Apple-Q and Return. Although this may seem too simple for a macro, you will return from the Desktop menus often, and Solid-Apple-Q is surprisingly convenient (see Figure 7.1).

Tip: *You can write similar macros for other options on the Other Activities menu.*

You can write a macro to list all files on the data disk from any point within AppleWorks. This catalog includes the awp, adb, and asp file types used for AppleWorks as well as other ProDOS files. Note, however, that you see the same catalog with the previous macro.

You can even write a macro to automate disk formatting from any point within AppleWorks. That may seem risky, but if the disk has already been formatted, the macro will stop where AppleWorks does—with a warning and a question that requires you to type YES to proceed. The message will display the volume name if the disk has a ProDOS format.

Caution: *Some things are better done manually.*

This is important because AppleWorks has a comfortable feeling in manual operation. There will be times when you may not want to have screens flying by during macro execution. If you prefer to do something manually, do as you please.

When you perform an operation infrequently, there is no point in writing a macro, because you can probably find a better use for the key combination needed to call it.

MACROS FOR THE DESKTOP

Macros for the Desktop use the token <all>, even when they are used only with the Main Menu and Other Activities menu. This really does make sense. If you use Solid-Apple-K for four macros, one each with <awp>, <adb>, <asp>, and <all>, the last works only in Desktop menus. In later sections we will discuss additional macros that spend at least part of their time in Desktop menus.

Tip: *You can reassign the Solid-Apple-<down> macro in Super MacroWorks.*

When AppleWorks displays the catalog for a volume or disk, you cannot use Open-Apple-↓ to move the cursor down a whole screen at a time. You therefore need to hold the key down or write a macro to move it more than one line at a time.

Super MacroWorks comes with a built-in Solid-Apple-<down> macro that moves the cursor down 18 lines at a time, even in file catalog displays. However, it is more convenient to have an intermediate control of 4–6 lines throughout AppleWorks. Super MacroWorks comes with a program to assign this built-in macro to Solid-Apple-Control-D, but you must modify Super Macro-Works before installing it on AppleWorks. That done, you can use the Solid-Apple-<down> macro shown in Figure 7.1. The latter macro also works in the catalog displays.

Tip: *Use Apple-Q to reach a predictable point in AppleWorks.*

In AppleWorks through version 1.3, when you load more than one file, a message suggests that you press the Space bar, which goes to the Main Menu. You should use Apple-Q instead, because you want the Desktop Index. In version 2.0, AppleWorks goes right to the Desktop Index when you load files.

Consider the significance of the Desktop Index. Apple-Q will get you there in one command from anywhere in AppleWorks. Once there, you are one keystroke (Escape) from the Main Menu and one keystroke (Return) from the file in use. When a macro must work from a predictable point outside a file, always use Apple-Q to establish that point.

Tip: *Use Solid-Apple-Esc to reach the Main Menu.*

The first macro in Figure 7.1 is one of the few you will write to replace just two keystrokes, but if you are an experienced AppleWorks user, you know that it makes good sense. Escape will sometimes take you from a file to the Main Menu, but Solid-Apple-Escape will always get you there, and it saves thinking about whether to use Escape or Open-Apple-Q, Escape.

Tip: *Write a macro to access either drive 1 or 2.*

When you load AppleWorks entirely into RAM, and your system has two disk drives, you can put data disks in both drives. For any given file, every other save can go to the backup disk in drive 1.

Open-Apple-S saves the file to the standard location of the data disk. On a two-drive system, drive 2 is normally the standard location. To select drive 1, use the following strategy:

1. Press Apple-Q and Escape to go to the Main Menu.

2. Select option 5 and press Return to reach the Other Activities menu.

3. Select option 1 and press Return within that menu to change the current disk drive.

4. Select option 1 and press Return within the Change Current Drive menu to select drive 1.

5. Press Apple-Q and Return to return to the original file.

To select drive 2 again, select option 2 in step 4 listed above. When you do all this manually, it takes 15–20 seconds and some thought.

When you do it with a macro, it takes three seconds. The macros for Solid-Apple-1 and Solid-Apple-2 appear in Figure 7.1.

Of course, you could write a macro, here Solid-Apple-S, that can save a file to drive 1 and then reset to drive 2:

```
S:<all><oa-Q><esc>5<rtn>1<rtn>1<rtn><oa-Q>
<rtn><oa-S><rtn><oa-Q><esc>5<rtn>1
<rtn>2<rtn><oa-Q><rtn>!
```

Note, however, that there are advantages to using modular design and retaining some manual control. Because the first two macros change the standard drive locations independently, you can also list files, delete files, and format disks from either drive. If you still want to replicate the function of the long Solid-Apple-S macro shown above, you can write a brief macro that incorporates Solid-Apple-1 and Solid-Apple-2.

```
S:<all><sa-1><oa-S><rtn><sa-2>!
```

When you have a choice, use modular construction in macro programs, just as you would in AppleWorks itself.

Tip: *Write a macro to throw out unwanted files.*

If you often bring files to the Desktop to print them or move parts from them, you know that AppleWorks lists them as changed when you attempt to remove them from the Desktop. You have to answer questions before AppleWorks throws them out.

This simple macro substitutes for 3, Return, Y. You can use the Z key for this one, as shown in Figure 7.1. If you use this macro in the Word Processor, Data Base, or Spreadsheet by mistake, it enters 3 and Y on separate lines.

WORD PROCESSOR MACROS

There are many ways to use macros to automate word processing tasks. This section includes some important basic macros. In the section on advanced applications we will cover more complex macros.

In the Word Processor you can often make use of temporary macros for repeating phrases used within a file. Because Super MacroWorks records text as you enter it, it takes almost no extra time. Beyond that, you can use a basic macro file in which most macros work in all programs or in the Word Processor alone. For special projects, such as this book, it makes sense to use a specialized macro file.

Tip: *Keep the screen display in layout mode.*

As you learned in Chapter 2, when you move or copy text, you need format settings to highlight text accurately—it makes a difference whether you take format markers with you. Thus, when you move or copy text, the Word Processor always displays the format settings automatically, often displaying additional lines on the screen. When the display changes, the text line your eyes are following will shift down or even off the screen, and it takes time to adjust to the new display.

When you write macros to automate keystrokes, the displays change rapidly, and the shifts to and from the layout mode can be disorienting. Use the layout mode for editing, and save the normal display mode for the best possible preview of what the printer will put on paper.

Tip: *A macro can change files quickly.*

There are many times when you need to use two Word Processor files together. For example, if you use footnotes, you really need one file for text and another for the notes. When two files appear on the Desktop Index, a macro that calls the next file will alternately call the second file, then the first, and so on in an alternating cycle. In Figure 7.1, the Solid-Apple-X macro does that. Note also, that you can always find the last Desktop file in a macro by going to the first file and using <up> once.

Tip: *Macros can set text formats.*

Everyone knows how to enter printer options for setting the left margin, right margin, bottom margin, and the characters per inch. If you write macros to do these tasks in exactly this order, you can overwrite unwanted entries at the beginning of the Word Processor file.

Solid-Apple-O in Figure 7.1 lists a set of printer options useful for pages of text. The 1.5-inch bottom margin works well when you use a header or footer on each page. Solid-Apple-W lists a set of printer options for wide lines that are sometimes needed to print macro lists in the Word Processor, tables-style reports in the Data Base, and wide worksheets in the Spreadsheet.

If you write macros that enter sets of printer options in different orders, the Data Base and Spreadsheet will never know. However, different orders can create a jumble of old and new options in the Word Processor. In Chapter 2, we noted that one option will automatically overwrite another option only if that option is of the same type on the same line.

There is one additional complication. In the Word Processor, you would normally use the Open-Apple-O macro at the beginning of the file in the layout mode. To make that automatic, you need an additional command. Super MacroWorks uses <zoom> to force the zoom *out* mode, which hides printer options in the Word Processor, shows multiple-record layout in the Data Base, and displays values in the Spreadsheet. That establishes a known point from which to use Open-Apple-Z. The revised macro notation appears below:

```
O:<awp><oa-1><zoom><oa-Z><oa-O>LM
<rtn>.5<rtn>RM<rtn>.3<rtn>BM<rtn>1.5
<rtn>CI<rtn>10<rtn><esc>!
```

Notice that this macro is limited to the Word Processor. It might be inconvenient in the Data Base or Spreadsheet. For example, in the Spreadsheet this leaves the cursor in row 1 with formulas displayed in the cells.

Tip: *You can insert spaces to indent block paragraphs.*

There are two basic types of paragraph formats. Block paragraphs require an empty line between paragraphs. Indented paragraphs require no empty line. You can change the former type to the latter by inserting spaces and later deleting empty lines. Indentations commonly use two to five spaces—five is the convention for typewritten documents. The Tab key will not insert spaces, but you can write a macro to enter the required number. In Figure 7.1, Solid-Apple-<spc> uses four.

Tip: *Use Solid-Apple-C to copy a line of text.*

When you need to copy a line of text from one file to another, write a macro to do what you would normally do. Start at the left margin, copy the line with the ↓ key, and use the ← key to end the highlighting cleanly (it would otherwise include the first character of the next line). Remember that Solid-Apple-U, the undo macro, can copy the line from the clipboard.

Tip: *You can automate the find and replace commands.*

When you first use the find command, you normally want to start from the beginning. When you find the initial occurrence of the text entry, you can choose not to find the next occurrence. That leaves you free to edit. When you repeat the find command, you want the same text entry, and you normally want to start where you left off. AppleWorks meets those common needs.

When you want to use the find command anew, you normally want to start from the beginning with a blank entry place. In this case, AppleWorks makes you erase the old entry first. The Solid-Apple-F macro in Figure 7.1 takes you to the beginning of the file and removes the old entry with Open-Apple-Y.

The Solid-Apple-R macro does almost the same thing, except that it needs Open-Apple-Q to erase both entries at once. Otherwise, you would have to erase the second entry manually.

Tip: *Use macros to set and find markers.*

The Word Processor can have text markers from 0 through 254, and 0 is the one you are least likely to use. As we noted in Chapter 2, markers are a good way to come back to the place you left (at least to the nearest paragraph break).

Solid-Apple-G and Solid-Apple-M quickly set and find marker 0. Note that there is no need to specify that AppleWorks start from the beginning of the file as you would in a macro for finding text. When searching for a marker, AppleWorks always starts from the beginning anyway.

Alternatively, you can write a macro to enter a unique character string, such as @@, directly into the text. This gives you more precise control over location. The Solid-Apple-G and Solid-Apple-M macros would then be written as follows:

```
G:<awp>@@!
M:<awp><oa-1><oa-F>T<oa-Y>@@<rtn>N
<oa-D><right><rtn>!
```

Notice that Solid-Apple-M deletes the characters individually rather than as a word, because this character string can inadvertently be joined with another word.

Tip: *Use temporary macros.*

Temporary macros work particularly well for capturing long words and phrases that will be repeated during a specific work session. Unused number keys work well for this. Open-Apple-X begins the temporary macro sequence, after which you specify a macro key and type what you would normally type anyway. Control-@ ends the recording.

Incidentally, you can use Open-Apple-X simply to make the blinking cursor disappear. The Escape key brings the cursor back. (You cannot allocate the Escape key for live keystroke recording.)

Tip: *Temporary macros and codes can work together.*

All macros require simultaneous keystrokes (Solid-Apple and another key), and that can slow down touch typists. As we noted in Chapter 2, good typists may find it faster to enter *xx* for a frequently used word and then replace all instances at the end of the session.

You can create a temporary macro to type out a long word and then use that macro when you want to see how long a printed line will be (in a list, for example). When you replace all instances of *xx* at the end of a session, use the temporary macro to specify the replacement text. In writing this chapter, I used SA- and OA- as codes and replaced them as case-sensitive text.

Tip: *Use macros to write macros.*

You can use macros to enter tokens such as <rtn>. Typing errors account for most of the mistakes a compiler finds. When a compiler accepts an incorrect token entry as text, the macro can go awry. That can leave a tell-tale clue—tokens on screen as text. The point here is that accurate entry is just as important as quick entry. The same concept applies to command words used in any kind of programming.

When you use macros to write tokens, the macro compiler must be able to tell the difference between the word and the command. To specify the command, enter a space and the <left> token before the closing bracket:

```
1:<awp><rtn <left>>!
2:<awp><right <left>>!
```

If you use temporary macros for tokens, you avoid this complication. The delimiting tokens never present problems; just write them after the actual delimiting token:

    3:<awp><all>!
    4:<awp><awp>!

Tip: *Write a macro to address envelopes.*

If you have a friction-feed daisywheel printer, you can probably address single envelopes as you would with a typewriter. You can convert a letter heading into a return address and mailing address for the envelope. For a business envelope, the return address should have a left margin of 0.2 inches. Five lines after the return address ends, the mailing address should begin with a left margin of 4 inches.

The macro listed below creates the format shown in Figure 7.2. It assumes that the date appears on the first text line, followed by the return address on lines 3 through 5, followed by the mailing address

```
File: Envelope               REVIEW/ADD/CHANGE              Escape: Main Menu
=====|====|====|====|====|====|====|====|====|====|====|====|====|====|====|===
--------Left Margin:  0.5 inches
--------Right Margin:  0.3 inches
--------Bottom Margin:  1.5 inches
    September 30, 1987

--------Left Margin:  0.2 inches
Thomas Farmer
12 Field Rd.
Jefferson, RI 02845




--------Left Margin:  4.0 inches
                              West Supply
                              108 Jefferson Pike
                              Westbrook, MA 02731

--------Pause Here
-------------------------------------------------------------------------------
Type entry or use @ commands         Line 7  Column 4      @-? for Help
```

Figure 7.2: Text format for addressing envelopes

on lines 7 through 10. The latter range can include either a three- or four-line address. This notation assumes that display mode is on and the cursor is on the first text line. It ends with a PH instruction to pause before the greeting and body of the letter:

```
E:<awp><down><down><oa-O>LM<rtn>.2
<rtn><esc><down><down><down>
<down><rtn><rtn><rtn><rtn>
<oa-O>LM<rtn>4<rtn><esc>
<down><down><down><down><oa-O>PH
<rtn><esc><oa-1><down><down><down>!
```

You can add a print routine that prints from the cursor line and enters Escape after reaching the PH instruction. You can even use a macro to restore the letter to its original state.

Tip: *A macro can load Document Checker's batch processing log.*

Pinpoint's Document Checker can batch process multiple Word Processor files automatically. It creates a text file log that includes the total number of words, the number of different words, the number of unmatched words, and a list of unmatched words for each file. This text file always has the name DOCUMENT.LOG, so a macro can use it to create a Word Processor file. Keeping with the convention used in this book, the volume name is /P. The macro is as follows:

```
8:<all><sa-esc>1<rtn>3<rtn>2<rtn>/P/
DOCUMENT.LOG<rtn>Log<rtn>!
```

Even though the macro creates a Word Processor document, it specifies <all> so that you can use it from the Desktop as well.

DATA BASE MACROS

The Data Base presents some unique problems, because its structure is the most difficult to understand well. In many ways, writing and testing macros can be the best way to master it. Once the macros are complete, you can almost forget how to use the Data Base manually.

Tip: *A macro can make the cursor jump to the right.*

In the Data Base and Spreadsheet, Open-Apple-→ and Open-Apple-← cannot move the cursor one word right or left. However, you can meet most of your needs by writing a simple macro to jump the cursor six characters spaces to the right. Solid-Apple-J in Figure 7.1 shows the notation.

You could write another macro to move the cursor six spaces to the left, but Super MacroWorks provides a built-in Solid-Apple-, macro that jumps back to the previous space character in any AppleWorks program. You could also use another increment for the jump, but six spaces seems to provide the best balance for moving quickly and getting close to the intended destination.

To return to the beginning of any category, press Return and ↑. Most people will probably prefer to do that manually. Note that when you use this method in the last category, you temporarily move to the next record before coming back (it will not work in the last category of the last record).

Tip: *Make record selection easier and faster.*

In AppleWorks version 2.0, the find command is slower than in previous versions, but record selection is faster. You can take some of the tedium from record selection by writing macros to begin the process. Temporary macros work well here.

For continuous on-line searching, you normally select from the same category each time. For example, you might be searching for records that contain a specific name in LAST NAME. Assuming it is category 2, the macro would be

```
1:<adb><oa-R>N2<rtn>7<rtn>!
```

Recall from Chapter 4 that the contains rule is often more useful than the equals rule. After the macro, you can type in the name (or delimiting part of the name) and press Escape. Using the macro in the following tip, you can return to all of the records in multiple-record layout.

Tip: *Macros can return you to a standard location.*

The concept of returning to a standard location applies throughout AppleWorks, but here we will use it to return to the multiple-record layout from anywhere in the Data Base. The macro is simple:

1:<adb><oa-R>Y<oa-Q><rtn><zoom>!

Try this routine from different locations. Notice that it also returns the Data Base file from a limiting record selection rule to all records. Open-Apple-R begins record selection, and Y (for Yes) selects all records.

Remember that Super MacroWorks uses <zoom> to force the zoom out mode, which hides printer options in the Word Processor, shows multiple-record layout in the Data Base, and displays values in the Spreadsheet.

Tip: *Add scrolling to the Date Base multiple-record layout.*

Super MacroWorks uses the right-angle bracket to denote the end of a token, so you cannot write <oa->> to switch a category to the right when you change a multiple-record record layout. However, that command is really just <oa-.>. Super MacroWorks uses the left-angle bracket to denote the beginning of a token, so you cannot write <oa-<>. However, that command is <oa-,> because the shift key is not used.

This means that you can build macros that effectively scroll the multiple-record display left and right. The macro listed below makes the first eight categories in multiple-record layout appear to scroll left (even if there are more than eight categories in the file). If you close your eyes and count to three each time you use the macro, you will not have to see the frantic action on screen.

    1:<all><oa-L><oa-.><oa-.><oa-.><oa-.><oa-.>
    <oa-.><esc><rtn>!

Notice that <oa-.> appears only seven times. In this macro, the first category in the multiple-record layout jumps over the next seven categories to become the eighth. Thus, by using <oa-.> 29 times, you can scroll 30 categories.

Tip: *Use a macro to convert dates in the Data Base.*

When you use DATE as a category name, AppleWorks will convert formats such as 9/30/87 to a Sep 30 87 format. The format 9.30 becomes Sep 30.

When you use a category name that does not contain DATE, formats such as 9/30/87 remain as entered. If you later change the category name to DATE, press the Space bar and Return to convert the entry to Sep 30 87. The macro is simple:

    1:<adb><spc><rtn>!

With the Data Base file in multiple-record layout, place the cursor on the DATE entry for the first record, and simply hold down Solid-Apple-1 until it makes all the changes you need.

SPREADSHEET MACROS

AppleWorks lacks some commands found in other spreadsheets. If you first learned another spreadsheet such as Advanced VisiCalc, and you continue to use it, write macros to give Apple-Works a more familiar command structure. The tips below describe some basic macros that almost everyone will want to install.

Tip: *Use a macro to bring the cursor to cell A1 quickly.*

The Spreadsheet has a useful ruler (divider) command: Open-Apple-1 takes you to the first row, and Open-Apple-9 takes you to the last row in use. However, there is no command to go home to cell A1. You can write a macro that finds the A1 coordinate. Solid-Apple-H in Figure 7.1 shows the notation.

You can write a macro to find any coordinate, but you have to enter the coordinate yourself. The example below requires three key entries, but it handles any cell from A01 through Z99—the area where you are most likely to be.

```
':<asp><oa-F>C<oa-Y><key><key><key><rtn>!
```

Super MacroWorks uses an additional command, <key>, to suspend a macro and accept a keystroke before continuing. Unlike the <input> command, <key> returns control to the macro on its own, avoiding the need to press Return. This makes it a faster-running macro.

Tip: *Use a macro to blank a cell and move right.*

When designing templates, you need the ability to blank a cell quickly. Solid-Apple-B in Figure 7.1 shows the notation. You can also write a macro to blank a cell and move down. It always helps to be heading somewhere else when you are on a blanking run, because nothing more can happen where you were. (If you wanted to write something else in the cell, you wouldn't be blanking it in the first place.)

Tip: *Write a macro to help set column width.*

The commands for setting column width are unusual and sometimes difficult to remember. Solid-Apple-C takes you to the point where you start using ← or → to change the column width.

Although it is easy to write a macro that narrows or widens a cell one character space at a time, there is no practical advantage to doing that.

Tip: *Set labels right and values to two places.*

The most common format requirements for single cells are for labels justified to the right and values set to two decimal places. Figure 7.1 shows the Solid-Apple-L macro for labels. The macro for values would be

    L:<asp><oa-L><rtn>V2!

When you set values, you should think about whether a related block, row, or column needs the same setting. When you start setting values to two decimal places one by one, it shows if you enter a value such as 12.20.

Tip: *Set manual recalculation and protection together.*

The process for setting manual recalculation is difficult to remember. When you begin a new worksheet, you need to specify manual recalculation early in the development process. It is also a good idea to enable cell protection at the same time, even if you choose not to define protection for individual cells until later.

This is one of those cases when a macro is clearly practical. Solid-Apple-V in Figure 7.1 shows the notation.

Tip: *Macros are good for entering commonly used values and formulas.*

You may have several commonly used values that require up to nine digits. Pi is a good example, and we can write it with seven places to the right of the decimal:

    1:<asp>3.1415927!

You can automate formulas, such as simple conversions. The following macro converts hectares to acres. It assumes that the hectare value is in the cell just to the left of the cursor cell. The cursor cell contains the formula and the acre result:

2:<asp> + <left>*2.4710538<rtn>!

Notice that once again we used a value with a decimal to seven places, although 2.47 would be adequate for most purposes.

The following macro converts a Fahrenheit temperature to Celsius. It assumes that the Fahrenheit temperature is in the cell just to the left of the cursor cell. The cursor cell contains the formula and Celsius result:

3:<asp> + <left>-32*5/9<rtn>!

Tip: *You can use macros to enter formulas for higher functions.*

In Chapter 4, we used formulas to generate higher functions. For example, we used the exponentiation capabilities of the Spreadsheet to find natural logarithms. You want to use the smallest power available in order to generate the most accurate value possible. Super MacroWorks can take only seven decimal places, even though we got eight places to work in the Spreadsheet itself.

This macro assumes that the starting value is one cell to the left of the cursor cell:

1:<asp> + <left> ^ .0000001-1/.0000001<rtn>!

The antilog is simply *e* taken to the log value. The macro for this assumes that the natural log is one cell to the left of the cursor cell:

2:<asp>2.7182818 ^ <left><rtn>!

Tip: *Use a macro to emulate the Data Base "ditto" command for the Spreadsheet.*

You cannot create a Solid-Apple-' macro, because Super MacroWorks uses that for a built-in macro that enters dates.

However, you can create a Solid-Apple-; macro that emulates the Date Base "ditto" function (Open-Apple-'). It begins with the cursor in the first cell to be filled, just below the cell to be copied. This is a simple macro function for copying labels and values (but not formulas):

> ;:<asp><up><oa-c>W<rtn><down>
> <rtn><down><down>!

You can also create a macro to copy across a row. You can assign a different key to make both available at the same time.

> 1:<asp><left><oa-c>W<rtn><right>
> <rtn><right><right>!

Tip: *Store report formats in macros.*

The Data Base can store up to eight report formats with a file, but in the Spreadsheet you must create the report manually each time you print it. However, you can store any block specifications, printer option settings, and final print menu selections as a complete macro.

When you write such macros, use characters that require the Shift key. You don't want to call these macros by mistake because when they take off, you may be too stunned to press the Escape key in time to bail out.

MACROS FOR TRANSFERRING DATA

In Chapter 5 we covered some complicated transfer problems and followed a few long paths. Once you automate these paths, the seemingly impractical transfers become routine.

Tip: *Macros can make difficult transfers routine.*

The route from the Word Processor to the Spreadsheet passes through the Data Base. Without macros, it might not be worth the effort. The notation appears in two macros: each takes two lines. In Solid-Apple-1, a dummy Silentype printer prints the Word Processor file to disk in a text file named simply A. The macro then creates a one-category Data Base file from file A and creates a tables-style report named X.

    1:<all><oa-P><rtn>3<rtn>/P/A<rtn><oa-Q>
    <esc>1<rtn>4<rtn>2<rtn>1<rtn>/P/
    A<rtn>X<rtn>!

In Solid-Apple-2, the Data Base prints report X to disk in a file named D. It then creates a Spreadsheet file from that DIF file. The macro ends at the point where AppleWorks asks what name the new Spreadsheet file should have.

    2:<all><oa-P><rtn>X<rtn><oa-P>8<rtn>/P/
    D<rtn><oa-Q><esc>1<rtn>5<rtn>2<rtn>/P/
    D<rtn>!

It is important to remember that this macro expects to see three printers installed. The numbers in the print menus will otherwise be incorrect, and the macro will go awry.

Tip: *Macros can automate graphing.*

In Chapter 4 you learned how to create a bar graph in the Spreadsheet. We transferred it to the Word Processor to remove all instances of −1. The following macro automates the transfer from the Spreadsheet to the Word Processor.

You can practice this with the graph example in Chapter 4. This macro assumes that all of the graph worksheet will be printed, but you can change the macro to specify a block. The macro creates a Word Processor file, widens the margins in that file to allow the maximum 77 characters, copies the graph to the Word Processor file, and removes the − 1 entries.

This macro expects option 4 to be for printing to the clipboard (for the Word Processor), and it assumes that three printers have been installed. The notation appears here in five lines, each followed by ; to indicate remarks within a line.

X:<all><oa-P>A 4<rtn>;	Print to clipboard
<oa-Q><esc><rtn>3	
<rtn><rtn>WP<rtn>;	Create WP file
<oa-O>lm<rtn>0<rtn>	
rm<rtn>0<rtn><esc>;	Set 77-character line
<oa-C>F;	Copy from clipboard
<oa-E><oa-R>T-1	
<rtn><rtn>A<oa-1>;	Remove all − 1 entries

You can rename the Word Processor WP file to something more meaningful. You can also copy the graph from it to another Word Processor file.

Tip: *You can use a macro to find and remove carriage returns from formatted text files.*

AppleWorks through version 1.3 prints unformatted text files from the Word Processor to disk. Version 2.0 prints formatted text files. If you want to create another Word processor file from formatted text files, you may need to add text or change margins. That means you have to remove carriage returns before reformatting.

Super MacroWorks includes a <find> command to locate the next carriage return in the Word Processor. The macro to remove them is simple:

    1:<awp><find><oa-D><rtn>!

You can substitute Open-Apple-Delete within the macro, but with combinations of programs that modify AppleWorks, you may find cases in which neither Delete nor Open-Apple-Delete can remove a carriage return.

Although <find> locates the next macro, you often want to remove a carriage return that is either under the cursor or one character space to the left of the cursor. You can handle these cases as well by modifying the macro:

1:<awp><left><left><find><oa-D><rtn>!

MACROS FOR MANAGING PRINTERS

Macros make it much easier to handle printers within the limitations of AppleWorks. It is no longer necessary to make repeated changes manually. A macro can quickly change specific codes for printers and printer interface cards. Although you can install only one custom printer, you can effectively store another custom printer in a macro.

Tip: *Use a macro to toggle the top-of-page command.*

When you have a page length other than the standard 11 inches, your printer should ignore the top-of-page command. In the Data Base and Spreadsheet you can enter a special code in the printer options. In the Word Processor you can use several tricks, including piggyback codes.

The most practical all-around solution is a standard toggling macro that works from each program and goes right into the printer configuration. Solid-Apple-T in Figure 7.1 shows the notation. You must have the Program disk in a drive, because Apple-Works writes the new information to the printer segment. The Open-Apple-Q command near the end of the macro keeps the Change a Printer menu in view while AppleWorks saves the new configuration. That gives you time to view the top-of-page status.

Tip: *Macros can enter control codes quickly.*

If you have a listed printer, you may also want to enter it as a custom printer to use all of its capabilities. Once you have a custom printer, you can use macros to change its control codes. In Chapter 6, we discussed a technique for entering two or more control codes together. For example, if you want to print an entire document in boldface at 10 characters per inch, you can piggyback the boldface code after the interface card control code.

The macros below use Control-I 0N for the Grappler card interface, and Esc-E for Epson MX boldface.

```
1:<all><oa-q><esc>5<rtn>7<rtn>4<rtn>5
<rtn><rtn><tab>0N ^ <oa-q><rtn>!
2:<all><oa-q><esc>5<rtn>7<rtn>4<rtn>5<rtn>
<rtn><tab>0N<esc>E ^ <oa-q><rtn>!
```

Tip: *You can design macros to alternate between printers.*

Suppose you want to use two custom printers. You need two macros: one to install all the codes for printer A, then another to install the codes for printer B. For this macro, assume the custom printer is the last on the list of printers. That means you will not have to remove and reinstall other printers.

```
1:<all><oa-q><esc>5<rtn>7<rtn>3
<rtn>3<rtn>2<rtn>12<rtn>......<oa-q><rtn>
```

The row of dots indicates where you can enter the sequence for revisions: first on the Change a Printer menu, and then on entries within the printer codes (option 6).

If the custom printer is listed first, you have more to reconstruct each time.

EXTRA FEATURES OF MACRO PROGRAMS

Most Beagle Bros programs come with unexpected extra features, and the macro programs are typical. In this section we will take a closer look at four additional improvements for Apple-Works. The most important of these allows AppleWorks to use Control-Reset.

Tip: *Super MacroWorks enables Control-Reset.*

As you learned in Chapter 1, when you use Control-Reset with AppleWorks, you go to the Monitor. With Super MacroWorks installed, you come right back to the Main Menu. If you need to hold down Control-Reset for two full seconds to empty the buffer on a Grappler interface card, you still come back to the Main Menu.

Incidentally, if you have MacroWorks rather than Super Macro-Works, the program comes close: When you go to the Monitor, simply enter

    33DG

to return to the Main Menu.

Tip: *You can change the AppleWorks beep.*

Super MacroWorks enables you to modify AppleWorks to minimize the error beep, so that it sounds more like a peep. This also changes any beeps you use within macros and control programs to signal that they have completed their work or need keyboard input.

Tip: *You can edit the Help screens.*

When people learn AppleWorks, they use the reference card rather than the Help screens. When they know AppleWorks, the Help screens have little value. Super MacroWorks lets you enter your own information on the Help screens.

You can add information about macros (the edit feature allows you to enter the Solid-Apple mousetext character). If you think that your printed list of macros will serve as well as the Apple-Works reference card did, use the help screens for other information. The only restriction is that each new line can be no longer than the original line.

Tip: *Bird's Better Bye provides a good way to quit AppleWorks.*

When most people finish a session with AppleWorks and want to use another program, they take out the AppleWorks disk, insert another program disk, and press Control-Open-Apple-Reset. But there is a simpler way to move on.

MacroWorks comes with a version of ProDOS 1.1.1 that includes Alan Bird's Better Bye. When you quit AppleWorks, it lists the volume, subdirectories, and system programs that you can use. You can still change the disk: when you press Escape, you get a listing for the new disk. Move the cursor to the program you want to run, press Return, and it starts. If you use a high-capacity disk, this is a particularly useful improvement.

You can modify this version of ProDOS 1.1.1 as described in Chapter 1, because it is otherwise the same ProDOS. Super MacroWorks includes the Better Bye on a later version of Pro-DOS 8, which is more suitable for the IIGS.

ADVANCED APPLICATIONS

Advanced applications are often highly specific. For example, you will find it worthwhile to write long macros when you process the same types of data and print the same reports week after week. This section provides information on strategy, along with specific examples.

Tip: *Make your applications modular and predictable.*

When you design applications, keep everything neatly defined and clearly connected. Nothing is ever so complex that it cannot be broken down into component parts, and you can make things easy to break down and build up.

When a macro does its work in more than one program, write the macro in commented lines that break at the program boundaries. In the previous section on transferring data, the macro for transferring Word Processor text to the Spreadsheet is an example.

Tip: *You can read AppleWorks disk catalogs to a Data Base file.*

Super MacroWorks includes a Solid-Apple-^ command that reads disk catalog information from the current data disk or sub-directory to a Data Base file that comes with the macro program. You simply load DISK.FILES, use the command, and watch the records fill. This command is particularly useful for documenting large collections of files. DISK.FILES includes only one note field among its seven fields, but you can add more later.

Tip: *Spreadsheet consolidation has many uses.*

You can sum totals from other worksheets by automating the manual consolidation process described in Chapter 4. Remember that AppleWorks version 2.0 can move and copy rows in a special way. If those rows include cells with formulas, you can choose to transfer either values-with-formulas or values-only from the clipboard. The Spreadsheet automatically offers you the choice.

There are minimal requirements for using this option. You must include at least two rows in the move or copy. The first row must contain a formula, and the second must contain at least a value or repeating label. You can transfer the rows directly from one worksheet to another.

Suppose you have four worksheets, each representing a geographical area: East, West, North, and South. You can quickly consolidate their totals in a file named Combined, but you need to establish some rules and guidelines.

The worksheets should be stacked on the Desktop in the following order from first to last: East, West, North, South, Combined. That allows the macro to go to the first file and move down the list. It can always find the last file by finding the first and moving up one to reach the bottom.

It is not necessary to have the total line in the same row on each regional worksheet. The macro can find the word "total" if it occurs first at the total line. Here is the macro notation in parts. The Solid-Apple macros are from Figure 7.1:

C:<all><oa-Q>1<rtn>	
<sa-H><oa-F>	
Ttotal<rtn>;	Find total line in file 1
<up><oa-c>T	
<down><rtn>;	Copy two rows
<oa-Q>1<up><rtn>;	Find last (Combined) file
<oa-F>CA4<rtn>	
<oa-M>FV;	Move from clipboard, values only
<oa-Q>2<rtn>	
<sa-H><oa-F>	
Ttotal<rtn>;	Find total line in file 2

Notice the new file number for the Desktop Index. The process otherwise remains the same, with each clipboard unloading at A4 and pushing the other rows down. That in turn pushes the summation row down and changes its formula. The only thing that changes with each cycle is the Desktop Index number: 1, 2, 3, and finally 4.

If you write a long macro, you can combine 11 worksheets into a Combined file this way. This process leaves the regional worksheets unchanged. If you repeat the same consolidation from week to week, this saves your time, because you can walk away from it.

Tip: *Use multiple sets of macros, and call them with macros.*

When you store macros in Word Processor files, you can manually load them, select them on the Desktop, compile them with Open-Apple-=, and expect them to begin work immediately. A macro can automate this process as well as any other process.

You might want to have three sets of macros named Macros-.Base, Macros.Edit, and Macros.Data. The first is for general use; the second, for writing reports; and the third, for specialized work with the Data Base and Spreadsheet.

CONTROL PROGRAMS

AppleWorks has become a standard program for the Apple II series, mainly because it works so well. It provides a dependable platform on which to build applications, including applications beyond the limits of AppleWorks itself. Super MacroWorks provides an example of control capabilities that will be used and extended by other programs. Concepts and examples in this section can be adapted for Beagle Bros TimeOut UltraMacros.

Tip: *Super MacroWorks is also a programming language.*

Beyond macros, Super MacroWorks offers a set of commands that can perform logical tests, store the results, and proceed in different ways based on those results. The Beagle Bros manual draws no line between macros and control programs.

Standard macros written for this chapter use only those tokens that represent AppleWorks commands. For selected macros, we have reviewed alternate versions that use commands added by Super MacroWorks.

In this section we will use still more commands added by Super MacroWorks—commands that provide conditional control in macros. Macros that use these control commands become, in effect, control programs. They use the same underlying logic you have already encountered with @IF in the Spreadsheet and the record selection rules in the Data Base.

Tip: *You can program up to 74 Spreadsheet recalculations.*

Chapter 4 includes a complex template for completing several iterations of a calculation. In the specific example we calculated an annual mortgage payment, but you can replace it with other types of calculations. Figure 7.3 is similar to the example in Chapter 4, except that it includes values in column E, beginning with year 1 of the payment schedule. Cell E16 equals 1 + E15, and so on down the column. These entries serve as relative reference values for formulas in columns F and G, making it easy to copy those formulas.

Remember that you can press Open-Apple-K twice for two calculations in succession, but what if you want to recalculate 4, 8, or 18 times in succession? Super MacroWorks allows you to do that, and we will discuss two options.

Suppose the iteration template had places for 18 years. That is the simpest case, because a Super MacroWorks macro repeats exactly 18 times when it calls itself. The notation is simple:

    1:<asp><oa-K><sa-1>!

However, suppose you want only 8 recalculations. Super Macro-Works allows you to use the token <rpt> to continue the macro forever. In the iteration example from Chapter 4, the iteration would continue after filling all available listing places, but no further results would be recorded. By pressing Escape, you can stop the macro.

```
File: Iteration.2                REVIEW/ADD/CHANGE            Escape: Main Menu
=====A=====B=====C=======D========E========F========G========H=======I====
   1|    Iteration.2
   2| --------------------------------------------------------------
   3|    99 Flag
   4|              0 Counter Seed
   5|              4 Counter
   6|            .01 Variable Increment
   7|            .11 Variable Seed
   8|                                     .15 Interest Rate
   9|                                      10 Years
  10|                                 1178.00 Amount (1000s)
  11|                           4.0455577 (1+I)^N
  12|                                  234.72 Annual Payment (1000s)
  13|
  14|
  15|                              1     .12    208.49 (1000s)
  16|                              2     .13    217.09
  17|                              3     .14    225.84
  18|                              4     .15    234.72
    -----------------------------------------------------------------
   F18: (Value, Layout-F2) @IF(C5=E18,F8,F18)

   Type entry or use @ commands                            @-? for Help
```

Figure 7.3: *Revised iteration model*

Alternatively, you can set a variable with the token <var = > and increase it by 1 with each cycle of the macro. The token for increasing the variable is <incvar>.

You can turn off a repeating macro by creating a test condition that it cannot meet. When you use a variable, the token <varnot> can test for a value. If you want to recalculate eight times, set the variable to zero with the following macro:

2:<asp><var = >0!

Then write another macro to increase the variable and check to see that the variable has not reached the value 8:

3:<asp><oa-K><incvar><varnot>8<rpt>!

Note that you must set the variable in a separate macro, otherwise it would be reset with each cycle of the Solid-Apple-3 macro. If you use the Solid-Apple-3 macro again without resetting the variable to zero, <incvar> increases the variable value to 9 before the next <varnot> test, and the macro continues forever (because the variable will never again equal 8).

If you want to recalculate more than 9 times, Super MacroWorks assigns values in ASCII order (see Appendix B). The ASCII symbol after 9 is the question mark, so for 10 recalculations the macro would read

    3:<asp><oa-K><incvar><varnot>?<rpt>!

The highest possible Super MacroWorks variable value is 74, which is assigned to the lowercase z.

Tip: *You can enter conditional text strings.*

There are times when you need to enter text information based on numeric values. For example, when teachers use the Spreadsheet for grading, they want to convert numeric averages to letter grades. AppleWorks does not allow you to enter characters as the result of a formula (although many other spreadsheets do).

You can use macros to make conditional tests and enter text in a worksheet after you use Open-Apple-K to recalculate. We will use a simple gradebook example for averages from 40 through 99. Figure 7.4 shows an example with letter grades assigned by the macros described below. Averages of 90 or greater are assigned the letter grade A, averages from 80 through 89 equal B, and so on. Averages below 60 are assigned the letter grade E. The sales must be values, not formulas, so copy the gradebook rows to the clipboard and then back from the clipboard, specifying values only.

The first macro tests for an initial digit of 9, so we will call it the Solid-Apple-9 macro:

    9:<asp><oa-U><if>9<rtn><right>A<down>
    <left><rpt>!

The cursor must be in cell G7 when the macro begins. In order to isolate the cursor on the first digit of the value, we must edit the cell. If the first digit is 9, Return completes the edit, the cursor moves right one cell, and enters the letter A. The cursor then goes down one cell and left one cell, in this case to G8.

```
File: Gradebook                REVIEW/ADD/CHANGE            Escape: Main Menu
======A======B======C======D======E======F=========G========H========I====
  1|
  2|
  3|
  4|    Student      Exam     Exam     Exam     Exam   Semester  Letter
  5|    Last Name      1        2        3        4    Average   Grade
  6|    --------------------------------------------------------------------
  7|    Abbott         94       88       89       98     92.2       A
  8|    Barnes         96       95       97       92     95.0       A
  9|    Collins        82       93       92       83     87.5       B
 10|    Darden         45       54       28       37     41.0       E
 11|    Eaton          76       68       55       54     63.2       D
 12|    Farmer         67       80       78       74     74.8       C
 13|    Graham         54       52       50       51     51.8       E
 14|    --------------------------------------------------------------------
 15|
 16|
 17|
 18|
    --------------------------------------------------------------------------
H13: (Label, Layout-R) E

Type entry or use @ commands                              @-? for Help
```

Figure 7.4: *Letter grades in Spreadsheet*

You can write similar macros for other cases:

8:<asp><oa-U><if>8<rtn><right>B
<down><left><rpt>!
7:<asp><oa-U><if>7<rtn><right>C
<down><left><rpt>!
6:<asp><oa-U><if>6<rtn><right>D
<down><left><rpt>!
5:<asp><oa-U><if>5<rtn><right>E
<down><left><rpt>!
4:<asp><oa-U><if>4<rtn><right>E
<down><left><rpt>!

What happens if the first digit is something other than 9? When that happens, the macro either stops or returns to the macro that called it. We therefore need a macro to call each macro in turn. The notation is

1:<asp><sa-9><sa-8><sa-7><sa-6><sa-5>
<sa-4><rpt>!

Solid-Apple-1 first uses Solid-Apple-9 to test for a lead digit of 9. If that digit is not 9, control returns to Solid-Apple-1, which then uses Solid-Apple-8 to test for 8., and so on until a match occurs. Solid-Apple-1 then repeats the process for the following entry. When the macro comes to a digit less than 4, it continues cycling on that entry. You can stop the Solid-Apple-1 macro at any time by pressing Escape. Alternatively, you can add a counter routine similar to that described in the previous tip.

In other applications you may want to test simply for 1 or 0. Depending on the application, a result can recall text such as

> Reorder immediately
> Failed test: Check for defects
> Unexpectedly high result
> Payment overdue

If you plan to be nearby while the macro is running, try including a <bell> token to note a desired result. In our original example, you can make your Apple II beep whenever it enters an A. The revised macro looks like this:

> 9:<asp><oa-U><if>9<rtn><right>A<down>
> <left><bell><rpt>!

Incidentally, you can also make your Apple II beep by entering a token that cannot be executed. In the Spreadsheet, Open-Apple-R and Open-Apple-G are invalid commands, so either can replace <bell>.

Tip: *More efficient control programs are yet to come.*

Super MacroWorks is the first AppleWorks macro system to include a programming language. Beyond the commands discussed here, it includes ten registers to store and retrieve numbers and text, including ProDOS volume, subdirectory, and file names. You can swap and compare the contents of registers, and make decisions based on those comparisons.

Beagle Bros also offers TimeOut UltraMacros, which combines further integration with macros. TimeOut modifies AppleWorks to load related TimeOut programs and access them from within AppleWorks. Macros created with UltraMacros can then work within TimeOut programs as well. The UltraMacros programming language includes a complete if-then-else structure for highly efficient control programs.

SUMMARY

This chapter explained how macros work and how they can automate tasks. It is a fitting final chapter for the book, because macros work most efficiently when they use the tips and techniques presented in earlier chapters. Most macros are simply recordings of what you would otherwise do manually.

Remember that macro programs can affect the time required to load AppleWorks and use different commands. You may well conclude that there are advantages to using AppleWorks version 1.3 with MacroWorks and version 2.0 with a more advanced macro program.

Appendix A continues the discussion of macros as a part of the overall development of AppleWorks. It will also discuss sources for templates and patch information. Appendix B includes information on using the keyboard efficiently.

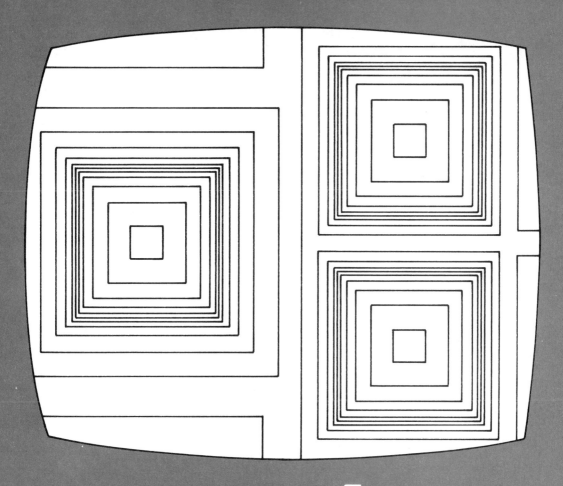

Appendix **A**

An AppleWorks Prospectus

*I*n a world of marketing hyperbole, it is easy to get carried away with new products. It is even easier to overlook worthwhile things that have not been widely promoted. In this appendix we will review what has happened in two years since the first edition of this book, and what might happen during coming years.

APPLEWORKS: A STANDARD APPLE II FEATURE

The strength of AppleWorks is its ability to start quickly and perform common tasks efficiently. Along with ProDOS and the Monitor, AppleWorks has become a common feature of the Apple II. You can almost expect an Apple II user to have some version of AppleWorks at hand. This is surprising in the sense that Apple has consistently chosen not to bundle AppleWorks with Apple II hardware. Even so, the bundling option remains so logical that it probably discourages the development of other general-purpose word processors, database managers, and spreadsheets. And that, in turn, makes AppleWorks an even more likely choice for Apple II users.

Because it has become so commonplace, and because it is so well designed, AppleWorks provides a good base for add-on programs, including aids for handicapped users. AppleWorks also provides a dependable complement to specialized programs that can read and create DIF, ASCII, and AppleWorks files.

VERSION 2.0 DESIGN CHANGES

AppleWorks was designed to provide fast operation and adequate Desktop memory within a 128K Apple II system and a 6502-series microprocessor. Hundreds of thousands of Apple II systems will remain within these boundaries for years to come. Thanks to software firms such as Norwich Data Systems, AppleWorks can also run on older Apple II models. AppleWorks can also share files with the Apple III and III E-Z Pieces. Any suggestions for changes in AppleWorks should respect these important facts.

AppleWorks version 2.0 adds a few features without giving up overall quickness. Because version 2.0 differs significantly from earlier versions in internal design, it will probably be the only version used for development of advanced add-on programs. In Chapter 7, I tried to minimize this divergence of paths by writing macros that work for both MacroWorks on version 1.3 and Super MacroWorks on version 2.0. The matching set of basic macros makes both versions work alike up to a point (I use version 1.3 with MacroWorks most of the time because it loads faster).

From the user perspective, there have been surprisingly few significant changes in the design of AppleWorks between versions 1.0 and 2.0. Table A.1 shows the most important differences. Version 2.0 probably should have been called version 1.4, as it was in the French and German editions.

The following commentary covers the important design choices for version 2.0 in light of other available modifications. After reading it, you may well understand why many people continue to feel comfortable using version 1.3.

AppleWorks version 2.0 saves files indirectly as described in Chapter 1, but when there is not enough space, it offers the option to overwrite the earlier version of the file. This is the best choice overall, but Checkmate utility software adds the same

---

Table A.1: *Comparison of features in AppleWorks versions*

Feature	V1.1	V1.2	V1.3	V2.0
Accepts interface card codes		*	*	*
Formats 3.5" disk			*	*
Runs on 64K Apple II	*	*	*	
Supports IIGS RAM card				*
Saves unformatted text files	*	*	*	
Saves files directly				*
Includes Mail Merge				*
@AND, @OR, @ROUND functions				*

option to version 1.3. Applied Engineering software has long offered direct saves that overwrite the earlier version of the file immediately, and that method is consistently fast because it never stops to ask questions.

The version 2.0 Word Processor prints formatted ASCII files to disk. Because you can do that anyway with a dummy Silentype printer, the original choice to print unformatted text files gives earlier versions of AppleWorks more file transfer capability.

Version 2.0 continues to use the Standard Apple Numerics Environment (SANE), so the question is how the Spreadsheet can best handle very close approximations of decimal fractions ending in 5. An @ROUND function makes sense, but it should probably incorporate the rounding techniques described in Chapter 4.

The AppleWorks Spreadsheet file format has always reserved a specific location for an @IRR function to calculate internal rate of return, but that function was not included in version 2.0. That was a good design choice: adding @IRR to the base program will never be worth the memory and processing time required. Chapter 4 includes a simple template to do this work when needed.

The decision to include a mail merge capability in version 2.0 is perhaps the most interesting design choice. Although everyone expected to see it in AppleWorks version 2.0, AutoWorks had already demonstrated that an inexpensive add-on macro program can provide an equally useful integrated mail merge function. In this case, one design choice is not necessarily preferable to the other.

REMAINING PROBLEMS

Each new version of AppleWorks solves more undocumented problems, but the changes create new ones. The first priority of any marketing-oriented firm should be getting the basics right, because that saves frustration for everyone. Here are a list of the basics:

1. ProDOS 1.1.1 and its CONVERT program still need to be fixed.

2. AppleWorks version 2.0 should at least display an error message for an @IF formula error.

3. There is still more work to do in making the record selection rules work correctly.

Apple should also make its list of reported problems available to AppleWork users, through dealers and through Apple user groups. This book has amply demonstrated that there are many ways around problems. The lack of information about a problem is invariably far more damaging than the problem itself.

AppleWorks has idiosyncracies that users might construe as problems, and the manuals need to address this issue. Compared to the original version 1.0 AppleWorks Reference Manual, the reference value of *Using AppleWorks* has been strengthened by adding chapters for essential tips. However, there remains a quiet disjunction between the program and the documentation for such features as Spreadsheet row capacity, @ROUND, record selection rules, page numbering, and printing ASCII files. Here are four suggestions for adding information from this book to AppleWorks manuals:

1. Many people want boldfacing for an entire Word Processor document, and the manual should explain how to do it using interface card codes for listed printers.

2. The manual should caution users about remaining record selection problems.

3. The Spreadsheet formula capacities for worksheet rows should be carefully explained with examples.

4. The @ROUND documentation should be corrected and completed to include the idiosyncratic rule for rounding.

PATCHING APPLEWORKS

AppleWorks can be easily modified at the byte level, and there are good byte modification programs available, including Pro-Byter from Beagle Bros. The problem is to learn where to go on the Startup and Program disks.

If you are looking for text entries, they are easy to find and change on your own. For example, you may think that "Type entry" is enough of a message for the lower left corner of the screen. You can replace the other characters in the message with space characters.

If you want to change listed printer codes, error messages, cursor controls, and default margin settings, scattered information appears in Open-Apple and CompuServe's Apple forum (see below). Applied Engineering, Checkmate Technology, and Beagle Bros have effectively created patch programs for use with their respective programs. Randy Brandt, author of Super Macro-Works, has developed a disk of patch routines that will make patching easier for AppleWorks 2.0.

Here is one example for the intrepid. My copies of Apple-Works version 2.0 include a patch that makes @NA produce two space characters, so that graphs look complete in the Spreadsheet. To make the necessary patch, use a copy of your original Pro-DOS Filer disk or System Utilities disk. Unlock the ProDOS file and then go to Applesoft BASIC. When the right bracket character (]) appears, place the AppleWorks Program disk in drive 1 and enter the following:

```
BLOAD SEG.M1,T$00,A$300,L2,B$CB85
POKE 768,32 : POKE 769,32
BSAVE SEG.M1,T$00,A$300,L2,B$CB85
```

For version 1.3 use B$D10D instead of B$CB85 at the end of the first and last lines. The only letter O's in these patches are in BLOAD and POKE. Remember that when a value used with @LOOKUP is less than the smallest lookup value in the table, NA appears as the result. After the modification, you will get a blank.

RELATED SOFTWARE

The strength of the Apple II is open design. Open systems allow everyone to learn quickly and add to what they have learned. AppleWorks is not copy protected, nor should related software be copy protected, because that compromises too much, including essential trust.

If advanced VisiCalc reappeared for $80 and without copy protection, it would be well received even without further development. VisiCalc justified the decision to use left-to-right notation in the AppleWorks Spreadsheet. It is some consolation to know that many VisiCalc templates remain in the public domain.

Pinpoint's Document Checker is an unprotected spelling checker that combines speed and accuracy with efficient packaging. Note that Pinpoint Publishing offers some excellent programs that do not require Pinpoint itself.

We still need an innovative mapping and graphics program that uses methods described by Edward Tufte for the visual display of quantitative data. Read the graphics section of Chapter 4 on this subject, and note that Tufte is one of several important sources in this emerging field.

The important remaining question is whether a macro program can provide a practical shell to integrate AppleWorks with other programs — without needing a hard disk.

RELATED HARDWARE

During the next two years, AppleWorks users will probably continue to benefit most from hardware items that are already available. During the autumn of 1984, Applied Engineering developed a memory card and software patches that made AppleWorks a serious program for professional applications development on the Apple IIe. They also developed a memory extension for the Apple IIc (making it something you can take apart). Both products have been continuously improved, and other firms developed similar products. Apple now has its own extended memory cards of a different design, and third-party firms have followed that design path as well.

Extended memory has encouraged larger applications and longer sessions on the Apple II. That reality makes nonglare monitor screens even more important. AppleWorks users often work in too much light and glare. As noted in Chapter 1, the Apple II uses relatively few dots to create letters on the screen, so you need every other available advantage in differentiating between letters. Amber monitors are slightly easier to read when light levels are above the preferred level of 30 footcandles, but a non-glare screen or shield is even more important.

The most important path not yet taken is the 360K disk drive. No one has offered a dual-purpose disk drive controller that can use IBM-compatible drives and 360K disks. That would allow the Apple II to read and write ASCII and DIF files in ProDOS or MS-DOS format. Ironically, you can purchase such a controller for use in IBM-compatible systems.

BASIC PROGRAMMING

The Beagle Compiler has given the ProDOS version of Applesoft BASIC a new life. Compiled programs run fast enough to be worthwhile: three to ten times faster than interpreted BASIC. You can use the compiler on existing BASIC programs, including the AppleWorks Mailing Program.

Beagle Bros Extra K is a related software package for writing larger programs. Applesoft BASIC programs can normally occupy and access only 48K of memory, even when the Apple II has 128K. Among other things, Extra K allows BASIC to use variables in the auxiliary (or extended) memory, thus permitting larger programs. Incidentally, Extra-K also includes a program that copies 5¹/₄-inch disks in less than 35 seconds on a two-disk drive system.

The standard texts on writing BASIC programs to create and read DIF files have been included in the annotated bibliography in Appendix D. You can also review AMP for programming insights. Open-Apple has published information on using BASIC programs to read (and even write) Data Base files directly (see Appendix D).

APPLEWORKS SUPPORT SERVICES

Apple relies heavily on its dealer network for technical support of hardware and software, including AppleWorks. It provides dealers with an on-line information service accessible from a Macintosh.

Many other hardware and software firms use technical support centers. The firm typically includes a support telephone number in the users manual. The user makes a long-distance call, provides the software registration number for identification, asks a question, and receives an accurate answer.

This kind of technical support has significant benefits for the firm. Because one technical support center handles all the questions, staff members learn to answer common questions efficiently, and they can then provide important insights for upgrading instructional materials. A technical support center also learns about undocumented problems from the relatively few users who find such problems during advanced applications development. Staff members can run tests to identify causes and limits of these problems, and that makes it easier to improve subsequent releases of a software package. Given potential productivity advantages, technical support centers will increasingly integrate product testing, development of technical support databases, development of user manuals, and publication of advanced materials.

Professional Support

Specific professions, such as agricultural management, library science, and health care, are often called vertical markets, because their hardware, software, and information needs tend to be at least partly specialized. A users group for a specific profession can provide needed specialized information about hardware and software, as well as information about applications development and current events in the field.

If such a users group does not exist, an interested hardware or software firm can start one. Its newsletter can be little more than an extension of direct-mail advertising, or it can be a serious publication reflecting long-term commitment to a profession. The best example of the latter is the Apple Library Users Group quarterly newsletter. Apple's own librarian, Monica Ertel, has made it one of the most useful publications currently available in information science. The address is 1038 Bandley Drive, Cupertino, CA 95014.

Books and Periodicals

Appendix D provides a bibliography that includes some of the most useful books for AppleWorks users. The bibliography also includes articles from representative periodicals. One periodical in that bibliography is all but indispensible.

Open-Apple is an essential monthly newsletter published by Tom Weishaar, author of Beagle Bros Pronto-DOS. The newsletter contains no advertising, no nonsense, and incredibly useful information. It focuses on standard features of the Apple II series, including ProDOS and AppleWorks. *Open-Apple* asks the right questions and tracks down the important bugs.

Topics of interest include reading and writing Data Base files, sending Spreadsheet files by modem, using AppleWorks as a phone dialer, fixing bugs in various versions of ProDOS, and modifying the AppleWorks cursor. You can order indexes and back issues. The address is P.O. Box 7651, Overland Park, KS 66207.

The Apple Program Developers Association offers Apple II development tools and technical publications that may otherwise be difficult to find. Their address is 290 S.W. 43rd St, Renton, WA 98055.

If you use the Data Base or Spreadsheet for difficult applications, back issues of *Lotus* magazine are surprisingly useful, especially for technical applications development in specific professions. Check with a friend who uses a Lotus-type spreadsheet.

Appleworks Users Groups

Most Apple Users Groups cover specific geographic areas, and most have AppleWorks special interest groups. You can call Apple at (800) 538-9696 to find the one nearest you. User group newsletters often publish articles or a continuing column on Apple-Works. In some of these groups, AppleWorks users are available to answer questions by telephone.

For AppleWorks users interested in templates on disk, the prime source is The AppleWorks Users Group, P.O. Box 24789, Denver, CO 80224. TAWUG has no membership fee; you become a member when you order a disk. Members donate templates and programs to the public domain. You can order a disk that catalogs the collection, and with that you can search through the AppleWorks attic. Beyond templates, the files include reviews, technical information, utility programs, and interesting AppleWorks columns from Apple user group newsletters.

The National AppleWorks Users Group publishes *AppleWorks Forum,* a comprehensive newsletter. Their address is P.O. Box 87453, Canton, MI 48187. NAUG also runs a well-organized telephone support system and offers public domain disks, including templates from The AppleWorks Users Group and the Apple Library Users Group.

Other national users groups include the Apple Puget Sound Program Library Exchange, a cooperative in Washington state, which publishes the monthly *Call-A.P.P.L.E.* and offers THE Spreadsheet. Their address is 290 S.W 43rd St., Renton, WA 98055. See Chapter 4 for a list of *Call-A.P.P.L.E.* articles on spreadsheet statistics.

International Apple Core is the source for the AppleWorks Mailing Program. Their address is P.O. Box 880388, San Francisco, CA 94188. CompuServe has an Apple forum run by the Micronetworked Apple Users Group. It maintains a library of AppleWorks information and related utility programs (see Appendix C).

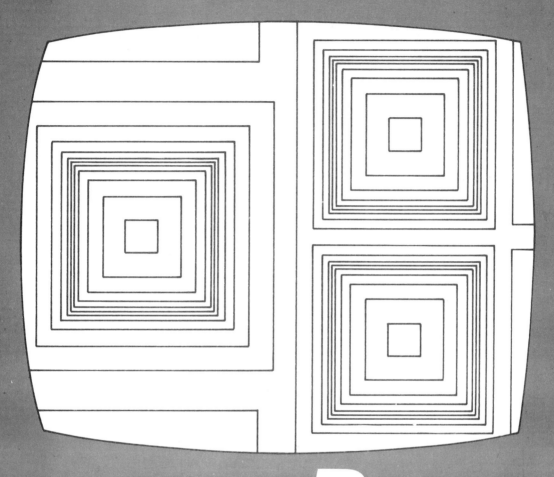

Appendix **B**

The AppleWorks Keyboard

ppleWorks uses the keyboard differently for each of several purposes: text entry, number entry, editing, and control code entry. This appendix explains how to work more efficiently in each case, as well as how to make your own keyboard templates.

TEXT ENTRY

The interaction between the user and the keyboard is the slowest interface in AppleWorks. If you know touch typing, you can significantly speed up your work. If you don't know touch typing, your thoughts will always run ahead of your fingers. Moreover, touch typing lets you think about your writing rather than about where the next key might be. If you want to learn touch typing, Jeremy Grossman's *Quick Typing* (John Wiley and Sons, 1980) is a good paperback self-teaching guide that includes additional information useful for typing on a word processor.

Touch typing is basically the ability to use all ten fingers on the correct keys without looking at the keyboard. To do this you need to know at least the following: the four fingers of the right hand touch keys J K L and the semicolon, reach up to U I O P and also 7 8 9 0 on the higher rows, and reach down to M , . / on the bottom row. The four fingers of the left hand touch keys A S D F, reach up to Q W E R and 1 2 3 4, and reach down to Z X C V. The index fingers reach to the middle keys, and the right thumb controls the Space bar. The little fingers cover the keys to the right and left of the alphanumeric keys—most importantly the Return and Shift keys.

The D and K keys on the Apple each have a little bump on them so your middle fingers know when they are home. (The → key is also embossed.) Note that the right Shift key is used with the left-hand keys (such as A and S), while the left Shift key is used with the right-hand keys (such as L and P).

Practice using each finger until the muscles seem to remember on their own. The little fingers have the most difficult work. Remember that this keyboard layout was a 19th-century scheme to keep people from jamming mechanical linkages while typing. There are faster keyboard designs: the Apple IIc converts to the Dvorak layout, on which the most commonly used keys are the most easily accessible.

NUMBER ENTRY

If you enter numbers often, as accountants do, you may want to use the equivalent of touch typing for number entry. On many personal computers, the number keys appear both on the top row of the keyboard and on a numeric keypad to the right of the keyboard. If you learn the keypad by touch, you can type numbers quickly with your index, middle, and ring fingers.

You can purchase a separate numeric keypad for the Apple II series. Left-handed users will appreciate the fact that this keypad can be used on either side of the keyboard. Most numeric keypads cluster the number keys in four rows: 7 8 9 at the top, then 4 5 6, then 1 2 3, and finally 0 and the decimal point at the bottom. Most keypads include basic arithmetic function keys. Some keypads also include unexpected keys: for example, > may be included because it quickly moves a VisiCalc cursor to a specified cell coordinate.

EDITING

Editing is typically a process of correcting spelling, changing punctuation, and moving text. Sometimes you will need to add whole sentences or paragraphs, but editing is generally quite different from text entry.

During editing you will spend most of your time on the bottom rows of the keyboard, using the Apple and arrow keys. The zoom, copy, move, and file-naming commands are all on those rows.

The Apple-E command, for changing between the insert and overstrike cursors, is one of the most frequently used commands in editing. Because the letter E is directly above the Open-Apple key, it is almost always easier to use Solid-Apple-E during editing. Learn to change back and forth between the insert and overstrike cursors quickly, even when replacing just a few characters.

ASCII VALUES

Entering control codes for printers requires no special typing skills, but you must know which keystrokes to enter for ASCII values. Keep a table of ASCII values near at hand for reference. You will most likely need to convert ASCII decimal values found in your printer manual into keystrokes. Table B.1 provides all the information you will need. (You may want to add a tab to this page to make it easier to find.) Pay special attention to the first 31 ASCII values, and remember that when you add printers to AppleWorks, pressing Control-[is the same as pressing Escape.

KEYBOARD TEMPLATES

Keyboard templates offer a simple but effective way to remember the things you need to know to work most efficiently with the keyboard. You can design your own templates, print them on paper or card stock, make several backup copies, highlight specific information, and pencil in comments as needed. You can make more templates for specific applications or use self-adhesive Post-It notes for reminders.

There are basically two kinds of templates. The first is for people who are learning AppleWorks or using it only occasionally. The template sections shown in Figures B.1 and B.2 work together as a template for beginners. The template is designed for getting around in the Word Processor and for using existing Spreadsheet and Data Base applications. The abbreviations WP, SS, or DB are used whenever a command is limited to one or two programs.

The letter keys for AppleWorks commands were wisely allocated for mnemonic purposes (they are easy to remember). However, some people need time to adapt to using AppleWorks

Table B.1: *ASCII character codes*

ASCII	Hex	CHR	Control Code	ASCII	Hex	CHR	Screen
0	00	NUL	Control-@	32	20	space	
1	01	SOH	Control-A	33	21	!	!
2	02	STX	Control-B	34	22	"	"
3	03	ETX	Control-C	35	23	#	#
4	04	EOT	Control-D	36	24	$	$
5	05	ENQ	Control-E	37	25	%	%
6	06	ACK	Control-F	38	26	&	&
7	07	BEL	Control-G (Bell)	39	27	'	'
8	08	BS	Control-H (←)	40	28	(	(
9	09	HT	Control-I (Tab)	41	29	)	)
10	0A	LF	Control-J (↓)	42	2A	*	*
11	0B	VT	Control-K (↑)	43	2B	+	+
12	0C	NP	Control-L	44	2C	,	,
13	0D	CR	Control-M (Return)	45	2D	-	-
14	0E	SO	Control-N	46	2E	.	.
15	0F	SI	Control-O	47	2F	/	/
16	10	DLE	Control-P	48	30	0	0
17	11	DC1	Control-Q	49	31	1	1
18	12	DC2	Control-R	50	32	2	2
19	13	DC3	Control-S	51	33	3	3
20	14	DC4	Control-T	52	34	4	4
21	15	NAK	Control-U (→)	53	35	5	5
22	16	SYN	Control-V	54	36	6	6
23	17	ETB	Control-W	55	37	7	7
24	18	CAN	Control-X	56	38	8	8
25	19	EM	Control-Y	57	39	9	9
26	1A	SUB	Control-Z	58	3A	:	:
27	1B	ESC	Control-[	59	3B	;	;
28	1C	FS	Control-\	60	3C	<	<
29	1D	GS	Control-]	61	3D	=	=
30	1E	RS	Control-^	62	3E	>	>
31	1F	US	Control-—	63	3F	?	?

Table B.1: *ASCII character codes (continued)*

ASCII	Hex	CHR	Screen		ASCII	Hex	CHR	Screen
64	40	@	@		96	60	`	`
65	41	A	A		97	61	a	a
66	42	B	B		98	62	b	b
67	43	C	C		99	63	c	c
68	44	D	D		100	64	d	d
69	45	E	E		101	65	e	e
70	46	F	F		102	66	f	f
71	47	G	G		103	67	g	g
72	48	H	H		104	68	h	h
73	49	I	I		105	69	i	i
74	4A	J	J		106	6A	j	j
75	4B	K	K		107	6B	k	k
76	4C	L	L		108	6C	l	l
77	4D	M	M		109	6D	m	m
78	4E	N	N		110	6E	n	n
79	4F	O	O		111	6F	o	o
80	50	P	P		112	70	p	p
81	51	Q	Q		113	71	q	q
82	52	R	R		114	72	r	r
83	53	S	S		115	73	s	s
84	54	T	T		116	74	t	t
85	55	U	U		117	75	u	u
86	56	V	V		118	76	v	v
87	57	W	W		119	77	w	w
88	58	X	X		120	78	x	x
89	59	Y	Y		121	79	y	y
90	5A	Z	Z		122	7A	z	z
91	5B	[	[		123	7B	{	{
92	5C	\	\		124	7C	|	|
93	5D	]	]		125	7D	}	}
94	5E	^	^		126	7E	~	~
95	5F	_	_		127	7F	DEL	

commands, particularly if they have used other programs. For example, VisiCalc users may have difficulty remembering Apple-L for layout (rather than /F for format). Unlike the AppleWorks reference card and help files, the sample template sections in Figures B.1 and B.2 redirect you to the AppleWorks terminology where appropriate. You can photocopy these template sections, paste them up side by side, and photocopy them again onto card stock. Make some copies for friends.

When you make your own templates, consider their layout carefully. With the Apple IIc it is best to use freestanding templates. Print or copy needed information sideways on $8^1/_2 \times 11$-inch

---

ARRANGE (means sort)
Apple-A arranges SS rows,
    DB records

BLANK
Apple-B blanks SS cells

CALCULATE
Apple-K calculates WP page breaks,
    recalculates SS
Apple-V, R, F, M set SS manual recalc

CHANGE (see QUICK CHANGE, EDIT,
    LAYOUT, NAME, REPLACE, WIDTH)

COPY (see also MOVE)
Apple-C, W copy within files
Apple-C, T copy to clipboard
Apple-P to menu for printing SS, DB
    to clipboard (for use in WP)
Apple-C, F copy from clipboard

CURSOR MOVES
Apple-→ moves one word right in WP;
    one screen right in SS
Apple-↓ moves one screen down
Apple-1 moves cursor to first line
Apple-9 moves cursor to last line
Apple-2. . .8 moves cursor to first
    line of each eighth-section

DEFAULT VALUES
Apple-V sets SS, DB default value

DELETE
Control-Y deletes to end of WP line,
    SS edit line, or DB category
Apple-D deletes selected segments
Delete erases character to left

EDIT
Apple-E switches between insert and
    overstrike cursors
Apple-U edits SS cell

ESCAPE
Escape to menu, file, or status listed
    in upper right of screen

FIND
Apple-F finds word or text block in WP,
    SS cell coordinate,
    DB record

FORMAT (see LAYOUT)

HELP
Apple-? lists available commands

INSERT
Apple-I inserts SS row or column,
    DB record

LAYOUT (means format)
Apple-L changes SS cell layout,
    DB record layout
Apple-O for Printer Options menu

Figure B.1: AppleWorks template, sections A–L

white card stock, using up to about 6 inches. Then fold back the rest of the card to serve as a base. (Note that the top slots of the Apple IIc should never be covered because they vent heat.)

Templates for the Apple IIe can fit just above the keyboard. Print or copy needed information sideways on $8^{1}/_{2} \times 11$-inch white card stock, using up to about 4 inches. Cut the card to make a template that is $4^{1}/_{2} \times 11$ inches. Fold back a quarter-inch

---

MARGINS
Apple-O for options menu

MOVE (see also COPY)
Apple-M, W move WP text, DB records,
　　SS rows, columns within files
Apple-M, T move to clipboard
Apple-M, F move from clipboard

NAME
Apple-N new name for file in use

PRINT
Apple-P to printing menus
　　Note: Allows printing to text
　　file, clipboard (SS, DB),
　　DIF file (SS, DB),
　　screen (DB)
Apple-H prints hard copy of screen

QUICK CHANGE (means change files)
Apple-Q quick change to another file
　　on the Desktop

QUIT
Escape to main menu, then option 6
　　Note: use option 3 to save
　　Desktop files instead

RENAME (see NAME)

REPLACE
Apple-R replaces WP text,
　　DB record-selection rules

REPORT
Apple-P for DB report menus
　　Note: Apple-P goes to report menu
　　before print menu
Apple-J justifies DB report category
Apple-G adds or deletes DB group totals

SAVE
Apple-S saves file to data disk

SORT (see ARRANGE)

TAB
Apple-T sets tabs in WP
Tab moves to next setting in WP,
　　next SS cell,
　　or next DB category

VALUES
Apple-V sets SS, DB default values

WIDTH
Apple-L, C, Return, C, Apple-→ widen
　　selected SS column(s)
Apple-L, Apple-→ widen DB category

WINDOWS
Apple-W creates SS windows
Apple-J jumps to other SS window

ZOOM
Apple-Z to WP layout mode and back,
　　to SS formulas and back,
　　to DB single record and back

Figure B.2: AppleWorks template, sections M–Z

at the bottom of the card (below the last line of information), and fit it into the space just above the top row of keys. You will need to trim one-eighth inch off each end of the insert tab. (You may also want to round off the top corners of the template to the radius of a nickel or quarter.)

If you need to include more information than these guidelines allow, print it first on a larger sheet. Later you can copy it onto 8¹/₂ × 11-inch card stock. Many quick-print shops can make reduced photocopies to about 77% of original size, and sometimes to any specified reduction.

More specialized templates are used primarily by people who design applications. For example, Figures B.3 through B.5 provide information that could appear on such a template—in this case for use on the Spreadsheet. Figure B.3 includes less frequently used commands that even experienced users can forget. For example, after several days away from AppleWorks, you may need to check the template before resetting manual recalculation in the Spreadsheet.

ARRANGE (means sort)
Apple-A arranges selected rows
     Note: A–Z option for labels

CALCULATE
Apple-V, R, F, M set manual calculation

COPY
Apple-C, W copy rows, columns,
    and "blocks" within file
Apple-C, T copy to clipboard
Apple-P to menu for printing to
    clipboard for use in WP
Apple-C, F copy from clipboard
    Note: You can copy complete
    rows only. You can copy from
    the clipboard repeatedly.

LAYOUT (means format)
Apple-L changes cell layout
Apple-O changes print format options

PRINT
Apple-P to printing menus
    Note: options include printing
    to printer, ASCII file, DIF
    file, clipboard

TITLES
Apple-T fixes row or column titles
    from cell below or to right

VALUES
Apple-V sets global default values
    for column width, formats, cell
    protection, recalculation

WIDTH
Apple-L, C, Return, C, Apple-→ widen
    selected column(s)

WINDOWS
Apple-W creates windows
Apple-J jumps to other window

Figure B.3: Selected Spreadsheet commands

Figure B.4 provides a list of all the Spreadsheet column letters with corresponding numbers for each column. The list can be simplified to show only columns E through O, then every fifth column thereafter.

A	1	AG	33	BM	65	CS	97
B	2	AH	34	BN	66	CT	98
C	3	AI	35	BO	67	CU	99
D	4	AJ	36	BP	68	CV	100
E	5	AK	37	BQ	69	CW	101
F	6	AL	38	BR	70	CX	102
G	7	AM	39	BS	71	CY	103
H	8	AN	40	BT	72	CZ	104
I	9	AO	41	BU	73	DA	105
J	10	AP	42	BV	74	DB	106
K	11	AQ	43	BW	75	DC	107
L	12	AR	44	BX	76	DD	108
M	13	AS	45	BY	77	DE	109
N	14	AT	46	BZ	78	DF	110
O	15	AU	47	CA	79	DG	111
P	16	AV	48	CB	80	DH	112
Q	17	AW	49	CC	81	DI	113
R	18	AX	50	CD	82	DJ	114
S	19	AY	51	CE	83	DK	115
T	20	AZ	52	CF	84	DL	116
U	21	BA	53	CG	85	DM	117
V	22	BB	54	CH	86	DN	118
W	23	BC	55	CI	87	DO	119
X	24	BD	56	CJ	88	DP	120
Y	25	BE	57	CK	89	DQ	121
Z	26	BF	58	CL	90	DR	122
AA	27	BG	59	CM	91	DS	123
AB	28	BH	60	CN	92	DT	124
AC	29	BI	61	CO	93	DU	125
AD	30	BJ	62	CP	94	DV	126
AE	31	BK	63	CQ	95	DW	127
AF	32	BL	64	CR	96		

Figure B.4: *Spreadsheet column letters and corresponding numbers*

You may also want to print important formulas on your template. Figure B.5 shows an example of how this can be done. Here the brief comments are the most useful part, because you will often copy the actual formulas from a PARTS file like the one described in Chapters 4 and 5.

No matter how experienced you are with AppleWorks, you will always be learning something new that you have not quite mastered. This is the kind of information that belongs on a keyboard template. Save some space to pencil in additional information during the life of the template. And when the template is no longer needed, set it aside and make another for your present needs.

	B	C	D	E
1	.5	.22	.52	2
2	.12	10	20	40
3	3.99			

FORMULAS (data above)	RESULTS	COMMENTS
+B2+C2/D2*E2	20.24	Left-to-right order of operations
+E1^.5	1.414214	Same as square root of 2
@IF(B2<=1,C2+D2,0)	30	.12 is less than 1
@INT(B1*B3*100+.5)/100	2.00	Rounding formula for accounting
@SUM(E1. . .E3)	42	Includes E2
@COUNT(E1. . .E3)	2	Empty E3 does not count
@AVG(E1. . .E3)	21	Sum divided by count
@MAX(E1. . .E3)	40	Finds maximum value in series
@MIN(E1. . .E3)	2	Empty E3 not considered
@NPV(B2,C2. . .E2)	53.34	C2 is year 1 (or period 1)
@CHOOSE(E1,20,10,40)	10	E1=2, so second value is chosen
@LOOKUP(B1,C1. . .E1)	10	.5 is less than .52, hence the value beneath .22 is selected

Figure B.5: *Sample formulas with comments*

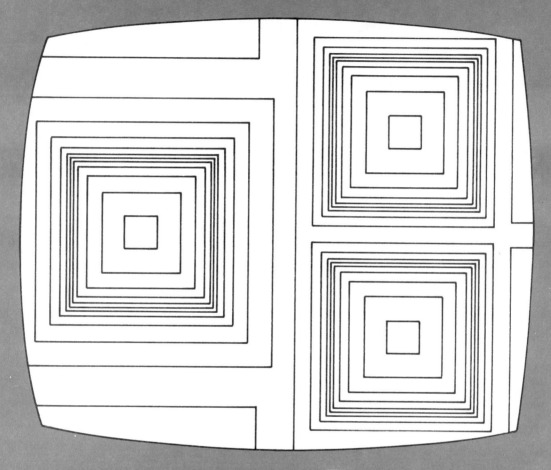

Appendix **C**

On-Line Information Sources

*T*his appendix reviews essential concepts about when, where, and how to obtain on-line information about AppleWorks and data for processing in AppleWorks. Some people think that access to on-line information services will someday be the prime reason for using an Apple, but only a small fraction of Apple II systems have modems installed. In the process of comparing on-line sources with more traditional sources, you will begin to understand why. This appendix will not cover everything you need to know, but it will point you in the right direction.

A practical 300-baud modem costs $80 to $150. Commerical on-line information services typically cost $20 or more to join, roughly the cost of the users manual. Connect costs are typically between $5 and $15 per hour, with the lowest rates for 300-baud modems on nights and weekends. Noncommercial bulletin board services are usually free, but you may have to pay long distance telephone rates. In short, you can spend money quickly on-line.

CompuServe is probably the best-known on-line information service. You can read its ASCII files and capture them in Apple II memory at the same time. Good communications programs, such as the ProDOS version of ASCII Express, have at least a 28K text trap in memory. The program saves to disk when the memory buffer is full. You can then use AppleWorks to create a Word Processor from the text file. (If you have DOS 3.3 communications software, you must convert downloaded text files to the ProDOS format before using them in AppleWorks.)

Each on-line information service has its own procedures for connection. To reach CompuServe from a metropolitan area, you can dial a local telephone number and avoid long-distance rates. After a brief procedure of entering an ID number and password, you can go directly to the Apple forum and read its files. (If you are not already a member, you must sign on and come back the next day to access the most useful information.)

When you know what information you need, the important questions are when, where, and how to acquire the data at the least cost. Specialized on-line databases are generally more expensive than broader-based information services. However, information costs vary considerably from source to source, even for the same information. Always plan your strategy before dialing.

When you read menus and scan files on-line, a 300-baud connection transfers text as fast as you can read it. Many services charge higher rates for 1200-baud connections, and 1200-baud modems are more expensive. If you download large files often for research purposes, use the faster transmission rate. However, consider keeping a 300-baud account as well, so that you can run the 1200-baud modem at the slower rate when you simply need to read screens.

This is the essential information you need to get started. Most on-line services advertise widely and offer free printed information about information content and rates. Read on, though, because you may not need to go on-line.

INFORMATION ABOUT APPLEWORKS

If you need information about your Apple II and AppleWorks, check your bookshelf. Do you have an AppleWorks manual, an Apple II manual, a printer manual, and back issues of Open-Apple? Unless you have all of the above, get those sources first. Then call Apple to find the name, address, and location of a nearby user group. No matter where you live, you can join almost any Apple II or AppleWorks users group and receive a newsletter by mail.

If a users group has an on-line bulletin board system, the group probably has public domain programs on disk as well. In cost per kilobytes of information transferred, the disk mailer is one of the most remarkable technical innovations in the history of communications. Use it whenever you can.

If you already have a modem, check out noncommerical bulletin board systems in your local dialing area. Use long-distance services only for information you cannot get locally. For example, if you are developing a program related to AppleWorks, Robert Lissner maintains his own AppleWorks bulletin board system at (702) 831-1722 (Nevada). But if you simply need AppleWorks file format documentation, you can get that on disk by mail from The AppleWorks User Group.

Although CompuServe charges for connect time, it does not have a minimum charge per month. Even minimal users receive *Online Today,* a monthly journal with good reviews and telecommunications articles. On CompuServe itself, you can find AppleWorks information on the Apple forum, which is run by the Micronetworked Apple Users Group (MAUG).

One example of useful Apple forum information is the ProDOS Text File Splitter, an Applesoft BASIC public domain program by Larry Miller. It splits ProDOS text files into a specified number of parts approximately equal in size. This program has two important uses. First, if you want to use CONVERT to convert a large ProDOS ASCII file to DOS 3.3, you can break it into files of less than 30K (see Chapter 6). Second, if you download a large file from an information service, and it exceeds Desktop memory, you can break it into smaller files. You can download files while reading it, or by using the XMODEM protocol. It goes to the disk as a text file, and you can quickly EXEC it to a working BASIC program.

Another example is Binary II, a set of programs by Gary Little for transferring ProDOS binary files, including AppleWorks Spreadsheet files. For a reference article on this subject, see the *Open-Apple* newsletter index.

INFORMATION TO USE IN APPLEWORKS

If you need data for processing in AppleWorks, check your bookshelf again. Do you have at least a paperback dictionary, grammar book, almanac, paperback encyclopedia, and the most commonly used reference book in your own field? Unless you have all of the above, get those books first. Then go to your public library (or college library), and check the card catalog, periodicals, and reference section. For example, on the subject of low-cost information from the federal government, read Matthew Lesko's *Information USA* (Viking Books, 1986).

For small amounts of data, enter it from the printed source using the Apple II keyboard. For large amounts of data, you may be able to purchase it already loaded on disk. Small firms specialize in loading to disk such things as standard business letters, recipes, and population data. Check the classified advertisements in current Apple II journals. Many firms and government agencies offer data on 360K disks in MS-DOS format. You can transfer this data to the Apple II by using ASCII files and a modem connection from an IBM-PC.

Although the printed word still serves us well for most information, some things change too quickly for efficient distribution in print. A classic example is the Official Airlines Guide (OAG), available on CompuServe and other information services. In a deregulated airline industry, fares, routes, and schedules change frequently. The electronic edition of the OAG keeps track of that with daily fare updates and weekly schedule updates. It also provides information content and format that may not be available to a given travel service. This is the kind of information that belongs in an on-line information service.

In summary, when you need information about AppleWorks, or data for processing within AppleWorks, think of on-line services as one option among many. Use it for what it does best, and remember that more traditional sources still have advantages of their own.

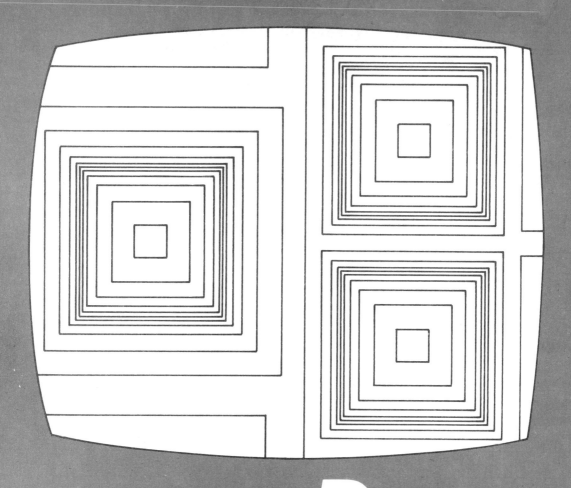

Appendix **D**

An AppleWorks Bibliography

*I*nformation on AppleWorks comes from many sources: the on-line Micronetworked Apple Users Group, books, articles, users-group newsletters, and advertisements. The following annotated bibliography, although not comprehensive, suggests the range and quality of sources for intermediate and advanced users. It includes references that are not specifically AppleWorks-related but can be quite valuable to AppleWorks users.

Hardware and software manuals can sometimes be unexpectedly useful AppleWorks sources. The Checkmate Technology MultiRam manual is a good example: in addition to installation instructions, it includes AppleWorks performance tests and information on practical uses of the enlarged Desktop. User's manuals for scientific calculators can also be invaluable.

ANNOTATED BIBLIOGRAPHY

Alexander, Penny. "Automating the Miniledger." *Business Computing.* 2, 5 (May 1984), pp. 68–72.
> Good example of a periodical column (from a periodical that is no longer published). Each template respects the limits of VisiCalc. Other particularly useful topics include project scheduling (September 1984) and invoicing (November 1984).

Arganbright, Deane. *Mathematical Applications of Electronic Spreadsheets.* New York: McGraw-Hill, 1985.
> Carefully designed templates in mathematics and statistics, with useful insights on circular references and iteration.

Beil, Donald. *The DIF File.* Reston, VA: Reston Publishing, 1983.
> Thorough and easily understood reference; a landmark book.

Cerati, Rodolfo. "Spreadsheet in BASIC." *Byte.* IX, 6 (June 1984), pp. 154–56, 457–62.
> Thought-provoking discussion of a single-purpose program that looks exactly like a spreadsheet.

Checkmate Technology. *MultiRam Software Manual.* Tempe, AZ: Checkmate Technology, 1986.

A remarkable manual that includes many performance tests and tips on AppleWorks.

Date, C. J. *Database: A Primer.* Reading, MA: Addison-Wesley, 1983.

Introduction to database management in theory and practice, by the author of a more extensive two-volume classic on the subject.

Dickinson, John. "The Third Annual Survey: Printers." *PC Magazine.* 5,19 (November 11, 1986), pp. 135–138.

Introduction to the PC annual comparative test report. A surprisingly useful reference for Apple II users.

Dooley, Thomas, and David Spiller. *Financial Planning in Transit.* Washington: US Dept. of Transportation, 1983.

Good example of spreadsheet information from an unexpected source. The concepts can be generalized.

Englander, Jim. "Making a Utilities Diskette for Spreadsheet Creation." *Spreadsheet.* 1, 19 (June 1983), pp. 1–2.

Article that inspired the PARTS file, in a monthly newsletter no longer published.

Engles, Richard. "How AppleWorks Handles Arithmetic Operations," *AppleWorks Forum.* 2,8 (August 1987), pp. 21–23.

Carefully researched explanation of problems with AppleWorks version 2.0.

Flast, Robert. *54 VisiCalc Models.* New York: Osborne/McGraw-Hill, 1983.

Sound reference for finance and statistics, with formula listings for everything, including labels.

Frazier, Howard. "Customers on File." *inCider.* 2, 10 (October 1984), pp. 56–65.

Good Quick File II article that applies to the AppleWorks Data Base as well.

Grupe, Fritz. "Tips for Better Worksheet Documentation." *Lotus.* 1, 4 (August 1985), pp. 68–70.

One of many articles in *Lotus* that has broad utility for spreadsheet users.

Hergert, Douglas. *Mastering VisiCalc.* San Francisco: SYBEX, 1983.

Useful information on BASIC programs for handling DIF files.

Jacques, Jeffrey. "THE Spreadsheet Sheet: Data Analysis." *CALL-A.P.P.L.E.* 6, 12 (December 1983), pp. 21–25.

First of a continuing series on statistics. See Chapter 4 for a table describing the complete series.

Johnson, Tricia. "Doing the Impossible with @LOOKUP: An Automated Invoice System," *Spreadsheet.* 33 (August 1984), pp. 3–4. Continued in combined issue number 34/35, pp. 5–7.

How to use @LOOKUP with data that cannot be listed in ascending order. Based on an idea by Trevor Smith.

Kersey, Bert, and Jack Cassidy. *Pro-Byter.* San Diego: Beagle Brothers, 1985.

All software manuals should be this interesting, informative, and fun.

Koons, J.B. "SANE Programming on the Apple." *CALL-A.P.P.L.E.* 8, 7 (July 1985), pp. 19–20.

Good review of the Standard Apple Numerics Environment discussed in Appendix A.

Linzmayer, Owen. "Spelling Checkers," *Nibble.* 8,3 (March 1987), pp. 24–31.

Review of seven spelling checkers. A good example of what a comparative review should be.

Oliva, Ralph et al. *The Great International Math on Keys Book.* Lubbock: Texas Instruments, 1976.

Classic collection of useful formulas, written for a scientific calculator. TI manuals continue to be invaluable for spreadsheet users.

Ross, Paul. "Letter Quality Printing with AppleWorks and Epson FX-80." *Washington Apple Pi.* 7, 4 (April 1985), pp. 30–31.

Good example of printer installation information found in Apple users group newsletters.

Rubin, Charles. *AppleWorks.* Bellevue, WA: Microsoft Press, 1985.

Well-written, intermediate-level book, with considerable detail on information transfer.

Tufte, Edward R. *The Visual Display of Quantitative Information.* Cheshire, CT: Graphics Press, 1983.
A landmark book, finely crafted and with many illustrations.

Tymes, Elna. *Mastering AppleWorks,* 2nd Ed. San Francisco: SYBEX, 1987.
Thorough treatment of AppleWorks version 2.0, with additional information on DIF files and BASIC programming.

Van Buren, Chris. "Special Patch for Printing Blank Cells," *AppleWorks Exclusive Reference.* 2,1 (January 1987), pp. 6–7.
One of the most insightful patches I have seen, from a well-written newsletter.

Weishaar, Tom. "Making AppleWorks relational," *Open-Apple.* 3,5 (June 1987), pp. 3.33–3.37.
Perceptive, efficient writing about the Data Base and relational database management. One of many remarkable Open-Apple articles about AppleWorks. The March, August, and September 1987 issues include related information.

INDEX

Selections from The SYBEX Library

APPLE/MACINTOSH

Mastering ProDOS
Timothy Rice/Karen Rice
260pp. Ref. 315-5
An in-depth look at the inner workings of ProDOS, for advanced users and programmers—with discussion of system programming techniques, sample programs in BASIC and assembler, and scores of ready-made ProDOS utility routines.

Programming the Apple II in Assembly Language
Rodnay Zaks
519pp. Ref. 290-6
This tutorial on 6502 programming is for newcomers to assembly language, as well as programmers interested in an Apple IIc/IIe-specific presentation. Topics include the 65C02, the Apple mouse, the ProDOS interface, graphics and animation.

Mastering AppleWorks (Second Edition)
Elna Tymes
479pp. Ref. 398-8
New chapters on business applications, data sharing DIF and Applesoft BASIC make this practical, in-depth tutorial even better. Full details on AppleWorks desktop, word processing, spreadsheet and database functions.

Inside the Apple IIGS
Gary Bond
459pp. Ref. 365-1
An inside look at the hardware and system organization, with numerous programming examples showing how to access the system's ROM calls, soft switches, and tool calls using 65816 assembly language. Includes sound and graphics programming. The author, Gary Bond, was a member of the Apple IIGS development team.

Mastering Excel on the Macintosh (Second Edition)*
Carl Townsend
550pp. Ref. 439-9
Hands-on tutorials cover all the basics of using Excel on the Macintosh: worksheet functions, database management, graphs and charts; plus in-depth treatment of advanced features, and extensive coverage of macros.

Also:
Mastering Excel
Carl Townsend
454pp. Ref. 306-6

Advanced Excel Solutions
David K. Simerly
253pp. Ref. 389-9
High-level business applications using linked spreadsheets serve to demonstrate Excel's most advanced database, report, chart, table, and macro capabilities. Also: data interchange, optimizing disk storage, and the Switcher.

Mastering ThinkTank on the Macintosh
Jonathan Kamin
264pp. Ref. 305-8
The complete guide to "idea processing" on the 512K Mac. Covers every aspect of the program, from starting a first outline to advanced applications: logging sales calls, maintaining a resume, creating a marketing plan, and more.

Using the Macintosh Toolbox with C
Fred A. Huxham/David Burnard/Jim Takatsuka
559pp. Ref. 249-3
The complete C programmer's guide to creating full-featured Mac applications, in one succinct handbook. Covers graphics, windows, menus, controls, text editing,

resources, alerts and dialogs, and disk I/O, with detailed reference material.

Programming the Macintosh in Assembly Language
Steve Williams
779pp. Ref. 263-9
A comprehensive tutorial and reference covering assembly-language basics, the 68000 architecture and instruction set, the Macintosh Toolbox, linking with high-level languages and more; plus an extensive macro library and sample programs.

Programming the Macintosh in C
Bryan J. Cummings/Lawrence J. Pollack
294pp. Ref. 328-7
A comprehensive introduction to C programming, especially for Macintosh users. Covers the design philosophy and special advantages of C, as well as every feature of the language. With extensive reference material.

SPREADSHEETS AND INTEGRATED SOFTWARE

The ABC's of 1-2-3 (Second Edition)
Chris Gilbert/Laurie Williams
245pp. Ref. 355-4
Online Today recommends it as "an easy and comfortable way to get started with the program." An essential tutorial for novices, it will remain on your desk as a valuable source of ongoing reference and support. For Release 2.

Mastering 1-2-3
Carolyn Jorgensen
466pp. Ref. 337-6
Get the most from 1-2-3 Release 2 with this step-by-step guide emphasizing advanced features and practical uses. Topics include data sharing, macros, spreadsheet security, expanded memory, and graphics enhancements.

Lotus 1-2-3 Desktop Companion (SYBEX Ready Reference Series)
Greg Harvey
976pp. Ref. 385-6
A full-time consultant, right on your desk. Hundreds of self-contained entries cover every 1-2-3 feature, organized by topic, indexed and cross-referenced, and supplemented by tips, macros and working examples. For Release 2.

Power User's Guide to Lotus 1-2-3*
Pete Antoniak/E. Michael Lunsford
400pp. Ref. 421-6
This guide for experienced users focuses on advanced functions, and techniques for designing menu-driven applications using macros and the Release 2 command language. Interfacing techniques and add-on products are also considered.

Lotus 1-2-3 Book of Style*
Tim K. Nguyen
350pp. Ref. 454-2
For users of 1-2-3 who want a definite and comprehensive guide to writing 1-2-3 spreadsheets in a stylistically correct and acceptable way. Lots of examples show how to create models that are powerful and efficient, yet easily understandable.

Mastering Lotus HAL
Mary V. Campbell
342pp. Ref. 422-4
A complete guide to using HAL "natural language" requests to communicate with 1-2-3—for new and experienced users. Covers all the basics, plus advanced HAL features such as worksheet linking and auditing, macro recording, and more.

Simpson's 1-2-3 Macro Library
Alan Simpson
298pp. Ref. 314-7
Increase productivity instantly with macros for custom menus, graphics, consolidating worksheets, interfacing with mainframes and more. With a tutorial on macro creation and details on Release 2 commands.

Data Sharing with 1-2-3 and Symphony: Including Mainframe Links
Dick Andersen
262pp. Ref. 283-3

The complete guide to data transfer between Lotus products (1-2-3 and Symphony) and other popular software. With an introduction to microcomputer data formats, plus specifics on data sharing with dBASE, Framework, and mainframe computers.

Mastering Symphony (Third Edition)
Douglas Cobb
840pp. Ref. 470-4

A complex program explained in detail. Includes version 1.2 with the new Macro Library Manager. "This reference book is the bible for every Symphony user I know...If you can buy only one book, this is definitely the one to buy." —IPCO Info

Focus on Symphony Macros
Alan Simpson
239pp. Ref. 351-1

An in-depth tutorial guide to creating, using, and debugging Symphony macros, including developing custom menus and automated systems, with an extensive library of useful ready-made macros for every Symphony module.

Focus on Symphony Databases
Alan Simpson/Donna M. Mosich
398pp. Ref. 336-8

Master every feature of this complex system by building real-life applications from the ground up—for mailing lists, inventory and accounts receivable. Everything from creating a first database to reporting, macros, and custom menus.

Better Symphony Spreadsheets
Carl Townsend
287pp. Ref. 339-2

Complete, in-depth treatment of the Symphony spreadsheet, stressing maximum power and efficiency. Topics include installation, worksheet design, data entry, formatting and printing, graphics, windows, and macros.

Andersen's Symphony Tips and Tricks (Second Edition)
Dick Andersen/Janet McBeen
321pp. Ref. 342-2

Hundreds of concise, self-contained entries point the way to optimal use of Symphony features, including trouble-shooting tips. Covers all five Symphony modules, plus macros and the command language, and Release 1.1.

Mastering Framework II
Douglas Hergert/Jonathan Kamin
509pp. Ref. 390-2

This business-minded tutorial includes a complete introduction to idea processing, "frames," and software integration, along with its comprehensive treatment of word processing, spreadsheet, and database management with Framework.

Advanced Techniques in Framework: Programming in FRED
Alan Simpson
320pp. Ref. 246-9

This introduction to the FRED programming language is for experienced Framework users who need to expand their word processing, spreadsheet, graphics, and database management skills.

Mastering Enable*
Keith D. Bishop
350pp. Ref. 440-2

A comprehensive, practical, hands-on guide to Enable 2.0 integrated word processing, spreadsheet, database management, graphics, and communications—from basic concepts to custom menus, macros and the Enable Procedural Language.

Mastering Q & A
Greg Harvey
399pp. Ref. 356-2

This hands-on tutorial explores the Q & A Write, File, and Report modules, and the Intelligent Assistant. English-language command processor, macro creation, interfacing with other software, and more, using practical business examples.

Mastering SuperCalc 4
Greg Harvey
311pp. Ref. 419-4

A guided tour of this spreadsheet, database and graphics package shows how and why it adds up to a powerful business planning tool. Step-by-step lessons and real-life examples cover every aspect of the program.

Also:
Mastering SuperCalc 3
Greg Harvey
400pp. Ref. 312-0

Understanding Javelin PLUS
John R. Levine
Margaret Levine Young
Jordan M. Young
558pp. Ref. 358-9

This detailed guide to Javelin's latest release includes a concise introduction to business modeling, from profit-and-loss analysis to manufacturing studies. Readers build sample models and produce multiple reports and graphs, to master Javelin's unique features.

ACCOUNTING

Mastering DAC
Easy Accounting*
E. Carl Merrifield
400pp. Ref. 442-9

This hands-on tutorial shows you how to run your own business accounting system from start to finish, using DAC Easy Accounting. Ideal for non-accounting professionals.

DATABASE MANAGEMENT

Mastering Paradox
(Second Edition)
Alan Simpson
463pp. Ref. 375-9

Comprehensive treatment of Paradox versions 1.0 and 1.1 from database basics to command file programming with PAL. Topics include advanced queries and reports, automatic updating, and managing multiple data tables.

Mastering Reflex
Robert Ericson/Ann Moskol
336pp. Ref. 348-1

A complete introduction to Reflex: The Analyst, with hands-on tutorials and sample applications for management, finance, and technical uses. Special emphasis on its unique capabilities for crosstabbing, graphics, reporting, and more.

dBASE III PLUS Programmer's
Reference Guide
(SYBEX Ready Reference Series)
Alan Simpson
1056pp. Ref. 382-1

Programmers will save untold hours and effort using this comprehensive, well-organized dBASE encyclopedia. Complete technical details on commands and functions, plus scores of often-needed algorithms.

The ABC's of dBASE III PLUS
Robert Cowart
264pp. Ref. 379-1

The most efficient way to get beginners up and running with dBASE. Every 'how' and 'why' of database management is demonstrated through tutorials and practical dBASE III PLUS applications.

Mastering dBASE III PLUS:
A Structured Approach
Carl Townsend
342pp. Ref. 372-4

In-depth treatment of structured programming for custom dBASE solutions. An ideal study and reference guide for applications developers, new and experienced users with an interest in efficient programming.

Also:
Mastering dBASE III: A
Structured Approach
Carl Townsend
338pp. Ref. 301-5

...puter Books

...ent.

...re is why . . .

At SYBEX, each book is designed with you in mind. Every manuscript is carefully selected and supervised by our editors, who are themselves computer experts. We publish the best authors, whose technical expertise is matched by an ability to write clearly and to communicate effectively. Programs are thoroughly tested for accuracy by our technical staff. Our computerized production department goes to great lengths to make sure that each book is well-designed.

In the pursuit of timeliness, SYBEX has achieved many publishing firsts. SYBEX was among the first to integrate personal computers used by authors and staff into the publishing process. SYBEX was the first to publish books on the CP/M operating system, microprocessor interfacing techniques, word processing, and many more topics.

Expertise in computers and dedication to the highest quality product have made SYBEX a world leader in computer book publishing. Translated into fourteen languages, SYBEX books have helped millions of people around the world to get the most from their computers. We hope we have helped you, too.

For a complete catalog of our publications:

SYBEX, Inc. 2021 Challenger Drive, #100, Alameda, CA 94501
Tel: (415) 523-8233/(800) 227-2346   Telex: 336311